THE COMPLETE BOOK OF

RUGBY

A CIP catalogue record for this book is available from the British Library

ISBN 1 86200 013 1

Project editor: Martin Corteel
Project art direction: Paul Messam
Production: Sarah Schuman
Design: Paul Cooper

Printed and bound in Dubai

CONTRIBUTORS' DETAILS

Howard Evans
One of Wales' foremost rugby statisticians, Howard Evans now works for the Sportsweb agency in Cardiff. His contribution to the Ultimate Encyclopedia included some Welsh greats and the great Welsh competitions.

Barry Glasspool
Barry is a South African free-lance journalist who has been writing on rugby for many years and is a regular contributor to the Johannesburg-based *Sunday Times*. His contribution to the Ultimate Encyclopedia consisted of pieces on the great South African players and a tribute to great coach Izak van Heerden.

Ron Palenski
The Sports Editor of the *Wellington Dominion*, Ron Palenski has long been acknowledged as one of New Zealand's foremost rugby experts. Also a contributor to *Inside Rugby* magazine, Ron's contribution to the Ultimate Encyclopedia consisted of pieces on the great New Zealand players, a history of New Zealand rugby, a tribute to great coach Vic Cavanagh, the history of the National provincial Championship and Dunedin's famous Carisbrook stadium.

Mark Reason
A well-known rugby journalist who has worked for the London-based *Sunday Times* and *Sunday Telegraph* for the past decade, Mark Reason contributed the chapter on scandals and pieces on legends Willie John McBride, Hugo Porta and Colin Meads.

Alasdair Reid
The rugby correspondent of the Scottish edition of *The Sunday Times*, Borderer Alasdair Reid contributed a piece on the great Scottish competitions.

Chris Thau
The Media Director for the Welsh Rugby Union and the Rugby World Cup, Romanian Chris Thau is one of the rugby world's best known figures and is almost certainly the best-travelled administrator the sport has ever seen. As well as contributing a wealth of knowledge and anecdotes on the world's smaller rugby nations, Chris also contributed pieces on the great French players and the history of French rugby.

(Opposite): **KIWI CRAZY** *New Zealand fans at the Hong Kong Sevens tournament in 1995;* (overleaf): **LETTING OFF STEAM** *London Welsh v Newport in 1988*

THE COMPLETE BOOK OF
RUGBY

General Editor: Richard Bath

Executive Editor of *Inside Rugby* Magazine

SevenOaks

CONTENTS

GREAT CLUBS *Edinburgh Academicals*

GREAT STADIUMS *Hong Kong*

THE COUNTRIES *New Zealand's All Blacks*

INTRODUCTION

Comparisons across the ages are invidious. Each generation is bigger than the one before, and if quantifiable sports such as athletics are any guide, we get quicker, stronger and fitter with each decade. This was brought home to me all too powerfully when I was researching the chapter on Great Players. Sifting through some old photographs I came across a 1992 photo of two Springboks, the great Sixties second row Frik du Preez and the up-and-coming Nineties scrum-half Robert du Preez. The second row was marginally the shorter of the two, and only slightly stockier. Would he, could he, survive today when he would have to concede almost half a foot to even the most average of international locks? I suspect not, yet size is not important in itself for the purposes of inclusion here; the only thing that matters is how a player or a match or a stadium measures up to his contemporaries and that is how every chapter in this book has been approached.

The importance of a yardstick by which to judge players and events is also a pre-requisite to a balanced appraisal of their historical importance, and this led to a problem peculiar to rugby union – how to gauge the impact of players when they have not played against each other with sufficient regularity to draw any reasonable conclusions. In this I refer particularly to my general principle of profiling players from within the Big Eight, (England, Wales, Scotland, Ireland, France, New Zealand, Australia and South Africa). This was a conscious decision taken on the basis that most players from outside the major countries have not had wide enough exposure to top level international rugby over a long enough period of time. The one exception is Argentina's Hugo Porta, whose 17-year Test career included several virtuoso one-man performances against the top sides in the world, including South American Jaguars' famous win over the Springboks.

Other than the exclusion of players from the second tier rugby nations, I have tried to stick to the format of giving equal billing to each of the Big Eight. In many cases this was unavoidable – the Legends and Great Players chapters, for instance, would have been little more than a list of the best New Zealand and South Africa have to offer unless I had strictly profiled just 25 players from each country for the Greats and one for the Legends. This has inevitably led to many players who readers might feel demand inclusion being left out, and it was certainly difficult to leave players like Springbok "Boy" Luow or All Black Ken Gray out of such a chapter. Wherever I have been unable to chose between two players, I have chosen the player I have seen play the most often. The choices I made are completely subjective and are mine alone. This is not the case with the Ten Great Matches. Although I have erred on the side of recent games, some contests are of such renown that it would be impossible to disregard them. I have therefore had to rely on written recollections rather than film or video of the game. Once again, there has been a conscious effort to reflect the spread of world rugby through the chapter, and all of the Big Eight countries are featured.

Of the more factual areas, such as the Chronology of the Game or the chapter on the Business of Rugby, there has been little or no attempt to be comprehensive. Rather, by highlighting examples of change, I have tried to explore trends in the game. I have also tried not to be completely dominated by rugby's abiding principle for over a century, amateurism. It has not been possible to dwell upon the effect that this has had on some of the game's institutions and competitions, and here I refer most particularly to the Great Competitions.

This book could not have been compiled without the help and perspective of many of the game's elder statesmen. In every country, there was at least one veteran rugby man willing to take the time and effort to sift through files and magazines to find a nugget of information that has remained buried for many years, and I am indebted to the following who contributed either their wisdom or their words to this Encyclopedia: John Reason, Terry O'Connor, Mark Reason and the staff at the RFU library (England); Sean Diffley and Peter McMullan (Ireland); Peter Thorburn, Norman Mair and Alasdair Reid (Scotland); Howard Evans (Wales); Ron Palenski (New Zealand); Barry Glasspool (South Africa); John Blondin (Australia); and Chris Thau (France, Romania and the world!).

The unsung heroes of this book also deserve a mention. My wife Bea, for having to read more than a quarter of a million of my words; all the staff at Brackenbury Publishing for their (sometimes faltering) help and support; and my son Oliver, for being the only Bath ever to arrive early.

Any errors you spot – and despite the best efforts of myself and copy editor Gavin Mortimer, there are bound to be a couple – are my responsibility. But I trust that they are minor and not enough to detract from your enjoyment of a work of reference which was, for me, a labour of love.

RICHARD BATH
Fulham, London
May 1997

THE ORIGINS OF THE GAME

There are so many conflicting reports of how the game of rugby came into being that the only thing that is for certain is that Rugby School's William Webb Ellis did not spontaneously invent the game when he picked up the ball and ran with it, showing "a fine disregard for the rules of football as played in his time", the time in question being 1823. Not only did a schoolboy contemporary of Webb Ellis refute the notion a few years later, but there is also the fact that rugby was by no means the first code of football to involve running and handling. In fact, before Webb Ellis did his party trick in 1823, all codes of football involved running and handling.

It is sometimes claimed by Irish historians of the game, for instance, that Webb Ellis was actually giving a demonstration of "Caid". This ancient Irish free-for-all is very similar to rugby, and Webb Ellis could have witnessed it as a young boy when his soldier father was stationed in Ireland with the Dragoons. But in truth the origins of the game go back even further than Caid, to the Roman Empire and a popular game of the time called "Harpastum". And even then it is said that the Romans actually imported that game from China and Japan where it had been played for many centuries, while some accounts have it that the game was an Ancient Greek pastime called "Episkyros". Whatever the case, Harpastum was very much like rugby in that it involved two teams whose sole objective was to carry a leather ball stuffed with cloth or feathers over their opponents' goal line.

A BLOODY AND MURTHERING PRACTICE

By the twelfth century, "foote balle" of one kind or another had become so popular in Britain that the chronicler Fitzstephen devoted a whole chapter to it in his Surveys of London. The game he described pitted one village against another in wrestling wars of attrition that ranged over distances of many miles and could go on for days at a time. The games were often brutal, savage affairs with blunt implements used as a means of gaining an advantage over the rival village. Certainly, the games were not popular with the chroniclers of the time; Philip Stubbs wrote in his "Anatomy of Abuses" in 1583: "Football playing ... may rather be called a friendly kind of fight than a play for recreation, a bloody and murthering practice than a felowly sport."

Versions of the game of football were played throughout Europe; the Irish called it "Caid", the Cornish "Hurling to Goales" (not to be confused with the Irish version), the West Country referred to it as "Hurling Over Country", East Anglians "Campball", the Welsh knew it as "Cnapan", the French played a version called "La Soule" or "Chole" and the Italians of Florence had "Calcio". Yet wherever the game was played, it was incredibly violent, with the Shrovetide clashes between Chester and Derby the nastiest of them all (hence the term "local

WHEN IN ROME... *play rugby. Three 6th Century Italian flankers!*

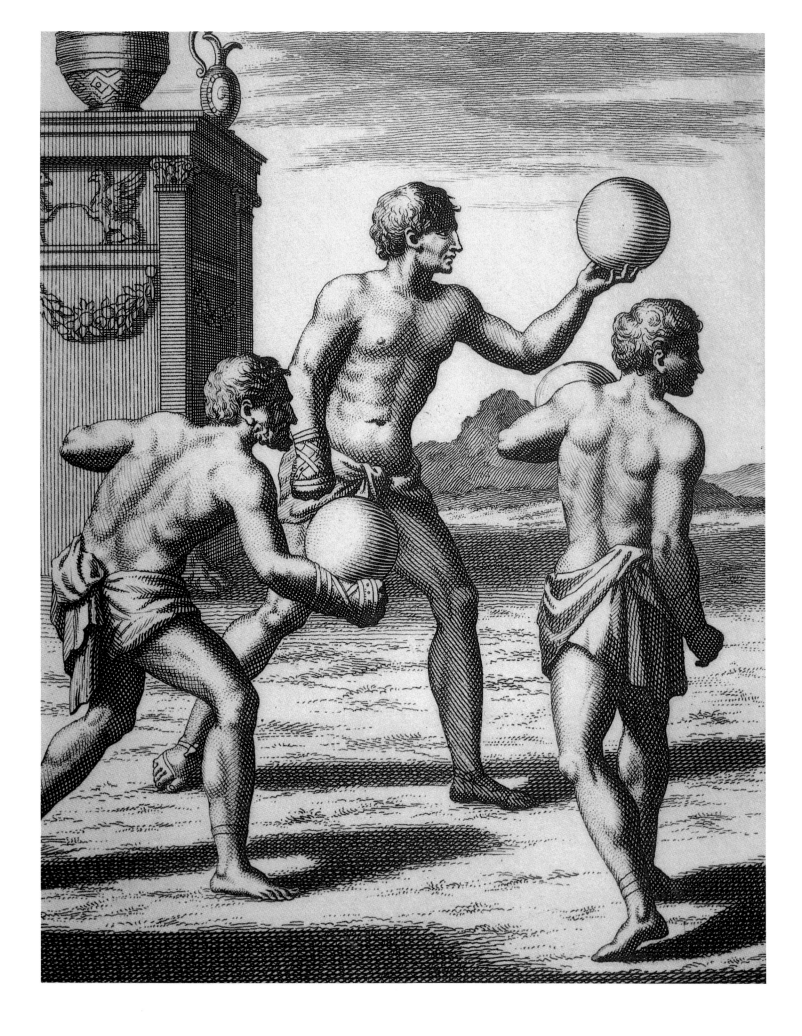

derby"). Most Sundays and every Shrove Tuesday, the ritual blood-letting would get underway, with the most noted games taking place at Cross of Scone near Perth in Scotland, Corfe Castle in Dorset, Alnwick in Northumberland, and Midlothian (where the married women played the single ones).

Gradually, though, the game began to develop beyond a good excuse for a brawl. By the 1600s the writer Boccalini was reporting in glowing terms of a highly organized game "Calcio", which was played by young Florentine nobles in two teams of 27, the Reds and the Greens. In Britain, the chronicler Richard Carew describes the Cornish game of: "Hurling to Goales" which had by then developed many of the essential features of modern rugby, including offside. "There are 15, 20 or 30 players on each side

who strip themselves to their slightest apparel, and then join hands in ranks one against another. Out of these ranks they match themselves by payres, one embracing another, every of which couple are especially to watch one another during the play. After this they pitch two bushes in the ground some eight or ten feet asunder, and directly against them, ten or twelve score paces off, other twain in like distance, which they term goales. Whosoever can catch or carry through the adversaries' goales hath won the game."

Yet football was no more popular with the authorities in the 1600s than it had been in the preceding centuries when virtually every English, Scottish and French monarch had tried at one stage or another to ban a pastime which took their men away from archery and could lead to some

extremely violent episodes. That began to change in the 1647 when Winchester College took up a round ball version of the game, ensuring that the code of football at last had a modicum of respectability that would allow it to flourish. Different versions of the same game were being played at schools around the country, although all exhibited many of the ingredients that now make up rugby. Winchester had a well-established game, while at Eton College a wall-less form of the famous Eton Wall Game had been played for almost half a century before the wall was built in 1717. Harrow, Charterhouse, Shrewsbury and Westminster all had distinct games, while a form of football with many of the features of current day Aussie Rules Football had been played at Rugby for almost a century before Webb Ellis intervened.

It was fortunate that the game was flourishing in the public schools, because football for the common man was increasingly suppressed from 1750 onwards, most notably by the 1835 Highways Act which forbade the playing of football on public land, where most of the games had taken place. Just for good measure, the Act was enforced by special constables and dragoons who quickly gained the reputation as killjoys.

THE CODIFICATION OF RUGBY

With so many different forms of football being played in England's schools, however, it was by no means certain that the Rugby code would prevail. Former pupils of Rugby school were the most evangelical advocates of their game and in 1839 Old Rugbeian Arthur Pell founded a club at Cambridge University and challenged a

THE CLUB *Blackheath became the first genuinely "open" club when it was formed in the early 1850s.*

group of Old Etonians to a game of football. The Etonians, however, were astounded at the Rugbeians' use of their hands and so it was decided that representatives from the major public schools of Eton, Rugby, Harrow, Marlborough, Westminster and Shrewsbury would codify what became known as the "Cambridge Rules" in 1848. Outside the universities and schools, other clubs were also beginning to form. Blackheath and Richmond played their first game under "Harrow Rules" in 1861, changing the next year to "Rugby Rules" after an influx of Old Rugbeians.

The ambiguous situation regarding rules continued until 1863, when supporters of the "Kicking Codes" played at Charterhouse, Eton, Westminster and Harrow met Blackheath and the other supporters of the "Carrying Codes" popular at Cheltenham, Marlborough and Rugby at the Freemasons' Tavern in London to thrash out a compromise. All went well at first, with the Kickers accepting the Carriers' insistence on retaining the customs of "hacking" (kicking an opponent's shins, a practice which was eventually outlawed in 1866) and "tripping". Things went awry when the Kickers decided to refer the compromise to Cambridge University, who refused to countenance hacking, tripping or the key Blackheath condition, "that a player may be entitled to run with the ball towards his adversaries' goal if he makes a fair catch." Blackheath walked out, leading to the final split that created the two separate codes of Association Football (soccer) and Rugby Football. Even then, several

RUGBY RULES *The packs close in during a typical game at Rugby School in the 1870s.*

clubs remained confused as to which code they should be playing, with the situation at Sale in 1870, where the club played rugby and Association Football on alternate weekends, by no means unique.

Rugby spread rapidly from that date, initially by the efforts of old boys of Rugby and Marlborough Schools, and in 1871 the Rugby Football Union was formed at a meeting convened at the Pall Mall Restaurant by Edwin Ash of Richmond. Three Rugbeians headed an organization of 20 clubs

of which Richmond, Harlequins and Blackheath remain the best known. (Wasps would have been there had its delegate managed to drag himself out of the pub!) An Old Rugbeian and member of the now defunct Wimbledon Hornets club, Leonard Maton, codified the Laws of Rugby Football in 1871, in which hacking and tripping were expressly forbidden under law 57. The Varsity Match was first played in 1872, and the Hospital's Cup was inaugurated in 1875 as the English game set in place institutions that are alive and well in 1997.

Yet England was not the only country where the game had taken root. North of the Border, Merchiston Castle School and the old boys of Edinburgh Academy first played the world's oldest continual fixture in 1858. While in Ireland the Old Rugbeian R.H. Scott founded a club at Trinity College Dublin in 1854, and in Wales the game took root when Reverend Rowland Williams became deputy-headmaster of St David's College, Lampeter, in 1850. Against a backdrop of rapid expansion at club level, the game took a mighty inter-

national leap forward in 1871 when an England team captained by Blackheath's Frederick Stokes accepted a challenge issued in *The Scotsman* newspaper by a Scotland side led by Edinburgh Academical F.J. Moncrieff. England were beaten by a goal and a try, to a try in front of 4,000 spectators at Raeburn Place. Twelve years later, when England played Wales at St Helen's, they started the Five Nations and put in place a structure that was to maintain the European game for the next century.

The rapid expansion of the game in Britain was to bring its own problems, however. When the number of players dropped from 20 to 15 in 1876, the nature of the game changed completely from a forward trial of strength to a genuine running code. The effect was dramatic, with the game taking off in the north of England, where it was at least as popular as Association Football. In 1879 a crowd of over 7,000 gathered to watch Wigan win the West Lancashire Cup, a figure far in excess of the number of spectators who watched the England versus Scotland 11-man game that

WINCHESTER'S YOUNG GUNS *Play their own version of football in 1866.*

NORTHERN STARS *The game in the north, such as this 1895 County Championship clash between Yorkshire and Lancashire, captures the imagination.*

year. Fierce inter-town rivalries quickly developed and cup rugby became one of the most emotive issues in the north. With such intense competition, standards rose more quickly in the north, and the southern gentlemen began to suspect (rightly in many cases) that money was changing hands. In fact, taking up a job as a barman in another rugby-playing town became something of a standing joke in those years, so accepted was it that it was a back-door means of paying players.

As the 1870s drew to a close, the social composition of the game had begun to change irrevocably, and throughout the 1880s it became painfully clear that there was a wide rift between the gentlemen Corinthians of London, Ireland and Scotland, and the working men who made up the bulk of the playing population in Wales, the West Country and the Northern counties of England. The rise of professional Association

Football meant that the rival code was beginning to attract huge crowds, and it became apparent that rugby would eventually fall behind in popularity. With the northern clubs also dominating rugby in England and closet professionalism rife in Yorkshire and Lancashire, matters began to come to a head in 1888, when the Halifax player J.P. Clowes was designated a professional after accepting £15 to buy equipment before departing on a nine-month tour of Australia and New Zealand. Indeed, the whole of the Anglo-Welsh team which toured Australia and New Zealand under the leadership of R.L Seddon and A.E. Stoddart was forced to sign an affidavit to the effect that they had received no money for touring (although it must also be noted that more than two thirds of the party were from clubs such as Batley, Dewsbury, Swinton and Rochdale Hornets who were among the founders of what became the Rugby League).

THE GREAT SPLIT

From 1888 onwards, the northern clubs mounted a campaign that would allow them to pay a "broken-time" allowance for money lost while playing rugby. At that time, the bulk of the England team were from Yorkshire and Lancashire sides, while such was the north's domestic dominance that Yorkshire won the County Championship trophy every year bar one between its inauguration in 1889 and the Great Split of 1895, with Lancashire winning in the one year Yorkshire failed to do so. The issue finally became unavoidable, and in 1893 a representative of the Yorkshire County, Mr J.A. Miller, argued: "that players be allowed compensation for bona fide loss of time". With RFU secretary G.R. Rowland Hill and president R. Whaley arguing strenuously against the broken-time proposal, it was rejected by 146 votes amid scenes of enormous rancour.

The northern clubs determined

to stay within the RFU and it was only when in 1895 the Union president R. Cail significantly tightened the laws concerning professionalism that the northerners decided to act. Convinced that they could never get fair treatment from a southern-dominated RFU (120 votes of that 1893 majority had been collected ahead of time as proxy votes), twenty of the top northern clubs met in the George Hotel in Huddersfield on 28 August 1895 and decided to form a Northern Union, which later became the Rugby League.

The split precipitated a steep decline in English fortunes and over the next ten years the number of clubs playing Rugby Union halved. So decimated was the national side that the Welsh began to dominate completely and it was not until 1910 that England next won the International Championship. And the matter was not finished there. In 1897 another thorny problem arose when the Welsh

Rugby Union honoured its star player, Newport's Arthur "Monkey" Gould, with a benefit game, which was clearly against the spirit of the professional regulations put in place in 1895. Despite fierce opposition from the Yorkshire delegates, Rowland Hill and the RFU, ever mindful of the damage wrought by the split of 1895, agreed to allow Gould to play against English clubs and to continue representing Wales. A disgusted Scotland was not so accommodating, however, and it was only in 1899 that Scotland and Wales resumed playing contact.

SPREADING THE GOSPEL

Not surprisingly, the vicious in-fighting of the 1890s also coincided with the first signs that Britain was not the centre of the rugby world any more. The once dominant British Isles touring sides, who lost only four matches in their first four overseas tours up to and including the visit to Australia in 1899, were beginning to find the opposition a tougher proposition (see page 46). Not that that should have come as any great surprise. When England played Scotland for the first time in 1871, the game had already begun to spread throughout the Empire at a prodigious rate and it was only a matter of time before the Colonies achieved parity.

The first nation outside Britain to embrace rugby was Australia, when the Sydney University club was formed in 1863, and by 1872 there were 13 clubs in Sydney. As in Britain, there was cross-code competition with the 1877 AGM eventually voting down a motion to "abolish scrimmages and running with the ball", at which stage the popularity of the sport exploded and by 1880 there were 41 clubs in Sydney as well as a burgeoning game in Brisbane. Despite developing rapidly in New South Wales and Queensland, with the latter one of only three sides to defeat the Reverend Matthew Mullineaux's British Lions in 1899, the game was always in competition with Australian Rules Football. From 1907, following a visit from the New Zealand Rugby League team, Union came under threat from League. Dr Moran's Australian Rugby Union side visited to Britain less than a year later, but on their return left *en bloc* to play Rugby League, a situation made even worse in 1914 when the Rugby Union authorities decided it was unpatriotic to play rugby while thousands of young Australian men were being sent overseas to fight in the First World War. With only one alternative, players switched in huge numbers to League, and although Union in Sydney gradually recovered, the effect upon Queensland can be gauged by the fact that no Union was played in the state again until the 1930s.

Across the Tasman Sea, New Zealand was introduced to the game by Charles John Munro on his return from schooling in north London in 1870, and took to it rapidly as it displaced the mixture of Association Football, Victorian Football (later to become Australian Rules Football) and an amalgam of carrying codes then in vogue. With the Maoris also displaying a natural aptitude for the game, many saw rugby as the social glue of New Zealand. (Indeed, some commentators of the time thought that it brought an end to the bloodshed over land that occurred between Maoris and settlers in the late 1860s.) By the time that A.E. Stoddart's British team arrived in 1888, the New Zealanders had improved to such an extent that both Auckland and Taranaki inflicted on the British their only two defeats of a monumental 35-match tour

Suitably buoyed with their progress, the New Zealanders dispatched a Maori side to tour Europe in 1888–89. The subsequent success of that tour forever etched the game of rugby into the Kiwi psyche. The tourists played 74 matches in all, winning 49 of them, this despite sometimes playing up to four matches in a week. The tour produced some legendary players such as three-quarter Davy Gage, forward Tom Ellison and half-back Paddy Keogh. When in 1905 another tour returned (called "The Originals"), this time led by Dave Gallaher, only one game was lost, and that to Wales by a try that was so hotly disputed at the time that it remains a talking point in New Zealand rugby circles even today. By the time New Zealand completed a third tour of Britain in 1924, during which they had gone unbeaten, thus earning themselves the epithet "The Invincibles", they had proved themselves the strongest rugby side in the world.

At the same time that rugby was expanding in Australasia, a third Southern Hemisphere nation was developing a taste for the game. Rugby was introduced to South Africa as early as 1858 by the Reverend "Gog" Ogilvie, who had played the game in Buenos Aires. In 1862 the first recorded match was played between civilians and military in Cape Town, and although Rugby had to compete against "Winchester Football" and the other kicking codes, the preference of Governor Cecil Rhodes for Rugby's rules soon settled the debate. Indeed, it was Rhodes' decision in 1891 to invite a British side led by Scotsman Bill Maclagan that saw South Africa enter the international game. Although the visitors won all of the games on that tour, conceding only one try in the process, enthusiasm for rugby became widespread in Southern Africa. By the time the British came back in 1896 they were to lose a Test, and when Mark Morrison led the third tour in 1903, they lost the series. When war broke out in 1914, Tom Smyth's 1910 Lions had been defeated on two tours of Britain and Ireland, in 1906 and 1912, South Africa were beaten in just one Test.

Elsewhere in the world, Rugby was beginning to take root. In 1872 the first French club was formed at Le Havre. The game also began to spread through North America where, after five years in the universities the first cross-border game took place when Harvard University played McGill University from Montreal in 1874. That year also marked the first recorded instance of the game being played in Japan when British sailors staged a game in Yokohama. Throughout the British Empire, the rugby gospel was spread by troops, and by the of the First World War in 1914, the game was established worldwide as a winter ball sport second only in popularity to soccer. They may not have ever heard of William Webb Ellis in Buenos Aires, Bucharest, Calcutta or Nandi, but they knew a good idea when they saw one.

THE ORIGINALS *Dave Gallagher (left) in action for New Zealand against Midland Counties during the 1905 tour.*

THE GREAT

Of all the sports in the world, Rugby Union is the one which has been the most reluctant to indulge in competitions. This was due in part to its administrators' genuine but misguided belief that quantifiable competition was too much of a temptation for ambitious clubs. This would lead to the poaching of players, monetary inducements and, ultimately, professionalism. History has proved they were right, for it was the biggest competition of them all, the Webb Ellis World Cup, that brought about the change from an amateur to openly professional game.

Rugby union was virtually the last major sport to have a world championship; the only sport not to possess a pan-European tournament and, until 20 years ago, the only team sport in which none of the major nations had any sort of league. Yet rugby is the most competitive of pursuits, and in such circumstances men always look for a marker to establish a pecking order. In rugby it has been cups that have done the trick. And rugby's

cup really has runneth over, with even the smallest countries boasting some form of fiercely contested knock-out competition.

Now, after a century of *ad hoc* confrontations and cup clashes, rugby has caught the competition bug. International, club and provincial friendlies are out, silverware is in – and the resulting fusion of tradition and spectacle has created some of the best sporting action on the globe.

COMPETITIONS

INTERNATIONAL COMPETITIONS

THE WORLD CUP

Given that the British Home Unions had so often taken a stand against the concept of expanding competition, it came as no surprise that England and Ireland were the last two nations to fall into line once the concept of a Rugby World Cup. As Dudley Wood, the then notoriously pro-amateur secretary of the RFU, was later to say: "We knew of course that once a World Cup competition got underway then the eventual outcome was always likely to be a professional game, and that is why we were so dubious about the concept.

Subsequent events have proved Wood's words prophetic. The World Cup has been a success on a scale that even its most ardent advocates could never have foreseen. The fourth tournament, to be held in Wales in 1999, will bring in receipts of well over £70m, and will be seen by three and a half billion television viewers in 150 countries, 70 of which will have teams competing in the tournament or its qualifying rounds. Two million people will have attended games at which the most highly paid superstars in the history of the game will strut their stuff in front of 4,000 journalists. It will also return the fourth highest television ratings ever seen in sport, with only the Olympics, World Cup football and the International Athletics Championship pulling in more viewers. Not bad for a tournament which was dragged kicking and screaming into the world and

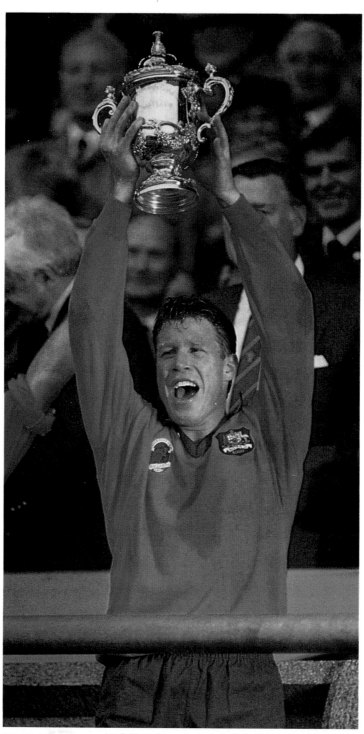

ON TOP OF THE WORLD *Nick Farr Jones holds aloft the 1991 World Cup.*

which many people doubted would ever break even.

But back in the mid–1980s those cynics and doubters certainly had a point as far as the early financial security of the tournament was concerned. Gates in 1987 varied from disappointing to downright poor, and even before co-hosts Australia were beaten by France in the semi-final, the modestly sized Concord Oval in Sydney was easily big enough to take the meagre crowds on the Aussie side of the Tasman. Only the keen interest of the New Zealand public allowed the crowd figures to hit 600,000 and the tournament to return a profit of £1.5m. The Rugby World Cup, though, was always intended to be more than just facts and figures and, with hindsight, it's clear that what happened on the pitch in New Zealand and Australia in 1987 was enough to capture thje imagination of the advertising and marketing men and set in train one of the greatest sporting tournaments anywhere in the world.

Much of the success of the 1987 World Cup was down to the fact that it was won by New Zealand on their own ground at Eden Park. The All Blacks were by far the strongest side in the tournament, and opened the proceedings as they meant to carry on, with a record 70–6 win over hapless Italy. Crushing all before them, David Kirk's New Zealand wiped out Fiji 74–13 and Argentina 46–15, before powering through the quarter-finals with what many later considered their toughest match in the tournament, a 30–3 win against Scotland, and on to the semi-finals where they annihilated Wales 49–6, a score that sent shockwaves around the rugby world. Even France, who had pipped Australia in one of the most exciting games of rugby ever played when they won the second semi-final 30–24 courtesy of an injury-time Serge Blanco try (see page 182), were no match for the Black steamroller. Two tries in two minutes in the second half finished off a game in which the plucky resistance of the French was always likely to prove insufficient to stop the best side in the world.

When Kirk lifted the Webb Ellis Trophy on 20th June 1987 in front of 48,000 screaming New Zealanders, it was the culmination of five years of planning since the sports entrepreneur Neil Durden-Smith had proposed just such a tournament in 1982 (even though a 1957 International Board regulation specifically forbade such a venture), and owed much to the tireless work of administrators such as John Kendall-Carpenter and Ces Blazey. Yet it was a very conservative revolution, in the best traditions of rugby. There were no qualifying rounds, with the sixteen competing countries being invited to attend. This rather arbitrary system of selecting the teams led to much rancour, notably on the part of Korea and Western Samoans who failed to receive an invitation. Nonetheless, one of the most encouraging signs was that the tournament would help drag some of the smaller nations up by the bootlaces.

While sides such as Italy, Zimbabwe and Tonga received fearful beatings, the spirited contribution of the Canadians and Japanese was a powerful signal that the world of rugby was beginning to change.

That signal was reinforced as the preparations for the 1991 World Cup got underway. Qualifying rounds were held throughout the world, with 40 nations competing in regional pools. Financial support from the profits from 1987 was a vital component in allowing small unions to travel thousands of miles to compete in what quickly became a genuine worldwide competition. The emerging nations were also engaged in a frantic round of Test matches to battle-harden their top players and by the time the second tournament kicked off in Europe, it was clear that the gap between the top sides and many of the more ambitious smaller nations had begun to narrow perceptibly.

This was proved in spectacular fashion when the tournament kicked off, with Wales the most high-profile casualties. Beaten 16–13 at Cardiff Arms Park by debutants and eventual quarter-finalists Western Samoa in their first game, Wales failed to advance beyond the pool stage. They were the only actual casualties among the traditional powers, but other emerging sides such as Italy and Canada also proved that the status quo was changing rapidly, both of them pushing the All Blacks to the wire. Virtually every game was genuinely competitive and almost every match was played to a full house, making the tournament a resounding and highly profitable success .

The 1991 World Cup also reflected a shifting balance of power in world rugby, with Australia playing the most attractive and inventive rugby and thoroughly deserving to lift the tro- phy. They confirmed their dominance of world rugby at the time by beating their two main rivals, England and the All Blacks, to win the tournament, the latter victory coming courtesy of a virtuoso performance by veteran wing David Campese. Although the 12–6 final win over England was a dour event dominated by Australia's outstanding defence and England's tactical naiveté, the tournament included some of the most outstanding games of rugby ever played in Europe (see pages 184 and 185). The presence of hosts England in the final also ensured that the sport received the biggest single shot in the arm in its history – it was the event which catapulted rugby into the premier league of sport.

The decision to hold the 1995 World Cup in South Africa was controversial to say the least. The Springboks only rejoined the international rugby community in 1992 following the abolition of Apartheid, and many felt that the country's infrastructure was too flimsy for a sporting event

---

1987

Pool 1

Australia	19	England	6
USA	21	Japan	18
England	60	Japan	7
Australia	47	USA	12
England	34	USA	6
Australia	42	Japan	23

	P	W	D	L	F	A	Pts
Australia	3	3	0	0	108	41	6
England	3	2	0	1	100	32	4
USA	3	1	0	2	39	99	2
Japan	3	0	0	3	48	123	0

Pool 2

Canada	37	Tonga	4
Wales	13	Ireland	6
Wales	29	Tonga	16
Ireland	46	Canada	19
Wales	40	Canada	9
Ireland	32	Tonga	9

	P	W	D	L	F	A	Pts
Wales	3	3	0	0	82	31	6
Ireland	3	2	0	1	84	41	4
Canada	3	1	0	2	65	90	2
Tonga	3	0	0	3	29	98	0

Pool 3

New Zealand	70	Italy	6
Fiji	28	Argentina	9
New Zealand	74	Fiji	13
Argentina	25	Italy	16
Italy	18	Fiji	15
New Zealand	46	Argentina	15

	P	W	D	L	F	A	Pts
NZ	3	3	0	0	190	34	6
Fiji	3	1	0	2	56	101	2
Argentina	3	1	0	2	49	90	2
Italy	3	1	0	2	40	110	2

Pool 4

Romania	21	Zimbabwe	20
France	20	Scotland	20
France	55	Romania	12
Scotland	60	Zimbabwe	21
France	70	Zimbabwe	12
Scotland	55	Romania	28

	P	W	D	L	F	A	Pts
France	3	2	1	0	145	44	5
Scotland	3	2	1	0	135	69	5
Romania	3	1	0	2	61	130	2
Zimbabwe	3	0	0	3	53	151	0

Quarter-finals

New Zealand	30	Scotland	3
France	31	Fiji	16
Australia	33	Ireland	15
Wales	16	England	3

Semi-finals

France	30	Australia	24
New Zealand	49	Wales	6

Third place match

Wales	22	Australia	21

Final
Eden Park, Auckland, June 20, 1987
New Zealand 29
Tries : Jones, Kirk, Kirwan
Conversion : Fox
Penalties : Fox 4
Dropped Goal : Fox

France 9
Try : Berbizier
Conversion : Camberabero
Penalty : Camberabero

New Zealand : Gallagher; Kirwan, Stanley, Taylor, Green; Fox, Kirk (Capt); Mcdowell, Fitzpatrick, Drake, Pierce, G.Whetton; A.Whetton, Jones, Shelford.

France : Blanco; Camberabero, Sella, Charvet, Lagisquet; Mesnel, Berbizier; Ondarts, Dubroca (Capt), Garuet; Lorieux, Condom; Champ, Erbani, Rodriguez.
Referee : K.V.J.Fitzgerald (Aus)
Attendance : 48,350

1991

Pool 1

NZ	18	England	12
Italy	30	USA	9
NZ	46	USA	6
England	36	Italy	6
England	37	USA	9
NZ	31	Italy	21

	P	W	D	L	F	A	Pts
NZ	3	3	0	0	95	39	9
England	3	2	0	1	85	33	7
Italy	3	1	0	2	57	76	5
USA	3	0	0	3	24	113	3

Pool 2

Scotland	47	Japan	9
Ireland	55	Zimbabwe	11
Ireland	32	Japan	16
Scotland	51	Zimbabwe	12
Scotland	24	Ireland	15
Japan	52	Zimbabwe	8

	P	W	D	L	F	A	Pts
Scotland	3	3	0	0	122	36	9
Ireland	3	2	0	1	102	51	7
Japan	3	1	0	2	77	87	5
Zimbabwe	3	0	0	3	31	158	3

Pool 3

Australia	32	Argentina	19
W.Samoa	16	Wales	13
Australia	9	W.Samoa	3
Wales	16	Argentina	7
Australia	38	Wales	3
W.Samoa	35	Argentina	12

	P	W	D	L	F	A	Pts
Australia	3	3	0	0	79	25	9
W.Samoa	3	2	0	1	54	34	7
Wales	3	1	0	2	32	61	5
Argentina	3	0	0	3	38	83	3

Pool 4

France	30	Romania	3
Canada	13	Fiji	3
France	33	Fiji	9
Canada	19	Romania	11
Romania	17	Fiji	15
France	19	Canada	13

	P	W	D	L	F	A	Pts
France	3	3	0	0	82	25	9
Canada	3	2	0	1	45	33	7
Romania	3	1	0	2	31	64	5
Fiji	3	0	0	3	27	63	3

Quarter-Finals

England	19	France	10
Scotland	28	W.Samoa	6
Australia	19	Ireland	18
NZ	29	Canada	13

Semi-Finals

England	9	Scotland	6
Australia	16	NZ	6

Third Place Match

NZ	13	Scotland	6

Final
Twickenham, 2 November 1991
Australia 12
Try : Daly
Conversion : Lynagh
Penalties : Lynagh 2

England 6
Penalties : Webb 2

Australia : Roebuck; Campese, Little, Horan, Egerton; Lynagh, Farr-Jones (Capt); Daly, Kearns, Mckenzie; Mccall, Eales; Poidevin, Ofahengaue, Coker.

England : Webb; Halliday, Carling (Capt), Guscott, Underwood; Andrew, Hill; Leonard, Moore, Probyn; Ackford, Dooley; Skinner, Winterbottom, Teague.
Referee : W.D.Bevan (Wales)
Attendance : 60,000

SPIRIT OF THE SAMURAI *Despite being regularly out-gunned, Japan proved that the "emerging" nations could come of age through the World Cup.*

of the magnitude of the World Cup. But rugby is a religion in South Africa, and Nelson Mandela's government of national unity made it a priority to ensure that the tournament was a spectacular success. And it was, largely because South Africa crowned their return by beating the in-form favourites New Zealand in a try-less but nail-biting final encounter that the Springboks won with a Joel Stransky drop-goal late into extra-time (see page 187). The national outpouring of joy that followed the famous win produced an amazing, spontaneous unity that transcended colour in a country in which colour played a central role. It was possibly rugby's greatest hour.

The 1995 World Cup was also the game's last as an amateur sport. The economic success and the huge television coverage of the event was too tempting for the satellite barons, and with All Black wing Jonah Lomu establishing himself as the game's first genuine world superstar after literally running over Wales, Scotland, Ireland and England, the game moved inevitably on to a new professional era. Preparations for the next World Cup, the biggest yet, are already underway. Revenue will be greater, profile higher and the number of teams larger, with the current format of four pools of four teams being expanded to five pools of four teams. Even the qualifying rounds, which are now well advanced, are half as big as they were in 1995, with 71 nations now competing. When 1999 comes around the thousands of fans guaranteed to descend on the Welsh capital will witness the final at a redeveloped Cardiff Arms Park, a fitting venue for one of the most glamorous and thrilling sporting events in the world today.

1995

Pool A

South Africa	27	Australia	18
Canada	34	Romania	3
South Africa	21	Romania	8
Australia	27	Canada	11
Australia	42	Romania	3
South Africa	20	Canada	0

	P	W	D	L	F	A	Pts
South Africa	3	3	0	0	68	26	9
Australia	3	2	0	1	87	41	7
Canada	3	1	0	2	45	50	5
Romania	3	0	0	3	14	97	3

Pool B

W.Samoa	42	Italy	18
England	24	Argentina	18
W.Samoa	32	Argentina	26
England	27	Italy	20

| Italy | 31 | Argentina | 25 |
| England | 44 | W.Samoa | 22 |

	P	W	D	L	F	A	Pts
England	3	3	0	0	95	60	9
W.Samoa	3	2	0	1	96	88	7
Italy	3	1	0	2	69	94	5
Argentina	3	0	0	3	69	87	3

Pool C

Wales	57	Japan	10
NZ	43	Ireland	19
Ireland	50	Japan	28
NZ	34	Wales	9
NZ	145	Japan	17
Ireland	24	Wales	23

	P	W	D	L	F	A	Pts
NZ	3	3	0	0	222	45	9
Ireland	3	2	0	1	93	94	7
Wales	3	1	0	2	89	68	5
Japan	3	0	0	3	55	252	3

Pool D

Scotland	89	Ivory Coast	0
France	38	Tonga	10
France	54	Ivory Coast	18
Scotland	41	Tonga	5
Tonga	29	Ivory Coast	11
France	22	Scotland	19

	P	W	D	L	F	A	Pts
France	3	3	0	0	114	47	9
Scotland	3	2	0	1	149	27	7
Tonga	3	1	0	2	44	90	5
Ivory Coast	3	0	0	3	29	172	3

Quarter-Finals

France	36	Ireland	12
South Africa	42	W.Samoa	14
England	25	Australia	22
NZ	48	Scotland	30

Semi-Finals

| South Africa | 19 | France | 15 |
| NZ | 45 | England | 29 |

Third Place Match

| France | 19 | England | 9 |

Final

Ellis Park, Johannesburg, 24 June 1995

South Africa 15 *
Penalties : Stransky 3
Dropped Goals : Stransky 2
New Zealand 12
Penalties : Mehrtens 3
Dropped Goal : Mehrtens

South Africa : Joubert; Small (Venter 97'), Mulder, H.Le Roux, Williams; Stransky, Van Der Westhuizen; Du Randt, Rossouw, Swart (Pagel 68'), Wiese, Strydom; Pienaar (Capt), Kruger, Andrews (Straeuli 90').

New Zealand : Osborne; Wilson (Ellis 55'), Bunce, Little, Lomu; Mehrtens, Bachop (Strachan 66'-71'); Dowd (Loe 83'), Fitzpatrick (Capt), Brown; I.Jones, R.Brooke; Brewer (Joseph 40'), Kronfeld, Z.Brooke.

Referee : E.F.Morrison (England)

Attendance : 63,000

* After Extra Time
9-9 After Normal Time

THE FIVE NATIONS CHAMPIONSHIP

The first instance of formalised contact sport between two British countries occurred on November 19, 1870, when England beat Scotland at Association Football at the Kennington Oval. The match, played in front of a crowd of 4,000, was a heated affair eventually won by the English. But such was the rancour generated by the win that the Scots determined to have another go at the "Auld Enemy" the next year, and this time it would be on their own ground and on their own terms. Their own ground was Raeburn Place and their own terms was the 20-a-side game of Rugby Football, which was then making huge strides North of the Border.

When Edinburgh Academical FJ Moncrieff and a group of Scottish players issued a challenge to English rugby via the pages of a newspaper in 1871, and then won the ensuing match by a goal and a try to one try, they could have had no idea what they had set in train. One hundred and twenty-six years and nearly 1,000 fiercely contested international encounters later, however, the fruit of the seed they planted that day is the International Championship, commonly known as the Five Nations, the most prestigious and historic rugby tournament in the world.

Although a silver cup that bears an alarming resemblance to an oversized cafetiere was presented to the Five Nations organisers by Lord Burghersh in 1993, and a points system put in place in the same year to ensure that there was a winner to present the trophy to, the Five Nations existed for over a century without any level of formal organisation. Instead it has evolved gradually, and it is even impossible to discern a date when the phrase "Five Nations Championship" was first used. Nevertheless, the competition is the longest established international rugby competition in the world.

The inaugural England versus Scotland fixture of 1871 started the ball rolling, and has been played in every peacetime year since. From 1879 onwards, the fixture was played for the magnificent silver trophy called the Calcutta Cup which was presented by GAJ Rothney of the Calcutta Rugby Club after dwindling membership forced the club to close. The trophy, which takes the form of a tapered cup with three snake handles and an elephant as the lid, was actually made from melted down silver rupees withdrawn from the central bank of Calcutta from the club's funds when it was wound down.

It was not long before the two nations became the three, when Ireland (or, as with all early international matches, a club side – in this case Trinity College, Dublin – masquerading as the national side) played England at The Oval in 1875 and lost by the then handsome margin of one goal, one drop goal and one try to no score. Another five years passed and the three sides became four when Wales followed a well-worn path to The Oval and went home with a humiliating defeat by the enormous score of seven goals, one drop goal and six tries to no score (equivalent to a defeat of 82–0 on today's scoring system).

With the existing annual round of matches being gradually expanded on an ad hoc basis as Ireland first played Scotland in 1877 and Wales in 1882, while Scotland first locked horns with Ireland in 1877, a genuine Home Unions Championship was in full swing by 1890.

Although the intensity of those early clashes was every bit as severe as in Five Nations games of today, the laws that governed the game in those early days were very different indeed. There was no set points scoring system until the early 1890s and in the very early years the matches were declared drawn unless one of the two teams scored a converted try (a "goal"). Until 1877 matches were played with 20 players on each side and with 13 of them as forwards,

and it was those forwards which led the great dribbling rushes of the time. Only with the formation of the International Board after an Anglo-Scottish squabble over the laws in 1884 were the various practices and laws harmonised in the interests of fair international competition.

Although England, and to a lesser extent Scotland, held the whip hand in those early years due to their advanced experi-

ence and greater player base, by the late 1880s the four sides were playing off a relatively level playing field, with any one of the nations genuinely capable of winning all three of its matches. From the moment that England completed the first mythical "Triple Crown" in 1883 at only the second time of asking (and then added insult to injury by repeating the act the next year) the pursuit of a clean sweep has become the over-

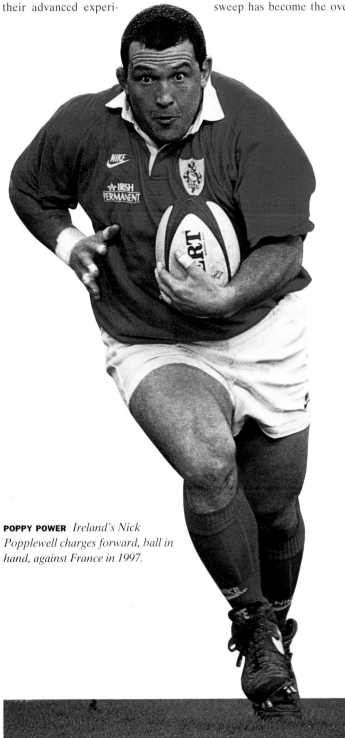

POPPY POWER *Ireland's Nick Popplewell charges forward, ball in hand, against France in 1997.*

TRY-TIME: *England winger Mike Slemen scorches over for a try against Scotland in 1980.*

riding aim of every British nation come the beginning of January. Just how much fortunes fluctuated between the four sides was obvious in the early 1890s when, in four consecutive years, each of the Home Unions won the Triple Crown in consecutive years: Scotland in 1891; England in 1892; Wales in 1893; and Ireland in 1894!

Although the Oxbridge connection was alive and well for England through players such as Harry Vassall and Alan Rotherham, the ultra-competitive club scene in the North of England in the 1880s and early 1990s provided the basis of England's strong international showing, while Wales were also beginning to prove themselves formidable adversaries in the annual round of increasingly less friendly internationals. The balance of power was to change radically in 1895, however, when England went into a spiral of decline after the heart of Northern rugby was ripped out by the decision of 20 top clubs and their players to form the Rugby League. Between 1895 and 1910, England were the whipping boys of British rugby with the Scots and Welsh only losing to them three times in 15 encounters, while the Irish lost only six times in the same period.

With a whole generation of outstanding players such as Gwyn Nicholls, Rhys Gabe and Percy Bush to call upon, it was the Welsh who took greatest advantage. Six times they won the Triple Crown between 1900–11, and with France joining the

competition in 1906, Wales completed the first ever Grand Slam in 1908 and repeated the feat the next season. Not that the Welsh had it all their own way. Scotland were also a force to be reckoned with at the time, and with men like the rough tough forward "Darkie" Bedell-Sivright in their side they also boasted a formidable record, notching up three Triple Crowns between 1900–10.

But as England regained its strength following the 1895 debacle, Britain's most populous rugby nation reasserted itself once more and, with Wales' 1911 Grand Slammers the only nation to put up a serious challenge and War the only interruption, dominated the Championship from the time the 1910 season kicked off until Scotland's Grand Slam of 1925. Even today the names that led England to the greatest period of dominance in its history are still revered, names such as Ronnie Poulton-Palmer and Cherry Pilman, celebrated halfbacks Cyril Kershaw and "Dave" Davies, and the outstanding back row in English history, Wavell Wakefield, Tom Voyce and Arthur Blakiston. The all-white army marched to eight shared or outright Championships in ten seasons, winning three Grand Slams in four years along the way.

It was only the emergence of a truly great Scotland team that stopped England's triumphant procession. Led from the back by Dan Drysdale, and drawing on the cunning of fly-half Herbert Waddell and the famous Oxford University threequarter line of Wallace, Aitken, Smith and Macpherson, they dominated the 1925 season in which they won a Grand Slam. They were to remain one of the strongest forces in world rugby for the rest of the Twenties.

By now, France had begun to figure in the equation, although the figures tended to be in the "points conceded" column. France only beat England and Wales once between 1906 and the outbreak of war, and while they had better luck against Scotland (four wins) and Ireland (five wins), they were generally the whipping boys of the tournament. In 1931, however, they became more like the kicking boys – well, they were unceremoniously kicked out of the Cham-

pionship when it became clear that their top clubs were openly paying their players.

France were not to reappear in the Championship until it restarted after the War. In the pre-war years, England and Scotland had been the two dominant forces, but as soon as post-war France took to the field it was clear that the balance of power had shifted dramatically. Although they only won two of their games, Jean Prat's France only lost to England by 6–3 and Wales by 3–0 and were clearly a force to be reckoned with. Although the Irish side led by mercurial Ulster genius Jack Kyle provided a flash of brilliance at the end of the Forties, collecting the only Grand Slam in Ireland's history in 1948 and a Triple Crown the next year, France, Wales and England dominated the Five Nations from the War to the present day.

For Scotland, a major pre-war power, the fall from grace was a heavy one. Seventeen matches were lost on the trot between 1951–55, including the famous 44–0 humiliation by Basil Kenyon's South Africa at Murrayfield in 1951, a thrashing akin to those endured by the Welsh at the hands of New Zealand in the 1987–8. Thankfully the late Fifties, Sixties and Seventies saw Scotland bumble along as also-rans, more often scoring a Wooden Spoon (ie: no wins) than a Championship win, but remaining competitive. That luck changed in the early Eighties when a crop of out-

standing players spearheaded by half-backs Roy Laidlaw and John Rutherford saw Scotland to a Grand Slam in 1984, its first since the glory days of 1925. Grand Slams in the modern era are uncannily like buses, and not only had one come along, but six years later Scotland were at it again. With inspirational prop David Sole and fullback Gavin Hastings as the main strike weapons, and with the back row of Finlay Calder, Derek White and John Jeffrey disrupting favourites England in the Grand Slam showdown (see page 183), Scotland scored the most famous victory in its entire history to complete a clean sweep in the 1990 Five Nations Championship.

The main reason why Scotland invariably missed out on the privilege of occupying the Wooden Spoon berth in the post-war years was because it had already been taken by the Irish. Indeed, at times it looked as if the men in green had taken out a long lease on the position. Despite the efforts of giants of the game such as Willie John McBride, Mike Gibson and Fergus Slattery, the lack of strength in depth all too often extinguished the Irish fire. The only relief from the misery of mediocrity came from the hand of fly-half general Jack Kyle in the Forties and the boot of his Eighties counterpart Ollie Campbell, who kicked Ireland to Triple Crowns in 1982 and 1985. The Nineties, have been particularly unkind to Ireland, who almost seem to have discarded any lingering

UNDER PRESSURE *But Wales' Rob Howley clears to touch against France.*

thoughts of sustaining a challenge for Five Nations honours.

Another country which has often seemed to have also fitted that bill during the Nineties is Wales, which is staggering for a country that has one of the proudest records in British rugby. After the War the Welsh carried on producing backs in the mould of Wooller, Tanner and Jones, with staggering talents like Cliff Morgan, Bleddyn Williams and Ken Jones dropping off the conveyor belt of talent in the late Forties and Fifties. Teak hard forwards such as Clem Thomas, Bryn Meredith and Rhys Williams were the backbone of sides which were among the most difficult to beat, and Wales were always formidable at the Arms Park. As the years wore on, so Wales became increasingly dominant, and after 1969, when Barry John and Gareth Edwards combined for their first full season together to bring Wales a Triple Crown, the men from West of Offa's Dyke became well nigh invincible.

Throughout the Seventies, it seemed that Wales was producing the best players in the world, certainly to judge from the evidence of the 1971 and '74 Lions tours. Greats such as JPR Williams, Gerald Davies and Mervyn Davies ruled the Five Nations and the world, and the prize was a hatful of honours, with the Grand Slams of 1971, 1976 and 1978 punctuating a run of Triple Crowns. Only as the Eighties dawned did Wales begin to decline, and even then it was a slow decline. England's Grand Slam of 1980 involved the narrowest of 10–9 wins against Wales, who were reduced to 14 men after dismissal of flanker Paul Ringer for a stiff arm tackle, and even in 1987 Wales were able to pull themselves up to a third-place showing in the first World Cup and winning the Triple Crown in 1988. Yet the Five Nations is not a vacuum, and two huge defeats in New Zealand in 1988 led to numerous defections to League and crushed Welsh morale to the point where only now is a new generation coming through which genuinely believes itself capable of challenging for top honours on a regular basis.

England's post-War performances were in almost direct reverse to those

NOT A PRETTY SIGHT: *French prop Christian Califano leads out the French team for their 1995 Five Nations clash with Wales.*

of the Welsh. Despite possessing far and away the biggest playing constituency upon which to draw, England's most conspicuous talent until the late Eighties was underachievement. Despite producing backs of the class of Peter Jackson and forwards of the durability of Eric Evans, England's return was very meagre, with Triple Crowns in 1954, 1957 and 1960, and a solitary Grand Slam under Bill Beaumont in 1980. A lack of consistency in selection and the inability of the English club system to bring talent to the top meant that for the most part mid-table mediocrity was England's staple diet.

Only when manager Geoff Cooke combined with young captain Will Carling in the late Eighties did that situation change. That England 1988 vintage was certainly a quality one, although the continued decline in Welsh, Irish and Scottish fortunes, allied to the existence of a hard core of veterans in a pack centred around Wade Dooley, Dean Richards and Mike Teague, did suggest that England were to have the rub of the green at last. The results were amazing, with England winning back-to-back Grand Slams in 1991 and 1992, and then going on to win another in 1995 to rival the great England side of the Twenties.

The final piece of the Five Nations puzzle is that most enigmatic of rugby countries, France. After expulsion in 1931 and rehabilitation in 1947, France prospered under the inspirational leadership of Lourdes legend Jean Prat. Far from being the perennial losers, France became the most vibrant force in the competition, invariably providing the main opposition to the top dogs if they were unable to assume that position. France have long played the closest thing in Europe to total rugby, with backs like the Boniface brothers, Joe Maso and Serge Blanco combining with some gigantic forwards such as Jean Prat, Walter Spanghero and Jean-Pierre Bastiat to make France the most consistently entertaining side in the Championship. Grand Slams in 1968, '77, '81, '87 and '97 – the last one achieved when coming from 14 points behind after a ten-year losing streak at Twickenham – have underlined the strength of French rugby.

Grand Slam Winners
England: 1913, 1914, 1921, 1923, 1924, 1928, 1957, 1980, 1991, 1992, 1995
Wales: 1908, 1909, 1911, 1950, 1952, 1971, 1976, 1978
France: 1968, 1977, 1981, 1987, 1997
Scotland: 1925, 1984, 1990
Ireland: 1948

Five Nations Winners

1883 England	1942 No comp
1884 England	1943 No comp
1885 No comp	1944 No comp
1886 Eng & Scotland	1945 No comp
1887 Scotland	1946 No comp
1888 No comp	1947 Wales & Eng
1889 No comp	1948 Ireland
1890 Eng & Scotland	1949 Ireland
1891 Scotland	1950 Wales
1892 England	1951 Ireland
1893 Wales	1952 Wales
1894 Ireland	1953 England
1895 Scotland	1954 Eng & Fr
1896 Ireland	& Wales
1897 No comp	1955 Fr & Wales
1898 No comp	1956 Wales
1899 Ireland	1957 England
1900 Wales	1958 England
1901 Scotland	1959 France
1902 Wales	1960 Fr & Eng
1903 Scotland	1961 France
1904 Scotland	1962 France
1905 Wales	1963 England
1906 Ire & Wales	1964 Scot & Wales
1907 Scotland	1965 Wales
1908 Wales	1966 Wales
1909 Wales	1967 France
1910 England	1968 France
1911 Wales	1969 Wales
1912 Eng & Ireland	1970 Fr & Wales
1913 England	1971 Wales
1914 England	1972 No comp
1915 No comp	1973 Quituple tie
1916 No comp	1974 Ireland
1917 No comp	1975 Wales
1918 No comp	1976 Wales
1919 No comp	1977 France
1920 Eng & Scot	1978 Wales
& Wales	1979 Wales
1921 England	1980 England
1922 Wales	1981 France
1923 England	1982 Ireland
1924 England	1983 Fr & Ireland
1925 Scotland	1984 Scotland
1926 Scot & Ire	1985 Ireland
1927 Scot & Ire	1986 Fr & Scotland
1928 England	1987 France
1929 Scotland	1988 Wales & France
1930 England	1989 France
1931 Wales	1990 Scotland
1932 Eng & Wales	1991 England
& Ire	1992 England
1933 Scotland	1993 France
1934 England	1994 Wales
1935 Ireland	1995 England
1936 Wales	1996 England
1937 England	1997 France
1938 Scotland	
1939 Eng & Wales	* No competition
& Ire	
1940 No comp	
1941 No comp	

THE TRI-NATIONS SERIES

When the Tri-Nations series was launched in 1996 as an integral part of the top Southern Hemisphere unions' deal with Rupert Murdoch's Sky satellite television channel, it promised the most exciting rugby ever played on an annual basis and the most ridiculously large Cup in any sport in any country in the world. The idea was a simple one: take the age-old rivalries between old adversaries New Zealand, South Africa and Australia (who also happen to be arguably the best three sides in the world) and create the equivalent of a Southern Hemisphere Five Nations, only with each of the three sides playing each other on a home and away basis every year.

Conceived in 1995 during the World Cup, the campaign pitted the world champions South Africa against the team that was generally regarded as the best in the competition but which had lost the final to the Springboks amid rumours of a poisoning scandal, the All Blacks. With Australia still smarting from a last-minute quarter-final exit at the hands of the dreaded Poms, the scene was set for a blistering six-match series. Throw in the fact that the each of the countries' players knew each other intimately from the Super 12 series, and the fact that New Zealanders had also thrown in a three-Test tour to South Africa on top of their two home and away games against the Springboks and the series took on an even more rosy hue. New Zealand versus South Africa on five consecutive weekends – the World Cup final may have said who was world champions on paper, but in both countries there was no doubt that this was seen as a real test of endurance, and that the winners would be *de facto* the best in the world.

Just for once, the hype was justified. An historic series featuring the three World Cup winners was worth every penny, or at least over half of the population of New Zealand thought so as they stayed up into the wee small hours to watch the Blacks bash the Boks in a choice of venues throughout South Africa. Hooker Sean Fitzpatrick's men were irresistible, and ended the most arduous season ever undertaken by any side as the undisputed champions of the world. For the first time ever, a New Zealand side had gone down to South Africa and won a series there. And they didn't just win it, they walked it in a series that never looked in doubt, eben though the Boks pulled back the last Test at Ellis Park 32–22. By the end of the tour coach John Hart summed up the party's feelings as he reflected upon four wins over the Springboks, three of them on South African soil: "This is the greatest day in the history of New Zealand rugby. It is a record that can never be bettered and will probably never be equalled." The revenge for the '95 World Cup, the Cavaliers and Fred Allen's 1949 tour party that was whitewashed 4–0 amid what Kiwis saw as heavily biased refereeing, was at last complete.

With the All Blacks sweeping the board during the Tri-Nations and winning the payback tour to boot, that left the Wallabies and Springboks to fight it out for second place, a battle that saw honours even in their mini two-Test series. It was one of the greatest Test series ever played, but it was not, in many senses, "new", for the three countries have long histories of playing each other on a very regular basis, particular between the Antipodean duo. Although there has been no formal competition, so intense has the rivalry been between these three countries that it is recorded here as if it was.

The Tri-Nations Series	
Season	**Winners**
1996	New Zealand

BLEDISLOE CUP
NEW ZEALAND V AUSTRALIA

The symbol of trans-Tasman supremacy since 1931, when it was presented by the then Governor-General of New Zealand, Lord Bledisloe, the Bledisloe Cup was so often won by the New Zealand All Blacks that they thought of it as virtually their property. Certainly that is the impression given, for after winning the Cup for the first time in 1932 when they defeated Australia 20–13, no mention of the Cup was made for almost half a century. That all changed after an historic afternoon in 1979 when the Wallabies defeated the All Blacks 12–6 in Sydney in one of the rare one-Test series between the two countries, thus claiming the Cup for the first time since 1949 (and that 2–0 series victory was regarded by most Kiwis as unimportant because it was achieved while the best 30 players in New Zealand were away in South Africa with Fred Allen – also getting whitewashed to make a unique double!).

Rare though it was, it wasn't the fact that the Wallabies had won the series that moved the goalposts (they had also won series in 1929, 1939 and 1949). No, it was the fact that, after having beaten the Blacks, they then proceeded to parade the huge and long-forgotten Cup around an ecstatic Sydney Cricket Ground. The New Zealand rugby public, watching the match live in their sitting rooms, were

PAYBACK *Frank Bunce carves through the Springbok defences as the All Blacks dominate the first Tri-Nations.*

THE WINNING WAY *New Zealand win the 1993 Bledisloe Cup.*

mortified. Not only had the All Blacks been beaten, but here were the easy-beats of world rugby – a side which had lost to Tonga on its own patch just six years before – lording it over the lords of rugby. The occasion put a great deal of spice into the relationship and, with the Wallabies on an upward curve that led to a World Cup win in 1991 and competitiveness at the highest level ever since, the keenly anticipated Bledisloe Cup is now one of the highlights of the rugby year.

No two Test sides have played each other more than New Zealand and Australia, who have now amassed over 100 Tests against each other since New Zealand first thrashed Australia 22–3 in Sydney in 1903, with more than half of those being for the Bledisloe Cup. New Zealand have, to date, won over 70.

NEW ZEALAND V SOUTH AFRICA

No Tests in world rugby, with the possible exception of a Lions tour, can create as much excitement and anticipation as the prospect of a meeting between the Springboks and All Blacks. Since the two countries first shared the series in New Zealand in 1921, the rivalry between them has been the most intense and unremitting in world rugby. Numerous clashes between them could have made it into the Ten Greatest Games chapter, but the one chosen was the World Cup final for the added dimension the silverware gave to the whole match (see page 187).

Of all the countries in the world, it was New Zealand which found it hardest to break with South Africa, when the country became a sporting pariah thanks to its adherence to the policy of Apartheid. It seems all the more odd given that New Zealand is possibly the most racially harmonious countries in the world, with race hardly an issue for most Maoris. Despite that, though, Maori players such as George Nepia were not allowed to play in South Africa before 1992. Even the first series was disrupted when row broke out after a member of the South African party, C.W.F. Blackett, sent a cable to South Africa following the Springboks' ill-tempered 9–8 victory over the Maoris at Napier. The offending passage read: "it was bad enough having to play a team officially designated New Zealand Natives, but the spectacle of thousands of Europeans frantically cheering on a band of coloured men to defeat members of their own race was too much for the Springboks who were, frankly, disgusted."

It says much for New Zealand's love of rugby that relations between the two nations continued until the 1980s, when matters reached a head. The 1981 South African tour to New Zealand, for instance, was nicknamed the "Barbed Wire Tour" because all games had to be played behind barbed wire fencing to stop anti-Apartheid protesters invading the pitch. That tour witnessed some of the most violent scenes of civil disobedience in New Zealand's history as the country was split in two over the issue, with rugby followers fighting in the streets with demonstrators. The Third Test of that series saw a plane dropping bags of flour, carpet tacks and smoke canisters onto the pitch, while anarchy ruled outside the ground. Even then, only a legal decision that touring South Africa would violate New Zealand's constitution by denying Maoris the same rights as white New Zealanders, stopped the tour, which then became an "unofficial" tour by the Cavaliers, who included virtually every All Black. That is how strongly New Zealand rugby people feel about South Africa, and it is an intensity that is reciprocated.

AUSTRALIA V SOUTH AFRICA

Before South Africa's international exile, Australia were not worthy of the intensity that Tests against the All Blacks generated. Indeed, up until that time, the Springboks had won 21 of the 28 Tests between the two, with the Australians only winning the home two-Test series in 1965 despite some strong showings, most notably the 1963 tour to South Africa where the Wallabies won two of the first three Tests before drawing the fourth to square the series.

In South Africa's enforced absence, however, the Wallabies went from strength to strength, becoming world champions when they beat England to win the 1991 World Cup, and underlined that status by touring South Africa in 1992, where they humiliated the South Africans at Ellis Park, thrashing them 26–3, in the process showing the Springboks how far they had regressed during their years of sporting isolation.

Winners — The Bledisloe Cup

Year	Team	Score	Team	Score
1931	NZ	20	Aus	13
1932	Aus	22	NZ	17
	NZ	21	Aus	3
	NZ	21	Aus	13
1934	Aus	25	NZ	11
	Aus	3	NZ	3
1936	NZ	11	Aus	6
	NZ	38	Aus	13
1938	NZ	24	Aus	9
	NZ	20	Aus	14
	NZ	14	Aus	6
1946	NZ	31	Aus	8
	NZ	14	Aus	10
1947	NZ	13	Aus	5
	NZ	27	Aus	14
1949	Aus	11	NZ	6
	Aus	16	NZ	9
1951	NZ	8	Aus	0
	NZ	17	Aus	11
	NZ	16	Aus	6
1952	Aus	14	NZ	9
	NZ	15	Aus	8
1955	NZ	16	Aus	8
	NZ	8	Aus	0
	Aus	8	NZ	3
1957	NZ	25	Aus	11
	NZ	22	Aus	9
1958	NZ	25	Aus	3
	Aus	6	NZ	3
	NZ	17	Aus	8
1962*	NZ	20	Aus	6
	NZ	14	Aus	5
1962*	NZ	9	Aus	9
	NZ	3	Aus	0
	NZ	16	Aus	8
1964	NZ	14	Aus	9
	NZ	18	Aus	3
	Aus	20	NZ	5
1967	NZ	29	Aus	9
1968	NZ	27	Aus	11
	NZ	19	Aus	18
1972	NZ	29	Aus	6
	NZ	30	Aus	17
	NZ	38	Aus	3
1974	NZ	11	Aus	6
	Aus	16	NZ	16
	NZ	16	Aus	6
1978	NZ	13	Aus	12
	NZ	22	Aus	6
	Aus	30	NZ	16
1979	Aus	12	NZ	6
1980	Aus	13	NZ	9
	NZ	12	Aus	9
	Aus	26	NZ	10
1982	NZ	23	Aus	16
	Aus	19	NZ	16
	NZ	33	Aus	18
1983	NZ	18	Aus	8
1984	Aus	16	NZ	9
	NZ	19	Aus	15
	NZ	25	Aus	24
1985	NZ	10	Aus	9
1986	Aus	13	NZ	12
	NZ	13	Aus	12
	Aus	22	NZ	9
1987	NZ	30	Aus	16
1988	NZ	32	Aus	7
	Aus	19	NZ	19
	NZ	30	Aus	9
1989	NZ	24	Aus	12
1990	NZ	21	Aus	6
	NZ	27	Aus	17
	Aus	21	NZ	9
1991	Aus	21	NZ	12
	NZ	6	Aus	3
1991**	Aus	16	NZ	6
1992	Aus	16	NZ	15
	Aus	19	NZ	17
	NZ	26	Aus	23
1993	NZ	25	Aus	10
1994	Aus	20	NZ	16
1995	NZ	28	Aus	16
	NZ	34	Aus	23
1996	NZ	43	Aus	6
	NZ	32	Aus	25
1997	NZ	31	Aus	13

* Indicates Two Separate Series Played During The Same Season
** Indicates World Cup Semi-Final Match

THE SUPER 12 TROPHY AND THE EUROPEAN CUP

Club or provincial rugby across countries or even continents is the latest and most exciting stage of rugby's development towards a truly global, professional game. As with soccer, rugby first embraced the concept of a World Cup and then, after the game went open in 1995, sought to move towards a wholehearted acceptance of competitions based along the same lines as European soccer's UEFA Cup, where the best that each nation has to offer goes into a round robin stage followed by a knock-out competition.

Such regional competitions are now firmly established in both hemispheres, with the top Southern Hemisphere provinces competing for the Super 12 Trophy and a mixture of Northern Hemisphere clubs and provinces contesting the European Cup. So successful has the innovation been in both cases that domestic competitions are now in real danger of becoming almost secondary to the real business of the Super 12 or European Cup competition. Indeed, in the five countries where domestic performance is the key to entry into the Super 12 or European Cup – England, Wales, France, New Zealand and South Africa – the rush for inclusion at the higher level is a spur that has added extra spice to domestic competitions as clubs and provinces fight to reach a high enough position to gain entry.

SUPER 12

The Super 12 series sprang into life in the wake of the 1995 World Cup when Union went professional. With the launch of the Rupert Murdoch-backed Super League and the Australian Rugby League's decision to target Union's top players by removing the salary cap only for players switching codes, it was clear that the status quo in Australia and New Zealand was no longer tenable. Something had to be done, and that something was a ten-year, £340m deal with Murdoch that built upon the existing

infra-structure of Southern Hemisphere competition. The first element was the Tri Nations (see page 22) and the second was the the Super 12.

The concept is a simple one: the best 12 provinces from New Zealand, South Africa and Australia battle it out to find the best provincial outfit south of the equator. Each team plays every other team once in the group phase, with the top four teams progressing to the semi-finals. First-placed plays fourth-placed, while second takes on third, culminating in a show-piece final. Only Australia knows in advance which provinces it will enter into the competition, with its two established sides Queensland and New South Wales being joined by ACT, which was upgraded specifically so that it could push Australia's representation up to three. New Zealand enters five expanded provinces (usually Auckland, Wellington, Otago, Waikato and Canterbury), chosen on the basis of performances in the National Provincial Championship. South Africa enters the four semi-finalists from the Currie Cup (with Natal, Transvaal and Northern Transvaal being the ever-presents with Western Province recently giving way to Orange Free State).

Although the competition was rushed into life as a response to the looming threat of the expansionist tendencies of Australian Rugby League, the format had been a long time in the making and was based on two previous versions stretching back to 1986, the Super Six and the Super Ten. The Super Six, played between Queensland, New South Wales and the top four New Zealand provinces, was first contested the year before the first World Cup in 1987. Dominated by the two New Zealand provinces of Canterbury and Auckland until 1992, when Queensland at last emerged victorious, the tourna-

AUCKLAND AGAIN Joeli Vidiri at the 1997 Super 12 final.

ment was a vital factor in the rise of the Wallabies and, more significantly, had put a framework in place for when South Africa's isolation ended in 1992.

As soon as South Africa were back in circulation, the Super Six format was radically extended to the Super Ten with the four New Zealand and two Australian provinces being joined by three South African provinces and, following the success of Samoa at the 1991 World Cup, the winner of the Pacific Championship played between Fiji, Tonga and Western Samoa. With two pools of five, the tournament was a huge success in almost every sense from its inception in 1993. Modest but steadily growing crowds ensured that the competition was financially viable, and Transvaal's stunning 20–17 win over Auckland in the inaugural final at Ellis Park ensured that the tournament got the kick-start it so badly needed. Sizzling competition and a willingness to run the ball characterised the tournament throughout its three-year lifespan, with Queensland's wins over Natal in 1994 and Transvaal in 1995 characteristic finales to this new level of provincial competition. The tournament also gave top players a taste of what professional rugby was like, which was to prove a decisive factor when events threatened to get out of control after the World Cup.

By the time the Super 12 came along in 1996, the groundwork had been done for what was quickly to become the greatest annual tournament in the rugby world. In terms of logistics, the number of matches, the size of crowds and the sheer pace of the rugby, the Super 12 has no equal in world rugby. Its crowds averaged almost 30,000 at each of the 69 matches last year, and the standard of rugby is unquestionably the highest and most entertaining in the world, not least because in the professional age every side seems to have taken it upon themselves to play open, running rugby. The "draft pick" system in place in Australia and New Zealand also ensured that the best players available were on show, while the decision not to poach players from one country to another and the decision to award bonus points to sides that score four tries in a match, as well as teams which stayed within seven points of the winning side, means that all sides are relatively strong. Every Super 12 side is capable of beating any other, either home or away.

The commitment to attack has produced some of the finest matches ever

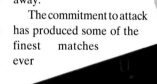

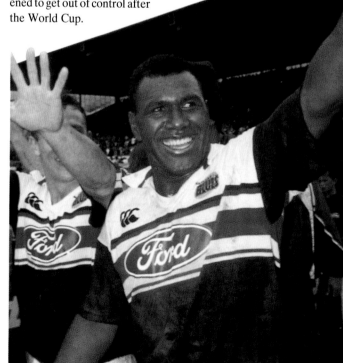

PASS MASTERS *Cardiff's Rob Howley manages to ship the ball on to Jonathan Davies despite the close attentions of Toulouse's Christian Califino.*

seen, and although the mistake rate is high, so is the endeavour, the player fitness and the try count. Auckland and Natal, in particular, have recorded some huge scores, such as Natal's 75–43 win over Otago, and Auckland's 43–43 draw with Northern Transvaal. Indeed, it was Auckland who dominated the Super 12 in its opening year, beating Natal 45–21 in a spectacular final at Eden Park.

Auckland retained the trophy in 1997 when they again showed they were a class above their rivals, remaining unbeaten on their way to a 23–7 victory over surprise package ACT at a rain–soaked Eden Park.

Super 12 Winners

Season	Winners		Runners-up	
1995	Queensland	30	Transvaal	16
1996	Auckland	45	Natal	21
1997	Auckland	23	ACT	07

EUROPEAN CUP

Although it was the go-ahead Unions from Australia and New Zealand who got the show on the road, it was actually in Europe that the first faltering attempt at getting a pan-national club competition underway were taken. That was in the early Sixties when the French-controlled FIRA organisation (see page 26) tried to inaugurate a European competition. Inevitably the British unions declined to participate, although it was wider financial problems which put paid to the idea after three years.

Europe had to wait until the 1995–96 season to develop the real McCoy for itself. Even then, the failure of the English clubs to commit themselves in the first year made the competition something of a Franco-Welsh affair, although the whole tenor was raised by a hugely entertaining

final between Toulouse and Cardiff at the Arms Park, which the Frenchmen won 21–18 in extra-time. Having seen the enormous potential of a European Cup, the following season saw England enter four clubs and Scotland put forward three districts to join representatives from Ireland (3), France (4), Wales (4) and Italy (2). The 20 teams competing were split into four pools of five, from which the top two sides went into the quarter-finals.

Despite pooling all their top players into provinces for the event, the Irish and Scottish fared little better than the Italians, and the quarter-finals were dominated by the English, Welsh and French big guns. Although not open running rugby in the Super 12 style, the matches were nevertheless gripping enough to ensure that the European Cup ties have taken on a mystique and aura

that the domestic competitions still lack. In particular, games at winners Brive's packed ground and the seething atmosphere of Wasps' Loftus Road when Cardiff came to town were a level of intensity up from domestic fare. The final, a contest between Leicester's strong-mauling pack and Brive's free-running backs was a classic encounter, with French passion overcoming English determination as Brive took a grip on the match late on, winning 28–9 at the Cardiff Arms Park.

Just to prove their domination of the competition, France also contributed seven out of eight quarter-finalists in the European Conference, the level below the Cup.

Heineken European Cup Winners

Season	Winners		Runners-up	
1996	Toulouse	21	Cardiff	18
1997	Brive	28	Leicester	9

ASIAN CHAMPION-SHIP

The struggle for supremacy in Asia began in 1969 when Japan won the first Asian Championship in Tokyo, hardly a shock outcome given that with a playing population in excess of 100,000, Japan have almost as many players to call upon as the rest of of the Asian Championship countries put together. Moreover, rugby has been established in Japan far longer than in any of the other countries, and Japan boasts a unique system where clubs are run by companies, making most of the country's top players virtual professionals.

Nevertheless, Japan have not had it all their own way in the bi-annual tournament, not by a long chalk. Hong Kong put up a strong challenge early doors, but the first nation to break Japanese hegemony was Korea, which won the 1982 tournament by beating Japan 12–9 at the eighth time of asking. That win was achieved after the scores were level 9–9 at full-time, with Korean fly-half Moon Yuang Chan kicking the winning drop-goal quarter of an hour into extra-time. From there on in the competition has been a two-horse race between the speedy Japanese and the larger Koreans, a rivalry spiced up by the historical and vicious history between the two countries (Korea was a Japanese colony for almost half a century, and the Seoul government is still in the process of dynamiting buildings constructed to spell "Long Live Japan" when viewed from above!). The most bittersweet moment in the many clashes between the two came in the Asian Championship which doubled as a qualifying round for the 1995 World Cup, when Japan recovered from a half-time deficit of over 20 points to sneak a win at the wire. Korea's best run was three wins on the trot between 1986–90.

Japan and Korea may have completely dominated the competition, but in conjunction with the Hong Kong Sevens it still provides an arena of meaningful international competition where the small frames of the Asian races will not be a factor. As well as the two habitual winners, the Championship is also contested by Hong Kong, Sri Lanka, Malaysia, Thailand, Singapore and Taiwan, although quite what impact the adoption of the game by China will have upon the involvement is unclear.

The Asian Championship Winners

Season	Winners		
1969	Japan	1994	Japan
1970	Japan	1996	Japan
1972	Japan		
1974	Japan		
1976	Japan		
1978	Japan		
1980	Japan		
1981	Japan		
1982	Korea		
1984	Japan		
1986	Korea		
1988	Korea		
1990	Korea		
1992	Japan		

PACIFIC CHAMPION-SHIP

Although the qualifying rounds for the 1995 World Cup showed that rugby is alive and well on Pacific Islands such as the Cook Islands, Tahiti, Papua New Guinea and Soloman Islands, the long-established Pacific Championship is restricted to a three-way tournament between the three regional giants, Fiji, Tonga and Western Samoa. The Championship kicked off in 1924 when Fiji travelled to Tonga and drew the three-Test series, and consolidated its position as a three-way affair the next year when Fiji visited to Samoa and beat the hosts 6–0 on a field which had a large tree between the goal line and the 25-yard line! Since then finances and the difficulty of travel have often disrupted the tournament, which is played on an ad hoc basis.

At one stage before the last World Cup, the winners of the Pacific Championship were granted entry into the Super 10 provincial series, but the tournament's evolution into a Super 12 tournament in 1995 sidelined the islanders and the proposed replacement, the Pacific Rim Series, bit the dust at the last minute due to financial problems. Another feature of the Pacific Championship has been the fierce rivalry between the island races, which has sometimes threatened to get out of hand. When Fiji played in Apia in 1993, for example, the Samoans had to cancel police leave and put the army on standby!

Plans are underway, however, to include some form of Pacific Island side in the next Super 12.

FIRA

Once a powerful administrative body encompassing most of the world's unions outside the Big Eight, the Federation Internationale de Rugby Amateur – FIRA – is now essentially a European competition for all those countries not in the Five Nations (except France, which competes in both although it invariably plays an "A" team in the FIRA competition). The organisation was initially started in 1932, the year after France were thrown out of the Five Nations. Desperate for alternative international fixtures, France approached Germany, and the two countries formed an organisation which also had Romania, Italy, Holland, Catalonia, Portugal, Czechoslovakia and Sweden as fellow founder-members. After the war, when France were readmitted to the Five Nations, FIRA had grown in stature as it widened its net in Europe and took on associate members from outside the continent, and it sought wider aims such as regaining rugby's Olympic status and establishing a European clubs competition (which it did briefly in the early Sixties before financial considerations finished the tournament).

Although FIRA's days as a direct alternative to the International Board are over, thanks to the IB's decision to embrace the concept of a World Cup and to extend membership to

THEY COULD BE GIANTS *Hong Kong celebrate after posting a world record score of 154–18 over Singapore in 1994.*

every rugby-playing country in the world, the FIRA Championship which was first played in 1974 still provides Europe with a valuable outlet for national competition.

Played in three divisions containing virtually every country in mainland Europe and Francophone North Africa, France have invariably headed the First Division, although Romania have also won it five times and the USSR once.

In the 1997 match between Italy and France, the Italians caused a major upset when they defeated a near full-strength French side shortly after they had won the Grand Slam for the first time in a decade.

The FIRA Championship

Season	Winners	Season	Winners
1965–66	France	1978–79	France
1966–67	France	1979–80	France
1967–68	No comp	1980–81	Romania
1968–69	Romania	1981–82	France
1969–70	France	1982–83	Romania
1970–71	France	1983–84	France
1971–72	France	1984–85	France
1972–73	France	1985–87	France
1973–74	France	1987–89	France
1974–75	Romania	1989–90	France
1975–76	France	1990–92	France
1976–77	Romania	1992–94	France
1977–78	France	1994–97	Italy

NORTH AMERICA

The Americans and Canadians have markedly different rugby traditions, but share two common bonds: huge geographical and financial problems in attempting to devise any national competitions and the Can-Am Series. The problem of finances and geography has infiltrated both the national and the domestic level, with the Can-Am Series, which has been played between the US national side, the Eagles, and Canada every year since 1977, only going ahead most years after players paid their own air fare. Perhaps because most of its players come from the same province, British Columbia, the Canadians have dominated the series, winning on all but six occasions.

The USA"s inaugural club championship was played in 1979, but with the country's two strongest rugby communities 3,000 miles apart in California and on the East Coast, only with the recent injection of $10 million from Sky (see page 198) has a genuine national championship been financial or logistically feasible.

Much the same goes for Canada, where the Carling Bowl has long been the measure of domestic success. Inter-Provincial competition has been a recent innovation, but the climatic problems that exist in many areas (New Foundland, for example, only play rugby in the summer), the huge distances involved, a lack of serious funding and the dominance of the British Columbians limits its usefulness.

The Pan-Pacific Rim Championship

Season	Winners
1996	Canada
1997	Canada

SOUTH AMERICAN CHAMPION-SHIP

The South American Championship has been contested between Brazil , Argentina, Paraguay, Uruguay and Chile since the early 1970s, and has been won by Argentina whenever the Pumas have put in a side. Brazil have been the traditional whipping boys of the tournament, suffering several humiliating defeats, while Chile and, more recently, Uruguay, have provided the main opposition to the Argentinians.

WOMEN'S WORLD CUP

The Women's game has come on apace since the first international in 1982, when France beat the Netherlands 4–0. With momentum building throughout the Eighties, the first World Cup was held in 1991, with the two main world powers – USA and England – meeting in a match of all-out commitment. The Americans' swifter backs gave them the edge and they ran out 19–6 winners. Three years later in Scotland, the scenario was much the same, with the England pack dominating the Americans, scoring two penalty tries after continued pressure in the scrum. Even with two late American tries, the result was a 38–23 victory to England.

A WOMAN'S TOUCH *England captain Emma Mitchell fires out a pass as her side are overwhelmed by the USA.*

SEVENS TOURNAMENTS

Sevens first poked its head out into the rugby world in 1883 in the tiny market town of Melrose, centre of Scotland's rugby heartland in the Borders. At the time Melrose were on the verge of bankruptcy and were desperately looking for a way to bring in some paying punters to fill up their empty coffers. The halfbacks of the side, two butchers from the town called David Sanderson and his apprentice Ned Haig, hit upon the idea of using the forthcoming sports day as a way of raising money.

The passion for rugby is etched deep into the psyche of the tightly-knit Borders community, and the pair knew that if they could harness this spirit and enthusiasm they could have a potential money-spinner on their hands. As Haig said many years later:

"Want of money made us rack our brains as to what was to be done to keep the club from going to the wall, and the idea struck me that a football tournament might prove attractive. But it was a hopeless task to think of having several games in one afternoon with 15 players on both sides so the teams were reduced to seven men."

In fact, although Haig has always received the praise for being the founding father of sevens, the birth of the game was as much down to Sanderson, who came up with the idea after playing an abbreviated code of the game while working south of the border. Posterity has denied him his rightful place in the history of the game however, mainly because of a argument he had with the Mel-

rose club years later which led to his role being downplayed (and often even deleted) from official histories of the sevens.

But whoever came up with the idea, the important thing is that it stuck. Even more importantly, the innovation was an instant success at the Melrose Sports day, as this extract from the Border Telegraph of May 2, 1883, shows: "By the time of the event, an enormous crowd of spectators had assembled, special trains having been run from Galashiels and Hawick and about 1,600 tickets being taken at Melrose during the day.

The competition had been looked forward to with great interest, as most of the clubs of the district were expected to compete for the prize – a silver cup presented by the ladies of Melrose."

The success of the day was sealed when Melrose beat neighbours and great rivals Gala in a tense and excit-

ing final. With the scores level at full-time, a period of extra-time was decided upon, at which stage captain Sanderson scored a cheeky blindside try. As skipper, he immediately led his side off the pitch and claimed the Ladies Cup to howls of protest from the Gala players who thought that extra-time should be another 15 minutes. This is where the precedent for the first score in extra-time being the winning score comes from.

The tournament saved the Melrose club from bankruptcy, and established a tradition that was to flourish and, as Scots travelled the rugby world, spread until sevens became a respected code in its own right. Although the accompanying festivities, including foot races, dribbling races, drop-goal and place–kicking competitions, were later dropped, it was otherwise a format that was widely copied. A Borders sevens circuit soon sprang up and by the end of the cen-

SEVENS HEAVEN *In recent years Fiji, the 1997 World Sevens' champions, have established themselves as the most exciting and skillful of Sevens players.*

tury there were tournaments at Gala, Hawick, JedForest, Langholm, Selkirk and Kelso. Yet Melrose still remains the biggest and most prestigious competition to this day, with a Melrose winner's medal second only to a Scotland cap in the honours list north of the Border. Perhaps, explains Walter Allan in the Official History of the Melrose Sevens, that is why an episode in 1983 when several of the victorious French Barbarians, the first non-British winners of the tournament, handed over their medals to local beauties caused such deep offence in the town.

Far from spreading quickly from those ancient beginnings in the Scottish Borders, for the best part of a century sevens remained a minority pursuit generally played for a bit of fun and to keep fit at the end of the season. Even without Sanderson's recollections of having played the game south of the Border there is a good deal of evidence that an abbreviated rugby game was played in England on an informal basis in rugby's early years. Despite this, though, relatively few sevens tournaments raised their heads in England. Places like Caldy, in Lancashire, and the Snelling Sevens in Wales, still have tournaments that were started just after the turn of the century, but by and large sevens has never been big in Britain outside the Borders. Indeed, for many years it was known as "The Borders Game".

The one major exception was the Middlesex Sevens, which has been held annually at Twickenham since 1926 and which has regularly played to full houses of 60,000. Yet that tournament is as much a social occasion as a serious sporting day out, with beer and sunshine the priority on the last day of the season. Until

ALL THE WAY *Tim Rodber of England shows the Australians a clean pair of heels during the final of the 1993 World Cup Sevens.*

recently, it was restricted to clubs from the London area, but in recent years it has issued invitations to guest sides and recent winners include sevens specialists Fiji and Western Samoa.

It was not until the launch of the Hong Kong Sevens in 1976 that sevens spread outside Britain and became a truly global game. The Hong Kong tournament was the brainchild of a number of ex-pat Scots working in the Colony, chief among them was "Tokkie" Smith, now regarded as the father of modern sevens. From its first tournament, won by the Cantabrians side from Christchurch, New Zealand, it was abundantly clear that the Hong Kong event was something out of the ordinary.

In particular, the chance to compete on a more even playing field with the bigger sides in world rugby was welcomed by the people of Asia and the numerically smaller nations of world rugby. Sides such as Korea, Taiwan, Sri Lanka, Papua New Guinea, Holland and Germany all came to prominence at the sevens alongside the giants of the abbreviated code, New Zealand, Australia and Fiji, with the unique system of having three competitions – a bowl, plate and cup – making the competition esepcially "minnow friendly".

From the early Eighties, it was national sides only at Hong Kong, with the exception of the Home Unions who are in the middle of heavy domestic competitions when the sevens are held in late March. Instead, specialist sevens touring sides like the Barbarians (Britain), the Co-Optimists (Scotland), the Wolfhounds (Ireland), Crawshay's (Wales) and the Penguins (England) came out from Britain to try their luck at Hong Kong, although the only northern hemisphere side to win at Hong Kong so far was the Barbarians in 1981.

These days Hong Kong is a glittering event which essentially doubles as a world championship of sevens, although quite how the Chinese takeover will impact upon the fun-loving aspects that have done so much to popularise the tournament is anyone's guess. In many ways, though, Hong Kong has already fulfiled its important mission by establishing sevens as a missionary force in the game, a quick and easy introduction to the essentials of rugby without

many of the technicalities that baffle newcomers.

If nothing else, the success of Hong Kong as a tourist magnet has set off a trail of sevens tournaments in exotic locations around the world that has established an unofficial sevens circuit. Sevens specialists Fiji and a raft of invitation teams compete for cash prizes up to £25,000 in places as beautiful as Dubai, Singapore, Paris, Benidorm, Punta del Este in Uruguay, Lisbon, Barbados, Catania in Sicily, Tokyo, Suva in Fiji, Stellenbosch, Madrid, Denver and Victoria Falls in Zimbabwe. Sevens has become so popular that it will even feature as the new sport at the 1998 Commonwealth Games in Malaysia (which is the birthplace of the increasingly popular game of tens and the venue for the famous Cobra Tens).

Although it has yet to achieve anywhere near the popularity of the World Cup or even the Hong Kong Sevens itself, the rise of sevens has led to the introduction of a World Cup Sevens tournament every four years under the auspices of the International Board's commercial arm, RWC Ltd. Contested for the Melrose Cup, the first tournament was a low-key affair staged at Murrayfield in Edinburgh.

Despite the southern hemisphere sides being firm favourites at the outset of the tournament, England upset the form book beating Australia in the final.

Logic and form reasserted themselves four years later, however, as Fiji beat South Africa in a closely-fought final in Hong Kong. Indeed, not one of the northern hemisphere sides managed to reach the semi-final stage.

Unlike the 1993 World Cup Sevens, the 1997 tournament was played to packed crowds amid a cacophony of raucous singing and a deluge of warm beer.

Hong Kong Sevens Winners

1976	Cantabrians	1988	Australia
1977	Fiji	1989	New Zealand
1978	Fiji	1990	Fiji
1979	Australia	1991	Fiji
1980	Fiji	1992	Fiji
1981	Barbarians	1993	W.Samoa
1982	Australia	1994	New Zealand
1983	Australia	1995	New Zealand
1984	Fiji	1996	New Zealand
1985	Australia	1997	Fiji*
1986	New Zealand	* Indicates Tournament
1987	New Zealand	Doubled as World Cup Sevens

Middlesex Sevens Winners

1926	Harlequins	1963	London Scots
1927	Harlequins	1964	Loughborough
1928	Harlequins	1965	London Scots
1929	Harlequins	1966	Loughborough
1930	London Welsh	1967	Harlequins
1931	London Welsh	1968	London Welsh
1932	Blackheath	1969	St Luke's
1933	Harlequins	1970	Loughborough
1934	Barbarians	1971	London Welsh
1935	Harlequins	1972	London Welsh
1936	Sale	1973	London Welsh
1937	London Scots	1974	Richmond
1938	Met Police	1975	Richmond
1939	Cardiff	1976	Loughborough
1940	St Mary's Hos	1977	Richmond
1941	Cambridge Uni	1978	Harlequins
1942	St Mary's Hos	1979	Richmond
1943	St Mary's Hos	1980	Richmond
1944	St Mary's Hos	1981	Rosslyn Park
1945	Notts	1982	Stewart's-
1946	St Mary's Hos		Melville F.P.
1947	Rosslyn Park	1983	Richmond
1948	Wasps	1984	London Welsh
1949	Heriot's F.P.	1985	Wasps
1950	Rosslyn Park	1986	Harlequins
1951	Richmond II	1987	Harlequins
1952	Wasps	1988	Harlequins
1953	Richmond	1989	Harlequins
1954	Rosslyn Park	1990	Harlequins
1955	Richmond	1991	London Scots
1956	London Welsh	1992	W. Samoa
1957	St Luke's	1993	Wasps
1958	Blackheath	1994	Bath
1959	Loughborough	1995	Leicester
1960	London Scots	1996	Wigan RLFC
1961	London Scots	1997	Fiji
1962	London Scots		

World Cup Sevens Winners

1993 at Murrayfield

Final	England	21	Australia	17

Plate Winners: Argentina

1993 at Hong Kong

1997	Fiji	24	South Africa 21

Plate Winners: Tonga

THE BRITISH LIONS

Before the advent of the first World Cup in 1987, British Lions tours represented the apex of a player's career. To play for the Lions or against the Lions was the highest honour the game could bestow, and the coming of a Lions tour would dominate the sporting agenda in in the host nations for months before the tourists' arrival. There have been many great players to have played for their individual countries, but until 1987 it was virtually impossible for a player to achieve legendary status unless he had tested himself in the furnace of a Lions Test.

Although universally known as the British Lions since 1924, when the side gained the nickname due to the logo on their tour ties, the tours are in fact undertaken by the British Isles Rugby Union Team. The tour party is chosen from the geographical entity of the British Isles, which for these purposes include England, Wales, Scotland and Ireland (both North and South), and tours to either New Zealand or South Africa on average every four years. Only in 1989, when South Africa were still isolated after the 1980 tour and the Wallabies were emerging as a genuine third force in the Southern Hemisphere, did Australia feature as a destination in its own right rather than as a staging point on the way to the real challenge in New Zealand.

It was on a joint trip to Australia and New Zealand that the concept of the Lions was first born. The trip in question was James Lillywhite's 1876–7 cricket tour. Marvelling at the hunger of the Australians and New Zealanders for sporting competition, the English cricketers Alfred Shaw and Arthur Shrewsbury (the former was the first man to bowl a ball in Test cricket) eventually hit upon the idea of filling their winter with a rugby tour and promptly cabled the RFU. Typically, the game's English administrators had no interest in sending a representative party, but had no problem with a side travelling southwards. An agent was appointed and within six months a 21-strong tour party sailed for New Zealand and Australia under the leadership of Swinton's Bob Seddon. In fact, virtually all of the tour party came from either the Northern clubs or from the Scottish cotton mill town of Hawick, which had very strong ties with Yorkshire rugby. Only Welshman William Thomas and the Isle of Man's AP Penketh were drawn from other areas and only three of the squad were established internationals.

Before the tour had even left it hit controversy when it was discovered that at least two players had received "expenses" of around £15 each, yet on March 8, 1888 the party left for New Zealand, where it met up with England cricket captain Andrew Stoddart. He was later to assume captaincy of the rugby side as well after Seddon was drowned in Australia's Hunter River during a boating accident (making him the last man to captain England at both rugby and cricket). In Australasia, the clash of rugby cultures was intriguing, with the British introducing the concept of heeling back and passing from the scrum, while also playing several games under Australian Rules in Victoria. In all the side played 35 games and lost just two of them, to Taranaki and Auckland, scoring 292 points, conceding 98 and finding the going significantly harder in New Zealand than in Australia.

It has been one of the RFU's enduring characteristics that if a venture succeeds, it inevitably annexes it, and so it was three years later when Cecil Rhodes, then governor of the Cape Colony, requested that a British tour party be sent to Southern Africa. This time the tour party was to play Test matches and was accordingly placed under the leadership of experienced Scottish cap Bill Maclagan and made up of experienced English and Scottish players, of whom half were internationals. The result was a victorious trek around Southern Africa in which 19 unbeaten games were played and 221 points scored, with only one conceded. Bustling Blackheath centre Randolph Aston, who scored 30 tries, including two in the 3–0 Test whitewash, to be acclaimed the star of the tour, typified the outstanding back play of the British.

Although their first two tours were triumphant romps punctuated by glittering social occasions, it was not long before the British headstart had begun to be eroded. When Johnny Hammond returned to South Africa in 1896 with a team made up of English and Irish players, for instance, he was amazed to find how far the colonials had come on. Strong forwards and a better tactical appreciation meant there were less easy matches and for the first time the British lost a Test when they were defeated 5–0 by South Africa in the Fourth Test at Newlands. It was the same story in 1899 when the Rev Matthew Mullineux's party lost three of its 21 games in Australia, including the First Test 13–3. The 1891 tour to South Africa remains the only Lions tour where the tourists have completed a whitewash. By the time the new century dawned, the process of catch-up had been completed and British visits to the Southern Hemisphere began to take on a pattern that still exists today – the British provide weak forwards and inventive

SEEING EYE TO EYE *The Lions' mid-week side – AKA Donal's Doughnuts – lock horns with Canberra.*

NO ESCAPE: *British Lions winger Ieuan Evans feels the full force of the All Black tackling during the 1993 tour to New Zealand.*

backs, a combination which is reversed in their opponents.

Mark Morrison's 1903 side were the get a taste of the things to come when they lost the Third Test 8–0 and with it the series 1–0 in South Africa after the first two Tests were drawn. It was a similar situation the following year when Darkie Bevell-Sivright's hugely talented Welsh threequarters Percy Bush, Teddy Morgan and Rhys Gabe inspired the British side to a won 14, lost none record in Australia. In a foretaste of the future, however, the same side won only two of its five games in New Zealand, and lost the Test 9–3.

Worse was to come in 1908 when Scotland and Ireland refused to contribute players for the tour to New Zealand after an argument over All Black expenses on the 1905 "Originals" tour. The weakened Anglo-Welsh tour party lost one of its three major matches in Australia, was beaten by five New Zealand provincial Unions and despite managing to draw the Second Test 3–3 after the All Black selectors rested seven of its best players, lost the other two Tests by the unprecedented scorelines of 32–5 and 29–0. Even when Tom Smyth's 1910 party contained the cream of all four Home Unions, the result was depressingly familiar; only 13 of 24 games won and a 2–1 series defeat. The status quo had changed forever.

The shift in power was confirmed in dramatic fashion during the two tours to South Africa and one tour to Australasia between the wars. In twelve Tests, the Lions only managed to win two, scoring 90 points but conceding almost double that number. Yet if the tours were not successes in terms of playing results, they did at least consolidate the Lions reputation as a side which played some of the most attractive, open, running rugby in the world as men such as Haydn Tanner, Iain Smith, Carl Aarvold, Harry Bowcott and Vivian Jenkins cut a swathe through the Southern Hemisphere. Had the British tight forwards been able to live with their Southern Hemisphere counterparts, the roles may well have been reversed. Indeed, had the British sides been able to draw fully from the talent avail-

able, they would undoubtedly have proved far more competitive, but the long duration of tours undertaken by cruise liner, which could last up to six months, meant that many top players declined the invitation to tour.

After the war, the growing prestige of the Lions meant that virtually every top player was available to tour New Zealand, and in 1950 only two of Britan's leading players were unable to make the four-month tour. That tour, although unsuccessful, remains famous for the flair and inventiveness of Lions backs such as Irish fly-half Jack Kyle and Welsh centre Bleddyn Williams. Once again, forward deficiencies – in particular the inability to cope with the hard rucking percentage game pioneered by Viv Cavanagh and Otago – meant that the Lions lost three of the four Tests in New Zealand, winning both in Australia. But Karl Mullen's men played an attacking game of such fervour and in such stark contrast to the home sides that they were feted wherever they went. The 1950 Lions were also the first side to wear the now famous kit incorporating the colours of the four Home Unions: the red of Wales on the shirt; the white of England on the shorts, cuffs and collar; the navy blue of Scotland and the green of Ireland on the socks.

The 1950 tour set the standard for the remaining two tours of the Fifties. As with the 1950 tourists, Robin Thompson's 1955 side left an indelible mark on the history of South African rugby. Travelling by air for the first time, the tour was also cov-

ered extensively by newspapers and the new medium of television, with the result that the party became stars. As in New Zealand, the South African public were desperate to see talented backs given free rein, and they were not to be disappointed by the Lions. With a streetwise pack that was at last able to hold the Springboks at bay, backs like Irish wing Tony O'Reilly, English centres Butterfield and Davies, and half – backs Dickie Jeeps and Cliff Morgan ran rings around Stephen Fry's Springboks. The First Test in Johannesburg, which the Lions won 23–22 in front of 95,000 spectators after playing the whole second half with only seven forwards (see page 179) was reckoned one of the greatest games ever played and set the tenor for a series of high excitement which the Springboks counted themselves fortunate to eventually share.

1959 witnessed another spectacular series in Australia and New Zealand, with the Lions throwing caution to the wind in a run-at-all-costs strategy. And it almost paid off. After convincingly winning the two Tests in Australia, the forward frailty re-emerged and the Lions lost the New Zealand leg 3–1, yet it was a far from discreditable performance. Indeed, many New Zealanders conceded that the 18–17 First Test defeat, which came when All Black fullback Don Clarke kicked six penalties to the Lions four tries, was at the very least a moral victory (which would now be a 25–18 win that would have tied the series).

The Sixties were an unmitigated disaster for British rugby as the forwards continued to be battered by the Southern Hemisphere, while the conveyor belt of inventive threequarters which had sustained the Lions up to 1959 dried up almost completely. The '62 Lions in South Africa lost three Tests and drew one, but were at least competitive. The '66 Lions looked business like in Australia, but were humiliated so completely in New Zealand that captain Mike Campbell-Lamerton dropped himself amid a four-Test whitewash. South Africa in '68 was little better, with Tom Kiernan's charges avoiding defeat in just one of the Tests, a 6–6 draw in in Port Elizabeth.

If the Sixties was the Lions' dismal decade, then the Seventies was to emerge as its golden era. The major obstacle to success for the Lions had always been a lack of possession, but by the time of the 1971 tour to New Zealand, Britain had a set of outrageously talented backs and a pack able to dominate the best in the world. And that's exactly what the Lions did for the duration of the tour. Revitalised by the evidence of the 1969–70 Springbok tour of Britain, which showed the gap between Southern and Northern Hemispheres closing, the Lions played 26 games on that tour, losing just two against Queensland and the Second Test in Christchurch. With coaching genius Carwyn James in the background directing operations and Welsh fly-half Barry John providing peerless on-field tactical acumen, the Lions inflicted the first series defeat on New Zealand soil since the 1937 Springboks. The bedrock of the challenge was the forward power provided by men like Willie John McBride, Mervyn Davies and Ian McLauchlan. The decisive factor was the best set of backs ever dispatched from Britain – JPR Williams, Gerald Davies, John Dawes, Mike Gibson, John Bevan, David Duckham, Barry John and Gareth Edwards are all as revered now, quarter of a century later, as they were then.

Barry John's '71 Lions were the finest all-round side ever to have pulled on Lions' shirts, but there is equally little doubt as to which is the

GOING, GOING, GONE *All Black scrum-half Sid Going vs the Lions in 1971.*

best set of Lions forwards ever to have represented Britain. The pack that toured South Africa in 1974 destroyed the Springbok eight and any provincial forwards who had the gall to go head to head with one of the hardest packs ever to play the game. McBride had toured South Africa as a Lion in '62 and '68 and had come to fully understand the role intimidation played in top level rugby there. His reaction was, as he put it, "to get our retaliation in first." The Lions refused to take a step back as they brawled their way round The Republic, using the now notorious "99" call – where every forward punches the nearest Springbok on the basis that the referee has to send them all off or none of them off – and ending the tour unbeaten. With hefty wins in the first three Tests, only a controversial 13–13 draw (controversial because a Fergus Slattery try was disallowed on the stroke of full-time) marring the perfect record.

However, while the Lions of '74 had outstanding forwards, the back play had declined somewhat from its peak in New Zealand three years before. By the time Phil Bennett led the Lions back to New Zealand in 1977, the backs had become the Achilles heel of the side. The forwards were again outstanding, but with poor back play and a curious lack of spirit in the squad which many ascribed to the very high number of players (18) from one country (Wales), the Lions lost the series 3–1. It was again a similar scenario in 1980 when poor back play and injuries meant Billy Beaumont's fiercely competitive pack managed only one win over the Springboks from four Tests that could have swung either way. By 1983, when Ciaran Fitzgerald's Lions were destroyed by the All Blacks, who won the series 4–0, it was clear that the forward dominance of the Seventies had completely dissipated. By the time coaches Ian McGeechan and Roger Uttley led the Lions to Australia in 1989, the whole balance of power had shifted once more. The Wallabies had been building impressively since their unexpected failure to make the World Cup final, and the Lions arrived with a formidable pack

GOTCHA! *J.P.R. Williams is scragged by a Transvaal defender during the 1974 Lions' tour to South Africa.*

based on an experienced English eight which was completely dominating European rugby. Only Welsh lock Bob Norster had been capped by the Lions before, and he only played in the First Test defeat.

It was obvious after that First Test defeat that the quick, rucking game favoured by the Celts was not going to beat an ultra-fit Australian side, so the decision to draft in two more Englishmen in Wade Dooley and Mike Teague and base the gameplan around the strong-mauling English forwards was taken. It worked like a dream, with Teague taking the Man of the Series and the Lions totally outmuscling the Wallabies to win the Second Test 19–12, a win wrapped up by a virtuoso Jeremy Guscott try in the last few minutes of a pulsating match.

Unfortunately the Test series was played against a backdrop of lurid Aussie press headlines brought on by the Lions' aggressive but legitimate style of play. The deciding Test was settled by a Ieuan Evans try after a David Campese blunder behing his own try – line (see page 107). The Lions 2–1 series win may not have been pretty, but it was certainly effective as the tourists came back from 1–0 down to win the series for only the second time. Outmuscling the Wallabies with teak hard forwards

in their prime is one thing, but trying to do the same to the New Zealanders when the core of your pack is clearly past its sell-by date is a different proposition altogether. Yet that is what the Lions attempted to do in 1993, and it almost worked. With tyro twin tower locks Martin Johnson and Martin Bayfield dominating the lineout and with captain Gavin Hastings, centres Guscott and Gibbs, and wing Ieuan Evans in outstanding form, the Lions stormed back from a 20–18 First Test loss to take Second Test 20–7. Even though the midweek side performed woefully throughout the tour, the Lions had high hopes for the Third Test, but despite being 10–0 up at halftime, they were crushed 30–13 in the second-half display by the All Blacks.

With the advent of professionalism many people erroneously assumed the Lions' future would become increasingly parlous as club sides refused to release their prized assets for gruelling and demanding tours that could well bring their players back to them injured and therefore unable to play for them in September when the domestic season started.

But the 1997 tour to South Africa, the first time the Lions had visited the country since 1980, generated a

massive amount of media hype.

Given no chance of winning the three–Test series when they arrived in South Africa, the Lions stunned the Springboks, taking the series 2–1.

A superb goal–kicking display by full–back Neil Jenkins throughout, and some robust defending in the first two Tests gave the Lions a series victory that only the most ardent Lions' supporter would have predicted at the outset. More importantly, the success of the tour guarantees the future of the Lions into the next century.

British Lions Full Test Record							
Year	Country	P	W	D	L	F	A
1891	South Africa	3	3	0	0	11	0
1896	South Africa	4	3	0	1	34	16
1899	Australia	4	3	0	1	38	23
1903	South Africa	3	0	2	1	10	18
1904	Australia &	3	3	0	0	50	3
	New Zealand	1	0	0	1	3	9
1908	Australia &						
	New Zealand	3	0	1	2	8	64
1910	South Africa	3	1	0	2	23	38
1924	South Africa	4	0	1	3	15	43
1930	New Zealand &	4	1	0	3	34	53
	Australia	1	0	0	1	5	6
1938	South Africa	3	1	0	2	36	61
1950	New Zealand &	4	0	1	3	20	34
	Australia	2	2	0	0	43	9
1955	South Africa	4	2	0	2	49	75
1959	Australia &	2	2	0	0	41	9
	New Zealand	4	1	0	3	42	57
1962	South Africa	4	0	1	3	20	48
1966	Australia &	2	2	0	0	42	8
	New Zealand	4	0	0	4	32	79
1968	South Africa	4	0	1	3	38	61
1971	Australia &						
	New Zealand	4	2	1	1	48	42
1974	South Africa	4	3	1	0	79	34
1977	New Zealand	4	1	0	3	41	54
1980	South Africa	4	1	0	3	68	77
1983	New Zealand	4	0	0	4	26	78
1989	Australia	3	2	0	1	50	60
1993	New Zealand	3	1	0	2	51	57
1997	South Africa	3	2	0	1	60	66

CLUB COMPETITIONS

HARING TO GO *Dusty Hare, the former England full–back, can't hide his disappointment as he picks up his losers' medal at Twickenham following Leicester's 1989 Pilkington Cup final defeat at the hands of Bath.*

ENGLAND

It's fair to say the English have never been that keen on competitions. Or maybe it would be more accurate to say that English administrators have never been that keen on competitions. It was, after all, the white hot heat of competition in the Yorkshire and Lancashire Cups which eventually led to the breakaway of the northern clubs and the formation of the Rugby League. As experiences go, it was a pretty damaging one for the RFU and senior administrators were unanimously decided after the Great Schism of 1895 that competitive rugby would be kept to a minimum. "Friendlies" were to be the order of the day.

Not that there weren't many club players and administrators who yearned for some form of meaningful competition. The County Cups were always fiercely fought and the County Championship formed the bedrock of the representative level from which the national side was chosen. But as for leagues, the answer was a straight "no way". One of many such bids to bite the dust was at the RFU annual general meeting at the Palace Hotel on the Strand in Sep-

tember 1900. At that meeting a delegate representing Bristol argued cogently and passionately in favour of the introduction of leagues instead of cups, but all to no avail. Officialdom was firmly set against the idea, and the plan was firmly scotched when retiring president J Thorp, new president F Fox and the all-powerful secretary Rowland Hill spoke out strongly against the proposal, with the latter denouncing the plan from "the radical young gentleman from Bristol", adding that "all know the evils that must spring from the introduction of such a system."

So for the first 100 years of its existence, English rugby had to put up with a decidedly low-key competitive structure. Not that the RFU minded if the competing parties were from the right background and competing in the right atmosphere. Competition may have been too mighty a temptation for the working man, but for young professionals it was positively encouraged. So it was that events such as the Varsity Match between Oxford and Cambridge Universities and the Hospitals' Cup were

actively promoted at the same time that the idea of leagues was being poo pooed in Twickenham. The Varsity Match in particular was a high point of the season, with many of the country's finest players passing through either one of the institutions (see page 97) after 1871 when the first match was played between the two seats of learning. To date, out of the 115 matches played the Dark Blues of Oxford have won 49, while the Light Blues have won 53, and all matches since 1921 have been played at Twickenham.

As for the wider rugby world, the focus at club level was on the 27 County Cups, which were keenly fought in the early years but which have gradually declined in importance to the point where today they are seen by serious clubs mainly as a means of gaining entry into the national knock-out Cup. Of wider significance, still, is the County Championship, even if that has been declining steadily in influence since the war. The tournament, in which the counties draw on players from within their geographical boundaries, has a long and illustrious history. It started in 1889, when Yorkshire were declared county champions after an unbeaten season, and the history of the competition since then has been dominated by the northern counties and those from the West Country. Indeed, on only 30 occasions in the last 106 years has the (preposterously large) trophy ventured outside those two rugby heartlands, and seven of those wins were by Warwickshire in a Coventry-inspired eight year period of complete domination in the late Fifties and early Sixties.

It can come as little surprise then that the areas which retain the most enthusiasm for the County Championship are the north and south west of the country. Yet the rise of the leagues and of the national knock-out cup (and even of the much maligned Divisional Championship) in recent years means that the once-

proud championship has become something of a sideshow. Indeed, so minimal is interest that it seems the only time it ever manages to attract any profile is when Cornwall make it to the final and add some novelty value to the proceedings by packing out Twickenham. So secondary has the Championship become that it is no longer open to players from the top three national divisions.

The decline of the County Championship is down to more than fashion, however. In recent years it has been supplanted as a method of national selection by the artificially created and hugely unpopular Divisional Championship, a tournament born when the southern hemisphere provincial model was seen as the perfect prototype. Unfortunately, the English version never appealed to either the English rugby fan or player whose allegiance was always to their club. Subsequently, it died a death after just over a decade in 1996 when virtually every serious contender for a slot on the national side refused to play in it, and crowds had dwindled to only a few hundred. Yet while few ever bothered to watch the Divisional games, everybody tends to underestimate their impact on the national side in the Eighties and Nineties, a period when a whole generation of players – including Will Carling and Rob Andrew – came to prominence through playing for their division.

Today, the competitive emphasis is back where it started 125 years ago – with the clubs. All of the current competitions are club based, with the two hugely popular additions from this decade, the Junior and Intermediate Cups, proving that the appetite of players at all level for Cup competition is virtually insatiable. Those two competitions are, of course, offshoots of the National Cup competition which has been played in England annually since Gloucester beat Moseley 17–6 in the first final at Twickenham in 1972. Since then, the Cup has become one of the most eagerly awaited parts of the domestic season and has established a reputation as a competition capable of producing some outstanding games. Two that particularly stand out feature Bath, who have dominated the event to such an extent that they have won it ten times since their first victory in 1984. In 1992, they overcame Harlequins in the closing minutes of extra–time 15–12, courtesy of a Stuart Barnes' drop-goal from the half–way line , and in 1990 Bath put on a display of rugby the like of which Twickenham has rarely witnessed as they obliterated close rivals Gloucester 48–6 in the glorious May sunshine. The Cup final is always a sell-out, and with a capacity approaching 80,000 at Twickenham it is the largest club match in the world.

For all that the Cup is a fun day out, though, the really serious competition for ambitious clubs remains the league, which with 2,200 clubs is the largest organised league in any

sport anywhere in the world. It is perhaps a measure of English rugby's innate conservatism that a World Cup had come and gone before the inaugural league season got underway in September 1987, but it also says volumes about the public and the players' appetite for quantifiable results that the leagues have proved to be the success that they have. Last season, despite huge increases in ground admission as the professional game kicked in, almost half of the games in the first division of the leagues were sold out and interest is now at an all-time high. Bath remain the single most successful league side, with an amazing seven league titles in the last ten seasons, with only Leicester and Wasps (both twice) spoiling the party.

As with their footballing counterparts, English rugby clubs are now beginning to widen their horizon and have just completed their first year competing in a European Cup (see page 25).

The Pilkington Cup

Year	Winner		Runner-up	
1972	Gloucester	17	Moseley	6
1973	Coventry	27	Bristol	15
1974	Coventry	26	London Scottish	6
1975	Bedford	28	Rosslyn Park	12
1976	Gosforth	23	Rosslyn Park	14
1977	Gosforth	27	Waterloo	11
1978	Gloucester	6	Leicester	3
1979	Leicester	15	Moseley	12
1980	Leicester	21	London Irish	9
1981	Leicester	22	Gosforth	15
1982	Gloucester	12	Moseley	12*
1983	Bristol	28	Leicester	22
1984	Bath	10	Bristol	9
1985	Bath	24	London Welsh	15
1986	Bath	25	Wasps	17
1987	Bath	19	Wasps	12
1988	Harlequins	28	Bristol	22
1989	Bath	10	Leicester	6
1990	Bath	48	Gloucester	6
1991	Harlequins	25	Northampton	13
1992	Bath	15	Harlequins	12
1993	Leicester	23	Harlequins	16
1994	Bath	21	Leicester	9
1995	Bath	36	Wasps	16
1996	Bath	16	Leicester	15
1997	Leicester	9	Sale	3

* Title Shared

IRELAND

The four Irish provinces of Ulster, Munster, Leinster and Connacht have provided the basis for competition in Ireland virtually from the time that the game became established across the Irish Sea. The internal Cups that each province stage annually are the bedrock of rugby in Ireland, and have contributed to a thriving club scene that has engendered age old rivalries that are, by and large, still maintained to this day. That ancient rivalries are still as keen as ever is not surprising given that the meritocracy that comes with League competition only reached Ireland earlier this decade when the IRFU became the last major union in the world to have some form of

national competition when it introduced the the All Ireland League. Before that, the union had to rely upon the evidence of the Inter-Provincial series between the four main provinces and, latterly, the Exiles, which was made up of the large number of Irish players living, playing and working in Britain.

If the Irish were very tardy in setting up a national League, then it was a hesitancy in marked contrast to the speed with which competitions sprang up as rugby was becoming established in the early days. Within five years of Ireland's first international game, against England at The Oval in 1875, the Leinster Union (which is centred around the city of Dublin) had set up its own Cup competition which started the following year in 1882. Fittingly, the competition was won by the the birthplace of Irish rugby, Dublin's Trinity College – hardy much a shock given that the great institution had provided almost half of Ireland's non-Ulster players to that date, including men like the "heavy, hard-working forward" Michael Cusack. Needless to say, given Trinity's pedigree and tradition as a rugby hotbed, it dominated the early years of the Leinster Cup, winning in 12 of the first 19 years. Since then, however, its influence has gradually faded and it has only won the Cup once since 1926, with open clubs like Lansdowne, Bective Rangers, Old Belvedere, Wanderers, Blackrock and St Mary's all winning the Cup regularly, Indeed, the Leinster competition is the most open of all the Irish cups, with any one of up to ten clubs capable of staging a realistic challenge for the silverware.

The Ulster Cup, which is based around the northern rugby stronghold of Belfast, was the next competition to kick off in 1885 when the northern birthplace of rugby, NIFC, carried the trophy back to their Ormeau headquarters on the outskirts of Belfast. The Munster province, which is dominated by the clubs of Cork and Limerick, started its competition the next year, and 13 years later, in 1896, the rugby backwater of Connacht followed suit. All three Cups followed Leinster's lead, with one or two clubs dominating early

TOP DOGS *Bath have dominated the Leagues.*

on before the game became sufficiently well established outside the early centres for other clubs to be able to genuinely compete. Only in in the west in Connacht, where the comparatively tiny rugby population made strength in depth non-existent, has the Cup been dominated by just two clubs, Galweigans and University College Galway, who won the Cup 50 times in its first 70 years. In Munster, the triumvirate of Garryowen, University College Cork and Cork Constitution have also dominated the Cup, winning the competition 64 times in the first 83 years. Likewise, in Ulster, where the dominant forces have historically been NIFC (who won the Cup every year bar one between 1893–1902), Queen's University and Instonians.

The next tier up from the provincial cups since 1947 has been provided by the Provincial Championships. Although the provinces had played each other on an ad hoc basis until then, it was only after the war that the "Inter-Pros" provided the national selectors with a meaningful representative level by which to assess players. Ulster were the dominant force in the early years, but of late Leinster and, more particularly Munster, have begun to make it a two-horse race. Connacht are invariably whitewashed. The "state of origin" for-

mat of the four provinces playing each other on a round-robin basis has remained virtually untouched since, except with the addition of the Irish

Irish League Winners

1991	Cork Cons	1996	Shannon
1992	Garryowen	1997	Shannon
1993	Young Munster		
1994	Garryowen		
1995	Shannon		

Irish Interprovincial Championship

Year	Winner	Year	Winner
1947	Ulster	1974	Munster
1948	Munster	1975	Ulster
1949	Leinster	1976	Leinster & Ulster & Munster
1950	Leinster		
1951	Ulster	1977	Ulster
1952	Ulster	1978	Leinster & Ulster & Munster
1953	Ulster & Munster		
1954	Ulster	1979	Munster
1955	Munster & Leins	1980	Leinster
1956	Ulster & Connacht	1981	Leinster
1957	Ulster & Leinster & Connacht	1982	Leinster
		1983	Leinster & Ulster & Munster
1958	Munster		
1959	Leinster	1984	Leinster
1960	Munster	1985	Ulster
1961	Leinster	1986	Ulster
1962	Leinster	1987	Ulster
1963	Munster	1988	Ulster
1964	Leinster	1989	Ulster
1965	Leinster	1990	Ulster
1966	Munster	1991	Ulster
1967	Ulster & Munster	1992	Ulster
1968	Ulster	1993	Ulster
1969	Munster	1994	Leinster & Ulster & Munster
1970	Ulster		
1971	Ulster	1995	Munster
1972	Leinster	1996	Leinster
1973	Leinster & Ulster & Munster	1997	Munster

Exiles in 1992, and of the abortive efforts to widen the format to include the Scottish provinces in 1995. The advent of the European Cup, in which Ireland's top three provinces currently compete, may soon force a rethink of the format however.

Irish rugby is notoriously conservative, and was the last union to introduce a system of nationwide leagues in 1991. Since then, the All-Ireland League has revolutionised club rugby, taking on the role of the Provincial Cups and injecting an element of dynamism and meritocracy into proceedings. The Limerick clubs of Garryowen, Shannon and Young Munster have completely dominated the competition, winning every year but one.

WALES

Competitive rugby returned to Wales in September 1971 after a lengthy absence at the top level when the Welsh Rugby Union introduced a knock-out cup competition, that, despite problems, particularly in the opening years, has continued and now includes 229 clubs. The Welsh Cup or Schweppes Cup or SWALEC Cup, to give it the three hats it has so far worn, has been a resounding success, not least because it has given the small village clubs a tilt at toppling the traditional giants of the Welsh game. No better example could be made of the excitement of this particular competition than when St Peter's, from the Roath suburb of Cardiff, came to the Arms Park and to the joy of the majority of clubs in Wales, defeated Cardiff FC – the self-styled "Greatest Club in the World" – by 16–14 in 1992–93 in what was Cardiff's 100th cup-tie.

The Cup competition was eventually followed by the creation of a Welsh National League for the top 38 clubs in September 1990 that Heineken sponsored for six seasons with the clubs increasing to 60 in five divisions. In the 1994–95 season, the National League, though unsponsored, was increased to include all the 200-plus first-class clubs and fifteen divisions were added with five each

in the West, East and Central areas of Wales.

Cup rugby in Wales had for many years been restricted to regional competitions but the cup in South Wales had begun as early as season 1877–78. That competition was known as the South Wales Challenge Cup and attracted eighteen entrants who paid two guineas each but stood to win a cup valued at a massive fifty guineas. Newport were the first winners by defeating Swansea at Bridgend, but the win-at-all-costs ethos it engendered meant that the Cup was not universally popular. It was not long before the Cup competition became associated with some of the undoubted flouting of the amateurism regulations in South Wales, and in many ways it was the example of the Cup in Wales that led the English RFU to eschew a similar competition.

Scoring values of course were constantly changing in those days to confuse players and spectators alike but if points were level the amount of minors conceded (penalties) was the decisive factor. Scott Gibbs, the current Wales centre, was in his first season as an international when this system was explained to him as he researched the history of the game. He took a breath, thought for a while, and said: "No wonder we could usually beat England then, as we always had a lot of miners playing." He roared with laughter as he found that minors were not in fact real miners!

But Gibbs was correct in many ways as miners did form the tough background for those great early cup clashes before the turn of the century. Back then, teams were drawn from within the very tight mining communities and cup rugby meant very competitive rugby. The result was fiercely competitive games played in front of fiercely partisan supporters.

In 1879, winners Newport had to play twice after the Final to win the cup as Swansea and Neath had met in six drawn matches and were then thrown out but later brought back for a seventh match that Neath won by the dreaded minor as Swansea carried over their own line after 150 minutes of 0–0. Newport beat Neath in the second final but Swansea were not happy and a third 'final' saw New-

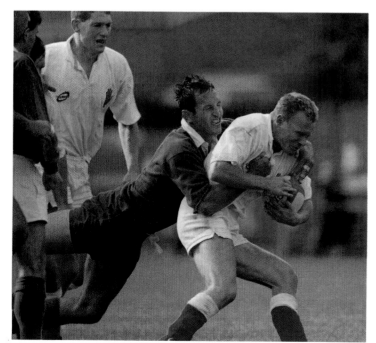

BACK TO THE WALL *Ulster's Maurice Field in an Interprovincial Cup clash.*

HANDS UP THE WINNERS *Cardiff celebrate their 1994 SWALEC Cup final victory.*

port defeat Swansea 48–0.

So bitter were many of the arguments and feuds thrown up by the Cup that the competition was eventually disbanded in 1887, only to resurface two years later as a series of cup competitions for the country's lesser sides. The District Cups, as the competitions have become known, are now fiercely fought local affairs, with Monmouthshire's Ben Francis Cup and Cardiff's famous Mallet Cup two of the most well known competitions.

At the top level, the reinstituted national knock-out cup has also been a huge success. The most recent final in 1997, saw Cardiff beat Swansea in front of a packed Cardiff Arms Park. Fittingly, this thrilling contest was the last ever match to be staged at the famous Cardiff Arms Park, but the try scored by Cardiff wing Nigel Walker will no doubt be remembered for years to come as one of the finest ever witnessed at the Arms Park. The following week, the builders moved in and began demolishing the ground in time for the 1999 World Cup when hosts Wales will have a spanking new stadium with a 73,000 capacity.

Yet the introduction of both cup and league rugby has been a far more artificial process in Wales, where the geographical proximity and ancient rivalries have meant that an unofficial league and cup competition has been running for the best part of a century. Veteran observers who have

witnessed the 'derby' matches such as Llanelli vs. Swansea, Neath vs. Aberavon, Cardiff vs. Newport and Bridgend vs. Maesteg, etc would realise that matches billed as 'friendlies' were in fact every bit as intense as the formal competitions of today. Indeed, it was this very intensity that ensured that Wales were such a force for so many years at international level.

The recollections of Wales and British Lions forward Allan Martin explain just how intense the unofficial competition in Welsh club rugby was. "My first match was on a Bank Holiday as a teenager," said Martin. "It was a Neath vs. Aberavon 'friendly' and it was just like a cup final. My opposite number was a seasoned international who hit me constantly. My skipper, also a Wales cap, told me what to do. I hit my opponent hard in full view of the grandstand and referee. The official smiled, understood, and we all got on with the game."

With an influx of foreigners now coming to play rugby in Wales, including Brive's Tony Rees, league rugby looks set to remain a potent force.

Welsh League Winners

1991	Neath	1996	Neath
1992	Swansea	1997	Pontypridd
1993	Llanelli		
1994	Swansea		
1995	Cardiff		

SWALEC Cup Results

1972	Neath	15	Llanelli	9
1973	Llanelli	30	Cardiff	7
1974	Llanelli	12	Aberavon	10
1975	Llanelli	15	Aberavon	6
1976	Llanelli	16	Swasnea	4
1977	Newport	16	Cardiff	15
1978	Swansea	13	Newport	9
1979	Bridgend	18	Pontypridd	12
1980	Bridgend	15	Swansea	9
1981	Cardiff	14	Bridgend	6
1982	Cardiff	12*	Bridgend	12
1983	Pontypool	18	Swansea	6
1984	Cardiff	24	Neath	19
1985	Llanelli	15	Cardiff	14
1986	Cardiff	28	Newport	21
1987	Cardiff	16	Swansea	15
1988	Llanelli	28	Neath	13
1989	Neath	14	Llanelli	13
1990	Neath	16	Bridgend	10
1991	Llanelli	24	Pontypool	9
1992	Llanelli	16	Swansea	7
1993	Llanelli	21	Neath	18
1994	Cardiff	15	Llanelli	8
1995	Swansea	17	Pontypridd	12
1996	Pontypridd	29	Neath	22
1997	Cardiff	33	Swansea	26

* Cardiff won on "most tries" rule

SCOTLAND

By tradition, the two strongholds of rugby in Scotland have been the public schools of Edinburgh and Glasgow, and the cluster of towns that flank the River Tweed in the Border country. Between them those two camps have, directly or indirectly, provided the vast majority of Scotland's international players, but their different traditions have also produced an enmity based as much on

class as on geography.

That tension was apparent even in the late Victorian period, when rugby's popularity was growing in both areas. In the Borders, where clubs such as Hawick, Gala and Jed-Forest were largely working class institutions, there was a resentment of the haughty control exercised by representatives of city schools on the Sottish Football Union, the forerunner of the SRU. On more than one occasion, their mutual distrust almost led to the creation of a breakaway group that would have mirrored developments in England, where the rebel Northern League produced the game of Rugby League.

The Border sides, however, remained in the Scottish fold. Yet their desire for more meaningful rugby at a time when the SRU viewed that concept with disdain, was to produce, in season 1901–02 the Border League, the championship that is now the game's oldest and most established competitive club league.

The League's original members were Gala, Hawick, Langholm, Melrose and Jed-Forest. In 1912, Selkirk and Kelso joined to bring the complement up to seven teams – a number that did not change until 1996, when Peebles, after years of lobbying, were admitted to the competition. Throughout its history, the League has been contested on a home-and-away basis, surviving even the introduction of National Leagues in 1973. Then, with a fine sense of irony, the Border clubs opposed the arrival of the national championship, fearful of the effect it would have on their own competition.

By the end of season 1996–97, Hawick's 43 Border titles – outright or shared – made them easily the most successful side. Melrose had won 14, Jed-Forest 10, Gala six, Kelso five, Selkirk three and Langholm one. Recent innovations have included play-offs, when the League produces a tie, and a points-for-tries system backed up by sponsorship from the Bank of Scotland.

In a professional age, with increasing pressure from representative games, the Border League has lost some of its status, with top sides now regularly fielding under-strength

BREAK FOR THE BORDER *Jed Forest take on Melrose in a typically feisty Borders Cup clash in 1990.*

teams. As it approaches its hundredth birthday, however, there is little risk that the tenacious Borderers will ever allow their league to die.

SCOTTISH LEAGUE AND CUP

The motion before the annual general meeting of the Scottish Rugby Union in 1969 was innocuous enough. Tabled by Glasgow High School and Heriot's FP it suggested that the "committee of the SRU should investigate the introduction of a system of competitive club rugby in Scotland, such a system to be introduced at the earliest possible date."

Four years later, after numerous redrafts of plans by umpteen sub-committees, the SRU Clubs Championship, the first official national league competition in the British Isles, came into being. After more than a century of unofficial Scottish championships, drawn up by newspapers and decided by an incomprehensible system of percentages, Scotland thereby stole a march on the other home nations – an initiative that was widely credited with delivering their 1984 Grand Slam.

Scotland, where democratic control of the running of the game rests with the clubs, was always likely to be the first to introduce league rugby. Ironically the chief obstacle to the

development was the reluctance of the South of Scotland clubs, who had overcome official opposition to set up their Border League in 1901, to lessen the status of their own competition. The irony is heightened by the fact that they have dominated the National League since its inception.

Only thrice since 1973 has the title been won by clubs outside the Borders: Heriot's (1979), Boroughmuir (1991) and Stirling County (1995) breaking the hegemony of the South clubs. By the end of season 1996–97, however, Hawick had taken ten titles, Melrose six, Gala three and Kelso two. By far the most remarkable achievement, though, was by Stirling County, who rose through seven divisions to reach the top of the game.

Conflicting concerns over the leagues being too small, or too large, have led to numerous changes of format over the years. The most significant change, however, came in 1995 when the championship was divided into a Premiership for top clubs and a National League contested by junior sides, both competitions being played on a home-and-away basis.

A second innovation that season was the inauguration of the SRU Cup, Scotland's first national knock-out competition. Fittingly given their historic domination of Scottish rugby, it was won by Hawick who had also triumphed in the first seasons of both the National and Border League. In

the same year, the SRU Shield and Bowl were instituted for sides which had dropped out of the Cup in the third and fourth rounds.

However, despite these innovations, Scottish rugby has been badly damaged by the migration of large numbers of players to English clubs.

Scottish McEwans League Winners			
1974	Hawick	1986	Hawick
1975	Hawick	1987	Hawick
1976	Hawick	1988	Kelso
1977	Hawick	1989	Kelso
1978	Hawick	1990	Melrose
1979	Heriot's FP	1991	Boroughmuir
1980	Gala	1992	Melrose
1981	Gala	1993	Melrose
1982	Hawick	1994	Melrose
1983	Gala	1995	Stirling County
1984	Hawick	1996	Melrose
1985	Hawick	1997	Melrose

Scottish Tennant's Cup Winners			
1996	Hawick 17	Watsonians	15
1997	Melrose 31	Boroughmuir	23

FRANCE

The French Club Championship is without a doubt one of the rugby world's most enigmatic competitions, with the country's top sides simultaneously displaying violence so severe that it is unequalled anywhere in the world and flair so flamboyant that it is enough to make even the most jaded

rugby watchers weep with joy. Since France's clubs first locked horns in pursuit of glory in the first French Championship in 1892, competition for the famed shield called the Bouclier de Brennus has been tough and uncompromising, providing an insight into French rugby's jekyll and hyde character.

Stephen Jones, the well-respected correspondent of London's Sunday Times, once referred to the French Championship as the "most savage and gladiatorial contest in world rugby" and at times that sustained violence, displayed for all to see in a set-piece final and in modern times covered live on television and pumped into every household in France, has been enough to make the rest of the rugby world wince. One time where matters got out of hand was in the late Twenties, when the professionalism and crowd violence that the intensity of the tournament encouraged reached such a pitch that the Home Unions suspended France from the Five Nations in 1931. That ban was certainly motivated to a large degree by the decision of 12 top French clubs to flout the laws on amateurism, but it also owed much to the violence of the French Championship and, in particular, to the danger in which referees officiating at home losses were placed in.

That led to a terse communique from the Home Unions Committee, which had the effect of banning France from the Five Nations until 1947, and which included the following: "After examination of the documentary evidence ... we are compelled to state that owing to the unsatisfactory state of the game of Rugby Football in France, neither our Union, nor the clubs or Unions under its jurisdiction, will be able to arrange or fulfil fixtures with France or French clubs until we are satisfied that conduct of the game has been placed on a satisfactory basis in all essentials."

Yet the great passions that produce such violence in the Championship also produce rugby of such stunning intensity that it cannot be bettered anywhere in the world. This is particularly true in the south and south west of the country, where the rugby club is an integral part of the

Winners

Sydney Premiership

1900	Glebe	1921	Manly	1943	Manly	1965	Randwick	1987	Randwick
1901	Glebe & Sydney Uni	1922	Manly	1944	Eastern Suburbs	1966	Randwick	1988	Randwick
	(Shared)	1923	Sydney University	1945	Sydney University	1967	Randwick	1989	Randwick
1902	Western Suburbs	1924	Sydney University	1946	Eastern Suburbs	1968	Sydney University	1990	Randwick
1903	Eastern Suburbs	1925	Glebe-Balmain	1947	Eastern Suburbs	1969	Eastern Suburbs	1991	Randwick
1904	Sydney University	1926	Sydney University	1948	Randwick	1970	Sydney University	1992	Randwick
1905	South Sydney	1927	Sydney University	1949	Gordon	1971	Randwick	1993	Gordon
1906	Glebe	1928	Sydney University	1950	Manly	1972	Sydney University	1994	Randwick
1907	Glebe	1929	Western Suburbs	1951	Sydney University	1973	Randwick	1995	Gordon
1908	Newtown	1930	Randwick	1952	Gordon	1974	Randwick	1996	Randwick
1909	Glebe	1931	Eastern Suburbs	1953	Sydney University	1975	Northern Suburbs		
1910	Newtown	1932	Manly	1954	Sydney University	1976	Gordon		
1911	Newtown	1933	Northern Suburbs	1955	Sydney University	1977	Parramatta		
1912	Glebe	1934	Randwick	1956	Gordon	1978	Randwick		
1913	Eastern Suburbs	1935	Northern Suburbs	1957	St George	1979	Randwick		
1914	Glebe	1936	Drummoyne	1958	Gordon	1980	Randwick		
1915	No competition	1937	Sydney University	1959	Randwick	1981	Randwick		
1916	No competition	1938	Randwick	1960	Northern Suburbs	1982	Randwick		
1917	No competition	1939	Sydney University	1961	Sydney University	1983	Manly		
1918	No competition	1940	Randwick	1962	Sydney University	1984	Randwick		
1919	Sydney University	1941	Eastern Suburbs	1963	Northern Suburbs	1985	Parramatta		
1920	Sydney University	1942	Manly	1964	Northern Suburbs	1986	Parramatta		

village and where a team's home record is everything. It is from that southern heartland that the clubs which have come to dominate the Championship have come. With the exception of Jean Prat's Lourdes, who were the most potent force in the Championship in the Fifties and early Sixties, and Beziers, who retained the Shield for the better part of the late Sixties and Seventies, no side has managed to dominate the French Championship. This is in large part due to a bafflingly intricate system of sudden death games which, as well as changing on a regular basis, also mitigates against any one side dominating unless it is of overwhelming strength.

After being played for many years in the grounds of southern France, the Championship final has been played at the Parc des Princes in recent times. The final is not only full of passion, but is also one of the most colourful occasions in the rugby calendar, with both fans and players alike entering into the spirit of the occasion.

In 1990, for example, when Racing Club de France played Agen in the final, the Racing backs decided to wear bow-ties and berets to brighten up proceedings. If that wasn't bemusing enough for Agen, the sight of the Racing players sipping champagne at half-time was a moment they are not likely to forget, particularly as they lost in extra–time.

French League Winners

1892	Racing Club	1946	Section Paloise
1893	Stade Français	1947	Stade Toulousain
1894	Stade Français	1948	F.C.Lourdais
1895	Stade Français	1949	Castres Olympique
1896	Olympique	1950	Castres Olympique
1897	Stade Français	1951	U.S.Carmausine
1898	Stade Français	1952	F.C.Lourdais
1899	Stade Bordelais	1953	F.C.Lourdais
1900	Racing Club	1954	F.C.Grenaoble
1901	Stade Bordelais	1955	U.S.Perpignanaise
1902	Racing Club	1956	F.C.Lourdais
1903	Stade Français	1957	F.C.Lourdais
1904	Stade Bordelais	1958	F.C.Lourdais
1905	Stade Bordelais	1959	Racing Club
1906	Stade Bordelais	1960	F.C.Lourdais
1907	Stade Bordelais	1961	A.S.Biterroise
1908	Stade Français	1962	S.U.Agenais
1909	Stade Bordelais	1963	Stade Montois
1910	F.C.Lyon	1964	Section Paloise
1911	Stade Bordelais	1965	S.U.Agenais
1912	Stade Toulousain	1966	S.U.Agenais
1913	Aviron Bayonnais	1967	U.S.Montalbanaise
1914	A.S.Perpignanaise	1968	F.C.Lourdais
1915	No comp	1969	C.A.Beglais
1916	Stade Toulousain	1970	La Voulte Sportif
1917	Stade Nantais	1971	A.S.Biterroise
1918	Racing Club	1972	A.S.Biterroise
1919	Stadoceste Tarbais	1973	Stadoceste Tarbais
1920	Stadoceste Tarbais	1974	A.S.Biterroise
1921	U.S.Perpignanaise	1975	A.S.Biterroise
1922	Stade Toulousain	1976	S.U.Agenais
1923	Stade Toulousain	1977	A.S.Biterroise
1924	Stade Toulousain	1978	A.S.Biterroise
1925	U.S.Perpignanaise	1979	R.C.Narbonnais
1926	Stade Toulousain	1980	A.S.Biterroise
1927	Stade Toulousain	1981	A.S.Biterroise
1928	Section Paloise	1982	S.U.Agenais
1929	U.S.Quillanaise	1983	A.S.Biterroise
1930	S.U.Agenais	1984	A.S.Biterroise
1931	R.C.Toulonnais	1985	Stade Toulousain
1932	F.C.Lyon	1986	Stade Toulousain
1933	F.C.Lyon	1986	R.C.Toulonnais
1934	Aviron Bayonnais	1987	R.C.Toulonnais
1935	Biarritz Olympique	1988	S.U.Agenais
1936	R.C.Narbonnais	1989	Stade Toulousain
1937	C.S.Vienne	1990	Racing Club
1938	U.S.Perpignanaise	1991	C.A.Beglais
1939	Biarritz Olympique	1992	R.C.Toulonnais
1940	No comp	1993	Castres Olympique
1941	No comp	1993	Stade Toulousain
1942	No comp	1994	Stade Toulousain
1943	Aviron Bayonnais	1995	Stade Toulousain
1944	U.S. Perpignanais	1996	Stade Toulousain
1945	S.U.Agenais	1997	Stade Toulousain

NOTHING TO LOSE *Toulouse celebrate their 1995 Championship win.*

AUSTRALIA

ACT have recently come of age through the Super 12, and there are also many country unions who have made an invaluable contribution to Australian rugby union, but the pinnacle of domestic rugby Down Under remains the State of the Union challenge between the Reds of Queensland and the Blues of New South Wales. Although rugby union was effectively not played in Queensland between 1920–29, the State of the Union challenge has an otherwise unbroken record stretching back to the day the two states first locked horns ih Sydney in 1882.

Although the more populous rugby state of New South Wales has often held the whip hand, such is the rivalry between the two sides that results can see-saw dramatically within a single year. Nowhere else in the world do two sides play three or four games against each other *every* season, and that makes for a uniquely intense rivalry. Although New South Wales have won 175 of the 265 State of the Union clashes, as opposed to Queensland's 79, virtually every series has been a close one, with both states winning at least one match. The statistics are skewed by Queensland's weakness in the period immediately after the whole state went deserted Rugby Union for Rugby League just before the First World War. Recent history however, shows that the pendulum has swung Queensland's way. Of the 25 matches played since 1983, Queensland have won 15 and New South Wales 10.

As well as a gruelling inter-state competition, club rugby is alive and well in both Sydney and Brisbane.

The Sydney Premiership, where clubs play for the Shute Shield, has been in existence since 1900 and is one of the most fiercely contested club competitions in the world. Randwick, with 25 wins in Grand Finals, and Sydney University with 21, have been the most consistent performers in the 92 times that the Shield has been played for, although Gordon, Manly, Parramatta and Eastern Suburbs have also made significant contributions.

The rise of Randwick began in the 1970s and owes its origins to two factors. First there was the arrival at the club of a new, young and ambitious coach called Bob Dwyer. Dwyer had played for Randwick himself in the 1960s and, although he was never an outstanding player, he did possess an analytical brain that was to turn him into one of the world's greatest coaches.

One of Dwyer's biggest influences was a man called Cyril Towers, a centre for Randwick in the 1930s. Towers was a rugby visionary who introduced to Dwyer a whole new concept of back play that soon became standard not only for Randwick but for the Australian national side.

The second important factor in Randwick's success was the Ella brothers. Gary, Glenn and Mark were all spotted and coaxed to the club by Dwyer, because in these three outrageously talented backs, Dwyer saw the means by which he could put into practice his ideas to revolutionize back play.

The combination proved irresistable, and the arrival of David Campese added a further string to Randwick's bow. Such was their dominance of the Sydney premiership that between 1978 and 1994, they won the title a staggering 13 times.

Although competition in the modern day Brisbane Club Premiership is every bit as fierce as that in the Sydney competition, the history only

HEAD LOCK *ACT and Australian scrum-half George Gregan is going nowhere during a match in the 1997 Super 12 tournament*

stretches back as far as the Second World War.

Since then, Brothers (the club of current Wallaby captain John Eales) have been the most consistent performers, although in the early years Varsity were a force to be reckoned with, while more recently University have begun to show and in the very recent past the Souths club has put in a very strong performance, winning the Grand Final five years in a row after 1991 mainly due to the presence of the outstanding centre pairing of Tim Horan and Jason

Little at the club.

As mentioned in the beginning of this section, ACT has of late emerged as a very real threat to the duopoly of New South Wales and Queensland.

Although ACT have no comparable state competition, they have been strengthened in the last couple of seasons by the arrival of several former NSW and Queensland players, enticed by large sums of money and a chance to resurrect careers affected by the increased competition for places in their original states.

SOUTH AFRICA

THE CURRIE CUP

South Africa's Currie Cup is the oldest inter-union competition in the world and it is almost certainly the hardest fought. Contested by the provincial unions, the competition is so intense that it was credited with maintaining the standards of play during South Africa's sporting isolation so successfully that when the New Zealand Cavaliers toured South Africa in 1986, they were subjected to a 3–1 mauling in the Tests.

The creation of the Currie Cup was the fault of the British. When Bill Maclagan's embryonic British Lions toured Southern Africa at the invitation of Cecil Rhodes in 1891, a British rugby supporter called Donald Currie – who also happened to double up as the head of the Castle Shipping Line, the company which owned the ship called the Dunnotar Castle upon which the British party sailed to Cape Town – decided he wanted to leave some sort of lasting memorial to the event. The method he chose was to commission an elaborate gold trophy for the then huge sum of £40, and ask Maclagan to present it to the first side to beat the British side on the tour.

Given that the British stormed around the tip of the Dark Continent sweeping all before them, scoring 221 points yet conceding only one point while winning all 19 tour games, this was not possible. But Maclagan had little trouble identifying the side which gave the tourists the most problems and so awarded the trophy to the tough country outfit of Griqualand West, who had managed to stay within a score of the tourists. When the Cup was displayed in the window of Burmester's shop in Kimberley's main shopping boulevard, Adderley Street, it drew many admiring glances. Nevertheless, in accordance with Donald Currie's wishes, the Cup was donated to the SARB with the express intention of setting up an inter-union tournament (despite this the Griquas somehow managed to get the story out that it was they who, out of the goodness of their hearts, donated the Cup for this purpose!).

And so the Currie Cup competition was born. Not that it seemed like a competition for many years afterwards; more like a walkover as the all-powerful Western Province wiped the board with monotonous regularity. Western Province won the Currie Cup at the first time of asking in 1892, when it was combined with the existing South African Rugby Board trophy in the rugby equivalent of a boxing unification bout, and from there on in dominated the competition until its grip began to loosen in the early 1960s.

The original Currie Cup had only six provinces fighting for it in 1892: the winners Western Province, Griqualand West, Eastern Province, Transvaal, plus Natal and Border. The Orange Free State and Rhodesia were the next provinces to join the club in 1894 (at that time what is now Namibia, Kenya and Zimbabwe came under the auspices of the SARB).

Western Province had conceded their first points to Griqualand West in 1892, and in 1898 their unbeaten record was almost shattered by Transvaal, who lost a closely-fought match by just three points. On the way to the match the high veldters suffered a tragic blow when fullback David Cope and centre "Boy" Tait were killed in a railway accident, and it was commonly held that had this not happened they would have beaten the Cape Town crew. Even before the outbreak of the Boer War in 1899, the staging of Currie Cups had been

TIP TOP TRANSVAAL ... *notch up yet another Currie Cup win with a 56–33 victory over Orange Free State in 1994.*

irregular, with a competition being held on average every two years, but with the war necessitating the suspension of play for four years and then resuming only intermittently after the end of hostilities, it was not until 1911 that Western province relinquished their hold on the Cup, losing to the original holders, Griqualand West.

In the years following the end of the Second World War, the basis of the tournament began to change.

Matches had already moved to a home and away formula after 1920, but after 1945 there were several other changes of format, such as playing in two sections on either a geographical or merit basis. The question of format continued to dog the SARB, and in 1974, a bitter dispute broke out when, in the wake of the Lions' triumphant tour of the Republic, a top tier of ten provinces was created – fine if your province was in the elite, not so clever of yours was not. With some

minor amendments since, however, that arrangement still forms the basis of the now annual Currie Cup competition.

On the playing side, Western Province's early domination, which had seen them win 19 out of 27 possible titles between 1892 and 1960, began to wane in the late Sixties when Northern Transvaal won the cup in successive years. By the time the 1974 Lions visited South Africa, it was the high veldt sides Transvaal and

The Currie Cup							
1889 Western Province	1907 No competition	1924 No competition	1939 Transvaal	1956 Northern Transvaal	1972 Transvaal	1987 Northern Transvaal
1892 Western Province	1908 Western Province	1925 Western Province	1940 No competition	1957 No competition	1973 Northern Transvaal	1988 Northern Transvaal
1893 No competition	1909 No competition	1926 No competition	1941 No competition	1958 No competition	1974 Northern Transvaal	1989 Northern Transvaal
1894 Western Province	1910 No competition	1927 Western Province	1942 No competition	1959 Western Province	1975 Northern Transvaal	& Western Province
1895 Western Province	1911 Griqualand West	1928 No competition	1943 No competition	1960 No competition	1976 Free State	(Shared)
1896 No competition	1912 No competition	1929 Western Province	1944 No competition	1961 No competition	1977 Northern Transvaal	1990 Natal
1897 Western Province	1913 No competition	1930 No competition	1945 No competition	1962 No competition	1978 Northern Transvaal	1991 Northern Transvaal
1898 Western Province	1914 Western Province	1931 No competition	1946 Northern Transvaal	1963 No competition	1979 Northern Transvaal	1992 Natal
1899 Griqualand West	1915 No competition	1932 Western Province &	1947 Western Province	1964 Western Province	& Western Province	1993 Transvaal
1900 No competition	1916 No competition	Border (Shared)	1948 No competition	1965 No competition	(Shared)	1994 Transvaal
1901 No competition	1917 No competition	1933 No competition	1949 No competition	1966 Western Province	1980 Northern Transvaal	1995 Natal
1902 No competition	1918 No competition	1934 Western Province &	1950 Transvaal	1967 No competition	1981 Northern Transvaal	1996 Natal
1903 No competition	1919 No competition	Border (Shared)	1951 No competition	1968 Northern Transvaal	1982 Western Province	
1904 Western Province	1920 Western Province	1935 No competition	1952 Transvaal	1969 Northern Transvaal	1983 Western Province	
1905 No competition	1921 No competition	1936 Western Province	1953 No competition	1970 Griqualand West	1984 Western Province	
1906 Western Province	1922 Transvaal	1937 No competition	1954 Western Province	1971 Northern Transvaal	1985 Western Province	
	1923 No competition	1938 No competition	1955 No competition	&Transvaal (Shared)	1986 Western Province	

Northern Transvaal who had begun to call the shots. During isolation, it was the Blue Bulls of Northern Transvaal who established an ascendancy every bit as complete as that enjoyed by Western Province in the first half of the century, even if a little shorter-lived. With the province sustained by the phenomenal kicking talents of Naas Botha from 1977 until his retirement in 1992, Northern Transvaal dominated the Currie Cup with Botha contesting thirteen finals and winning eight of them.

Since Botha's retirement however, Transvaal have become the single strongest province, with Western Province, Natal and Northerns just behind.

NEW ZEALAND

NATIONAL PROVINCIAL CHAMPIONSHIP

New Zealand rugby existed for 106 years before it had a structured championship between its provinces. The National Provincial Championship, played in three divisions, began in 1976 and was an immediate success, making rugby people wonder why it hadn't happened sooner. Before 1976, the premier domestic trophy was the Ranfurly Shield but because it is a challenge competition, not all provinces were regularly involved. The 26 provincial unions (North Harbour in 1985 became the 27th) organised matches among themselves but all counted for nothing. They were what is known in Britain as "friendlies", though some of the encounters were far from that.

Unions would have their traditional fixtures, Auckland against Waikato for example, or Otago against Southland, and every two or three years the bigger unions would go on tour, playing three or four matches just for the honour and the glory of winning. The advent of the National Provincial Championship,

known in New Zealand as the NPC, changed all that. Some traditional fixtures fell by the wayside as unions concentrated their energies on the NPC and the weekly goal of achieving two points for a win. The systems have varied over the years, but each competition has had some form of promotion-relegation and, since 1992, a major round of semi-finals and finals has been played.

The Ranfurly Shield remains as a challenge trophy and home NPC matches automatically double as defences for the holder, though the shield is not at stake in semi-finals or finals. Bay of Plenty, now a second division union, won the inaugural first division title in 1976 but the most dominant union by far has been Auckland, especially since its resurgence under coach John Hart dating from 1982.

For several years, NPC matches were played when convenient to the two Unions involved, with the result that some might be played in April or May, extending the championship over the whole season. The New Zealand Union took control in 1992 and decided the NPC needed a more structured, cohesive look and ruled that all championship matches must be played after August 1, and the semi-finals and finals for the three divisions are played on the same weekends.

The championship gained even more organisation in 1996 with the advent of professionalism and the New Zealand season is now clearly split into thirds: the Super 12 is played in the first third; internationals in the second; and the NPC in the third.

The well-defined pyramid structure of New Zealand rugby – clubs at the base, then provinces then national teams – has long been the envy of other rugby-playing countries though the introduction of Super 12 has subtly altered the shape with some people, including leading administrators, arguing that to ease the workload of top players, the NPC should be downgraded to in effect be a feeder for the Super 12. Such a move would probably be strongly resisted by most of the 27 provinces.

RANFURLY SHIELD

The first Ranfurly Shield was contested in 1904, and from then on its possession has come to be seen as the symbol of dominance in New Zealand rugby. The format is simple, with provincial unions challenging the holders, and the holders playing games at a time to suit them and at a venue of their choice. As this generally means that games are played at the holders' home ground and when

they have a full-strength side available, possession is nine tenths of the battle as far as the Shield goes (it is so well known in New Zealand that, like the FA Cup in England, it is generally referred to as "The Shield". Only an outright win will wrest the Shield from the holders.

The story of the Shield began in 1901, when the offer of a trophy from the governor of New Zealand, the Earl of Ranfurly, was accepted by the NZRFU. A suitable trophy was commissioned from a Sheffield silversmith and the Englishman sent over an elaborately engraved Shield … complete with soccer goalposts and a soccer ball on it! After some hasty changes, the Shield was presented to Auckland, who were the dominant force in New Zealand provincial rugby that year. Rather like the Bledisloe Cup, which was left to gather dust in a darkened room for decades, the Shield was stuck in the Auckland locker room until Wellington challenged the Aucklanders to a game. The challengers duly came, saw and conquered, winning 6–3 to become the first winners of the Ranfurly Shield.

Since then seven Unions – Canterbury, Wellington, Otago, Hawke's Bay, Auckland, Southland and Waikato – have dominated the Shield. As the population has shifted

SET IN WINNING WAYS *Auckland have dominated both the NPC and Ranfurly Shield in recent years.*

SMILE OF SUCCESS *Auckland's Zinzan Brooke lifts the Ranfurly Shield as Canterbury's Mike Brewer applauds another stunning Blues performance*

to urban centres of late, though, the challenge of sparsely populated unions such as Southland, Taranaki, Hawke's Bay and Wairarapa has gradually faded, leaving the Big Five to dominate proceedings. Of the mega-unions, Auckland have established such an impressive run in the Shield that in recent years it has seemed as if the silverware almost belonged to them. The longest and most complete domination in Shield history was at the hands of John Hart's Auckland, who retained the "Log" through an amazing 61 defences over eight years between 1985 and 1993. It was a defence that was all the more amazing because Auckland defied tradition by going on the road for a high proportion of those defences. Even more commendably, the Shield was retained when New Zealand rugby in general was at its strongest – it was no surprise that the core of the All Blacks side which won the World Cup came from that outstanding Auckland side.

Auckland also enjoyed two other periods of dominance, the first spanning eight years and 23 defences after wresting the Shield from long-time rivals Wellington in 1905 and the second when former All Black captain Fred Allen coached the province to a then record 25 defences between 1960 and 1963.

The other sides to have enjoyed lengthy Ranfurly Shield runs are the wildmen from Canterbury on the South Island; Hawke's Bay, the home of the feared Brownlie brothers; and the other South Islanders from the House of Pain, Otago.

Hawke's Bay were the first of the great Ranfurly Shield sides. After securing the Shield from Wellington in 1922, a star-studded Hawke's Bay side containing Maurice, Cyril and Jack Brownlie and George Nepia, retained it over 24 challenges. It was a period of dominance that they were not to repeat until the Sixties when the great flanker Kel Tremain masterminded a 21-match defence of the Shield that was to last until 1969.

Hawke's Bay have not been a major power in Shield rugby since then.

Canterbury, the team which beat Hawke's Bay in 1969 to take the Shield, had two major Shield runs. The first came in the years after 1953 when the hard men from Christchurch Park withstood 23 challenges, and the second was in the early Eighties when former back–row legend Grizz Wyllie brought a ferocity to Canterbury's play that saw them sweep all aside in 25 record-equalling successes. It was at Wyllie's insistence that Canterbury went for the record against Auckland, a monumental clash that saw Auckland win 28–23 despite a magnificent Canterbury comeback that started when they were 24–0 down at half–time. For the next few years Canterbury could only lwatch enviously as Auckland's city slickers amassed an unprecedented 61-match winning streak. Although Wellington have also featured strongly at various stages of the Shield's history, the southern duo of Otago and, more occasionally Southland, have been

the two provinces to string together any sort of consistency.

Either side of the war Vic Cavanagh's Otago successfully defended the Shield 18 times, during which it won six matches while 11 of its top players were away with Fred Allen's '49er All Blacks in South Africa. For 15 years between 1935 and 1947, the Shield remained continuously on the South Island with either Southland or Otago.

National Provincial Championship			
Year	*Winners*	*Year*	*Winners*
1976	Bay Of Plenty	1992	Waikato
1977	Canterbury	1993	Auckland
1978	Wellington	1994	Auckland
1979	Counties	1995	Auckland
1980	Manawatu	1996	Auckland
1981	Wellington		
1982	Auckland		
1983	Canterbury		
1984	Auckland		
1985	Auckland		
1986	Wellington		
1987	Auckland		
1988	Auckland		
1989	Auckland		
1990	Auckland		
1991	Otago		

THE COUNTRIES

Initially confined to a small part of the English upper-class, rugby is now played in nearly 100 countries throughout the world, and boasts a World Cup that is the most watched sporting event after the Olympic Games and soccer's World Cup.

In the 175 years or so since William Webb-Ellis first picked up the ball and ran with it at Rugby School, the game has undergone a dramatic transformation.

With China joining the rugby community in earnest in 1997, the game has at last become truly international with virtually every corner of the globe now boasting a clubhouse and band of rugby enthusiasts. Played from Argentina to Japan, from Canada to New Zealand; rugby has put down deep roots in all four corners of the world.

After the first international, which took place between England and Scotland in 1871, the game quickly spread throughout the British Empire, crossing the Channel and becoming an established part of life in the large ex-pat communities in the Far East, North America and Argentina before gaining widespread popularity amongst the wider population.

By the beginning of this century, the game was a firm fixture in the original "Big Eight" – the original International Rugby Football Board (IRFB) members, England, Ireland, Wales, Scotland, France, New Zealand, South Africa and Australia – and had established a firm foothold in countries as diverse as Argentina, Japan, Canada, Romania and Fiji. And now, with the game going openly professional and the number of rugby playing countries expanding remorselessly, the future looks rosy for the world's fastest growing team sport.

WE HAVE LIFT-OFF *England scrum–half Kyran Bracken gets his pass away.*

44

FOUNDER MEMBERS

AUSTRALIA

YEAR FOUNDED: 1874
COLOURS: Gold shirts with olive green trim, olive green shorts, olive green socks with gold trim
NO. OF CLUBS: 350
NO. OF PLAYERS: 40,000

In rugby terms, Australia, as a nation, is a little misleading, for the game has never been widely played across the country. Indeed, for long periods, New South Wales – or, more precisely, the metropolitan area around the state capital Sydney – was the only area to fly the Rugby Union flag in the face of intense competition from the competing codes of Australian Rules Football and Rugby League.

That Rugby Union has had a precarious existence in Australia is all the more strange considering that it was the first country outside Britain to adopt the game. The Wallaroo Football Club was formed in 1870, followed in the same year by Sydney University and The King's School, and the game was first played on an organized basis in 1875. Although the explosion in clubs in Sydney – from three in 1870 to 13 two years later – makes it look as if the code quickly established itself in Sydney, the truth is a good deal less simple.

In its early days, rugby football was competing with "Victorian" football (later to become Australian Rules) and soccer. Although the Southern Rugby Football Union (SRFU) was formed in 1874, virtually all of the member clubs played all three codes or a hybrid mixture of the three. Matters came to a head in 1877 at the SRFU annual general meeting, when J.H. Carruthers, a representative of the University Club, introduced a motion to: "abolish scrimmages and running with the ball", a proposal which the Wallaroo club, for one, denounced as: "in reality a hidden attack upon the most vital aspects of the Rugby game." The proposal was roundly defeated and, although advocates of the Victorian code, and those who wanted a hybrid game, continued to press their case, the SRFU went from strength to strength, climbing from 17 member clubs in 1878 to 41 in 1880. Crowds of 5-6,000 were not uncommon in Sydney by 1880, but it was not until 1882 that the game was successfully transplanted to Queensland.

The progress of the game in Queensland – again, essentially the metropolitan area surrounding the state capital, Brisbane – was far less smooth than in New South Wales where, by 1880,

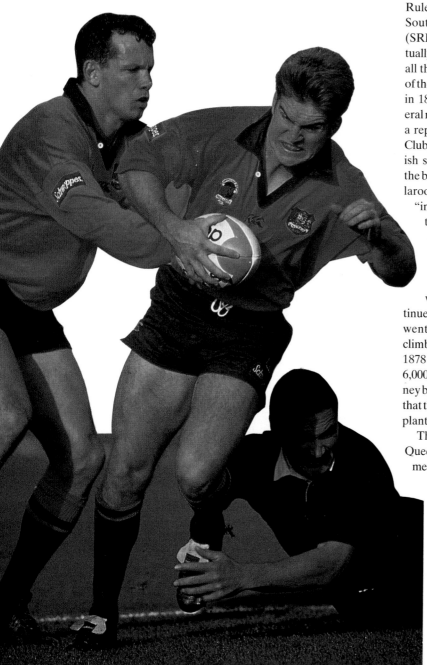

ADVANCE AUSTRALIA *Aussie Centre Tim Horan in characteristically agressive mood against the old enemy, the All Blacks.*

it had established itself as the premier code. In Queensland, the game struggled to put down deep roots, although the state did go through something of a golden period in the decade leading up to 1900, when its side beat New South Wales a total of 11 times in the original "State of Origin" games. New South Wales were not the only casualties, as Queensland stunned an unofficial British team led by the Reverend Matthew Mullineaux – the first British side to visit Australia since the ill-fated 1887 British touring party, whose captain, R.L. Seddon, drowned in the Hunter River.

In 1903, Queensland and New South Wales combined to meet New Zealand in Sydney, losing that initial encounter 22–3. It was a result that the Wallabies – as the Australian national side became known – were to get used to. All Black great Dave Gallaher returned two years later with his Originals, winning 14–3 on their way to whitewashing the British Isles. Until Australia became a force in the 1970s, wins over their closest rivals were agonizingly hard to come by, the Wallabies managing just 14 in the first 67 games of what became the Bledisloe Cup series (after a donation by Lord Bledisloe, Governor-General of New Zealand, in 1931).

The first full Wallaby touring side, however, did not leave Australia's shores until 1908, when Dr Paddy Moran's party came, saw and conquered by beating England 9–3 at Blackheath. The players were in England at the same time as the Olympic Games were held in London, and they returned home triumphant having also won a stack of Olympic gold medals in the process.

Seen at the time as the start of Australia's pre-eminence, that tour in fact marked a dramatic downturn in the fortunes of Australian Rugby Union as the touring party converted almost *en masse* to Rugby League. It was a body-blow from

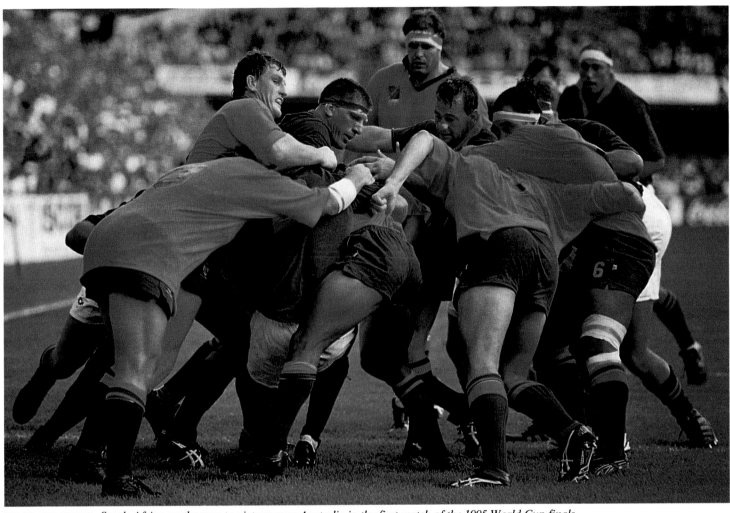

WORLD CUP OPENER *South Africa on the way to victory over Australia in the first match of the 1995 World Cup finals.*

which the 15-man code in Australia has long struggled to recover. If the effect on the Sydney competition was dramatic, it was as nothing compared to Queensland where the game ceased to exist for a decade following the First World War before eventually being re-established in 1929.

The story of Australian Rugby Union from the 1908 tour is one of a code fighting for survival against Rugby League.

League quickly established itself as the top game in Queensland and NSW, where union remained the preserve of the middle-class elite from a handful of private schools. There were also clubs scattered throughout parts of Western Australia, Victoria, Tasmania and South Australia, but they were based around schools and the expatriate community, and it seemed little effort was made to spread the gospel.

In the face of League's challenge, tentative steps were taken to make the Union code more appealing. The clearest example was the "Australian dispensation", which essentially said that players could not kick directly to touch from outside their own 25-yard line (22-metre line). Union, though, remained very much the poor relation in terms of playing numbers, crowds and profile.

Far from being allowed to plough their own furrow, Australia's Union followers have always had to cope with League raiding parties arriving at top clubs, such as Gordon, Manly and Randwick, chequebook in hand, to whisk away the brightest young talent. For every player who reached the top level, two would have taken the League dollar. It was amazing that Australia still turned out a string of outstanding backs, men such as Trevor Allan, Cyril Towers, Ken Catchpole and Cyril Burke.

In fact the problem wasn't a lack of pace and power behind the pack, but in it. Despite fielding teak-hard men such as Steve Finane and Graham Cooke, the Wallabies were vulnerable up front, a shortcoming which the New Zealanders profited from in Bledisloe Cup battles.

Australia's elevation to the elite of the modern game began in 1973, after Tonga had humiliated them, winning 16–11 in Brisbane.

Spurred into action, the Australians enlisted the help of the best coach in the world at that time, Welsh visionary Carwyn James. With his help, they began to graft some forward grit and purpose onto their good back play. and by 1984, when Alan Jones brought a young Wallaby side to Britain, the Australians had developed 15-man "total rugby" to a fine art.

This was the Grand Slam tour in which Mark Ella marshalled a flat back-line that bewitched British defences as the Wallabies easily won all four Tests.

Australia continued to make steady progress throughout the eighties, winning the Bledisloe Cup series against the All Blacks, and reaching the semi-final of the 1987 World Cup where they lost a thrilling match 30-24 to the French.

Four years later they went one better and reached the final, beating England at Twickenham. Undoubtedly the secret of the Wallavbies' success during this era was the astute captaincy of scrum-half Mick-Farr-Jones and the tactical nouse of coach Bob Dwyer.

Although disappointingly beaten by England in the 1995 World Cup, Australia's performance in the Tri-Nations Cup – against New Zealand and South Africa – has proved that the Wallabies are at the pinnacle of the world game.

ENGLAND

YEAR FOUNDED: 1871
COLOURS: All white except black socks (with white trim)
NO. OF CLUBS: 2,200
NO. OF PLAYERS: 200,000

Although William Webb-Ellis is said to have picked up the ball and run with it in 1823, it was not until 1863 that the game of rugby really existed in England in the sense that we would now understand it. Although Rugby School continued to play its own code, it was not until the historic meeting of 1863, when schools and clubs from the "kicking code" (soccer) and the "carrying code" (rugby) finally reconciled their differences to form one code, that rugby was really born.

Eight years later, on 26 January 1871, the Rugby Football Union was born when 20 clubs met under the chairmanship of Edwin Ash at the Pall Mall Restaurant in London. Of those clubs, less than half still exist (Blackheath, Richmond, Guy's Hospital, St Paul's School, Civil Service, Wellington College, Harlequins and King's College), with the remaining clubs now defunct (Law, West Kent, Belsize Park, Mohicans, Gipsies, Addison, Lausanne, Clapham Rovers, Flamingoes,

Wimbledon Hornets, Marlborough Nomads and Queens House). It was under the auspices of the RFU, less than a year after its formation, that a 20-strong England team led by Blackheath's Fred Stokes met and lost to Scotland, led by F.J. Moncrieff of Edinburgh Academicals, the famous club formed in 1859.

The game soon found enormous popularity in England, particularly in the north. Indeed, until the great schism of 1895, when 20 of the north's most prestigious clubs withdrew from the RFU to form the Rugby League, the north was a Union hotbed, producing some of the finest players ever to have played either code. With the split, men such as R.L. Seddon of Broughton Rovers, who captained England on their tour to Australia in 1887 (and tragically drowned in the Hunter River in NSW), were lost to the Union code.

Rugby Union in the north has never recovered the supremacy it enjoyed in the 1880s and early 1890s. After 1895, the direction of the game was dictated by the leading London clubs and the Oxbridge brigade. This, plus the fact that an unusually high percentage of administrators came from the top rugby-playing public schools, meant that English rugby has generally retained the conservative and Corinthian values that were so evident at the debate of the broken-time issue in 1893. Indeed, was England was steadfast in its refusal to contemplate a Rugby World Cup, and was one of the stiffest opponents of professionalism.

As the inventor of Rugby Union, England remains the spiritual homeland of the game, although the ascendancy of the southern hemisphere nations has gradually eroded that status over the past century. The most populous of all the world's rugby nations with 2,200 clubs and 200,000 players, England has conspicuously failed to make this weight of numbers count at international level, oscillating between the European supremacy of the mid-1920s and the early 1990s, and the dismal Five Nations form of the late 1970s. England have rarely been able to live with the southern hemisphere triumvirate, winning only 15 of the 50 Tests it has played against South Africa, New Zealand and Australia.

At international level, England has yet to develop a set style of play, with the adventurous pre-Second World War running game of men such as Adrian Stoop, Wavell Wakefield and Alexander Obolensky eventually giving way to the more muscular mauling game typified by forwards in the mould of Billy Beaumont and Dean Richards. Many of the problems in the English game can be traced to a century-long structural malaise: without a Currie Cup, Ranfurly Shield or Bouclier de Brennus to bring talent to the surface and help it develop in a genuinely competitive atmos-

DOUBLE ACT *England centres Will Carling and Jeremy Guscott lead the way against Ireland.*

phere, many of England's finest players played out their days in endless friendlies at unfashionable clubs.

Until the 1970s, when the knock-out competition was first played, the County Championship and cross-Border clashes with Welsh clubs provided the only real benchmark of performance. The County Championship, the pinnacle of the English game since it was first contested in 1889, has been dominated by seven counties, in essence players from the 15 or so top clubs. Unlike Wales, Ireland and Scotland, which all had five or six main clubs, the huge pool of players and clubs England was able to draw on was, paradoxically, its main weakness. Not until the Mallaby Committee recommended that an annual cup be started was there any attempt to overhaul the structure of English rugby. The commencement in 1970 of what was to become the Pilkington Cup revolutionized domestic rugby by bringing in the Merit Table which, a decade later, led to the of a full league structure in the 1987–88 season.

The introduction of leagues in 1987 changed English rugby forever. Famous old clubs such as Moseley, Coventry and Bedford slipped down the ladder while a whole batch of aggressive and less well established clubs such as Bath, Orrell, West Hartlepool and Saracens finally had an objective benchmark by which to judge themselves, and prospered accordingly. The traditional giants of the game had to look at their priorities and adjust. Harlequins and Leicester did so without breaking sweat. Others, such as Richmond and Northampton, took longer to get into gear.

The club game soon became the dominant force in domestic rugby, with the County Championship fading to the point where, from 1996, only players from the lower leagues were allowed to play.

An attempt to implant a Divisional Championship in the early eighties finally ran out of steam around the same time.

Between 1987 and '96 the League was dominated by Bath and Leicester, with only Wasps able to breake the two-club duopoly. With club

CHEERS *England celebrate their third Grand Slam in five years after defeating Scotland in 1995.*

rugby the domestic be-all and end-all, the entry of the top four club sides into the European Cup has taken rugby in England towards a Super 12-style set-up.

Bolstered by a strengthened domestic game, England have prospered since the mid 1980s. With a new management team in coach Geoff Cooke and captain Will Carling, England started a new era in 1988 when a 28–19 defeat of Nick Farr-Jones' Australians launched a run of success unprecedented since Wavell Wakefield's side won back-to-back Grand Slams in 1923 and '24, two of six Grand Slams won from 1913 to '28.

Whereas post-1988 England were a muscular crew who bludgeoned their way to success, this had not always been the case with English international teams.

While strong up front, the early England sides were renowned for their innovative and adventurous back play. Men such as W.J.A. Davies, Wavell Wakefield, Cherry Pillman, Harry Vassall and Alan Rotherham delighted fans with audacious running, and they were by no means alone. Theirs was a legacy passed down to the post-war generation, as the conveyor belt of superb backs turned out world-class

players in the shape of Bev Risman, Richard Sharp, Dickie Jeeps, Peter Jackson and Jeff Butterfield.

The decline in back play and the emergence of the more predictable forward-based game of today has its roots in the weakness of the England forwards in the 1960s and 1970s.

Despite men of the calibre of Peter Wheeler, Fran Cotton, Roger Uttley, Chris Ralston and a host of exceptional forwards, England were regularly out-gunned up front during this period. Some of the blame lay in poor and inconsistent selection policies, and some in the failure to define a tactical framework for England players to fit into. Yet the end result was a scarcity of ball for backs such as David Duckham and Keith Fielding, and an obsession with out-muscling sides up front.

Although Carling's men looked as if they were about to break the mould with some sparkling performances between 1988 and '90, defeat by Scotland in the 1990 Murrayfield Grand Slam decider saw England retrench and adopt a leaden (if effective) approach that still remains the closest England have to a national style.

Yet if England have found that

a conservative game plan is often enough to overwhelm their Home Union rivals, it is certainly an attitude that has failed miserably against the three southern hemisphere sides.

Tours to England before 1960 were generally attempts to halt the progress of outstanding sides such as New Zealander Dave Gallaher's "Originals" in 1908, or of the famous 1932 Springboks, or of Cyril Burke's all-conquering Wallaby side of 1948.

England did not venture on a major southern hemisphere tour until the Australasian tour of 1963, in which they were whitewashed. Apart from the odd, brief, respite, England have never been able to dominate outside Europe as they have within it.

In three World Cups, England have only once won a game against southern hemisphere opposition when they beat Australia in the quarter-finals in 1995.

Then, they were completely steamrollered by Jonah Lomu and company in the semi-final. In 1987, England lost to Australia before being put out by Wales at the quarter-final stage, and in 1991, after losing to New Zealand at the group stage, England lost to Australia in the Final.

DEFENSIVE WALL *Olivier Roumat of France gets plenty of protection against Wales in 1996.*

FRANCE

YEAR FOUNDED: 1905
COLOURS: Blue shirts and socks (with white trim) and white shorts
NO. OF CLUBS: 1,782
NO. OF PLAYERS: 150,000

The successful establishment of rugby in France has long provided a puzzle for sporting historians. At the end of the 19th Century when the game first took root, France was recovering from its crushing defeat at the hands of the Prussians and education was far higher up the agenda than sport for the gallic elite. Indeed, sport was barely on the agenda at all.

Nevertheless, he first recorded game of rugby on French soil occurred in 1872 between the English wine merchants of Le Havre, who organized a game at a ground somewhere between Rue Francis 1st and Rue Augustin Normand. Not surprisingly, to this day the colours of the first rugby club in France, Havre Athletic Club, are the dark blue of Oxford and the light blue of Cambridge.

For the next twenty years, rugby in France remained the preserve of the English abroad and the next club to emerge was in 1877 when English textile merchants in Paris formed the cunningly named English Tailors Club. At this stage, though, the game was gradually being taken up by small numbers of Frenchman and in 1879 the Paris Football Club was formed. In 1885 the Parisians toured England, but returned with a record of played four, lost four. Shattered, the club folded the following year. Despite this setback, Parisian rugby was improving steadily and the Racing Club de France, formed in 1882, was acting as a powerful missionary force for the game in the north of the country.

Yet as the clubs led the way, one of the most important developments in French rugby was happening at schools level. Baron Pierre de Coubertin, who was to enjoy greater fame for his Olympic vision, became a convert to rugby after visiting Thomas Arnold at Rugby School in the early 1870s, when the game was in expansionist mood. De Coubertin was instrumental in laying the foundations for rugby's successful germination into France's sporting psyche. An educationalist, he took an active role in promoting the game in schools and rugby at that level took off. In 1890 the first Schools Championship, featuring the three Lycées of Lakanal, L'Ecole Monge and L'Ecole Alsacienne, was launched by the enterprising Baron.

The final of the first French Championship (as opposed to the Schools Championship) was contested by Racing Club and their arch-rivals Stade Française, the only two entrants, but it was a tremendous success. Baron de Coubertin, its organizer and referee, presented the winners with a superb wooden trophy, described by an eye-witness as "a magnificent trophy of breath-taking beauty and nobility". This trophy, which is called the Bouclier de Brennus, went on to become French rugby's equivalent of the Ranfurly Shield or Currie Cup.

The tournament was such a success that the number of entries for the second Championship went up to five, with all the clubs hailing from the Ile de France in Paris. In 1896, however, the emphasis shifted from Paris, when the Toulouse club challenged its Bordeaux counterpart to a game of rugby. That game, eagerly awaited and raucously attended, acted as a catalyst and, within months, rugby was taking the country by storm.

In 1900, when the second Olympic Games were held in Paris, France selected its first national team to compete in the new tournament and emerged triumphant, winning the gold medal by beating Frankfurt Fusball Club 27–17 in the first game and Moseley Wanderers 27–8 in a surprisingly one-sided final.

At this time rugby was sweeping through France, moving from village to village, symbolizing regional and local rivalries, although quite how the game made its dramatic transition from a middle-class game enthusiastically adopted by the students of the north to become the favourite pastime of the farmers and labourers of the rural south is a moot point. Explanations have varied from a theory that the game followed in the footsteps of the medieval game of Soule, to the thought that it was the anti-clerical south's reaction to the priests of the north for whom soccer was the game of choice. Whatever the origins, however, "Le Jeu Anglais" soon came to represent to the south of France its own unique identity which, in turn, explains why the sport's progress faltered in the north.

The growth of the game was also helped by the addition of some high profile players from Britain. In particular, Percy Bush, of Cardiff, Wales and the Lions, joined the British Consulate in Nantes as his playing career drew to a close and gave rugby in France a real boost.

By 1905–06 the French Federation felt strong enough to throw down the gauntlet to the perfidious Albion and took on England in Paris. Any optimism proved to be sorely misplaced, however, as the

English steamrolled the home side to win by a massive 35–8. Further setbacks followed against Wales (36–4 in Cardiff in 1908), Ireland (19–8 in Dublin in 1909) and Scotland (27–0 at Inverleith in 1910). The diet of defeats continued relentlessly, until the tide finally turned in the spring of 1920 when the Irish succumbed by 15–7 in Dublin.

However, while the French were becoming increasingly competitive, it brought problems off the field. A culture apart, the amateur ethic which the British held so dear to their hearts was not quite as well entrenched in either French rugby or the French psyche. With domestic rivalries so great, and the incentive to poach players more intense than in Britain – except in Wales, where rugby was the game of the people rather than the professional classes – the result was petty professionalism and extreme violence.

It was not a situation which found favour with the amateur die-hards, but when, in March 1931, 12 of France's top clubs overtly started to pay players, the conflict came into the open and France's international development was abruptly curtailed. The Home Unions sent a communiqué to CF Rutherford, the secretary of the FFR, saying: "Owing to the unsatisfactory state of the game in France ... neither our Unions or clubs will be able to arrange fixtures with France or French clubs ... until we are satisfied that the conduct of the game has been placed on a satisfactory basis."

It was not until after the war that France was allowed to re-enter the community of rugby playing nations, and the four Home Unions soon found out that post-war France was a unrecognizable from the pre-isolation team. In the 1920s, France had produced outstanding flair players, such as Jarreguy, Ribere, Gallia, Cassayet-Armagnac and Mauriat, yet the side lacked the cohesiveness and grit to succeed at international level. The 1946 version, with magnificent Lourdes forward Jean Prat leading from the front and Basquet, Dufau, Pomathios and Alvarez following, was a different proposition.

That transformation was completed with a gritty 3–0 win over the touring 1956 All Blacks at the Stade Colombes and France soon became a real force in the Five Nations, which they first topped in 1954 when they shared top spot with England and Wales, although they had to wait until 1968 for the first of their four Grand Slams (others followed in 1977, 1981 and 1987).

The impact of France has been more than simple statistics or even that the game has flourished. Above all, France provides top-flight world rugby, with a bit of colour, but offers a completely different cultural experience. Domestically, the ferocity on the pitch is matched only by the internecine warfare at committee and management level. As a touring destination, France offers a remarkable change, while as a rugby nation, the savagery of domestic competition has produced, on one hand, uncompromising, teak hard forwards – men like Gerard Cholley and Olivier Merle – while on the other, sublime three-quarters such as Jo Maso, the Boniface brothers, Jean Trillo, Claude Dourthe and Philippe Sella.

It is this potent mixture which threatens the Anglo-Saxon hegemony. At the first World Cup in 1987, France stole the show with a last-minute 30–24 win over hosts Australia in one of the best matches of all time. Only they ever seemed likely to resist the all-conquering All Blacks before finally falling 29–9 in the Final. Although they were less successful in 1991 – losing to England in the quarter-finals – France soon proved their mettle in a remarkable 18 months that started in 1993. After a drawn series against Australia, they recorded an unprecedented away series victory in South Africa, and whitewashed the All Blacks 2–0 in the one of the most thrilling series ever in New Zealand.

The 1995 World Cup turned out to be something of a damp squib for the French. They had improved with every match and reached the semi-final, where hosts South Africa were the opponents. Unfortunately a deluge left the pitch at Durban flooded and, after a delay of 90 minutes, the game – more water polo than rugby – went ahead, but South Africa scraped though by 19–15.

SHORT BACK AND SIDES *The French backs show off their streamlined look against Tonga in 1995.*

IRELAND

YEAR FOUNDED: 1879
COLOURS: Green shirts and socks (with white trim) and white shorts
NO. OF CLUBS: 200
NO. OF PLAYERS: 15,000

Barry McGann, the Irish outside half of the late 1960s and early 1970s tells a story that perfectly sums up what the Irish mean to rugby. "Towards the end of my international career, Syd Millar was the coach and I had the reputation of being a very laid-back player. Because of work I was late to a training session, and it was in full swing when I got there. I went over to Syd and apologized for being late and asked him what he wanted me to do. I had a strong feeling he didn't believe I had made much of an effort to be there but he told me to warm up. Instinctively, I rubbed my hands together and blew on them and said: 'Okay, coach, I'm ready.' He just looked at me."

Yet if the Irish have long been the flag-bearers for the off-field bonhomie that distinguishes Rugby Union from other sports, once on teh field they play with a passion and commitment other countries find hard to match.

It is no coincidence that "the Garryowen" – where the fly-half kicksthe ball high and deep into the opposition half, giving his team time to charge up and flatten the catcher – is named after one of Ireland's greatest clubs. As England's veteran back-rower Mike Teague once said: "No pack of forwards in the world is more frightening than the Irish in full cry – it's just a good job they all drink so much Guinness that they can only keep it up for 20 minutes. A full game of that would be murder!"

Given Ireland's small player base of around 15,000 players in 200 clubs (greater London has seven times more players than Ireland), the Irish have until recently managed to remain remarkably competitive in international terms. A nation with such little strength in depth will always be prone to peaks and troughs, but as well as producing

outstanding players such as Willie-John McBride, Jackie Kyle and Mike Gibson, Ireland have also managed to claim the Triple Crown six times, while also winning the Grand Slam in 1948.

There is a story that Ireland is the real home of rugby union, and that William Webb-Ellis actually learnt the game during the period when his father, James, was stationed in Tipperary whilst serving with the 18th Royal Irish Regiment. There, it is said, the young Webb-Ellis came into contact with a thousand-year-old Irish game called "Cad", which was the traditional game played in rural areas, particularly in Munster. A game in which crowds of youths battled to gain possession of the Cad – an inflated bull's scrotum – it was a game in which the emphasis was in running with the ball. Hence the theory.

It is more likely, however, that rugby was introduced into Ireland from 1850 onwards by former pupils of Rugby School and Cheltenham

College, who began to play the game on an organized basis at Trinity College – the spiritual home of Irish rugby – as early as 1853. Perhaps it was because the game was so closely related to Cad that "football" made rapid progress throughout Ireland, with NIFC (North of Ireland Football Club) being established in

Belfast in 1859 as the number of clubs mushroomed. But as in Australia, where the code of rugby had to compete for space and players with Association Football and Victorian Football, so too did Irish rugby have to compete with Gaelic football and Association Football, while hurling was also a popular pastime.

The difference, according to Jacques McCarthy, that famous chronicler of Irish rugby's early days, was as follows: "Football in Ireland may be said to consist of three parts, Rugbeian, Associationist and Gaelic. The rule of play in these organizations has been defined as follows – in rugby you kick the ball; in Association you kick the man if

you cannot kick the ball; in Gaelic you kick the ball if you cannot kick the man!"

In 1868 two Trinity students, Charles Barrington and Robert Wall, laid down the ground rules for rugby in Ireland. About this time several football clubs (such as the famous Laune Rangers in Kerry)

opted for Gaelic football, yet the number of rugby clubs continued to increase rapidly and in 1879 the Irish Football Union was formed ... precisely four years after Ireland's first international against England at The Oval. The delay, which was caused by a spat between the Dublin and Belfast factions, was resolved just in time for a 20-strong united Irish side to register its first win, over Scotland, in 1881. Matters remained chaotic, however, down to the point where during the 1882 match against Wales, two Irish players were so appalled at the violence that they simply walked off the pitch never to be seen again, while two years later against Wales,

CELTIC FIRE *Ireland raise the roof before their defeat of Wales in the 1995 World Cup finals.*

Ireland turned up two players short and had to borrow two Welshmen.

The early years of international rugby were trying ones for the Irish. Naturally relaxed characters, the thought of training did not even occur to the earliest Irish sides, with the consequence that the team beaten by England at The Oval in 1875 was described in one newspaper report as: "immaculately innocent of training … one player looked like Falstaff – a mountain of tummy." With a write-up like that, it is hardly surprising that it took until 1881 for Ireland to register its first international win, beating Scotland by one drop-goal and one try to nothing in Belfast. Another six years passed before Ireland claimed another scalp, England being beaten at the thirteenth time of asking with Wales succumbing the next year. That victory heralded one of Ireland's purple patches and in 1894 and 1899, Ireland completed a clean sweep to claim a brace of Triple Crowns. However, it took until 1948 before Ireland won their first and, to date, only Grand Slam.

In 1964 prop Ray McLoughlin was appointed captain, a decision that proved a watershed for Irish rugby. A meticulous planner, McLoughlin frowned upon the: "it'll be all right on the night" approach, preferring instead to hold long training sessions and lengthy team talks, striving all the while to develop an "Irish" style of play. He did not last as captain for more than two seasons, but McLoughlin's influence has stayed ever since.

No matter how successful (or otherwise) Irish rugby is, however, the game in the Emerald Isle is maintained by the wealth of characters who have graced its rugby fields. There have been many eccentrics, such as D.B. Walkington of NIFC who wore a monocle throughout games, taking it off only to tackle and replacing it as soon as the man was downed. Then there was Basil Maclear of Cork County and Monkstown, who used to wear snow-white evening gloves throughout each game. It is larger than life characters – and clashes between

them – which do so much to endear the Irish to the rugby world. And, with the Irish famously loving a heated debate, one of the most famous rows in Irish rugby history occurred in the late 1970s and early 1980s when the whole of Irish rugby raged with debate on which Dubliner should play fly-half for Ireland: the free-running Tony Ward or the metronomic kicker Ollie Campbell. The debate came to a head in 1979 when Ireland sent a party to Australia and Campbell famously kicked the tourists to victory while Ward kicked his heels. In many ways, the depth of division and the passions raised said as much about rugby in Ireland as the debate itself.

Campbell also helped Ireland win two Triple Crowns in 1982 and 1985, but since then Ireland has struggled to maintain its traditional position in the world pecking order, a position that is challenged in 1997 as never before, recent home defeats against emerging nations Western Samoa and Italy have underlined the deceline in standard of Irish rugby over the last few years.

An intensely conservative rugby country, change does not come easily to the IRFU, although change is now being foisted upon it by force

of circumstances. At a domestic level, the Union has responded and competition is increasing on a year by year basis. The All-Ireland League started in 1990 (Ireland were the last major nation to inaugurate such a tournament) and participation in the European Cup from 1995 will inevitably raise standards, but whether Ireland can compete in the professional era when virtually all of its current international squad are plying their highly-paid trade with top English clubs, remains to be seen. Economic realities make it more likely that Irish rugby will end up with the same feeder-league relationship that Irish soccer has with its English counterparts.

The All-Ireland League has been implanted alongside the existing structure, the pinnacle of which is the Inter-provincial series between the four provinces, Ulster, Leinster, Munster and Connacht. This has long been a regular feature of Irish rugby, while Leinster started its own Cup competition in 1882, Ulster in 1885, Munster in 1886 and Connacht in 1896. The nature of the game in each of the provinces varied wildly, however. In Leinster and Ulster, the game is predominantly a game of the professional classes, while in Munster – or certainly in the City

of Limerick – it is stoically and proudly a game that crosses all social boundaries. Connacht, the smallest and most rural of the four provinces, has a relatively small playing population and no major clubs save for Galwegians. Schools rugby is very strong throughout Ireland.

Strangely, given the initial fallout between Belfast and Dublin, the IRFU remains the only major sporting body to encompass both sides of the divide in Ireland.

Although sectarian politics have inevitably intruded on the game at times – it is generally perceived by the nationalist community in Ulster as a Protestant game – there has always been a concerted effort not to involve politics in rugby, and neither the British nor Irish national anthems are played before games. As Garryowen bruiser Tom Reid replied in 1955 when asked what he thought of the political situation in South Africa at a reception for the Lions: "As a southern Irishman with me own political problems, I keep me views to meself." Virtually the only way that politics have become involved in Irish life is through the fact that two of Ireland's most famous statesmen – Eamonn de Valera and Dick Spring – were devoted players of the game.

SAFETY FIRST *Ireland's Niall Hogan clears the ball from under the noses of the English in 1996.*

NEW ZEALAND

YEAR FOUNDED: 1892
COLOURS: Black shirts, shorts and socks (with white trim)
NO. OF CLUBS: 1,000
NO. OF PLAYERS: 100,000

Historically the strongest of rugby countries and home of the famous All Blacks, New Zealand sides are sometimes feared but always respected and not beaten anywhere near as often as other countries would like. In a sentence that has been echoed by countless players before and since, Gareth Edwards, the great Welsh scrum-half, said, after first playing against New Zealand in 1967: "There is something about the All Black jersey that sends a shudder through your heart."

The All Blacks have habitually founded their game on a strong pack of forwards – believing that possession is everything – though it has seldom been at the expense of effec-

tive, and sometimes brilliant, back play. The All Blacks echo the domestic New Zealand game with a methodical, no-nonsense approach and the long-held belief that it is winning that matters, not the taking part.

New Zealand rugby is based on a playing structure that has been the envy of other rugby-playing countries. The All Blacks, the national team, membership of which represents an entree to New Zealand's most exclusive club, forms the apex of the playing triangle. Below them are the 27 provincial unions which have a tradition of home and away "friendly" fixtures and – since 1976 – a national provincial championship in three divisions.

Since the introduction of professionalism, a new tier has appeared, fitting between the provinces and the national side: the Super 12 teams, which are regional groups of provinces, play Australian states and South African provinces in an early-season com-

petition from March until May.

Provincial teams also contest the Ranfurly Shield, a challenge trophy named after the Earl of Ranfurly, Governor of New Zealand early this century. Challenges are usually at the holder's home stadium and though smaller unions have previously held the shield, it is now almost exclusively first division property – in particular Auckland's, who held it for a record 61 challenges between 1985 and 1993. Auckland have also won the National Provincial Championship first division 11 times since 1976.

The base of the New Zealand playing triangle is the clubs, who play in competitions organized by the provincial unions. Since professionalism, the top 140 or so players have been contracted to, and paid by, the New Zealand union. Some provinces separately contract other players and there is commercial movement of players at club level as well, but it is not widespread.

However, such has been the level of international, Super 12 and provincial commitment in recent years, that it has become increasingly rare for the top players to also play for club sides.

Rugby was introduced to New Zealand in 1870 by Charles John Monro, son of the Speaker of the New Zealand Parliament at the time. He had been sent to England for his education and attended Christ's College in Finchley. At CCF he learned to play rugby (where another devotee was Percy Capmael, founder of the Barbarians) and on his return to his native Nelson in 1870, Monro persuaded the boys of his old school, Nelson College, and a town club to play the game.

Using a steamer provided through his father, Monro took the Nelson College team to Wellington and arranged games there and formed New Zealand's oldest continuous rugby club, the Wellington Football Club. As boys left school

MAORI MENACE *The All Blacks scare the daylights out of the 1993 Australians with their traditional "Haka" war dance.*

and went to work around the country, they took rugby with them establishing it in a remarkably short time. New Zealanders took to rugby not only because of the influence of the well-educated (and therefore wealthy), but also because it was a game that suited the rugged individualism of early New Zealand, anxious to retain its British roots but just as anxious to prove itself an independent force.

Rugby's appeal to its indigenous people, the Maori, was another great benefit. Unlike in some other countries, there were no social or legal impediment to their playing alongside the Europeans ("the Pakehas"). Maori have always had a profound influence on rugby, not least by organizing the pioneering tour of Britain and Australia in 1888 by the New Zealand Native team, a tour that allowed New Zealanders to compare their standard and style of play with what they saw in Britain. A British team also toured New Zealand in 1888, but Tom Ellison, a Maori and one of the seminal men of early New Zealand rugby, remarked rather archly in his book, The Art of Rugby Football, that they learned little from the British team.

Ellison, who had toured Britain with the Native team, was instrumental in the development of two unique features of the New Zealand game, the evolution of the five-eighth positions (as opposed to inside-outside centres) and the introduction of the wing-forward, a position that was abolished in 1931. But Ellison's most enduring claim to rugby fame came at the New Zealand Rugby Football Union's first annual meeting in 1893, when he suggested that the New Zealand team uniform consist of a black jersey with a silver fernleaf motif. He also proposed white shorts but this was changed to black in 1901.

After the playing success of the 1888 Natives, the New Zealand Union yearned and planned for nearly a decade a tour of Britain by a full New Zealand team; and they achieved their aim in the season of 1905–06 when the Originals, led by wing-forward Dave Gallaher, made a pioneering and historic tour.

POWER BEHIND THE THRONE *Forwards Olo Brown (with ball) and Sean Fitzpatrick (left) lead the charge.*

When the New Zealanders beat Devon 55–4 in their first match, one London newspaper sub-editor was so sceptical of the result he reversed the scoreline. It wasn't long before the team, sweeping all before them, became known as the All Blacks. The name evolved from the colour of their uniform rather than the apocryphal tale that another sub-editor changed the phrase "all backs" (because of the forwards' speed) to All Blacks.

Their one defeat in the 32-match tour was to Wales, 3–0, a try to nothing. The match has grown in rugby folklore because Bob Deans was said to have scored what would have been an equalizing try, but had been dragged back over the line before the referee, in street clothes, could catch up with play. The All Blacks avenged that defeat in 1924, when "The Invincibles" – as the party became known – made their first unbeaten tour of the British Isles, although sadly that tour did not include a game against Scotland, who were then at one of their peaks.

New Zealand also developed enduring and, at times, troubling relations with South Africa, who they regard as the most consistently difficult opponents. Indeed, it took until 1996 for the All Blacks to win a series in South Africa.

The relationship with South Africa was made difficult for more than purely playing reasons. Under apartheid and before, South Africa had refused to host New Zealand teams containing Maori, and as the anti-apartheid movement increased internationally, New Zealand was seen to be at fault for bowing to the South African wishes. Contact between the two countries was completely severed after the 1981 tour of New Zealand was marred by widespread protests – a planned 1985 tour to South Africa was stopped by legal action – and the rivalry was renewed with all its old intensity only when the abolition of apartheid began in 1992.

New Zealand's other enduring international relationship is with her closest neighbour, Australia. Regular test series between the two countries are for the Bledisloe Cup, although the All Blacks had almost permanent possession until the late Seventies. New Zealand rugby used to regard Australian rugby in much the same way as Australian cricket regards New Zealand cricket, but there is now intense and unpredictable competition between the two with the Bledisloe Cup matches guaranteed sell-outs.

New Zealand has contributed many of rugby's greatest players, from full-back Billy Wallace and captain Gallaher of the first British tour and the full-back in every game of that tour, George Nepia, to John Kirwan and Michael Jones of the 1987 World Cup winning side.

Bob Scott of the post-World War II era was another of the standout full-backs, but it has been for hard, uncompromising forwards that New Zealand rugby has best been known.

Players syuch as the legendary Colin Meads – who most New Zealanders would regard as the best player ever to have pulled on a black jersey – or the captains in Britain in 1963. Other greats include Wilson Whineray, 1967, Brian Lochore, the flanker, Graham Mourie, who led the first All Black side to achieve a Grand Slam in 1978, and the remarkably durable hooker, Sean Fitzpatrick, who played in New Zealand's World Cup-winning team in 1987, and led the All Blacks to their first series win in South Africa in 1996.

STANDING TO ATTENTION *Scotland line up at Twickenham prior to their 1995 Grand Slam decider against England which their hosts won.*

SCOTLAND

YEAR FOUNDED: 1873
COLOURS: Navy blue shirts and socks (with white trim) and white shorts
NO. OF CLUBS: 276
NO. OF PLAYERS: 25,000

Although the game of rugby union was famously first played in England in 1823 at Rugby School, it is Scotland which boasts the oldest club not based in a school or university. Edinburgh Academicals, the Raeburn Place club, was founded in 1858, four years before Blackheath – or "The Club" as the London outfit styles itself. Indeed, Raeburn Place was the venue for the first ever international, in 1871, when England were beaten by one try and one goal to one try by Scotland in front of a crowd of several thousand in a forerunner of the Calcutta Cup.

Edinburgh Academicals, the old boys club for Edinburgh Academy, represents a distinct brand of rugby in Scotland, that of the Old Boys clubs, upon which much of domestic Scottish rugby has always been based. Edinburgh Academicals may have been the first, but it was not long before they were vying for supremacy with a host of other old boys sides, such as Heriot's FP (former pupils), Watsonians, Stewart's Melville FP, Dundee HSFP and Glasgow Academicals.

Throughout the mid to late 1870s, another almost parallel world of club rugby grew up in the sparsely-populated and rural Borders area. This brand of rugby, imported from Yorkshire through the burgeoning woollen industry, was a world away from the refined old boys circuit of the major cities. The Borders remains the only area in Scotland – outside the predominantly middle class atmosphere of the Edinburgh elite – where rugby really managed to take root. In small towns where there was little or no association football, clubs such as Gala, Hawick, Selkirk, Kelso, Jed Forest and Melrose soon became the sporting focus for the hardy farming communities living nearby.

As well as being geographically and culturally divorced from their city counterparts, the Borders clubs soon developed a competition of their own, the Borders League, which is still contested and remains the oldest organized league competition in world rugby. Although the population of the Borders is only 100,000, its unique cauldron of local rivalries has produced many of the best players to come out of Britain, and tradition has it that the best Scotland sides are those which contain a majority of Borderers. It says much for the area that the three most enduring club sides in Scotland – Hawick, Gala (Galashiels) and Melrose – have populations of 10,000, 5,000 and 2,500 respectively.

The Borders was also the birthplace of the abbreviated code of Sevens, somewhat ironic given the fact that Borders rugby is traditionally founded on forward muscle rather than fluent back play. The code was invented in 1883, when Melrose butcher and fly-half Ned Haig suggested a shortened version of the game as a means of raising money at a local fair. The idea was a roaring success, with Melrose beating Gala in extra time to win the competition, and soon most towns in the Borders staged their own annual sevens tournaments in April and May. So seriously do the Borderers take the game that when in 1983 the victorious French donated their Melrose Sevens winners' medals to local lasses as tokens of affection, there was uproar in the town – all Borderers see a Melrose Sevens winner's medal as the next best thing to a Scottish cap.

As with the rest of the European nations, the power in Scotland has always rested with clubs rather than any province or other grouping, although there has been a concerted but as yet unsuccessful attempt to create a divisional aspect to Scottish domestic rugby of late, with an Inter-District competition featuring five sides (the North & Midlands, the South, Glasgow, Edinburgh and the Exiles).

With a small playing population of just around 25,000 and almost 250 clubs, it has been a marvel that Scotland has managed to remain consistently competitive at international

level. Much of the credit for that goes to a well defined national style of play at Test level which is based squarely on a fierce rucking game. It echoes the domestic club game, a no-frills approach owing much to fitness, speed of movement away from the breakdown and speed of thought, rather than sheer forward muscle. If Scottish rugby has traditionally had one great strength, it has been in tenacious back-row players and hard-running halfbacks. Without regular front fives physically strong enough to impose themselves, Scotland have long looked to move the ball away from set-piece and tight loose play by adopting an all-action, fast rucking game designed to unsettle heavier opposition and create space for the fit Scots.

A small playing base means that Scotland have often struggled at the top level. Indeed, only against Ireland of the major rugby-playing nations, do Scotland still have a positive record, while in the early 1950s they suffered 17

consecutive defeats. Nevertheless, they have by far the most well defined style of play among European nations, especially since coaches such as Ian McGeechan, Jim Telfer and Richie Dixon made a conscious effort to ensure that every potential international player understood how the national side played. This, plus a wide-ranging search for Scottish grandparents, has allowed Scotland to play beyond their resources, allowing players struggling at international level to take the step up more easily than they could in England or Wales.

Although Scotland have yet to beat New Zealand, they have recorded wins over South Africa and Australia, and have

completed the Five Nations Grand Slam three times: in 1925, 1984 and 1990. Of those, the 1990 win will always be best remembered, not least because it was won during a highly-charged Grand Slam play-off decider at Murrayfield against the Auld Enemy, England.

Scotland had won their first three games relatively comfortably, but had done little to suggest that they could beat an England side which had played some of the finest rugby ever seen in Britain and which clearly saw itself as ready to claim only its third Grand Slam since 1928. However, Scotland captain David Sole gained a vital psychological edge when he calmly walked his men onto the pitch before wreaking havoc on the English for the most famous 80 minutes in Scottish rugby history.

Although Scotland came close to repeating the feat, when they met England at Twickenham in a 1995 Grand Slam decider, but they were totally overwhelmed, and the achievements of Sole's men stand as Scotland's finest hour.

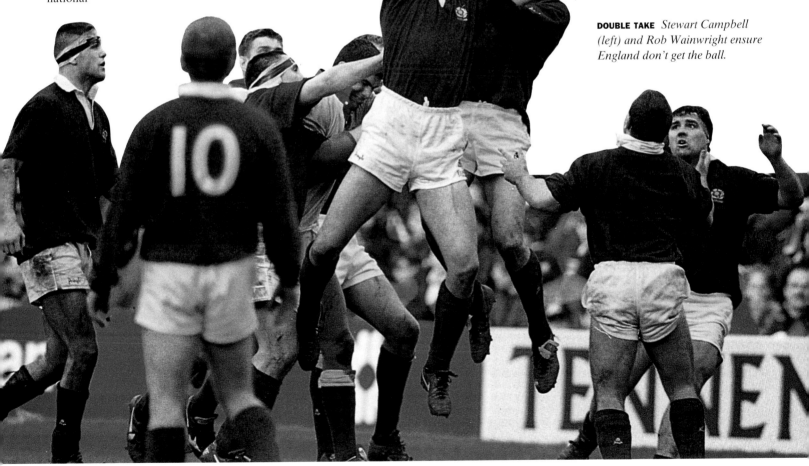

DOUBLE TAKE *Stewart Campbell (left) and Rob Wainwright ensure England don't get the ball.*

SOUTH AFRICA

YEAR FOUNDED: 1889
COLOURS: Olive green shirts and socks (both with gold trim) and white shirts
NO. OF CLUBS: 1,000
NO. OF PLAYERS: 100,000

When Cecil Rhodes, then governor of the Cape Colony, invited Scottish rugby missionary Bill MacLagan to put together a British side to visit South Africa in 1891, he could never have guessed the scale of the sporting love affair he had set in train. This relationship was consummated 104 years later as the South African Springboks

ALL THE PRESIDENT'S MEN *Nelson Mandela congratulates François Pienaar.*

claimed the game's greatest prize, lifting the World Cup in front of 80,000 screaming fans at Ellis Park in Johannesburg.

The most uncompromising and physically demanding of opponents, the South African Springboks are rivalled only by the New Zealand All Blacks in their capacity for recognizing that it is the winning, not the taking part, that matters to them. Because the Springboks are so rarely bettered, claiming the Springbok head – awarded to the first team to beat the touring Springboks – or winning a Test on South African soil is the pinnacle of achievement for touring players and national sides alike. As New Zealand leg-

end Colin Meads said: "This is what it has all been about. This is South Africa and these are the players you most want to beat. If you're ever going to play good rugby, you'll play it in South Africa. The atmosphere demands it of you – to beat South Africa in South Africa, what a dream!"

As with New Zealand and Australia, the basis of South African domestic rugby is the provincial system which has the Currie Cup as its pinnacle. First presented by Sir Donald Currie, the founder of the Currie shipping line, in 1891 to the side which performed the most creditably against MacLagan's tourists (which turned out to be Griqualand West, who lost 1–0), the golden cup is now played for by South Africa's top provinces. In its early years, Western Province virtually

owned the mug, winning it 19 times out of 27 attempts, with Transvaal as the Capetonians' main challengers.

Although there are over 1,000 clubs and 100,000 players in South Africa, virtually all the top talent is concentrated in the six provinces in the Currie Cup top flight: Eastern Province, Natal, Northern Transvaal, Orange Free State, Transvaal and Western Province. Rather than playing for both province and club, the top players now play exclusively for a provincial side.

The Currie Cup was so successful even when the ugly spectre of Apartheid cast its shadow across South African rugby and led to the cessation of international playing contacts for almost a decade, the competition sustained the standard of play to the point where the incoming "rebel" tours that did play during this period were all well beaten.

Rugby was introduced into South Africa in the 1860s, but really made strides in 1875 when the British garrison in Cape Town took on a team from the city. Within fifteen years, the game had become established enough for the South African Rugby Board to be formed and MacLagan's men invited to tour. Although routed by MacLagan's men, who scored 224 points while conceding only one in twenty games, the South Africans were nothing if not quick learners, and by 1896 they were able to win one of three tests against a strong British touring side led by Johnny Hammond, MacLagan's vice-captain in 1891.

The Boer War broke up the pattern of incoming tours, but the Brits were back in 1903, when Scotsman Mark Morrison came, saw and went home with a series loss to his credit. Resplendent in green and sporting the Springbok emblem for the first time, this was South Africa's first series win and set a pattern of success against British tourists that was not to change until the 1974 Lions memorably whitewashed the Springboks.

Such was the strength of South African rugby that when Paul Roos led the first touring party to Britain in 1906 and won 25 of the 28 matches

SPRINGBOKS MAULED *New Zealand put South Africa to the sword during their historic series win against the Springboks in 1996.*

played, the consensus in Britain was that his side was even better than Dave Gallaher's 1905 All Black "Originals". This feeling was consolidated in 1912, when Billy Millar's touring Springboks gave several virtuoso demonstrations of back play to overcome the elements and win all five tests on their tour of Britain, beating Ireland by the record score of 38–0.

Success kept coming, even after South Africa had their first contact with New Zealand and Australia when Theo Pienaar led a touring party south in 1921. But the manner in which the success was achieved began to change as the century wore on. Where the early Springboks had been famous for adventurous and scintillating back play, the later teams became notable only for their belief that Test match-winning teams are the ones which make the fewest mistakes. This approach was exemplified by Bennie Osler, the fly-half, kicker and captain of the 1931 side. Using huge forwards such as Boy Louw and Chris Koch to gradually wear down opposing packs, Osler would only unleash his backs

within hailing distance of the opposition goal-line, preferring to use his own cross field kicks or raking grubbers from scrum-half Danie Craven up to that point.

In a country blessed with strapping Afrikaners, it was never more popular than when Fred Allen's 1949 All Blacks were intimidated and outmuscled into a 4–0 series defeat. While results justified the approach, the safety-first, stick-it-up-your-jumper policy prevailed, but when the 1955 British Lions arrived and shared the series while playing some very exciting rugby, the momentum for a more interesting approach to the game became virtually unstoppable. The mood was reinforced by the 1956 tour to Australia and New Zealand when the All Blacks called up former heavyweight boxer Kevin Skinner, who proceeded to pummel one Springbok prop after another into submission as the New Zealanders won the series 3–1. As well as forcing a rethink of attitudes, the 1949 and '56 series created a rivalry between the Springboks and All Blacks that remains as keen today as it was then.

Unlike New Zealand, however, Apartheid meant that the indigenous South Africans were unable to play rugby alongside whites, a situation that inevitably provoked problems, particularly as a substantial number of New Zealanders were either Maoris or Polynesians. A remark attributed to Dr Danie Craven, effectively the administrator who ran rugby in South Africa – that a black player would play for the Springboks over his dead body – hardly improved matters.

Although the black rugby union, SARU, refused to play touring sides, the SARB did make token efforts at multi-racialism such as scheduling tourists to play township sides from 1972 onwards, and picking gifted black fly-half Errol Tobias for his first cap against Ireland in 1981. By this stage, however, whether or not rugby was getting its house in order was virtually irrelevant, and after the 1981 tour to New Zealand caused serious civil disturbance, isolation beckoned. After England toured in 1984, South Africa's only taste of international competition came from rebel tours,

until reintegration into international sports came about in 1992.

It took a while for the Springboks to recover from the years of isolation, and in the first year there were defeats on home soil by Australia and New Zealand, plus defeats in England and France. Yet with an unrivalled rugby infrastructure, South Africa soon began to string together some favourable results. In a country where touring is particularly hard – especially when the itinerary alternates fixtures between the thin air of the high Veldt and the coastal venues – South Africa quickly managed to regain their form.

The culmination of the Springboks' rehabilitation was when they hosted the 1995 World Cup. South Africa won in thrilling style via a Joel Stransky dropped-goal in overtime, but the enduring memory of post-Apartheid rugby in South Africa will remain captain Francois Pienaar's dedication of the victory to the new "Rainbow Nation" and Nelson Mandela's emotional support for a sport that once stood for everything he despised.

WALES

YEAR FOUNDED: 1880
COLOURS: Red shirts and socks (with white trim) and white shorts
NO. OF CLUBS: 440
NO. OF PLAYERS: 25,000

Of all the countries in the northern hemisphere, only Wales can claim that rugby is the national sport. So deeply embedded is the game in the Welsh psyche, and so deep is the love for it in Wales, that rugby is almost a national barometer charting the state of the nation. Success on the rugby field is, for many Welshmen, one of the main props of their national identity and self-esteem, and the Welsh have long acted as rugby missionaries. Where else, for instance, could a comedian/entertainer like Max Boyce become a spokesman for the people?

Rugby in Britain has always been a middle-class game, save for fanatical pockets like the West Country, the Scottish Borders and the Irish city of Limerick. Yet as the sport of all men, the game in Wales is markedly different, one where doctors and lawyers have traditionally rubbed shoulders with miners and dockers on a Saturday afternoon. Indeed, as with New Zealand, much of the immense strength of Welsh rugby has been in the fact that, despite being a relatively small country, virtually all sports-inclined youngsters were exposed to the sport and few athletes were left uncovered or their talents unused. As Gareth Edwards once said: "Growing up in Wales meant two things to me: rugby on Saturday and chapel on Sunday. The thought of doing anything else just never crossed our minds as youngsters."

Although the game is sewn into the fabric of the whole of Welsh society, it was in the industrial south, rather than the rural north, where the game took root. The wide belt of steelworks and coal mining areas stretching from English-speaking Newport in the East, through the Valleys of the Rhondda and across to Welsh-speaking Llanelli in the West, have provided some of the greatest players the game has ever seen. Yet while the industrial base conjures up images of iron-hard hulking forwards, the defining trait of Welsh rugby has long been its outstanding backs.

While Welsh rugby can boast some of the hardest forwards ever to lace up a pair of boots, men such as Clem Thomas, Rhys Williams, Delme Thomas and Graham Price – who were never renowned for their gentle temperaments once the red mist descended – and Welsh club rugby has long been recognized as among the most physically testing in the world, if you ask any Welshman what sets the pulses racing, the answer is not a foot-slogger, but a twinkle-toed, dancing brave at fly-half. So powerful is the legend of Wales as a fly-half factory, that if there was to be a Welsh Rugby Hall of Fame, then it is easy to imagine which would be the first names pencilled in: famous No.10s Barry John, Cliff Morgan and Phil Bennett would undoubtedly hog centre stage.

But if Welsh rugby is all about the forward fury Welsh-speakers call "hwyl" and three-quarter panache, it has also been enlivened by a fanaticism of support that can only exist in a country where rugby is the sporting be-all and end-all, and where singing is revered. But while the legions of followers of the game in the Principality have been united behind the national side since it first took on the English at Blackheath in 1881, the regional and club rivalries that were once the lifeblood of domestic rugby have now conspired to hold back the development of Welsh rugby.

With occasional interruptions since the mid-1870s, club rugby west of the Severn river has been dominated by a small coterie of City clubs.

SLIPSTREAM *Scotland can only watch as Ieuan Evans powers his way to the try-line to seal a win for Wales in the 1997 Five Nations championship.*

Swansea, Newport and Cardiff (the club which in 1885–86 introduced the three-quarters formation we have today and which is the self-styled "Greatest Club in the World"), were the original "Big Three" and have dominated ever since, while Llanelli, Pontypool, Neath and Bridgend have also enjoyed spells of pre-eminence. The fierce rivalries between these clubs – plus a continual diet of shockingly brutal clashes with top English sides, particularly mighty West Country neighbours Bath, Bristol and Gloucester – ensured that Welsh rugby was always very competitive.

Touring sides also gave Welsh rugby some of its greatest moments. Cardiff's wins over South Africa in 1906, Australia in 1947 and, most particularly, New Zealand in 1953 are mentioned in hushed tones, while Pontypool's 1927 double victory (over the Australian Waratahs and the New Zealand Maoris), Swansea's defeat of the All Blacks in 1935 and Newport's lowering of the Springbok standard in 1912 are all discussed in clubhouses as if they occurred just last week.

For all the great deeds of derring-do, however, Welsh rugby suffers from its insularity and has gradually lost ground against the main forces in world rugby in recent times. The incursion of Rugby League, which has claimed almost one in four of all Welsh internationals, has not helped the cause of the 15-man game, and the steady decline of heavy industry has also contributed to a worsening record (where once the majority of top players were miners or steelworkers, now it is possible to count the number on one hand). More than anything else, however, Welsh rugby has had to fight against the sheer weight of numbers of players in the super-powers: England, France, South Africa, Australia and New Zealand have all had access to at least three times as many players as Wales, and with just 440 clubs and 25,000 players, the lack of numbers has told.

The outstanding generation of players that emerged at the beginning of the 1970s papered over some of the structural problems that have subsequently appeared in Welsh rugby. Throughout the 1970s, a procession of gloriously talented players, including Barry John, Gareth Edwards, J.P.R. Williams, Mervyn Davies, John Taylor, Phil Bennett, J.J. Williams and the Pontypool front-row of Price, Faulkner and Windsor, held sway over Britain and the world. As the core of the victorious British Lions tour of 1971 to New Zealand and to South Africa in 1974, that generation of Welshmen represented the finest group of players ever to pull on a Lion's jersey.

As that pool of players dried up, Welsh fortunes began

WITH A LITTLE HELP
Wales' most-capped lock Gareth Llewellyn rises to the challenge against Scotland in 1996.

to change. By the mid-eighties, the national side was on the wane, and in the World Cup semi-final against New Zealand in 1987 the chickens came home to roost in spectacular fashion as Wales were humiliated

49–6, a reverse that was to be repeated the following year when Wales lost 52–3 and 54–9 on their tour of New Zealand. Worse was to follow in the 1991 World Cup in their opening game at the National Stadium they lost to the unfancied Western Samoans, a blow from which the national side are only just threatening to recover.

The era from 1985 to 1995 was the most miserable in Welsh rugby history, but there is a new realism with structures in place to ensure that national and club sides prosper. The benefits are beginning to show, while the emergence of the European Cup has enabled the top players to widen their experience. The return of Rugby League players has given the national side some much needed experience in the lead-up to the 1999 World Cup, which Wales is to host.

REST OF THE WORLD

ANDORRA

YEAR FOUNDED: 1986
YEAR JOINED IRFB: 1991
COLOURS: Blue/Yellow/Red
NO. OF CLUBS: 2

The game in Andorra is only 30 years old. Started by students returning from France and Spain, the game has been nurtured by Anick Musolas, a teacher and radio personality who learnt a love of the game from her rugby-mad father when they lived in La Rochelle.

Although Andorra has just two clubs (plus a recent addition made up of ski instructors from around the world!), it reached the Spanish Cup final in 1966, and was kicked out and have been playing in the French fourth division ever since.

Most of the players are locally bred, with No. 8 Tony Castillo, scrum-half Alonso Ricart and Roger Font to the fore, but there is some outside help, for example, in the form of 39-year-old Jimmy Jordan, a winger from Kilmarnock, and Gustavo Tumosa, a fly-half who once played for Argentine province of Rosario.

ARABIAN GULF

YEAR FOUNDED: 1977
YEAR JOINED IRFB: 1990
COLOURS: White/Maroon/Black/Green
NO OF CLUBS: 27

Rugby in the Gulf is almost exclusively the preserve of 500-odd Commonwealth ex-pats at eight clubs, although the Dubai Sevens has done a lot to bring attention to the game in the Middle East.

A team regularly enters the Hong Kong Sevens, and the Gulf made their first attempt to enter the World Cup fray in 1994, losing all three matches at the qualifying tournament in Kenya.

The Bahrain RFU and the Kuwait RFU also come under the general banner of the Gulf.

ARGENTINA

YEAR FOUNDED: 1899
YEAR JOINED IRFB: 1987
COLOURS: Light Blue/White
NO. OF CLUBS: 250

Of all the touring venues outside the "Big Eight", none is more testing than Argentina. A land where they breed 'em big, Argentina is one of the great touring venues but is notoriously a country where visitors invariably leave nursing physical and psychological bruises. Of the British sides to visit Argentina, few have found the Pumas (the national side's nickname) a soft touch: indeed, in four Tests from 1981–90, England could only win two, while Scotland fared even worse, losing both tests on their 1994 tour.

Argentina is a land of striking paradoxes and contrasts. The game was started by the British community in Buenos Aires as long ago as 1886 and remains a fiercely amateur sport played by the elite of the establishment. Yet travel a few hours up country from the refined grounds of the Rosario Athletic Club or the Buenos Aires Football Club and you reach Tucuman, the land where passions run high on the terraces and the ceremonial burning of the opposition flag is *de rigueur*. Traditionally it has been this region that has provided Argentina with some of its toughest forwards.

The game was implanted into the Argentine as far back as 1886, when Buenos Aires Football Club and Rosario Athletic Club met in a fixture that was a mix of rugby and football. The flavour of the early game in Argentina becomes clear through a glance down the names that comprised what was then called the River Plate Rugby Union: Elliot, Anderson, Thurn, Baikie, Taylor, Corry-Smith, Jacobs, Leicht, Brodie and Bellamy. Brits to a man.

Although boasting almost 200 clubs and 30,000 players, Argentina have long been out on a rugby limb. Ever isolated, Argentina's first contact with the wider rugby world was in 1910, when an England team led by J. Raphael turned up, won all six matches and left with a record of 213 points scored, 31 conceded. Further contacts went along much the same lines, David McMyn's England scoring 295 points while conceding only nine in their 1927 whitewash tour, while the Junior Springboks fared much the same in 1932, as did the British side in 1936.

Eager for wider competition (there is a South American Championship which the Pumas have won all 14 times they have contested it since 1958), the Pumas turned their sights overseas after 1945. The most significant tour, however, was to South Africa in 1965. Despite faring badly, the Argentineans made contact with Izak van Heerden, a coaching genius from Natal who was to revolutionize Argentine play in the late 1960s.

KNIGHTS OF ARABIA *Two Arabian Gulf players cadge a lift during the 1996 Dubai Sevens tournament.*

If the Pumas were lucky to discover Van Heerden, they were even luckier to possess in fly-half Hugo Porta (1974–90) an exquisite talent to go with the outstanding packs that were coming off the Pampas production line after 1945. Porta led the ultra-competitive Argentine sides of the late 1970s, and reached his zenith in South Africa when he stood out for the South American party which controversially toured the republic in defiance of the ban.

Although a tricky proposition on their own patch, the Pumas do not generally travel well and have under-performed in all three World Cups. In the 1995 tournament they finished at the bottom of their pool having lost all three matches. However, their most recent international fixture was against England in December 1996 at Twickenham, although they again lost, the margin was only two points, raising hopes for the future.

AUSTRIA

YEAR FOUNDED: 1990
YEAR JOINED IRFB: 1992
COLOURS: Black/White
NO. OF CLUBS: 7

Rugby in Austria goes back to 1900, and despite an enthusiasm that saw 10,000 spectators turning out for a demonstration game between two French sides in 1930, it remained largely a game played by Vienna-based students.

That changed with the influx of military personnel after 1945. The main rivalry has always been with Germany and Hungary, with whom the national side contested a 1993 FIRA match in front of 8,000 Viennese. The driving force in recent years was a former Italian cap, Dr Giancarlo Tizanini, who worked hard to establish an informal middle European "Five Nations" between Slovenia, Croatia, Hungary, Bosnia and Austria before his death in 1994.

In the 1996 FIRA Junior Championships, Austria played in the lowest division with Hungary and Slovenia. Although they beat the latter, they struggled against the bigger Hungarian pack from the start, before going down 21-8. With soccer and skiing still as popular as ever, rugby will have to be content with its status as a minority sport in Austria.

BELGIUM

YEAR FOUNDED: 1935
YEAR JOINED IRFB: 1988
COLOURS: Black/Yellow/Red/White
NO. OF CLUBS: 41

Although bordering France, rugby has struggled to gain a foothold in Belgium; gradually the game has spread into the north of the country, among the Flemish, but in the south rugby players continue to be a rarity. Nevertheless, Belgian rugby's most high profile personality remains the former international referee Teddy Lacroix, who is now president of the union. A relatively new union, formed in 1931, Belgium has 41 clubs and almost 2,500 players.

POISED PUMA *Argentine lock German Llanes, now with Bath, takes a line-out during their 20–18 defeat by England at Twickenham in December 1996.*

BERMUDA

YEAR FOUNDED: 1964
YEAR JOINED IRFB: 1992
COLOURS: Blue/Black
NO. OF CLUBS: 4

It's difficult to expect too much from a rock which is ten miles by ten, but Bermuda have managed to have fun while dominating Caribbean rugby. Largely played by white Bermudans and a few incomers – such as former Bristol wing Barry Whitehead – the highlight of the rugby year on the island is the annual Bermuda Classic Tournament, where teams of over 35s play each other in a super-annuated World Cup with vast quantities of alcohol thrown in for good measure.

While the Kiwis – sporting names such as Haden, Going, Kirwan and Shelford in recent years – have ruined the ambience a tad, at least the rugby is as feisty as the under-age version.

BRAZIL

YEAR FOUNDED: 1972
YEAR JOINED IRFB: 1995
COLOURS: Gold/Green
NO. OF CLUBS: 35

Rugby was first played at the Sao Paolo Club in 1888. Even then, because the game was only played in four provinces instead of the five required by Brazil to become a national sporting association, the Union only joined the International Board in 1995, and still only has about 800 players, mostly students.

Because Brazil was not a part of the IB in the 1970s and 1980s, it became a favoured destination for South African teams. Mervyn Sinclair, brother-in-law of Springbok legend Morne du Plessis, is heavily involved in coaching there, as is former Romanian coach Arthur Vogel. Brazil remains overshadowed by Argentina, and has fallen behind the new power, Uruguay in the South American pecking order. Add to that a recent 41-0 drubbing by Trindad and Tobago, and rugby in Brazil does not look particularly healthy.

BOTSWANA

YEAR FOUNDED: 1992
YEAR JOINED IRFB: 1994
COLOURS: Black/White/Blue
NO. OF CLUBS: 8

The game in Botswana, just to the north of South Africa, is along the lines of that in Kenya and, to a lesser extent, Zimbabwe – a hangover from colonial days. There are eight clubs in Botswana, all centred around Gaborone, although there has always been a steady trickle of touring sides from South Africa and other neighbouring African states.

BULGARIA

YEAR FOUNDED: 1962
YEAR JOINED IRFB: 1992
COLOURS: Red/White
NO. OF CLUBS: 12

Although the Union was formed in 1962, the first international was not until 1976, when Bulgaria got off to an inauspicious start losing 54-0 to a rampant Czechoslovakian side. The worst day in Bulgarian international rugby was a 100–0 defeat by Romania in 1973, when the try was still worth three points. There are a little over 500 active players, almost all of whom are based in Sofia.

CANADA

YEAR FOUNDED: 1929
YEAR JOINED IRFB: 1986
COLOURS: Red/White
NO. OF CLUBS: 175

Canada will always means the land of big hits and even bigger second rows. The country finally broke through into the top-ranked nations in 1991 when a win over the touring Scots was followed by an outstanding showing at the World Cup where hard-fought wins over Romania and Fiji, plus a narrow defeat by France, saw the Canucks reach the quarter-finals. Once there, they impressed everyone in a second half of sheer guts and determination which saw them outscore and out-All Black the All Blacks. Despite losing, it was clear Canada had arrived at last, a fact confirmed by the stunning 26–24 victory over Wales at Cardiff and a defeat of France the following year.

That 1991 vintage was typical of Canadian rugby. Huge forwards such as Norm Hadley, Al Charron, Dan Jackart and Eddie Evans, feisty half-backs Chris Tynan or John Graf, and a fly-half with a howitzer boot, Gareth Rees. That is the Canadian way: tackling hard and giving little or no quarter.

Even great Canadian backs, such as Spence McTavish and Mark Wyatt, conform to a pattern that owes much to a British heritage. The star players of this era grew out of the competitive Vancouver circuit, which makes British Columbia Canada's centre of rugby excellence. Yet few people realize that, numerically, the game is not actually centred around the West Coast city. In fact Ontario has as many players as BC, while there is a liberal spread over the rest of the country. Yet for all that, there has been a gradual migration of top Canadian rugby talent to Vancouver clubs – or at least there was until the top players moved to play professionally in Europe. The major miracle, however, is that Canada can deal with its climate – or that rugby was ever established in the country in the first place.

Not only do the distances make inter-province competition difficult, but with many grounds under ice and snow for much of the year, the country has to make do with a "split season".

While becoming increasingly cosmopolitan – especially as Vancouver looks West to the Pacific Rim for its inspiration rather than back to Europe – the game in Canada owes much to the mass emigration from Britain throughout the century.

Indeed, the game was first introduced to Canada in the 1880s by A St G Hammersley, an Englishman who played in the first Calcutta Cup match in 1871. From there on in, the bulk of international contact was with All Blacks sides returning from Britain, the first on which was the visit of Dave Gallaher's "Invincibles" in 1905.

UP AGAINST IT *Bulgaria, Europe's newest rugby nation, take on Spain, in the 1999 World Cup qualifiers.*

PASS MASTER *Canada's talented flanker Al Charon clears his lines.*

CHILE

YEAR FOUNDED: 1953
YEAR JOINED IRFB: 1991
COLOURS: Red/Navy
NO. OF CLUBS: 119

The game was first established in Chile during the 1920s around Santiago and Valpolariso. Living in the shadow of Argentina, Chile has always thought of itself as the best of the rest, a belief reinforced by its 1981 win in the South American Championship when Argentina was absent from the competition.

With 119 clubs and nearly 4,000 players, Chile's belief that it was streets ahead of Paraguay (seven clubs, 450 players) and Uruguay (11 clubs and 700 players) should have seemed well founded. However, the 1995 World Cup qualifiers when it lost 25–24 to Paraguay, 14–6 to Uruguay and 70–7 to the Pumas, sent it back to square one and shattered its illusions of progress.

CHINA

YEAR FOUNDED: 1945
YEAR JOINED IRFB: 1988
COLOURS: Red/Blue/White
NO. OF CLUBS: 15

Largely ignorant of rugby until 1990, China has now taken up rugby with a vengeance and will soon be a member of the International Board. The impetus for this swift adoption of the game came from Hong Kong, when some local Chinese players based in the British colony saw a game of rugby between two teams from Beijing Agricultural University in the north of China.

Further investigation revealed that a professor at the university called Chao Xihuang had been introduced to rugby by a Japanese businessman and had taken the game to his heart.

The intervention of the Hong Kong Rugby Union's energetic Kiwi supremo George Simpkin has helped to kick-start the game, which has gone from having 30 players in 1991 to over 1,000 trained instructors today.

Olympic status has also helped with the growth and stature of the game, but it is the adoption of Rugby Union by the million-strong People's Revolutionary Army that ensured a healthy future for the game in China.

COOK ISLANDS

YEAR FOUNDED: 1948
YEAR JOINED IRFB: 1995
COLOURS: Gold/Green
NO. OF CLUBS: 35

Although long established, and nurtured by British, Australian, Japanese and New Zealand sides from visiting ships, the game has only recently been put on a formal footing in these islands to the north of Australia. The side even beat Papua New Guinea in a recent World Cup qualifier. General factotum Anthony Turua is doing a great job and has good material and 35 clubs to work with. Almost all players play both union and league. The islands' most famous sons are former Australian Rugby League captain Mal Meninga and All Blacks Graeme and Steve Bachop.

CROATIA

YEAR FOUNDED: 1994
YEAR JOINED IRFB: 1992
COLOURS: Red/White/Blue
NO. OF CLUBS: 14

The break-up of Yugoslavia meant that there was little time for rugby. Even so, Croatia managed to play impromptu games against forces serving in Bosnia, and now have 14 clubs with in excess of 1,000 registered players. A big, mentally strong people, rugby suits them, and there are nearly 50 Croats playing in France's top three divisions.

OUT WITH A BANG *The 1996 Hong Kong Sevens saw China's debut.*

CZECH REPUBLIC

YEAR FOUNDED: 1926
YEAR JOINED IRFB: 1988
COLOURS: White/Red/Blue
NO. OF CLUBS: 18

40 years of Communism hardly helped, yet rugby in Czechoslovakia remained popular within a section of the middle class. Slovakia and the Czech Republic split shortly after the fall of Communism in eastern Europe, but as most of the rugby was played around Prague, the Czechs retained a playing strength of 2,400 players and 18 clubs.

Although better known as a touring venue (thanks to the cheap beer and beautiful surroundings of Prague), rugby has a long history in Czechoslovakia. Introduced to the country by Czech writer Ondrej Skkora on his return from France, the first competitive match took place in the Moravian provincial capital Brno, the cradle of Czech rugby, where SK Moravian Slávia fielded a side against AFK Zizka.

A founder member of FIRA in 1934, rugby only really took off after 1945, when players such as Zdenek Bárchanék, Eduard Krützner and Bruno Kudrna helped in games against rivals Poland and Germany, and in their losing battles against Rugby "super-power" Romania.

An interesting aside: in the 1960s, sports minister Antonin Himi asked captain Eduard Krutzner what quantity of steroids the team needed to win.

DENMARK

YEAR FOUNDED: 1950
YEAR JOINED IRFB: 1988
COLOURS: Red/White
NO. OF CLUBS: 29

Since the formation of the union in 1950, Denmark traditionally lagged behind the top Scandinavian side Sweden. Until 1980, they had never beaten the Swedes, but since then honours have been shared equally, and in 1995 the Danes beat regular visitors Welsh Districts for the first time ever.

The Danes now have one of the healthiest domestic structures in Northern Europe with 29 clubs and almost 2,000 players, although much of the work at the sharp end is done by ex-pat Britons in the form of coach Alan Giles and manager Bernard White (the national team has a style which reflects this input). On the playing side, the Danes have a real find in 6ft 6in No.8 Michael Anderson.

FIJI

YEAR FOUNDED: 1913
YEAR JOINED IRFB: 1987
COLOURS: White/Black
NO. OF CLUBS: 600

With huge men possessing vast natural talent, Fiji has often threatened to break into the game's top flight. Rugby was introduced to Fiji in the 1880s by Britons and Kiwis. In the early years Fiji's white and coloured inhabitants played in separate leagues. Once exposed to the wider world, the Fijians at one stage looked as if they were could be ranked alongside the Big Eight.

As far back as the 1950s, when Fiji twice toured Australia, sharing the series with their hosts on both occasions, the Pacific Islanders showed themselves to be fine athletes. So much so that when they played Australia at the Sydney Cricket Ground in 1952, a record crowd of 42,000 turned up.

Yet the Fijians remain on the margins of the game's elite at international level. Of late they have even been overtaken by Western Samoa and Tonga, the other two island nations in the Pacific Championship. Much of the blame for this lies in Fiji's love affair with Sevens, a game in which the islanders' penchant for running with the ball in hand has been given free reign. Masters at the abbreviated code, Fiji has of late produced some of the world's outstanding Sevens' players, such as mercurial fly-half Waisale Serevi and giant lock Mesake Rasaril. Yet the infatuation with Sevens, and the concentration on it to the growing exclusion of the full game, has taken its toll on Fiji's competitiveness at international level. Where once the Fijians were top of the Pacific Championship tree, these days it is Western Samoa who are setting the pace, with Tonga not far behind.

In 1987, it as Tonga and Fiji who were invited to take part in the inaugural World Cup, during which Fiji suffered a 74–13 drubbing by the All Blacks and failed to advance beyond the pool stages.

In 1991, they lost all three games. In 1995, they did not even make it to the tournament.

Latterly, the Fijian Rugby Union has tried to put its house in order, but exclusion from the Super 12 when Australia, New Zealand and South Africa formed a cosy cartel, not only set back the progress pf the Fijians in playing terms but also came as a severe blow to the morale

KICKING UP A STORM *Fiji's Mesake Resavi squelches through the mud in a Hong Kong Sevens match.*

of the naturally exuberant islanders. The only way smaller countries such as Fiji, Tonga and Samoa can develop their game is to play regularly against Australia, New Zealand and the Northern Hemisphere,. The sooner this happens the better it will be for the rugby world as a whole. Professionalism has also seriously harmed Fiji's game, with stars such as Waisale Serevi, Mesate Rosari, Paula Bale and Joeli Vidri lured to Japan and New Zealand. And, the pre-occupation with the Sevens code, makes the prospect of Fiji as a major force remote in the near future.

GEORGIA

YEAR FOUNDED: 1964
YEAR JOINED IRFB: 1992
COLOURS: Wine/White
NO. OF CLUBS: 15

The Georgians regularly had six or seven players in the USSR side before the break-up, as well as supplying the Soviet club champions in Dinamo Tbilisi.

One of the best players outside the eight founder members, flanker Dimitri Oboladze, was a Georgian. Perhaps this has something to do with the similarities between rugby and Georgia's national sport "Lelo", a full contact ball game.

Although rugby has been played in Georgia since the 1930s, the first official test was in 1989 against the touring Zimbabweans. Although the civil war that followed the end of communism didn't help the game, crowds as large as 10,000 to 15,000 have still been reported for derbies in the capital.

GIBRALTAR

YEAR FOUNDED: Not known
YEAR JOINED IRFB: Not affiliated
COLOURS: Not applicable
NO. OF CLUBS: 4

Although tiny, the Gibraltar RFU has four regular sides and is also sustained by the presence of British servicemen, friendlier relations with Spain have inevitably meant a wider fixture list.

ORANGE MARCH *Holland's talented scrum-half, Marcel Emon, prepares to launch another attack.*

GERMANY

YEAR FOUNDED: 1900
YEAR JOINED IRFB: 1988
COLOURS: White/Black/Red/Yellow
NO. OF CLUBS: 83

It is one of the great mysteries of rugby that the game has not taken off in Germany, despite having been implanted as long ago as 1872 when the Heidelberger Flaggenklub were formed. Long the preserve of the middle-classes, the game's main claim to fame is that it was the favourite pastime of Albert Speer, War Minister in Hitler's inner cabinet. Rugby reached its peak in 1938, when Germany recorded a second win over France (the first was in 1927) by 3–0. The presence of the British Army on the Rhine in the post-war years helped maintain a relatively high level of interest, and Germany now has 87 clubs and over 8,000 registered players. Yet, although the national side regularly play at Hong Kong and have produced some gifted players (Horst Kemmling, Claus Himmer, Dietrich Volkmer and Dietmar Kopp chief among them), it still remains predominantly the domain of students and visiting Europeans.

Efforts are being made to transport the game to the east of the country, which was virtually rugby-free from 1945 to fall of the Berlin Wall.

HOLLAND

YEAR FOUNDED: 1932
YEAR JOINED IRFB: 1988
COLOURS: Orange/White
NO. OF CLUBS: 81

The Dutch, one of the tallest peoples in the world, remain one of European rugby's true enigmas. Despite the fact that the game is well-entrenched among students and the fact that the Dutch possess an enthusiastic and well-run union which has a showcase tournament in the Amsterdam Sevens, Dutch rugby has yet to make real headway at international level. Much of this is due to the post-war advent of professional soccer, which decimated the healthy rugby scene in both Germany and Holland.

With 104 clubs and between 7,000 to 8,000 players to choose from, however, there are signs that this may be about to change. Holland has produced several outstanding players – including lock Michael Van Der Loos from the Hague, who was twice asked to consider naturalization after making a huge impact in Wales and in France.

An inspired win over a full-strength Moseley side in 1996 augurs well for the future of the game, although the tragic injury in 1988 when 22-year-old fly-half Marcel Bierman broke his neck dur-

ing the Hong Kong Sevens has not helped the cause of the game in Holland. With Germany still the biggest rivals, Holland is now on the same level as Spain, on the next rung down from Romania and Russia. Top players of the past few years have included Yves Kummer, Andre and Mats Marcker and wing Paul Bloom.

HONG KONG

YEAR FOUNDED: 1953
YEAR JOINED IRFB: 1988
COLOURS: Blue/Red/White
NO. OF CLUBS: 26

Known mainly for its Sevens tournament, a powerful missionary force for the game in Asia, Hong Kong almost single-handedly made the abbreviated game a force to be reckoned with outside the Borders of Scotland where it originated. The 1997 World Cup Sevens was played in the colony as it prepared for the Chinese take-over just months later.

Although the game was founded on the large number of Commonwealth military stationed there, the HKRFU has been trying to lay the foundations for the game to be sustained once British rule ends. Under the energetic Director of Rugby George Simpkin, efforts have been made to spread the game to the colony's Chinese population, as well

67

as to the mainland itself.

Perhaps because of its missionary contribution to the game's development in Asia, Hong Kong has been allowed to compete at the Asian Championships as a fully fledged nations. However, despite using the full offices of the British Army, Hong Kong have scored only fleeting successes against the region's perennial super-powers, Korea and Japan.

HUNGARY

YEAR FOUNDED: 1990
YEAR JOINED IRFB: 1991
COLOURS: Red/White/Green
NO. OF CLUBS: 15

Rugby in Hungary is a relatively new sport which owes its origins to a group of Italian diplomats who founded a number of teams in the late 1960s and 1970s. Although the game almost died after these originators made their return to Italy, the hard work of a few enthusiasts kept the game alive in Budapest. By 1981 the sport had even mananged to find support outside the capital, and spread to the provincial town of Kecskmet.

In 1990, Hungarian rugby was strong enough to stage its first international against East Germany, which it lost 3–7. Although growing – there are now 16 clubs and almost 1,000 players – the hold of the game on the hearts and minds of the average Hungarian is still tenuous and a recent 39–19 World Cup qualifier defeat by Sweden will not have raised spirits. Olympic recognition will help, though.

INDONESIA

YEAR FOUNDED: Not known
YEAR JOINED IRFB: Not affiliated
COLOURS: Not applicable
NO. OF CLUBS: 8

Indonesian rugby, like the rest of south-eat Asia, is a game sustained by small brigade of ex-patriate Britons and Australasians.

Virtually all organized rugby is played around the capital Jakarta in multi-sport clubs which occasionally stage rugby matches.

SILVER SERVICE *Hong Kong show off the Plate trophy they won at their own Sevens tournament in 1992.*

INDIA

YEAR FOUNDED: 1874
YEAR JOINED IRFB: Not affiliated
COLOURS: Not applicable
NO. OF CLUBS: 12

Although implanted into India almost as soon as Webb-Ellis had picked up the ball at Rugby School, the game was not to last. The odd game still takes place (the Indian RFU is run out of the Irish Consulate at the Royal Bombay Yacht Club chambers!), but the last formal club in India disbanded as long ago as 1877, just four years after its creation by a group of ex-pat Old Rugbeians. For all that, though, there is now a very successful campaign to revive the game in India, while the memory of the Calcutta Club lives on in the form of the Calcutta Cup. The trophy played for annually between Scotland and England came into existence when the club disbanded, and withdrew all its funds from Calcutta's central bank then melted them down and turned into an exquisite tapered cup.

ISRAEL

YEAR FOUNDED: 1971
YEAR JOINED IRFB: 1988
COLOURS: Blue
NO. OF CLUBS: 14

Rugby was introduced to Israel during the British Mandate period and was played intermittently by small groups in the army and among immigrants during the 1950s thanks largely to the efforts of Leo Camron, a former Springbok and Natal regular, but virtually disappeared until a new wave of immigrants arived from rugby-playing countries in the 1970s. Again it was a group of South Africans – this time based at Kibbutz Yisreel in the North West of the country – who provided Israeli rugby with a much-needed push.

After contacts with France, South Africa and the British military in Cyprus, the game was given a further shot in the arm when it was included in the four-yearly Maccabiah Games — the Jewish Olympics, where it was won in 1993

by South Africa. There are 10 senior and 12 junior clubs in the country, and roughly 70 per cent of players are now locally born.

To date, the high point of the country's rugby history was a shock 67–8 World Cup win against Hungary that did much to promote the sport within Israel.

ITALY

YEAR FOUNDED: 1929
YEAR JOINED IRFB: 1987
COLOURS: Blue
NO. OF CLUBS: 430

The game in Italy has come on so quickly in the last 15 years that, outside of the Five Nations, Italy are head and shoulders above the rest of Europe. This fact has been recognized by the inclusion of Italian clubs into the top tier of the recently formed European Cup and by the growing number of voices calling for the inclusion of "The Azzurri" in an expanded Five

Nations tournament. There are voices that have been vindicated by recent wins over both Ireland and Scotland.

If Italy have only come of age as a rugby power recently, then a look back at the history of the country should prove the recent pre-eminence is no fluke. Rugby was first introduced into the small country towns of the Po Valley and Northern Italy in the late 1920s by workers returning from France; and it is still in towns such as Rovigo and Treviso where the game is strongest, helped in part through the proximity to France's rugby heartland. Enthusiastic approval from Mussolini's cronies in the years leading up to the Second World War also did the game no harm.

Yet if it was France who planted the seed and helped nurture it for so many years, it was Italian efforts and a peculiar set of economic circumstances which saw Italian rugby develop a momentum all of its own throughout the eighties. In an effort to promote, sinking money into rugby became virtually tax-free in Italy, and the amounts sponsorship money that came into the sport were huge as companies such as Benetton sponsored club sides. The next step was an influx of foreign stars – many with Italian ancestry because this gave them the same employment rights as Italian nationals – into sides such as Benetton Treviso, and a dramatic rise in standards. Argentina was raided of top players with Italian ancestors, while stars such as Frano Botica, David Campese, John Kirwan and Michael Lynagh also plied their trade in Italy's top flight.

Although the rise in standards was not immediate, with the help of top foreign coaches such as Mark Ella and Bertrand Fourcarde, Italy gradually began to develop its own stars. The pace of change is per-

INSPIRED ITALIAN *Massimo Giovanelli, the "Azzurri's" captain.*

haps best illustrated by two meetings with New Zealand at two World Cups: in 1987 the Italians were walloped 70–6, while by 1991 they lost by as little as 31–21 in a close match. By 1994, World champions Australia hosted the Italians and received the shock of their lives when they won the first test 23–20 courtesy of a highly dubious last-minute try, and struggled to win the second 20–7. Italian rugby had arrived.

Notwith-

NEW BOYS ON THE BLOCK *Ivory Coast, 1995 World Cup debutants.*

standing that some of the best players among Italy's 16,500 registered players in 266 clubs remain foreign-bred – such as Argentinean fly-half Diego Dominguez, South African-born prop Massimo Cuttitta and former Wallaby open-side Julian Gardner – Italy now have at their disposal many truly talented young players, of which utility backs Ivan Francescato and Paolo Vacarri, plus breakaway Carlo Checchinato are examples.

IVORY COAST

YEAR FOUNDED: 1961
YEAR JOINED IRFB: 1988
COLOURS: Orange/White/Green
NO. OF CLUBS: 35

Although they only played their first international in 1990 against Zimbabwe, the Ivory Coast burst onto the international scene when they beat the much-fancied Namibians to qualify for the 1995 World Cup finals in South Africa. Once there, they were outclassed by the Scots (89–0), French (54–18) and Tongans (29–11), and had the dreadful experience of seeing wing Max Brito carried paralysed from the field during the game against Tonga. He remains a quadraplegic.

Although the Ivorians were soundly defeated, they at least left the rugby world with the sense that black Africa was beginning to emerge

as a force. The truth, however, is that most of the rugby played in the capital Abidjan, where there are some 13 teams and 2,000-odd players, is inspired by the close ties with the former colonial power France. A paid French official, Jean-Francois Turon, managed to get the game adopted by Abidjan University fifteen years ago and, with some enthusiastic help from the father of Ivorian rugby François Dali (who also happens to be the father of the current Ivory Coast captain, Athanase Dali), the game made great strides.

Max Brito played his rugby in France, as do most players in the national side. While this exposes the top Ivorians to a better standard of rugby, the exposure to French club rugby also has some regrettable drawbacks. The path to the World Cup finals, when Tunisia, Morocco, Namibia, Kenya and Zimbabwe were dispatched, for instance, was littered with all-out brawls and the sound of a referee's whistle.

JAPAN

YEAR FOUNDED: 1926
YEAR JOINED IRFB: 1987
COLOURS: Red/White
NO. OF CLUBS: 4,800

It is fitting that rugby reached Japan less than three decades after the American navy first employed "gunboat diplomacy" to break Japan's isolation from the world. As with every other facet of West-

NOT SO FAST *Japan's Tsutomu Matsuda is tackled as he tries to kick.*

ern life, the Japanese took to rugby with great alacrity, prizing the game for the way in which it enshrined the conflict and courtesy that was a basis for Bushido, the code of the warrior.

Although rugby was first played in Japan in Yokohama in the early 1870s between British sailors, the game only took hold when introduced to Japan in 1897 by two students who had been studying in London. After that, rugby swept through the Universities, which remain the heartland of rugby in Japan, and by the 1920s, there were nearly 1,500 rugby clubs in Japan and in excess of 60,000 players. Despite the intervention of the Second World War, interest has remained amazingly high in Japan, even though their lack of height and weight makes the Japanese peculiarly uncompetitive against top international sides – particularly at the lineout. It is partly for this reason and partly because of the sheer number of opportunities

to play at home, that the Japanese have tended to be a rather insular rugby community. The first tour to Japan did not take place until 1934, when an Australian Universities side was defeated in four of its nine games.

Although international contacts have been maintained, Japan have generally fared badly except for a 1990 win over a Scotland XV which was the national side in all but name. Despite the increasing threat from Korea, Japan have managed to retain the position of Asian champions, a status that has allowed them to compete at all three World Cup finals, where their solitary success came against Zimbabwe in 1991.

Stoically true blue amateur, the Japanese have managed to engage in an ingenious form of double-think over the past 30 years, with some of their top companies or universities employing elite players from around the world and then releasing them to play for their company or university sides (i.e. the Japan-

ese top flight). In this way, players such as Wallaby Ian Williams and Tongan international Sinali Latu have ended up playing for Japan, while a whole range of top internationals from Norm Hadley to Joe Stanley have plied their trade for one of the Japanese company sides.

Rugby in Japan is different from almost anywhere else in the world. With 2,900 clubs and almost 100,000 players it is a huge constituency, while the lack of pitches means that games start at 6 a.m. on grassless grounds and finish late into the night. Furthermore, it is a game almost devoid of violence: the legend is that when one game between two army units in 1975 got out of hand and had to be abandoned, the units were disbanded, the commanding officer sacked and every played involved banned *sine die*. There has not been a problem with violence since!

The domestic Japanese game is run by Shiggy Konno, a lovable amateur die-hard who was educated in Britain and whose favourite anecdote is how he would have become one of the last kamikaze pilots had his plane not run out of fuel.

KENYA

YEAR FOUNDED: 1970
YEAR JOINED IRFB: 1990
COLOURS: Navy/White
NO. OF CLUBS: 20

The first game in Kenya took place in 1909 when the predominantly British "Officials" took on the Dutch "Settlers" in Eldoret. Playing as East Africa, Kenya provided a test for the best in the world, playing the Lions in 1955, the Springboks in 1961 and Wales in 1964. "Nondescripts" and "Harlequins" were for many years two of the better club sides in Africa.

Unfortunately, the employment restrictions that applied to Britons and South Africans – and to white Kenyans – after independence, took a heavy toll on Kenyan rugby. However, under new president George Kariuki, the multi-racial KRFU is frantically promoting the game, which is now thriving. Former Gloucester man Dave Protherough

helped out before his recent death, and there are now 20 clubs in Kenya and almost 1,500 players. The Safari Sevens have also become a regular feature of Kenyan rugby.

KOREA

YEAR FOUNDED: 1946
YEAR JOINED IRFB: 1988
COLOURS: White/Red/Blue
NO. OF CLUBS: 4

Since 1990, when the Koreans first beat Japan to claim the Asian Championship, South Korea have emerged as the main rivals to Japan in Asia, and the Asian Championship final is now routinely played between the two countries. It is a fierce rivalry given extra spice by the historical legacy of Japan's occupation of Korea. The most demoralizing match in Korea's short rugby history was when the Japanese came back from a 20-point half-time deficit to defeat Korea in the qualifying decider for the 1995 World Cup. Ultra-aggressive and physically bigger (both taller and stouter) than most Asian nations, the Koreans play an energetic brand of rugby that is common to all clubs because the game is army based. This military background is hardly surprising, given that the game only reached Korea after the war thanks to the influx of Commonwealth forces. However, the increasingly affluent Koreans are also benefiting from the involvement of big businesses on the Japanese model, and works teams are now beginning to challenge the military's hegemony. They currently possess several outstanding players in Lee Ken Yok, captain Kim Yeon Ki and play-maker Sung Hae-Kyoung.

LATVIA

YEAR FOUNDED: 1963
YEAR JOINED IRFB: 1991
COLOURS: Red/White
NO. OF CLUBS: 8

Emerging from the ashes of the Soviet Union, the tiny state of Latvia was a surprise qualifier for the Rugby World Cup Sevens of 1993, not least because the only two pitches in the country (both in Riga) spend a great deal of the year under a thick layer of snow. It showed when losing heavily to Fiji, Wales, South Africa and Romania. At least Latvia defeated close neighbours Lithuania in Vilnius when they met in the 1995 World Cup qualifiers.

Efforts are being made to promote the game, hence the appointment of Latvian player-coach Vladimiris Nikonous as rugby development officer earning a "massive" £300 a month.

LITHUANIA

YEAR FOUNDED: 1961
YEAR JOINED IRFB: 1992
COLOURS: Green/Yellow
NO. OF CLUBS: 14

Pretty much a carbon copy of Latvia, with the proviso that they failed to reach the World Cup Sevens final, and lost out to Latvia and Germany in the 1995 World Cup qualifiers.

LUXEMBOURG

YEAR FOUNDED: 1973
YEAR JOINED IRFB: 1991
COLOURS: Blue/Navy/Red
NO. OF CLUBS: 3

Despite bordering France, the tiny Grand Duchy sees Andorra as their main rivals in Europe. This is not entirely surprising considering Luxembourg's similar lack of resources (three clubs, 180 players). After bursting on to the scene in 1975 with a 28–6 loss to neighbours Belgium, Luxembourg had to wait until 1989 to register their first win (10–6 against Andorra).

MALAYSIA

YEAR FOUNDED: 1927
YEAR JOINED IRFB: 1988
COLOURS: Navy/Yellow
NO. OF CLUBS: 180

Rugby in Malaysia has thrived since the turn of the century, and the Malay Cup, which is contested between Malaysia and Singapore, is one of the oldest competitions in the rugby world. The Malaysians have worked hard to overcome their shortcomings by inventing the game of tens and also by starting up an Asian round-robin tournament featuring Malaysia, Thailand, Singapore, Sri Lanka and Indonesia. The inclusion of Sevens in the 1998 Commonwealth Games will give the Malaysia a huge fillip.

MALAWI

YEAR FOUNDED: 1922
YEAR JOINED IRFB: Not affiliated
COLOURS: Not applicable
NO. OF CLUBS: Not known

Rugby has a long history in Malawi, formerly Nyasaland. The union was formed in 1922, back when Malawi was a British colony, and then most of the competition was against other British colonies. A series was played against Rhodesia (Zimbabwe) in 1934, while a regular competition was held against Beira for the Woury Cup throughout this period. In addition, the Leslie Sevens (from 1948) and Grainger Cup (from 1946, for clubs in Malawi) were regular features of rugby in central-southern Africa. Although the game is still played on an ad hoc basis – there have been recent tours to the Zambian copper belt and Zimbabwe – virtually all of the participants are whites and ex-pats from Blantyre.

MOROCCO

YEAR FOUNDED: 1916
YEAR JOINED IRFB: 1988
COLOURS: Green/Red
NO. OF CLUBS: 15

Introduced to rugby after France's occupation in 1919, this north African nation is another area which falls under France's sphere of influence and which owes the implantation of the game to the French. Nevertheless, the game did not really take root until the 1950s, when Mohammed Benjaloun (now in his eighties and president of the Moroccan Olympic Committee) emerged as the catalyst for rapid growth in the game. Through his efforts, there now 15 clubs and over 6,000 players.

As ever, the Catch 22 facing Morocco is that its best young players face intense pressure to play in France, and then to represent France. It was in this way that outstanding Agen utility forward Abdelatif Benazzi won his first cap for France back in 1990 at the same time as he was supposed to be playing for Morocco. Had Benazzi played for Morocco in the 1995 World Cup qualifyiers, it is likely that Morocco would have gone through to the next round. As it was, they drew 16–16 with Namibia when a win would have sent them – instead of the Ivory Coast – to South Africa for the finals. Nevertheless, partly thanks to an intense rivalry with neighbours Spain, the game still thrives in Morocco and once in a while a great player comes through: both Rachid Karmouchi and Said Bouja were capable of playing at a much higher level.

NAMIBIA

YEAR FOUNDED: Not known
YEAR JOINED IRFB: 1990
COLOURS: Blue/Red/White
NO. OF CLUBS: 27

Namibia burst on to the world scene in 1991, when after beating the up-and-coming Italians, the nation from South West Africa defeated the touring Irish in two tests, beating Phil

OUT OF AFRICA *Morocco take on Zimbabwe in a World Cup qualifier.*

Matthews' men 15–6 in the First Test and 26–15 in the Second during a match in which the Irish were completely outclassed just two months before they started their 1991 World Cup campaign. But if the Irish were caught unawares, it was hardly surprising. Namibia had only pulled away from South Africa to emerge as an independent nation in 1989, and had before that languished in the "B" division of South Africa's Currie Cup.

Yet despite being a backwater of South Africa, Namibia were always tricky opposition. As John Robbie, the former Ireland and Lions scrum-half who made his home in South Africa, said: "Namibia could never be fancied to win the Currie Cup against the big sides such as Transvaal and Western Province, but none of the top sides ever travel to Windhoek expecting anything but the hardest of matches."

As with the South Africans, Namibia play an aggressive, fast-moving game perfect for the hot and arid conditions. Big, hard forwards like Johann Barnard are complemented by hard-running backs such as Henning Snyman, Gerhard Mans and Andre Stoop (now a Rugby League player in England). In this post-Apartheid era, a conscious effort to bring in black and coloured players has resulted in several black caps, of which wing Eden Meyer has been the most successful. There are now over 50 clubs and 2,000 players in a rural country where players regularly travel huge distances to games. Since independence, Namibia (whose large number of evangelical Christians among their players means on-field prayer meetings before the match, after the match and at half-time) had to make do mainly with matches against Zimbabwe, most of which they won. The first major hitch in Namibian rugby was a shock 13–12 loss to the Ivory Coast at the 1995 World Cup qualifiers. A series of missed penalties in the 16–16 draw with Morocco saw them miss a widely predicted berth at the finals in South Africa.

The lesson has been learned and Namibia seem almost certain to qualify for the 1999 World Cup in Wales.

SHOCK OF THE NEW *Namibia gained international prominence in 1991 by beating Ireland and Italy.*

NORWAY

YEAR FOUNDED: 1975
YEAR JOINED IRFB: 1993
COLOURS: Red/White/Blue
NO. OF CLUBS: 4

Rugby in Norway is a relatively recent phenomenon, large parts of which are under snow for much of the year. Imported from Denmark and Sweden, where the game is of longer standing, the Norway Rugby Union was only formed in 1985, and the country still has only four clubs, all of which play regular matches against sides from visiting British ships. Norway played its first international game in 1996, under the leadership of a Welsh fly-half Huw Howells, but was beaten 44–6 by Latvia in a World Cup qualifier.

PAPUA NEW GUINEA

YEAR FOUNDED: 1989
YEAR JOINED IRFB: 1993
COLOURS: Black/Red/Yellow
NO. OF CLUBS: 40

Papua New Guinea is one of those regions that comes within the catchment area of Australia and where Rugby League has made determined efforts to take hold over the past 15 years. Nevertheless, thanks largely to the efforts of the ARU and Brendan Moon, the Grand Slam Wallaby who has now been resident on PNG for five years, Rugby Union is making a comeback in a shambolic fashion peculiar to PNG. There are 40 clubs and 3,000 players on PNG, although the national side has yet

to make the sort of international impact enjoyed by the main three Pacific Island nations: Fiji, Tonga and Western Samoa. The PNG "Puk-Puks" were one of the most entertaining and fiercely competitive sides at the Hong Kong Sevens throughout the 1980s.

PARAGUAY

YEAR FOUNDED: 1970
YEAR JOINED IRFB: 1989
COLOURS: Red/White/Blue
NO. OF CLUBS: 7

As with Argentina some 80 years earlier, it was the high number of foreign nationals – particularly from Britain, France and Argentina – working in mineral-rich Paraguay that saw rugby introduced into the country. The game has been nurtured from afar, particularly by the French who have provided a paid director of coaching in Jean-Pierre Juan Chich. Paraguay has about 1,150 players.

POLAND

YEAR FOUNDED: 1957
YEAR JOINED IRFB: 1988
COLOURS: White/Red
NO. OF CLUBS: 21

First established in the Warsaw Military Academy in the 1930s, the game was going great guns until 1939. Poland have threatened to become a force in Europe, most particularly in the late 1970s when Italy and Spain were accounted for. Even Romania were lucky to leave Poland with an unconvincing 37–21 win in 1977.

There are currently over 50 Poles playing in the French first and second divisions. The best is Gregor Kacala, the 18-stone Brive openside flanker, who was the find of the 1996 European Cup, when his immense driving helped Brive to win the competition in emphatic style. And, as with Adbel Benazzi, his success was swifly followed by a French passport. With 25 clubs and nearly 4,000 players, it is only a matter of time before the Poles begin to make a greater impact.

PORTUGAL

YEAR FOUNDED: 1957
YEAR JOINED IRFB: 1988
COLOURS: Red/Green
NO. OF CLUBS: 36

The first game ever played in Portugal occurred at Cruz Quebrada, on the outskirts of Lisbon, late in 1903, but it was only in 1922 when the game first began to be played on an organized basis. By 1927, rugby was well enough entrenched for the clubs of Benfica, Royal Football Club, Carcavelinhos, Ginasio and Sporting to form the Lisbon Rugby Union. Although Portugal is an Anglophile nation with close ties to Spain and France, it took until the 1950s for the game to spread outside of Lisbon. Even then it has remained the province of students and ex-students. However, this and a shortage of facilities are states of affairs the Portuguese are currently addressing, and the game is going through something of a boom which

should see the numbers of players doubled from 3,000 in 1995 to around 6,000 by 1998. Best remembered for a 102–11 home thrashing by Wales in the 1995 World Cup qualifiers, Portugal play in a style heavily influenced by the French. A relatively small physique and weaknesses in scrummaging, rucking and mauling, however, mean that the Portuguese are unlikely to make strides at international level in the near future.

ROMANIA

YEAR FOUNDED: 1914
YEAR JOINED IRFB: 1987
COLOURS: Yellow/Blue/Red
NO. OF CLUBS: 65

A country that historically has close links with France, rugby was introduced into Romania shortly after the turn of the century. It quickly became established in Bucharest, where it was enthusiastically taken up by the large number of students who had been exposed to the game

in France, and by the capital's burgeoning middle class. The first non-French exposure to the Romanian game came in 1954, when the famous Welsh judge Rowe Harding took his Swansea side to Bucharest to play Locomatavia, the Romanian champions. On his return, Harding spoke of a standard of game on a par with that in Britain, and a popular enthusiasm for the game unparalleled in Europe outside the Five Nations.

The following year, a Romanian side toured Britain, playing Swansea, Cardiff, Bristol and Harlequins, winning one, drawing two and losing one (to Cardiff by three points). Later that year, Romania defeated Llanelli at a tournament in Moscow, and then beat Cardiff and Harlequins in Bucharest. Only France, who played Romania before almost 100,000 fans in Bucharest, could beat the Romanians, and then only 18–15 after an epic battle.

Since then, however, Romania have been unable to deliver on their early promise in anything but a

fitful manner. They have beaten Scotland (1984 and 1991) and Wales (1983 and 1988, the latter in Cardiff), but the true benchmark of progress has always been the ongoing battle with France. Since their first meeting in 1924, Romania have got the better of France eight times, the most famous coming in 1990 at Auch when the legendary French-based No. 8 Hari Dumitras led Romania to a historic 12–6 victory.

Based around tremendous forward power – the Canadian's lock Norm Hadley reckoned the 1991 World Cup game against the Romanians was more physically sapping than playing either France or New Zealand – the Romanians have the long-term capability to emerge as a real force in European rugby, especially now that Dinamo Bucharest play in the European Cup.

Romanian rugby was severely damaged by its association with the dictator Nicolae Caeuscescu, who had as insidious an effect upon sport as he did upon the wider Roman-

BUCHAREST BRUISERS *The game in Romania is characterized by fearsomely strong forwards and its physically-sapping nature.*

ian society. As one of the sports of choice for Caeuscescu, rugby was in desperate danger of being stigmatized: during the 1991 World Cup, almost 50 per cent of the Romanian squad were officially listed as "locksmiths". The revolution that saw Romanian lock Viorel Morariu lose his life in the first day of fighting, saw many more casualties among a Romanian rugby community heavily involved with the police and military.

RUSSIA

YEAR FOUNDED: 1966
YEAR JOINED IRFB: 1990
COLOURS: Not known
NO. OF CLUBS: 222

Banned in the 1930s because it was too violent (the Moscow civil guard was called out when Llanelli and Bucharest were involved in a brawl in the final of a tournament), rugby took a long time to re-establish itself in the Soviet Union. The loss of Georgia, Ukraine, Latvia and Lithuania leaves a rump of 6,000 players concentrated mainly in Moscow and Siberia. There have, however, been several good players to come out of Russia, such as back-row forward Dimitri Mironov who played for the Barbarians several times during the 1980s.

SINGAPORE

YEAR FOUNDED: 1966
YEAR JOINED IRFB: 1988
COLOURS: Red/White
NO. OF CLUBS: 18

Singapore's rugby community was dominated between 1945–91 by the a regiment of New Zealanders, on their departure the rugby scene almost fell apart. Some remedial and promotional work by, among others, Australians Peter Randall and Andrew Blades, has halted

the decline amid attempts to expand the game into the Chinese population. Nevertheless, the scene is still dominated by the 20-odd ex-pat clubs to the exclusion of the local population. The highlight of the year in Singapore is the Sevens competition, which is standing by should Chinese rule not prove conducive to an international sevens jamboree in Hong Kong.

SPAIN

YEAR FOUNDED: 1923
YEAR JOINED IRFB: 1988
COLOURS: Red/Yellow
NO. OF CLUBS: 215

The game in Spain is burgeoning and is concentrated in the Basque area of the north, around the Catalan city of Barcelona and the coun-

FULL STEAM AHEAD *Poland take the fight to Spain in a 1996 World Sevens qualifier in Lisbon.*

try's capital Madrid. At the last count, there were a little over 10,000 registered Spanish players and over 200 clubs, and that number appears to be rising rapidly of late, particularly at school level, despite the fact that the game has been established in Spain since before the First World War.

In playing standard, Spain occupy the third tier in Europe, behind Italy and Romania. Alberto Malo, the flame-haired flanker who once forced his way into the Taranaki first team when he was playing in New Zealand, remains the best player to have worn the Spanish colours, although good quality players in Gabriel Rivero, Jon Azkargorta, Jaime Gutierrez, Jon Etxeberria and Javier Morote have ensured the Spaniards have been competitive in recent years.

SRI LANKA

YEAR FOUNDED: 1908
YEAR JOINED IRFB: 1988
COLOURS: Green/Yellow
NO. OF CLUBS: 25

Sri Lanka, discovered the game of rugby at the same time as India and incorporated its union in 1878. Sri Lanka has been one of rugby's great success stories and interest has remained high, with crowds of 40,000 to 50,000 for some club games. The Lions stopped off for a game in 1950, winning 44–6, but one of the enduring aspects of Sri Lankan rugby is that winning is a side issue – competing with European sides is a dream for an island race with a slight physique. Numbers, however, continue to climb despite a lack of funds and a war-torn country. There are 50 clubs, mostly based in Colombo, and almost 7,000 players on the island, of whom the most famous is Len Saverimutto, father of scrum-half Christian, who won three caps for Ireland in the 1995–96 season.

SWEDEN

YEAR FOUNDED: 1932
YEAR JOINED IRFB: 1988
COLOURS: Yellow/Blue
NO. OF CLUBS: 50

Rugby was first played in Sweden in 1931, when two visiting British cruisers, the "Dorsetshire" and the "Norfolk", played a match in Stockholm. The sport soon became established, crucially helped by Yves Gylden, a Swede who learned the game in France and who established the first three Swedish clubs in Stockholm. The advent of the Second World War almost killed it off, but a small number of enthusiasts survived although by 1960 there were still only between five and ten active sides in the country.

During the 1960s and 1970s, the game took off on the back of a development programme to the point where, today, Sweden is now the biggest rugby playing nation in Scandinavia with 55 clubs and almost 4,000 players. The most high-profile player in Sweden is No. 8 Kari Tapper, the only Swede ever to have played for the Barbarians.

TO THE FRONT
Taiwan first came to prominence in the Hong Kong Sevens in the 1980s.

SWITZERLAND

YEAR FOUNDED: 1972
YEAR JOINED IRFB: 1981
COLOURS: Red/White
NO. OF CLUBS: 25

Although organized rugby was first played in Geneva as long ago as 1869 (and Lausanne RFC claim to have been inaugurated in the same year as Blackheath), rugby was essentially a game for expatriates drawn to Switzerland to work in the banking industry. It remained as such until the early 1980s when some intense development work by the Swiss Federation under Eveline Obersson saw the number of home grown players soar. Now, while the number of clubs and players remain steady at 27 and 1,200 respectively, most of the country's top players are home-grown, with scrum-half Eric Planes, No. 8 Jean-Marc Morand and captain Victor van Berg particularly influential.

TAHITI

YEAR FOUNDED: 1989
YEAR JOINED IRFB: 1994
COLOURS: Red/White
NO. OF CLUBS: 10

A Francophone Pacific island, Tahiti joined the International Board in 1994 and has just under 1,000 players, many in the French military. Tahiti's first internationals were in 1997, 92–6 and 40–0 losses to Papua New Guinea and the Cook Islands respectively

TAIWAN

YEAR FOUNDED: 1946
YEAR JOINED IRFB: 1986
COLOURS: Blue/White
NO. OF CLUBS: 10

Under the name Kuang Hua Taipei, Taiwan have been regular visitors to the Hong Kong Sevens since 1984, although whether or not the entry of China to the rugby family will create problems for the territory remains to be seen. The game was played in Taiwan – formerly Formosa – since just after the turn of the century, but has really begun to grow in line with the local economy and links with Japan over the past 20 years. Short of pitches, resources are not a problem and administrators such as Lin Chang Tang have helped the cause in schools. Taiwan's players have a height and weight disadvantage, but the speed and durability of men such as Chae Wei Che, Chang Chyi-Ming and Tseng Chi Ming means Taiwan are now just behind the big three (Japan, Korea and Hong Kong) in Asian rugby and could make a breakthrough over the next decade.

THAILAND

YEAR FOUNDED: 1938
YEAR JOINED IRFB: 1989
COLOURS: Yellow/Blue
NO. OF CLUBS: 50

The only country to maintain its neutrality as most of south east Asia was carved up by the imperial powers last century, Thailand had a sizeable British population, plus a substantial middle-class which took to rugby in the 1920s. The union was formed in 1937, but it was thanks to the military and police that the game became established and now boasts 45 clubs with 1,500 players (including Will Carling's brother, who has been capped for Thailand!).

TONGA

YEAR FOUNDED: Not known
YEAR JOINED IRFB: 1987
COLOURS: Scarlet/White
NO. OF CLUBS: 62

Introduced into Tonga's Tupo College and Tonga College in the 1920s by Irish missionaries, the game is naturally suited to the Tongans, who follow the pattern prevalent throughout the Pacific Islands: huge hits without regard for the life or limbs of either the tackled or tackler. Some of this is due to the natural strength of the heavily built Tongans, while the rest is due to a mindset that sees rugby as a game for warriors. Either way, thanks to the New Zealand missionaries who brought rugby to the Pacific, the Tongans have managed to graft no-nonsense Kiwi grit on to a physique that is perfect for the game. The result, as with the Samoans and Fijians, has been an ability to perform above expectations: a country of 300,000 with less than 65 clubs and 2,500 players just should not be as effective as Tonga is. Even then, many of the world's greatest players in recent years – such as the Australians' pile-driving blindside flanker Willie Ofahengaue and the All Blacks' wing sensation Jonah Lomu – are Tongans by birth and would have made Tonga even more

competitive were it not that the overriding aim for young Tongans remains to win an All Black cap. Although adept at Sevens, as their creditable performances in Hong Kong over the years have proved, the 15-a-side game is more important aspect to the Tongans. The high point of their history came in 1973, when the touring Tongans beat Australia 16–11.

TUNISIA

YEAR FOUNDED: 1972
YEAR JOINED IRFB: 1988
COLOURS: Not known
NO. OF CLUBS: 36

Another North African country into which rugby spread after the French expansion in the wake of

the First World War. Very much akin to Morocco in that most of its best players are resident and playing in France, (except that Tunisia does not produce big men as does Morocco), Tunisia has nevertheless made significant strides of late under the intelligent leadership of Dr Bouraoui Regaya. Similar in style and attitude to the Moroccans, the Tunisians tend to come off second best when they meet their closest rivals: the last two games have both been won by the Moroccans. Tunisia now has 35 clubs and 2,500 players, as opposed to Morocco's 6,000. The best day in Tunisia's rugby history was 1982 when the African minnows managed to overcome European giants Romania in Tunis.

UKRAINE

YEAR FOUNDED: 1991
YEAR JOINED IRFB: 1992
COLOURS: Yellow/Blue
NO. OF CLUBS: 20

Rugby in the Ukraine has long threatened to become a major sport although, as with Georgia, a random mixture of Rugby League and Union has often been played. The sport is played on a regularly by the armed forces, who provide the strongest Ukranian club side in Aviator Kiev. Former USSR coach Igor Bokov has a steady hand on the tiller, and the game in the Ukraine is currently enjoing a period of rapid expansion. At the moment there are 20 clubs and 750 players in this former Soviet republic.

SOUTH SEA PREDATORS *In common with the other South Pacific peoples, the Tongans start every game with a ritualized challenge.*

UNITED STATES OF AMERICA

YEAR FOUNDED: 1975
YEAR JOINED IRFB: 1987
COLOURS: Red/White/Blue
NO. OF CLUBS: 850

SLEEPING GIANTS *Despite a huge player base, geographical and cultural problems have held the USA back.*

Although a strange form of the game was played at Harvard, Yale and Princeton in the 1840s, rugby was dealt a major blow in 1862 when Yale banned it for being too violent and dangerous. As rugby began to take hold in the top universities, it also quickly came into competition with American Football, a game based on the rules of rugby and association football as devised by William Gummere of Princeton University. American Football's first game, between Princeton and Rutgers in 1869, was played at exactly the same time that rugby was first making headway at the American universities, although it was the home grown code that was eventually to prevail.

Nevertheless, while rugby failed to match the tremendous growth of American Football, it too was spreading through the American University and College system. The early concentration of players was on the east coast, where the Ivy League universities of Princeton, Harvard and Yale provided the bedrock of the rugby community. Before long, however, the game had begun to be played in earnest in the west coast colleges and, to a lesser extent, in the southern state of Texas.

Although rugby in the USA has always benefited from a large number of players, the geographical difficulties of building the game in such a huge country later led to the rise of "conferences", where the East and the West operated as different blocs. Logistical considerations mean that contacts with other nations at international level have always been problematic, although regular games with Canada have been maintained, while New Zealand and Australia have often played games in California and New York on the return leg from tours to Britain. Dave Gallaher's 1905

"Invincibles" played eleven games in California, while in 1913 the All Blacks won their only full test on American soil by 51–3.

The most amazing feat in American rugby, however, remains the 17–3 defeat of a full French XV in the 1924 Olympic final in Paris by a scratch XV from Stanford University. Such was the reaction from the hostile crowd that the Americans had to literally fight their way from the pitch.

Since then, however, international success has been very limited. Indeed, the US Eagles are now struggling to keep up with the Canadians to the north and the Argentineans to the south – so much so, in fact, that they failed to make the 1995 World Cup finals. Yet all of that may be about to change.

The USA has a huge number of clubs (1,370) and players (95,000) and the problem has always been how to harness that latent potential. In particular, athletic young Americans have always steered towards American Football, partly because of the financial rewards on offer and partly because of the dubious reputation rugby enjoys in the US because of the over-indulgence of many players in rugby's social side. The game's failure to have some sort of association with the Olympics has also been a problem for a country obsessed with the four-yearly event. However, as well as the game going professional and embracing the Olympic concept, new coach Jack Clark has also managed to tie up a $10 million deal with a satellite television company, which has enabled the USARFU to launch a development programme in schools, pay some of the top players and fund international tours. Now that the country has woken up to rugby, it is only a matter of time before the Americans begin to excel.

URUGUAY

YEAR FOUNDED: 1951
YEAR JOINED IRFB: 1989
COLOURS: Sky Blue
NO. OF CLUBS: 12

KICK START *Frederigo Sciarra stars for the exciting Uruguayans.*

Although the number of clubs and players in Uruguay remain small at 12 and 1,200 respectively, the game enjoys huge social kudos in

Uruguay (its head is Pedro Borde-berry, a cabinet minister) and is subsequently extremely well funded. Best known for the Punte del Este Sevens, which attracts many of the world's top sides to one of South America's swankiest beach resorts, Uruguay is also beginning to make a reputation for itself as the up-and-coming nation in the Americas. This status was assured during the 1995 World Cup qualifying rounds when they beat Paraguay 67–3, Chile 14–6 and held mighty Argentina to 10–19.

WESTERN SAMOA

YEAR FOUNDED: 1924
YEAR JOINED IRFB: 1988
COLOURS: Royal Blue/White
NO. OF CLUBS: 124

Although the game was introduced to Samoa around the turn of the century by New Zealand missionaries, and the union incorporated as long ago as 1927, play was confined to tests against Fiji and Tonga, the first of which took place in 1924 against Fiji and featured a large tree in the middle of the pitch!

It was only in 1986, after Western Samoa had toured Wales and lost the Test 32–14, that they emerged to be reckoned with as a nation. Prior to the inaugural World Cup in 1987 they had questioned whether they even wanted a national side. Despite the fact that rugby has always been Samoa's national game, top Samoan players desired to play for the All Blacks, much as Glamorgan cricketers often aspire to play for England, so the Pacific island sent its best players off to New Zealand.

The 1986 tour to Wales changed all that and Western Samoa looked to New Zealand for top players with Samoan antecedents. They struck gold, finding two exceptional youngsters – Michael Jones and Peter Schuster. After missing out on the 1987 World Cup, to which Tonga and Fiji were invited, the Samoans set about building a side to challenge for the 1991 World Cup in Europe. The man entrusted with the job was Bryan Williams, the stocky winger who had won 39 caps in an illustrious career for the All

NOT THIS TIME *Western Samoa celebrate a try during their 44–22 defeat by England at the 1995 World Cup.*

Blacks during the 1970s. Using a mixture of home-grown backs, such as Brian Lima and Matthew Vaea, and no-nonsense New Zealand-based forwards in the mould of Mark Birtwhistle, Pat Lam, Matt Keenan and Peter Fatialofa, Williams welded a disparate bunch of talented individuals into a side which quickly came to dominate Tonga and Fiji, gaining access to the World Cup at the same time.

Once at the World Cup, the shuddering tackles for which they are famous put Wales off their stride in the first game at Cardiff to give the Samoans an unlikely victory. Although Argentina were also overcome, it was the nail-bitingly close finish, a 9–3 loss to Australia – who went to become champions two weeks later – that really established the Samoans. Even a 28–6 loss to Scotland could not dent the impression that the Samoans had made. After 1991 Samoa quickly proved that they were no flash in the pan.

Despite a mixed showing in the Super Tens competition and the aberration of a 73–3 shellacking by Australia in 1994, wins were quickly notched up against a touring Scotland XV in 1993 and against a full Wales side in 1994 (34–9). Further progress was made at the 1995 World Cup where they beat Italy and Argentina, and lost to England and South Africa. The most notable statistic was the shockingly high number of opponents who had to leave the field injured.

WEST INDIES

NO. OF CLUBS: 700–800

There is no body equivalent to the West Indies cricket, several Unions contest the Caribbean Championship. These include Trinidad & Tobago, Bermuda, Martinique, the Cayman Islands, Barbados, Jamaica, Bahamas, British Virgin Islands, Antigua

and Guyana. Except for Bermuda, the game in the Caribbean is badly funded and relatively disorganized, despite having generally been established at the turn of the century. Excluding Bermuda, there are roughly 30 clubs in the Caribbean, and about 700 to 800 players.

YUGOSLAVIA

YEAR FOUNDED: 1954
YEAR JOINED IRFB: 1988
COLOURS: Blue/White/Red
NO. OF CLUBS: 10

Founded in 1954, the Yugoslavs are so remote in rugby terms that they were able to play Rugby League for 15 years before either they or anyone noticed. These days, the conflict in the Balkans means that the YRFU is reduced to six clubs in Serbia, Montenegro and Kosovo. To all practical purposes, all Yugoslavian rugby now centres around Belgrade.

ZAMBIA

YEAR FOUNDED: 1965
YEAR JOINED IRFB: 1995
COLOURS: Green/Yellow/Black/Orange
NO. OF CLUBS: 17

Zambia is packed with mineral experts from around the world, particularly South Africa. As such, there is a thriving rugby scene, which includes home-grown talent. Malawi recently toured here, while a Springbok Development XV played two games in Zambia in 1994. Although only formed in 1994, the Zambian union is making strides and its players recently received some expert coaching from the former All Black flanker Ian Kirkpatrick.

ZIMBABWE

YEAR FOUNDED: 1875
YEAR JOINED IRFB: 1987
COLOURS: Green/White
NO. OF CLUBS: 40

Formed in 1895, and split into northern and southern sub-unions based around Salisbury and Bulawayo in 1952, Rhodesia long had to be content with contesting the "B" division of South Africa's Currie Cup. Indeed, the country's main claim to fame prior to independence was that it provided several players for the Springboks, the most notable of whom remain Saltie du Rand, the great Northern Transvaal forward and Bok captain who won 21 caps between 1949 and 1956, and Ray Mordt, the bull-necked wing (whose charges were such that he was once famously described by Danie Craven as "a wounded rhinoceros in the body of a man") who won 18 caps and scored 12 tries before he went to Rugby League in 1985. Ian McIntosh, the 1993 Springbok coach, also hails from Zimbabwe. In a rugby sense, independence was a mixed blessing for Zimbabwe.

On the one hand, it was able to play against the rest of the world and take its place in the World Cup of 1987, yet on the other it became isolated because it lost its place in the Currie Cup, and some top players formed part of the exodus to South Africa.

Although there are several top black Zimbabwean players such as Richard Tsimba, Bedford Chibima and Honeywell Nguruve, the challenge now is to be able to increase the number of black players, thereby swelling a playing population that stands at 2,000 from 40 clubs. So far, it is a challenge that the multi-racial ZRFU are responding to admirably.

Like Namibia, rural Zimbabwe also suffers from the large distances players have to travel. The re-entry of South Africa into mainstream sport will help the cause of rugby in the country inordinately – not least because it will give talented players, such as prop-cum-hooker Adrian Garvey, now a regular with Natal, a chance to step up a level.

QUICK GETAWAY *Zimbabwe's Andy Ferreira moves the ball before Ireland's Phil Matthews can pounce during the 1991 World Cup.*

THE GREAT RUGBY CLUBS AND PROVINCIAL TEAMS

While the armchair fan is content to watch the occasional international, the true "rugger-man" knows his Bath from his Beziers. The grass-roots are where provide the glamorous and gritty internationals. The next section provides insights into who and what makes the game great.

AGEN
FRANCE

FOUNDED: *1900*
STADIUM: *Stade Armandie*
COLOURS: *Royal Blue and White*
MOST CAPPED PLAYER: *Philippe Sella (111 caps for France)*
RECENT HONOURS: *None*

More of an institution than a rugby club, Agen has long been a dominant force in French rugby both on and off the pitch. Their off-field domination comes from the patronage of the all-powerful Albert Ferrasse, a man who is to French rugby what Rupert Murdoch is to satellite television. A former club captain who led Agen to victory in the 1945 Club Championship, Ferrasse ruled French rugby with a rod of iron for almost three decades until he voluntarily faded into the background in the early 1990s. On the field, the power of this club from central southern France has been even more marked and has brought eight Club Championship wins at regular intervals between the first over Quillan in 1930 and the latest, over Tarbes in 1988, with a purple patch in the mid-1960s that yielded three Championships in five years.

The 1930 success was undoubtedly the sweetest for Agen, not just because it was their first Club Championship, but because on the way to the title, their 18 year-old winger, Michel Pradie, died from injuries received in an earlier round. It was his replacement, Marius Guirad, who dropped the winning goal in extra-time to give Agen an emotional win.

Agen have traditionally fielded well-balanced sides with tough packs and direct, hard-running backs. A name-check of Agen's past and present greats reveals a galaxy of gloriously talented players who have allowed the club to play a versatile 15-man running game. Grizzled tight-forwards like Daniel Dubroca, Daniel Erbani and Francois Haget combined with back row legends such as Philippe Benetton, Pierre Biemouret, Abdel Benazzi and Guy Basquet to provide perfect ball for talented backs, of whom Philippe Sella — the most-capped player of all-time, and Pierre Berbizier remain the best known.

AUCKLAND
NEW ZEALAND

FOUNDED: *1883*
STADIUM: *Eden Park*
COLOURS: *Navy Blue and White*
MOST CAPPED PLAYER: *Sean Fitzpatrick (83 caps for New Zealand)*
RECENT HONOURS: *Winners of the Super 12 in 1996 and 1997.*

As befits the province which contains a capital city of one million people in a country of some 3,500,000 rugby-mad souls, Auckland have dominated New Zealand rugby since the game was first introduced in the 1870s. By whatever criteria Auckland are judged, the province has a

SUPER 12S *Auckland, fittingly won the inaugral Super 12s versus Natal on home ground, Eden Park, on the 25th May 1996.*

record of success unrivalled in world rugby. Not only have they provided New Zealand with more All Blacks than any other province, but they have reigned supreme in both the Ranfurly Shield and the National Provincial Championship. As well as winning the NPC 11 times since its inception in 1976, Auckland also have a proud history in the Ranfurly Shield, that most gruelling of competitions in which the holders are subjected to constant challenges by would-be opponents. Three periods of Auckland dominance stand out: the first after Auckland won the Shield from Wellington in 1905 and kept it for 23 challenges before losing to Taranaki in 1913; the second when the Fred Allen-coached side successfully defended their title a record 25 times between 1960 and 1963; and the third when John Hart's Auckland became the greatest provincial side in New Zealand history by retaining the

Shield for an unprecedented 61 challenges over an eight year period from 1985 until 1993.

That last stint of 61 defences was put together at a time when New Zealand rugby in general was at its most powerful. The core of the Auckland side that wrested the Shield from Canterbury in a contest of the highest drama (Canterbury were trailing 24–0 at half-time only to claw their way back to 28–23) were regulars in the invincible All Blacks side which won the first World Cup in 1987, and five Aucklanders played in the 1995 World Cup final.

Although Auckland's grip on the Ranfurly Shield has been on and off since they relinquished it in 1993, they retained their now undisputed position as the top New Zealand province when they won the 1996 Super 12 competition (see page 24). Consistently the finest provincial side in the world, Auckland have long pro-

vided a formidably tough obstacle for touring teams to overcome. Australia have succumbed regularly, while Auckland claimed the Springbok head from the 1965 South Africans and have regularly been putting British teams to the sword since the 1908 Lions were beaten 11–0.

AUSTRALIAN CAPITAL TERRITORIES
AUSTRALIA

FOUNDED: *1974*
STADIUM: *Bruce Stadium, Canberra*
COLOURS: *White and Blue*
MOST CAPPED PLAYER: *David Campese (also NSW) 101 caps for Australia*
RECENT HONOURS: *Runners-up in the 1997 Super 12.*

After years of living in the shadows of New South Wales and Queensland, ACT were galvanized into action with an influx of Media Tycoon Rupert Murdoch's cash that led to the setting up of what was essentially a Super 12 franchise in 1995. Intent upon artificially strengthening a third province to boost Australia's representation in the Super 12 at the tournament's inauguration, the Australian Rugby Union chose ACT, a state centred around Canberra which was at the time vying with NSW Country for the position as the third state. In reality, ACT were a country mile behind the traditional powers of Queensland and New South Wales, but the ARU's financial largesse allowed a side to be constructed around the few home-grown players of genuine quality such as scrum-half George Gregan, hooker Marco Caputo and explosive utility three-quarter Joe Roff. A few grizzled veterans such as Troy Coker and Ewen McKenzie were thrown into the mix and, against all odds, the "new" province of ACT Brumbies (renamed after Australia's wild horses) performed outstandingly in its first Super 12 year, amazing the southern hemisphere with wins over Transvaal, eventual winners Auckland, and ending the season with a 70–26 thumping of Otago. The 13-9 win over former Super 10 champions Transvaal, whose owner Louis Luyt had derided ACT's prospects of avoiding humiliation, was particularly satisfying.

Despite the impact of the Super 12, the rugby history of ACT does not start and begin with the competition. As well as giving the world David Campese, who was born in the leafy Canberra suburb of Queanbeyan, ACT have notched up some famous wins over touring sides including a 21-20 victory over Wales in 1978 and a 35–9 win over Argentina in 1983. ACT also can boast the richest rugby club in the world, the Tuggeranong Vikings, a Canberra outfit whose wealth is built on the back of several hundred slot machines.

THE BARBARIANS
GREAT BRITAIN

FOUNDED: *1890*
COLOURS: *Black and White hoops*

A unique club, the Barbarians have no home, no ground, no clubhouse and traditionally conduct all their business by post, yet an invitation to wear their broad black and white hoops remains one of the most sought-after honours in the game. The club originated in Bradford in 1890 by the famous Tottie Carpmael, a Blackheath forward on tour with a scratch London side who was so enamoured with the concept of an invitation-only touring side that he formed one at an after-match dinner. Carpmael's Corinthian founding principles have long been enshrined in the Barbarians code of honour, and the club's motto tells its own story: "Rugby football is a game for gentlemen in all classes, but never for a bad sportsman in any class." Accordingly, the

Barbarians have played an adventurous and free-flowing brand of rugby that places endeavour and entertainment way above victory. Players are invited to play for the club on the basis that they adhere to those principles, and the result has been many outstanding games down the years. The most famous of all was the 1973 game against the All Blacks at Cardiff Arms Park in which, with the match only three minutes old, the great Welsh scrum-half Gareth Edwards rounded off one of the best tries ever scored on British soil to spark a contest of sublime skill and endeavour (see The Great Matches, page 178).

The Barbarians have tried to keep the fun in rugby and have always included at least one uncapped player while, in another quirky custom, players always wear their club socks. In the years after the Second World War, the nature of the Barbarians changed slightly, and as well as extending invitations to non-British players and touring some of rugby's far-flung corners like Canada and Namibia, any major touring side to the Uk such as Australia or the All Blacks finish their tour with a match against the Barbarians in one of the four national stadiums

It is a mark of the esteem in which the Barbarians concept is held that most other major rugby nations now

have their own Barbarians side. The former Wellingtonian and All Black H.F. McLean set up a New Zealand equivalent in 1937, while Australia and South Africa followed suit two decades later. The most enthusiastic and the latest converts to the Barbarian ethos are the French, who were cajoled into forming a Barbarians club in 1980 by former French captain Jean-Pierre Rives who idolized the concept after playing for the Barbarians in the twilight of his career.

BATH
ENGLAND

FOUNDED: *1865*
STADIUM: *Recreation Ground*
COLOURS: *Blue, White and Black*
MOST CAPPED PLAYER: *Jeremy Guscott (48 caps for England)*
RECENT HONOURS: *English league and cup champions in 1995–96*

It was the introduction of the Courage leagues into English rugby in the mid-Eighties that transformed Bath from an average side into all-conquering English champions. Having drifted aimlessly from one friendly match to another, the leagues now gave Bath the motivation they craved.

Bath adopted a professional attitude before the game even thought about jettisoning amateurism and

amateur ways. A maelstrom of strong personalities constantly stirred by long-term coach Jack Rowell, Bath attracted players who wanted to push themselves and the club forged a self-sustaining ethos based around the ruthless pursuit of success.

Admittedly, they were helped by circumstances. A dedicated scouting duo in Tom Hudson and Dave Robson got the ball rolling by snapping up young talent from far and wide, while internal strife at traditional giants Bristol meant that players such as Gareth Chilcott, Nigel Redman and Richard Hill were driving through Bristol to play in the historic spa town of Bath. Two immense local talents in Jeremy Guscott and flanker John Hall also added to the potent brew of talent and spiky temperaments, and since 1984, when they beat arch-rivals Bristol 10–9 to win the Knock-Out Cup for the first time, Bath have remained virtually unchallenged as the country's top side. Since then, they have won the Cup ten times and the League six times since it was first contested in 1987 (including a run of four consecutive titles between 1990–94. Other players to feature heavily in the years of success include fly-half Stuart Barnes, full-back Jonathan Webb, flanker Andy Robinson, and centre Simon Halliday, while one of the new faces of 1997 was Argentine hooker Fredrico Mendez.

BA NONE *The "Ba Bas" have been copied the world over for their playing style, ethics and sense of rugby fun.*

parable open-side Fergus Slattery, and backs such as Hugo MacNeill and the 55-times capped Brendan Mullin.

BATH TIME *Once sleepy West Country bumpkins, Bath dominated with the advent of the Courage leagues.*

BRISTOL
ENGLAND

FOUNDED: *1888*
STADIUM: *Memorial Ground*
COLOURS: *Navy Blue and White*
MOST CAPPED PLAYER: *Robert Jones (54 caps for Wales)*
RECENT HONOURS: *None*

Schooled in the hard world of west country rugby and trips across "the bridge" to play the tough men from the Welsh valleys, it is perhaps surprising that Bristol has managed to keep up its reputation for enterprising and adventurous play throughout its long and illustrious history. Nevertheless, from the early days when hooker Sam Tucker was a regular in Wavell Wakefield's outstanding England Grand Slam winning side of the 1920s, through to today when forwards such as Simon Shaw and Mark Regan are Lions and England internationals, the west country club has consistently turned out exceptionally talented and competitive players. As well as forwards like Tucker, 42-times capped hooker John Pullin and teak tough flanker Tony Neary, Bristol have also produced a succession of fine backs such as prodigious wing Alan Morley, gifted fly-half Richard Sharp and L.J. Corbett, the "D'Artagnan of three-quarters"

BEZIERS
FRANCE

FOUNDED: *1911*
STADIUM: *Stade De La Mediterrane*
COLOURS: *Red, Blue and White*
MOST CAPPED PLAYER: *Didier Camberabero (36 caps for France)*
RECENT HONOURS: *None*

Unlike Toulouse, Agen, Racing and Lourdes, those other giants of French rugby down the years, Beziers founded their period of dominance in the 1970s and early 1980s on an abrasive forward game supplemented with a percentage game behind the scrum. Although neither popular nor pretty, it was a tactic that yielded spectacular results as Beziers' hardmen muscled their way to one adrenaline-fuelled Championship title after another. Taking over where Jean Prat's Lourdes had left off in 1960, Beziers won their first title in 1961, and have since gone on to lift the Bouclier de Brennus another ten times with a series of five back-to-back victories in 1971–72, 1974–75, 1977–78, 1980–81, 1983–84. French rugby tends to be very parochial, and most players stick with their local club. In that sense, the small provincial town of Beziers was lucky in the 1970s that it threw up monster forwards such as Alain Esteve, Alain Paco, Michel Palmie and a prop from the lunatic

fringe called Armand Vacquerin, who won 26 caps for France in the 1970s before killing himself in 1993 when he walked into a bar and played a (losing) game of Russian Roulette with himself after he failed to entice anyone else to play with! The guiding light who transformed these desperadoes into one of the most formidable forward units European rugby has ever seen was a prop called Raoul Barriere, a man who saw more poetry in the blood and guts of a Kingsholm or Boet Erasmus than in the typical French virtues of guileful running and sleight of hand. Barriere initiated, and for a long period sustained, Bezier's brutal assault on French sensibilities which lasted until the great pack finally began to fade in the late 1980s.

BLACKROCK COLLEGE
DUBLIN, IRELAND

FOUNDED: *1882*
STADIUM: *Stradbrook Road*
COLOURS: *Royal Blue and White*
MOST CAPPED PLAYER: *Fergus Slattery (61 caps for Ireland)*
RECENT HONOURS: *Runners up in the Irish league 1995*

One of the foremost rugby nurseries in Ireland, Blackrock College nes-

tles in a leafy middle-class suburb of Dublin and was originally conceived as an old boys club. Although many of today's players are no longer former Blackrock boys, the club still has a quiet and refined aura which belies the contribution that the club has made to Irish rugby since 1945. Before the war, "The Rock" were overshadowed by fellow Dublin outfits Trinity, Bective Rangers, Old Belvedere, Wanderers and Lansdowne, yet in the last 25 years the sleepy club has made a profound contribution to Irish fortunes by supplying forwards of the quality of Willie Duggan, Ray McLoughlin and incom-

BRISTLE *Not pleased with Bath's success, Bristol take it out on Saracens.*

who mesmerized defences throughout the 1920s. Bristol's greatest period was in the late 1950s, when the club scored 750 points in 42 games, conceding only 335, a huge differential in those days and proof that the all-action "Bristol Fashion" game was alive and well. Bristol have not always had it their own way, however, and one of the most infamous days in the club's history remains the 41–0 thrashing administered by Dave Gallaher's All Black "Originals" in 1905. More recently, the proud but somewhat hidebound club has seen a gradual decline in its fortunes, due in part to the emergence of local rivals Bath. The 28–22 cup win over Leicester in 1983 remains the Bristol's last major success, while the 10–9 loss to Bath in the following year's final signalled the start of a barren era from which the club has yet to emerge.

THE GREATEST *Cardiff rates itself highly, and with players such as Jonathan Davies it's sometimes hard to argue.*

CANTERBURY
NEW ZEALAND

FOUNDED: *1879*
STADIUM: *Lancaster Park, Christchurch*
COLOURS: *Red and Black*
MOST CAPPED PLAYER: *Richard Loe (48 caps for New Zealand)*
RECENT HONOURS: *None*

The strongest side in New Zealand's South Island, Canterbury have been the most consistent challengers to Auckland for the title of best province. Forward-orientated Canterbury have presented formidable opposition for touring sides and domestic rivals alike since its formation in 1879 and retain a Ranfurly Shield record that is second only to Auckland's. The proudest of Canterbury's two major Shield runs started in 1953 when Wellington were dispatched 24–3, a win which started a 23-challenge defence that kept them at the top of the pile for most of the 1950s. Arguably Canterbury reached their zenith during that decade in 1956 when they beat the touring South Africans 9–6, adding to their famous defeat of the Springboks in 1921. The men in red and black hoops also defeated the Lions, Australia and the All Blacks in the 1950s and have since gone on to notch

up wins against all the major touring sides. In doing so they have gained a reputation as New Zealand's most brutal province. Certainly 1971's 'Battle of Canterbury' when British Lions' prop Sandy Carmichael had his cheekbone fractured five times, gives credence to those who say Canterbury have trouble differentiating between aggression and downright violence.

Canterbury's second period of dominance started in 1982, when former All Black and Canterbury skipper Grizz Wyllie, a man who typified the harshly physical, no-nonsense attitude of his province, inspired Canterbury to win the Shield from Wellington.

A record-equalling 25 defences later, Canterbury were poised to win the record for the most number of successful defences when they met Auckland at Lancaster Park. But in a match of nail-biting tension, Canterbury were defeated and the powerbase of New Zealand Provincial rugby was transfered to the North Island where it has remained ever since.

In the 1990s it must be said that Canterbury have found it hard to match the pace set by Auckland, Waikato, Wellington and Otago in the Super 12 and in 1996 finished last in the competition.

CARDIFF
WALES

FOUNDED: *1876*
STADIUM: *Cardiff Arms Park*
COLOURS: *Light Blue and Black*
MOST CAPPED PLAYER: *Gareth Edwards (53 caps for Wales)*
RECENT HONOURS: *Winners of the Welsh Cup 1996-97.*

The self-styled "Greatest Club in the World", Cardiff have a playing pedigree and history that is unrivalled in the Northern Hemisphere. Originally a soccer club, Cardiff turned to rugby in 1876 four years before the formation of the Welsh Rugby Union, and started playing on a city centre site then owned by the Marquis of Bute, the now famous Cardiff Arms Park. A continual conveyor belt of talent from Cardiff has kept Wales well supplied and the roll of honour at the club is impressive. Yet it says something about Cardiff that its players have not just been outstanding on the pitch, but have left an indelible mark on the game. Gwynn Nicholls is accepted as the founding father of Welsh rugby, while Frank Hancock, a gifted centre who played for Cardiff before the turn of the century, invented the modern three-quarters

pattern that is standard today. So important was his contribution to the game that one of Wales's finest and most popular beers is named after him! Percy Bush had a decisive impact in launching the game in France, while other Cardiff backs such as Wilf Wooller, Cliff Jones, Bleddyn Williams, Cliff Morgan, Rhys Gabe, Barry John and Gareth Edwards have become true greats of the game in their own right.

Blessed with such a wealth of talent down the years, Cardiff have claimed some notable scalps when it comes to touring sides. The 1906 Springboks were beaten 17–0 in one of only two reverses on that tour (the other was against Scotland), while Australia have been beaten six time at the Arms Park, most memorably in 1947. But of all the wins in Cardiff's history, none is more sacred than the 1953 win over Bob Thomas's All Blacks, an event which is commemorated with a dinner each year.

So totally dominant were Cardiff in those years that they were able to provide ten of the Wales' side which beat Scotland 14-0 in 1948, including captain Haydn Thomas and they were able to field two first class XVs with identical fixture lists for a number of years.

In recent times, Cardiff have struggled to retain their pre-eminence, but have been aided by the vast riches they garner from the proximity to the National Stadium. Now, after a period in which Llanelli, Neath and Swansea ruled the roost with Cardiff restricted to a run of success in the Cup during the 1980s, they have emerged to become one of the strongest clubs in Europe.

CORK CONSTITUTION
IRELAND

FOUNDED: *1892*
STADIUM: *Temple Hill*
COLOURS: *White*
MOST CAPPED PLAYER: *T.J. Kiernan (54 caps for Ireland)*
RECENT HONOURS: *Irish Champions in 1990–91*

One of the great sides of Ireland and Munster, Cork Constitution have been enlivened by a century-long rivalry with the giants of Limerick rugby, Garryowen. Formed in 1892 when the staff of the Cork Constitution, a local newspaper, joined forces with Cork Bankers, the genteel professional men of "Con" have been doing battle on Cork's behalf ever since. The high point of Cork Constitution's rugby came in the decade after 1963 which saw the club win six out of ten Munster Cup titles as the two greats of the club's history, flanker Noel Murphy and full-back Tom Kiernan, led a side which dominated the Limerick clubs and Con's Cork rivals, University College.

Noel Murphy, who won 41 caps for Ireland, eight for the British Lions and coached the 1980 Lions to South Africa, is just one in a long line from the Murphy family who has seen service with the Cork club. Noel Murphy senior represented Cork and Ireland in the 1930s, and T.M. Murphy was a former chairman whose three sons all played for the club.

In recent years Cork Constitution have produced players of the calibre of Ireland captains Donal Lenihan and Michael Bradley, but look set for stormy waters after a spate of player poaching by English clubs and the IRFU's decision to favour provinces over clubs as Ireland's representatives in the European Cup.

COVENTRY
ENGLAND

FOUNDED: *1874*
STADIUM: *Barker Butts Lane*
COLOURS: *Blue and White*
MOST CAPPED PLAYER: *David Duckham (36 caps for England)*
RECENT HONOURS: *None*

Until the meritocracy of leagues foisted itself upon them in the 1980s, Coventry had enjoyed over a century of sustained excellence in which they had proved themselves one of the finest clubs in Britain. Formed in 1874, just three years after the RFU, Coventry soon established themselves as the dominant force in Midlands rugby and by 1908 had provided their first England cap in William Oldham. In the years that followed Coventry's status grew to the point where the club was seen as the main challenger to the Welsh "Big Three" of Cardiff, Swansea and Newport. The scintillating cross-border skirmishes of the late 1930s, in which Jimmy Giles and the Wheatley brothers took on the might of the top Welsh clubs, meant that the post-war clashes with Cardiff – the best club in Wales at that time – were eagerly awaited and drew sell-out crowds of over 40,000 whenever Coventry travelled to the

WHAT A CORKER! *Cork Constitution's ("Cons" to you and the rest of the rugby world) Barry McLaughlin distributes against Old Belvedere in 1997.*

Welsh capital. That period after the war was one of two halcyon periods for Coventry, with the Midlanders strutting their way through the 1950s in imperious style, often supplying two thirds or more of the Warwickshire side which won the County Championship seven times in eight years. Players like wing Peter Jackson typified the verve and elan of Coventry in those years, and it was no surprise when after a period of relative calm Coventry rose to prominence once again in the 1970s. As Coventry completed back-to-back Cup wins at Twickenham in 1973 and 1974, once again it was a stylish wing – this time called David Duckham – who captured the public imagination and came to symbolize the Coventry way.

The introduction of leagues in England in the 1980s, however, proved disastrous for Coventry as other clubs found the motivation and hunger previously lacking in their rugby and rapidly surpassed the once dominant Midlanders. Recently, however, post-professional Coventry have seen a large amount of cash come their way and have begun to knock on the door of big time rugby once again.

EASTERN PROVINCE
SOUTH AFRICA

FOUNDED: *1888*
STADIUM: *Boet Erasmus Stadium, Port Elizabeth*
COLOURS: *Red and Black*
MOST CAPPED PLAYER: *Hannes Marais (35 caps for South Africa)*
RECENT HONOURS: *None*

Eastern Province have a well-deserved reputation as one of the most intimidating and abrasive sides in world rugby and it is certainly true that some of the great rugby scraps of all time have taken place in Boet Erasmus. Wilson Whineray's All Blacks gave as good as they got in the pitched battle of 1960, the 1974 Lions had to be at their punchiest to survive 80 torrid minutes, and in 1994 England back-rower Tim Rodber's international career took a major step in the wrong direction when he

became only the second ever England player to be sent off following a punch-up in a bad-tempered clash with a Grizz Wyllie-coached Eastern Province. It is perhaps fitting that the most violent episode of the 1974 British Lions' tour, when the call of "99" went up and all-out mayhem ensued, was in the brutal Third Test at Port Elizabeth.

Yet, while Eastern Province's abrasiveness can cross the line, there is no doubt that the province has produced some fine forward packs in the past. The 35-times capped prop Hannes Marais is the best known Eastern Province forward, but by no means the only one. Prop Amos du Plooy masterminded the defeat of Robin Thompson's 1955 Lions (Eastern Province also downed Ronald Cove-Smith's tourists in 1924); second row Gawie Carelse was enormously influential on the 1969 Springboks tour to Australia; and Willem Delport was the enormous hooker who combined so effectively with equally large tighthead Jaap Bekker to throttle the life out of Nic Shehadie as the Boks overwhelmed John Solomon's Wallaby tourists in 1953. Eastern Province's favourite son remains centre Danie Gerber who, in a career ruined by the sporting boycott imposed on South Africa, still managed to accumulate 24 caps over 12 years.

EDINBURGH ACADEMICALS
SCOTLAND

FOUNDED: *1857*
STADIUM: *Raeburn Place*
COLOURS: *Sky Blue and White*
MOST CAPPED PLAYER: *D.M.B. Sole (44 caps for Scotland)*
RECENT HONOURS: *Scottish Division Two champions 1996-97*

The oldest club in Scotland and argued by some Scots to be the oldest club in the world, Edinburgh Academicals was formed in 1857 to provide the old boys of Edinburgh Academy with sport and recreation. Since then, it has occupied a special place in rugby folklore, not least because its Raeburn Place ground was the venue for the first international ever played

when England met Scotland in 1871. That fixture was a result of the celebrated 'Letter' which appeared in *The Scotsman* newspaper on December 8th 1870, challenging the English clubs to an international match. The challenge was accepted and on March 27th the game went ahead. Seven of the Scotland side were from the Academicals including the captain F.J. Moncrieff. The Academicals are also responsible for the oldest organized rugby game, that against Merchiston Castle School which was first played in 1859.

Immediately following their founding, however, matches for the Academicals were hard to come by, but gradually their fixture list increased, and by 1873-4 ten matches were played, all of which were won. Since then, the club has gone on to supply Scotland with over 100 internationals, including the present captain of the national side Rob Wainwright, and one of his predecessors and arguably the greatest leader in Scotland's history, David Sole. It was Sole who led his country to the Grand Slam in 1990. He is now back at Academicals as coach and is determined to re-establish the club as one of Scotland's finest following hte ignominyof being relegated from Division One at theend of the 1995-96 season.

Wit true Sole style the Academicals bounced straight back up again as 1996-97 Division Two champions, and it should be a re-juvenated Academicals side in Division One.

EXILES
GREAT BRITAIN

LONDON IRISH
FOUNDED: *1898*
STADIUM: *The Avenue, Sunbury-on-Thames, Middlesex*
COLOURS: *Emerald Green*
MOST CAPPED PLAYER: *Brendan Mullin (55 caps for Ireland)*
RECENT HONOURS: *None*

LONDON SCOTTISH
FOUNDED: *1878*
STADIUM: *Richmond Athletic Ground, Surrey*
COLOURS: *Blue*
MOST CAPPED PLAYER: *A.G. Hastings (61 caps for Scotland)*
RECENT HONOURS: *1991 Middlesex Sevens champions*

LONDON WELSH
FOUNDED: *1885*
STADIUM: *Old Deer Park*
COLOURS: *Red*
MOST CAPPED PLAYER: *J.P.R. Williams (55 caps for Wales)*
RECENT HONOURS: *None*

Due to the high number of non-English Britons living in London, the city has three main Exiles clubs in London, all of which are based in the south-west of the capital. There are fringe clubs such as London New Zealand, London Maoris, London Japanese and London French (and even London Cornish!), yet London

EDUCATED MEN The *Edinburgh Academicals take their ease in 1888.*

SLAINTÉ *London Irish in 1996.*

Scottish, Wales and Irish remain the best known Exiles clubs.

London Scottish, formed in 1878 and based in Richmond, are the oldest of the clubs and were the last to go "open" (in 1996). They have provided the most internationals of the three: Iain Laughland, 44-times capped lock Alistair McHarg, Lions Stuart Wilson and Paul Burnell, No. 8 Derek White and Gavin Hastings have all played for the club in recent years. In the past Lions captains Bill Maclagan and Darkie Bedell-Sivright also played for Scottish. In all, nearly 150 Scottish internationals have come out of LSFC, including the ten who played in the Scotland team which beat the 1906 Springboks and which won the Triple Crown that year. Also a club with a reputation for excellence at sevens, London Scottish teams led by Iain Laughland in the 1960s revolutionized the game winning the Middlesex Sevens four years in succession during the 1960s. Currently in Divison Two, London Scottish are recruiting extensively in 1997 and have strong ambitions for the future of the club.

London Welsh, formed in 1885, were at their zenith in 1971 and at that time were possibly the finest club side on earth. As well as providing the victorious 1971 Lions with a captain in John Dawes, London Welsh also supplied four key Test players in J.P.R. Williams, John Taylor, Gerald Davies and Mervyn Davies. Such quality players were in the mould of earlier London Welsh greats such as Wilf Wooller, Claude Davey and Haydn Tanner. The purple patch in the 1970s proved to be the end of an era, however, and since the advent of leagues, London Welsh have struggled to retain national status, although 1997 Welsh flanker Colin Charvis spent his formative years at the club.

London Irish, founded in 1898, have often been regarded as the weakest of the three Exile clubs, but in the last decade they have supplanted their Celtic rivals in the English league and were the only Exile club in Division One in 1997. The advent of professionalism has allowed the club to entice several of Ireland's leading players across the Irish Sea and at the start of the 1996-7 season, eight internationals, including the British Lion lock Jeremy Davidson, were at the club.

GALA
GALASHIELS, SCOTLAND

FOUNDED: *1875*
STADIUM: *Netherdale*
COLOURS: *Maroon*
MOST CAPPED PLAYER: *Derek White (41 caps for Scotland)*
RECENT HONOURS: *None*

It is one of the enduring mysteries of rugby that the Borders of Scotland have managed to produce such a disproportionately large number of internationals for a rural region with only 100,000 inhabitants. The Borders League, which was inaugurated in 1873, remains the oldest organized League in the world and is contested between the region's top seven clubs – Hawick, Melrose, Jed Forest, Kelso, Langholm, Gala and Selkirk. In an intense atmosphere permeated by ancient local rivalries, the Gala club has emerged as one of Scotland's finest outfits, supplying gritty players such as 27-times capped No. 8 Peter Brown, back rowers David Leslie and Derek White and the hooker who captained Scotland's 1984 Grand Slam side, Jim Aitken. Despite the fact that Gala's finest period in the 1970s came courtesy of some outstandingly combative packs with ferocious back rows, several of the club's most famous players have been backs of silky skills. Current British Lions and Scotland fly-half Gregor Townsend, a local lad born in Galashiels within a mile of the club's ground Netherdale, won most of his early caps out of the Bor-

ders club, while Lions centre Jock Turner and his scrum-half partner Duncan Paterson were an enduring duo for Gala in the late 1960s. Gala provided six of the Scotland team which beat England twice in eight days in 1971, Peter Brown kicking a conversion at Twickenham to lay the Twickenham bogey to rest once and for all. Gala also stage an annual Sevens tournament, and as a club have traditionally been accomplished experts in the abbreviated code.

GARRYOWEN
IRELAND

FOUNDED: *1884*
STADIUM: *Dooradoyle, Limerick.*
COLOURS: *Light Blue*
MOST CAPPED PLAYER: *Gordon Woods (29 caps for Ireland)*
RECENT HONOURS: *Irish Champions 1994*

Munster's premier club Garryowen play an adrenaline-pumping forward game that reflects the earthy nature of the club itself. Coming from Limerick, the one place in Ireland where rugby has always

GENERIC GIANTS *Garryowen's claim to fame is having had a kick named after their "up and at 'em" style.*

been a game for all classes and all men, the players of Garryowen have an enthusiastic "up and at 'em" approach to the game that has spawned countless rumbustious forward charges over the 113 years since the club was formed. Indeed, the word "garryowen", which is now an accepted name for an up and under, has become a part of the game in itself. First used in the 1890s when the men from Garryowen used the forward stampede forward in pursuit of a steepling up-and-under – all accompanied by the sound of the crowd's raucous baying – as a standard ploy, the tactic has remained synonymous with the club ever since. A man from Cork, on seeing the "garryowen" in operation for the first time is alleged to

have exclaimed: "Them Garryowen men are devils - they'd ate you without salt!" It was certainly an effective tactic, with Garryowen winning the Muster Cup ten times in eleven years before the turn of the century, a proud record of success which has slowed but not died. These days, Garryowen remain one of the finest clubs in Ireland, as befits a side which has boasted players of the calibre of 1950s prop Gordon Wood, his son Keith, 1980s fly-half Tony Ward and the Reid brothers, Paddy and Tom.

The origin of Garryowen's five pointed star sewn onto their jerseys dates from their early days. The star represents the five parishes of the city of Limerick and is considered a sign of good luck although not necessarily for visiting sides.

GLOUCESTER
ENGLAND

FOUNDED: *1873*
STADIUM: *Kingsholm*
COLOURS: *Cherry and White*
MOST CAPPED PLAYER: *Mike Teague (27 caps for England)*
RECENT HONOURS: *None*

Almost every major rugby country has a heartland in which rugby surpasses all other sports in popularity, and in England that heartland is the West Country in general, and the cathe-

dral city of Gloucester in particular. Nowhere in the country are townspeople as knowledgeable and passionate about the game as in Gloucester, where the game crosses all social boundaries. Hard and remorseless, the Cherry & Whites of Gloucester are egged on at their Kingsholm ground by some of the most partisan and vociferous supporters in rugby. A stoically forward-orientated club, Gloucester play a rugged ten-man game based around sheer power and a fly-half born to pump garryowens into opposition 22 – a combination which has long made them the most formidable of opponents. That emphasis on forward play has resulted in a long tradition of supplying England with streetwise bruisers, men such as the flanker Tom Voyce who, along with Arthur Blakiston and Wavell Wakefield, made up the best back row in the world in the 1920s. Other Gloucester men, such as 1981 Grand Slam tighthead prop Phil Blakeway, 1974 Lions loosehead Mike Burton and 1989 Lions man of the series Mike Teague, have typified the Gloucester approach to the game. Recently, the club has won plaudits by resisting the temptation to buy in the best players in the post-professional era, despite having the financial ability to do so. Sticking stoically to their network of traditional feeder clubs, the Kingsholm club have worked at developing

their existing talent, hoping that the traditional fire, commitment and togetherness of Gloucester rugby would see them through. It is to their credit that, despite worrying signs at first, the club's faith in the innate talent of Gloucester players like Phil Greening, has been borne out.

HARLEQUINS
ENGLAND

FOUNDED: *1866*
STADIUM: *Stoop Memorial Ground, Twickenham.*
COLOURS: *Light blue, magenta, chocolate, French grey, black and light green*
MOST CAPPED PLAYER: *Will Carling (72 caps for England)*
Recent honours: Pilkington Cup 1991

A founder-member club of the RFU, Harlequins have a famous tradition of elitism and a long and illustrious history. Well-heeled Londoners have always gravitated towards the club with the distinctive squares of blue, magenta, chocolate and grey, with sleeves of green and black. Situated in Twickenham, Harlequins played their club games at the RFU Headquarters for many years

(they played the first game there against Richmond in 1909) before moving to the nearby Stoop Memorial Ground, which was named after one of their finest early players, Adrian Stoop — who most to establish Quins as a side dedicated to producing brilliant running rugby, a tradition which is upheld to this very day. Over the past 131 years, Harlequins have had a major effect upon the game in England, producing talented backs such as Ronald Poulton-Palmer, John Currie, Will Carling and Bob Hiller, as well as some outstanding forwards in Wavell Wakefield, Jason Leonard, Paul Ackford and Brian Moore.

Yet despite such rich resources Harlequins have long been seen as a club of wealthy dilettantes. It has not been an easy tag to shake in recent years, as Quins have shown an inability to reproduce their sparkling Cup form in the Leagues, a fact often blamed on their plundering of other London clubs for talent giving the impression that they are not a "club" in the traditional sense – more a home for a collection of economic migrants who are brilliant at rugby. Nevertheless, with the arrival of professionalism, the London club have led the way in sponsorship by securing a five-year £4 million deal with a Japanese electronics firm. That money has been used to buy in the cream of the current northern hemisphere crop, and the construction of a magnificent new stand.

QUIN TONIC *Harlequins' Will Carling looks on as the pack forces Northampton in 1996.*

HAWICK
SCOTLAND

FOUNDED: *1873*
STADIUM: *Mansfield Park*
COLOURS: *Dark Green*
MOST CAPPED PLAYER: *J.M. Renwick and C.T. Deans (Both 52 caps for Scotland)*
RECENT HONOURS: *1996 Winners of the inaugural Scottish cup.*

The most consistently powerful of the Scottish clubs, Hawick have a record of success in Scotland which started with them winning the first unofficial Scottish Championship in 1895 and has remained second to none. Indeed, at one stage in the 1950s, so outstanding was the general standard of play at the club that all 15 of the first team had been approached by Rugby League scouts from Yorkshire.

The first organised rugby matches in Hawick, however, were far from outstanding. It took the club a while before goal posts were found, and for the first couple of seasons matches were played on a cricket pitch. Despite these rather humble beginnings, Hawick can lay claim to being the first Scottish side to host a floodlit match. In 1879 they played a game under electric light generated by two dynamos. Unfortunately, the experiment was not a success, with several players tackling shadows in the general confusion.

Like all Borders clubs, Hawick's game has traditionally been based on forward power and an intense rucking game, yet the Mansfield Park men have also blended in direct-running back play as part of a wider game plan.

That has allowed backs such as slippery 1970s' centre Jim Renwick and wing Tony Stanger to play a full role alongside a legion of forward greats such as Colin Deans, Willie Kyle, Jock Beattie, Hugh McLeod, Alan Tomes, and Adam Robson.

Another local lad who looked set for an illustrious career until injury intervened was Bill McLaren, the Hawick Academy teacher who has gone on to become the best-known and highly respected of rugby's British television commentators.

HAWKE'S BAY
NEW ZEALAND

FOUNDED: *1884*
STADIUM: *McLean Park, Napier*
COLOURS: *Black and White*
MOST CAPPED PLAYER: *Kel Tremain (38 caps for New Zealand)*
RECENT HONOURS: *None*

One of the giants of New Zealand's early rugby history, Hawke's Bay qualify as one of the Great Provinces largely because of two periods of dominance in the Ranfurly Shield that started in 1922 and ended in 1969, since when the rural province has gradually faded into the second tier. Its first period of dominance began in 1922 when peerless full-back George Nepia and the famous Brownlie brothers – the "moving tree trunk" Maurice, plus Cyril and Jack – led Hawke's Bay in what was then a record of 24 defences of the Shield that lasted until 1927. With coach Norman McKenzie at the helm, the side not only established a record of success, but also did it in style with some fine attacking rugby that was typified by Nepia's running from deep. Hawke's Bay's second period of success came thirty years ago when the great flanker Kel Tremain inspired his charges to first wrest the Shield from Waikato and then hold on to it for 21 defences in Fortress Napier until it was finally surrendered to Canterbury in 1969, having first being won in 1966. As well as Ranfurly success in the Sixties, the decade was also notbale for Hawke's Bay, not just because it produced the biggest ever attendance for one of its Provincial matches - 27,000 when Wellington came to play in 1967, but in 1963 the touring England side were thrashed 20-5.

HERIOT'S FP
EDINBURGH, SCOTLAND

FOUNDED: *1890*
STADIUM: *Goldenacre, Edinburgh*
COLOURS: *Blue and White*
MOST CAPPED PLAYER: *A.R. Irvine (51 caps for Scotland)*

Heriot's FP, the old boys side for George Heriot's College in Edinburgh, has a long and illustrious history in Scottish rugby, as do those other old boys sides in Edinburgh, Watsonians, Edinburgh Academicals and Stewart's Melville FP. What makes Heriot's different is its ability down the years to produce truly talented full-backs as if they were coming off a conveyor belt. Ken Scotland is reckoned to be the greatest of them all, but 51-times capped 1970s legend Andy Irvine is not far behind and nor is Dan Drysdale who played in all four Tests for the 1924 Lions in South Africa. Other Heriot's full-backs worthy of a mention in the same breath are Jimmy Kerr, Tommy Gray, Ian Thomson, Colin Blaikie and Ian Smith. Not to be outdone, the forwards have produced a mighty combination in recent years, with the Milne brothers Iain, Kenny and David all winning caps in Scotland's front row during the late Eighties and early Nineties. Former hooker Kenny, who won 39 caps, became coach of Heriot's at the start of the 1996 season, but met with little success in his first year as the Edinburgh finished second from bottom of the First Division.

LANSDOWNE
DUBLIN, IRELAND

FOUNDED: *1872*
STADIUM: *Lansdowne Road, Dublin*
COLOURS: *Red, Yellow and Black*
MOST CAPPED PLAYER: *Moss Keane (51 caps for Ireland)*
RECENT HONOURS: *Winners of the 1996-97 Leinster Cup.*

A founder-member of the Irish Rugby Football Union, Dublin club Lansdowne are almost akin to England's Harlequins in that they play an adventurous brand of rugby and in that their long-term home is also that of the IRFU, Lansdowne Road. Lansdowne have also managed to contribute a huge amount to Irish rugby, mainly through some of the outstanding players who have passed through their doors. In keeping with Lansdowne traditions, most of them are backs. There were two star performers from the 1920s in full-back Ernie Crawford and talented scrum-half Eugene Davey, and at one stage in 1931 Lansdowne supplied the whole of the Ireland back line, with Ned Lightfoot, Morgan Crowe and Jack Arigho joining Davey in his country's colours. Since then many other fine Lansdowne players have gone on to provide Ireland with distinguished service, including Des Fitzgerald, Alan Duggan, Michael Kiernan, Barry McGann and Eric Elwood.

Most of the club's original members were from Dublin University, Ireland's first rugby club, and Lansdowne's original name was in fact the Irish Champion Athletic Club. They became tenants of Lansdowne Road in 1872 and have been there ever since. Although the first international match was played there in 1878 against England, it wasn't until 1880 that the Wanderers Football Club became co-tenants. Another interesting aside concerning Lansdowne is that their colours of Red, Yellow and Black were adopted from the famous English cricket team, I Zingari.

LEICESTER
ENGLAND

FOUNDED: *1880*
STADIUM: *Welford Road*
COLOURS: *Green, Red and White*
MOST CAPPED PLAYER:
R. Underwood (England) 85 caps

RECENT HONOURS: *1997 Pilkington Cup winners and European Cup runners-up.*

Leicester's growth into a giant of the English game started soon after the club's formation in 1880 when the organizational talents of a local merchant called Tom Crumbie helped transform the club into a slickly run operation. His cash also helped the Tigers travel far and wide and by 1909, when the Barbarians began their annual Christmas fixture at Welford Road, Leicester were firmly established in the top flight. After that, the club with letters on their backs instead of numbers – only Leicester and Bristol still retain this old and

TIGERS! *Leicester, letters on their backs (and forwards) spell out their determination to play the game their way no matter what anybody else thinks.*

infuriating tradition – went from strength to strength and in 1931 the club provided 12 of the players, including captain George Beamish and play-maker Doug Prentice, who downed Benny Osler's touring Springboks by 30–21. Although Leicester continued to be a dominant force in English rugby, it was only in the 1970s that the club managed to pick up some silverware when the sides coached by Chalky White and containing players such as Dusty Hare, Les Cusworth, Clive Woodward, Paul Dodge and Peter Wheeler won 18 Cup matches in a row to take the Cup in the three consecutive years of 1979,80,81, thereby keeping the trophy forever. Since then the Tigers have gone on to contest the Pilkington Cup final six times, although they have been successful twice, in 1993 and 1997.

Despite being one of England's top teams over the last decade, Leicester have been unpopular among the country's rugby fans. A game-plan that involved keeping the ball in the forwards, only rarely letting the backs run with it, didn't endear them to the neutral spectator. However, the arrival of former Australian rugby coach, Bob Dwyer, at the beginning of the 1996 season, radically changed Leicester's approach to the game. As conservative stalwarts such as Dean Richards and John Wells were phased out, Leicester began to play some thrilling rugby with the likes of Austin Healey and Will Greenwood. Although they lost in the final of the 1997 European Cup to Brive, their pride was restored when six of their number were selected for the 1997 British Lions tour to South Africa, including the captain of the tour, the uncapped Martin Johnson.

LLANELLI
WALES

FOUNDED: *1872*
STADIUM: *Stradey Park*
COLOURS: *Scarlet*
MOST CAPPED PLAYER: *Ieuan Evans (71 caps for Wales)*
RECENT HONOURS: *Welsh Cup and League Champions 1992–93*

When Llanelli scored their first victory over a major touring side with their defeat of Australia in 1908, it was seen as an event which warranted an extra verse to be added to the famous old club anthem "Sospan Fach". That song ("Little Saucepan", which was named after the end product of the nearby tin mines), was to be amended twice more in Llanelli's history: firstly when a side led by lock Delme Thomas lowered the colours of the 1972 All Blacks and secondly in 1992, when the Scarlets beat World Champions Australia 9–3.

Those are the proudest moments in Llanelli's proud past, but they are by no means the only one for the small-town club from the far West of the land, where Welsh-speaking is the norm and rugby is the religion. In the past thirty years, the club have been Welsh club champions on six occasions and have won the Welsh Cup nine times, including in three consecutive years from 1991 onwards. Another less proud moment in the club's history was in 1957 when legendary lock Rhys Williams led a side to the final of the World Youth Games in Moscow. As an advert for the game it was a disaster: as well as losing to the Romanian side Grivita Rosie, Llanelli took part in a game of such hideous and appalling violence that it led the appalled Soviets to ban the game in the USSR for the best part of three decades!

Initially famed for tough packs which contained men such as Rhys Williams, the outstanding flanker for the 1930 Lions; Ivor Jones, Archie Skymm; 1966 Lion, Delme Thomas and two great back-rowers of the 1970s: Derek Quinnell and Tom David, Llanelli are also widely famed for their spirit of adventure, a spirit which was encapsulated in that famous instruction from legendary coach Carwyn James to fly-half Phil Bennett: "Now go out and show the world what all of Stradey knows." Bennett followed the instructions to the word, as have countless other Llanelli backs of immense talent down the years. Legends Rhys Gabe, Lewis Jones, Terry Davies, Wyn Brace, J.J. Williams, Ray Gravell, Ieuan Evans and Jonathan Davies have all worn the Scarlet colours with distinction, yet what few realize is that an adventurous game plan is no accident – Llanelli remain the only club in the world to have codified the running game so that it is part of their constitution. Every year John Maclean, who was Carwyn James's successor, sends out detailed instructions to every Llanelli player, of which the following forms a key part: "As in the past, the philosophy of Llanelli RFC is to try and provide entertainment and excitement for its supporters by playing effective and adventurous winning rugby which incorporates the belief that such an approach of justifiable risks, especially in running the ball from our own line and behind."

LOURDES
FRANCE

FOUNDED: *1896*
STADIUM: *Antoine-Beguere*
COLOURS: *Orange and Blue*
MOST CAPPED PLAYER: *Michel Crauste (63 caps for France)*
RECENT HONOURS: *None*

When the Second World War finished and it became apparent that France were about to become a major force in the Five Nations, it was the great Lourdes side which formed the core of Europe's new power. In particular, French captain and flanker Jean Prat was an inspiration and a seminal figure in the history of French rugby, yet he was by no means the only Lourdes player to play a key part in the coming of age of French rugby. Before the war, Lourdes had just made it into double figures in terms of internationals to have played for the club, with 16-times capped 1920s star Christophe Dupont – the best player to have represented the club. After 1945 there was an explosion of talent in the small provincial town, with the Prat brothers Jean and Maurice to the fore. Yet they were by no means alone, and many of the true greats of French rugby played for Lourdes in the club's heyday between 1945 and 1970 when they won nine French Championships, including a run of six under Prat's inspired leadership. The core of that side was formed by No. 8 Jean Barthe once described

by Danie Craven as the best forward in the world), Michel Crauste, Jean Gachassin, and many outstanding internationals whose names would not be out of place in France's Rugby Hall of Fame. As a major power, Lourdes faded in the early 1970s as Beziers began to dominate, yet they have still managed to produce players of the quality of Louis Armary and Jean-Pierre Garuet as well as accomplished scrum-halves Pierre Berbizier and Alain Hueber.

MELROSE
SCOTLAND

FOUNDED: *1877*
STADIUM: *The Greenyards*
COLOURS: *Yellow and Black*
MOST CAPPED PLAYER: *Craig Chalmers (52 caps for Scotland)*
RECENT HONOURS: *Scottish League and Cup Double Champions 1996-97*

For the last decade Melrose have been the 'Bath' of Scottish rugby. Like their English counterparts, they have dominated the League Championship, winning the title five times in the last six seasons. Even in 1997, having suffered the loss of two of their stars to English clubs – Doddie Weir and Craig Joiner – Melrose won another championship.

But away from the high-pressured business of winning league titles, the small Border town of Melrose (population just 2000) has become synonymous with the carnival atmosphere of

Sevens. It was in Melrose that Ned Haig, a local butcher, founded Sevens at the end of the last century, and since then the Melrose Sevens have become one of the most endearing tournaments in the rugby calander.

As one of the founder-members of the Border League and as a club with a wide rural catchment area, Melrose have long produced quality players such as 1980s wing Keith Robertson, Scotland captain and hooker in the 1960s Charlie Laidlaw and Lions No. 8 Jim Telfer. Much of the credit for turning Melrose from an average side into the most professionally run club in Scotland goes to the coaching influence of Telfer, a hard taskmaster who played for Scotland and the Lions and expects nothing less than total commitment.

NATAL BORN KILLERS *Natal take on Auckland in the 1996 Super 12s.*

NATAL
SOUTH AFRICA

FOUNDED: *1890*
STADIUM: *King's Park Stadium, Durban*
COLOURS: *Black and White*
MOST CAPPED PLAYER: *James Small (36 caps for South Africa)*
PRINCIPAL HONOURS: *1996 Currie Cup winners*

Known as the "Last Outpost of The British Empire", Natal and its main city Durban are the most English-influenced areas in South Africa, not that it helped them much when Bill Maclagan's British Lions side arrived in 1891 and administered a sound beating to a fledgling Natal side. Yet they improved quickly from those early days and by the time the Lions returned 33 years later under the leadership of Englishman Ronald Cove-Smith, the tourists were lucky to escape

with a draw against a Natal side which included Alfred Walker and Walter Clarkson, two of the five Natal players who toured New Zealand with South Africa in 1921 (although only four won caps). In the years that followed, Natal's Springbok representation became virtually continual, with the province's high point the selection of Greytown farmer Phil Nel as Springbok captain in 1933 – he even continued to captain South Africa in 1937 despite the fact that his Natal captain of the time, Ebo Bastard, was also in the Springbok side! By that time, Natal had become one of the mightiest provinces as the Big Six began to emerge, centred around the major cities.

As well as remaining the most stoically English-orientated of South African provinces culturally, Natal have also traditionally tried to play a game much closer to the style of the early English sides, with fast back rows and the ball moved wide at every attempt. In that they have been helped by the tropical conditions in Durban, which tend to be wet under foot and extremely humid above ground.

Playing an all-action style Natal have scored many famous victories over visiting sides, including the Wallabies in 1953, 1963 and 1969, the English in 1972 and a 6–6 draw with the All Blacks in 1960.

Past greats such as back row men Tommy Bedford and Wynand Claasen, who were both Springbok captains, and outstanding 1960s fly-half Keith Oxlee, provided a benchmark for aggressive running rugby which the Natalians today are living up to.

After winning the Currie Cup for the first time in the province's history in 1990, Natal repeated the feat against Western Province in 1995, and made a statement of intent for the rest of South Africa's Provinces in 1996 when they not only retained the Currie Cup, but reached the final of the Super 12 tournament.

With Springboks Gary Teichman, Andre Joubert and Henry Honiball among their number, Natal are without any shadow of a doubt the form team in South Africa as both its country and its sport prepare to enter the new millennium.

BAG SNATCHERS *The All Blacks of Neath have a tough reputation.*

NEATH
WALES

FOUNDED: *1871*
STADIUM: *The Gnoll*
COLOURS: *Black*
MOST CAPPED PLAYER: *Gareth Llewellyn (54 caps for Wales)*
RECENT HONOURS: *1996 Welsh Champions*

In 1992 Wallaby coach Bob Dwyer memorably described playing Neath at The Gnoll, that tightly-packed and most intimidating of grounds, as "an ordeal". But then Dwyer also described the no-nonsense Welsh All Blacks of Neath as "the worst bagsnatchers [scrotum squeezers] in rugby," adding a salutary piece of advice: "anyone considering playing here should think about bringing a cricket box with them." That is certainly advice that many players down the years would agree with, for Neath have proved themselves one of the most abrasive and aggressive of opponents, producing fearsome forwards such as Wales flankers Rees Stephens and Dai Morris, locks Roy John and Brian Thomas, and props Courtney Meredith and John Davies. Insular and tightly-knit with a "no one likes us we don't care" attitude, Neath have pursued success ruthlessly in the modern era winning the Welsh championship four times and the Cup twice in the late 1980s and early 1990s. But

a steep decline set in when club coach Ron Waldron was given the job of national coach. He tried to get Wales to follow Neath's in-your-face, all-action, 15-man game and drafted in the majority of the Neath side to help him along. However, what works at club level will not necessarily succeed at international level and Wales were humiliated in Australia in 1991, losing the Test 63–6, a dreadful state of affairs made worse by fighting between the pro and anti-Neath factions at the after-match dinner.

Nevertheless, despite no longer sweeping all before them after 1991, Neath's solidarity, self-belief and the consistency of players such as the Llewellyn brothers in the second row and full-back Paul Thorburn ensured that they remain competitive to the point that they won

the League in 1995–96. With a large catchment area and a tremendous feeder school in the all-conquering Neath Tertiary College, Neath remains a fine nursery for young talent, but may have to look further-afield in the future.

NEWPORT
WALES

FOUNDED: *1874*
STADIUM: *Rodney Parade*
COLOURS: *Black and Amber*
MOST CAPPED PLAYER: *Ken Jones (44 caps for Wales)*
RECENT HONOURS: *None*

Despite falling by the wayside in recent years, Newport were once regarded as one of strongest clubs in Britain. Much of their reputation was founded upon two of the best wins in Welsh rugby history, a 9–6 defeat of the 1912–13 Springboks and a 3–0 win over the otherwise undefeated 1963 All Blacks, courtesy of John Uzzell's famous dropped goal. (Uzzell was the son of Herbert Uzzell, another Newport forward who, as a member of the "Terrible Eight" played in what was reputed to have been one of the most violent games of rugby ever played when Wales met Ireland at Ravenhill in 1914.) Other famous wins were over South Africa by 11–6 in 1969, and over Australia by 11–0 in 1957, while even the 1924 All Black "Invincibles", a side featuring legends such as the Brown-

NEWPORT *The once-great Welsh side have some catching up to do.*

lie brothers, George Nepia and Mark Nicholls, struggled to beat a determined Newport side by 13–10. For all that, though, it is Newport's domestic record that really sets them apart. Formed in 1874 (three years before the Welsh Rugby Union was formed, which explains why the club was affiliated to the RFU in Twickenham as well), the Gwent club is the only first-class club in Britain to have gone through two full seasons undefeated. Even more remarkably, Newport did this while also establishing a reputation for brilliant back play that is completely at variance with the preference of today's Gwent sides for 10-man rugby in the mould of England's West Country giants. Chief among the players who established that reputation for adventure were Arthur Gould, who won 27 caps between 1885–97, and the 1904 Lions scrum-half and Newport tactical genius Major Tom Vile, who later

went on to referee 12 Five Nations internationals between 1923–31. Others followed in the same vein, most notably fly-half Roy Burnett who won only one cap thanks to the consistency of Cliff Morgan but who was idolized by the Rodney Parade faithful; and Keith Jarrett, who toured South Africa with the 1968 Lions.

NEW SOUTH WALES
AUSTRALIA

FOUNDED: *1874 (As Southern Rugby Union)*
STADIUM: *Sydney Football Stadium*
COLOURS: *Light Blue*
MOST CAPPED PLAYER: *David Campese (101 caps for Australia)*
RECENT HONOURS: *None*

In the two decades after Dr Moran's first Wallaby side returned from

Britain and defected to Rugby League en masse, in the process completely killing the game in Queensland until it was ressurected in 1929, rugby in Australia meant rugby in New South Wales (NSW). And although there were short periods of Queensland dominance after 1930, NSW remained the single most important source of international players until Queensland finally caught up with its long-term rivals in the 1970s. Based around the intense Sydney competition, which has spurred clubs like Manley, Eastern Suburbs, Gordon and Randwick to produce a steady stream of outstanding players, NSW rugby has proved itself to be one of the most fertile hotbeds in the world. To give a list of the great players who have represented the Blues would take up the whole chapter, but a quick glance at the Greats chapter – where there are entries for men like the Ella brothers, Ken Catchpole and

Trevor Allan – will give you a fair indication of just how many outstanding players have come out of Sydney over the years despite the regular raiding parties sent by League scouts.

Until 1955 NSW also encompassed areas which are now State sides in their own right, such as ACT and New South Wales Country. As that greater entity, NSW have a long and generally successful record of contact with non-Australian sides, starting with a tour to New Zealand in 1882, which was followed by a full "Test" series which New Zealand won 3–0. NSW eventually beat the All Blacks in 1907, and in 1922 defeated a full New Zealand side in a three-Test series.

The resurgence of Queensland in the 1970s and the recent rise of ACT means that NSW are not as dominant as they once were within Australia, yet that has to be seen within the context of Australia's enhanced

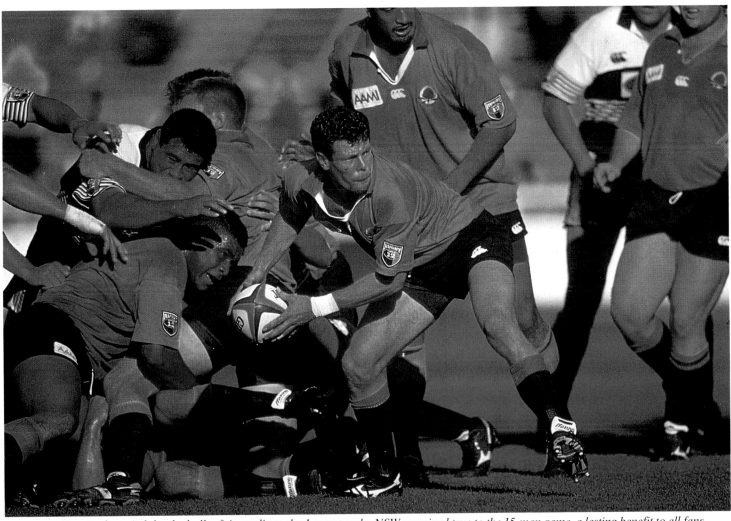

UNION MEN *Despite the switch by the bulk of Australia to the League code, NSW remained true to the 15-man game, a lasting benefit to all fans.*

standards in general. Since the late 1970s Australia have beaten the All Blacks on a regular basis, while Queensland have achieved parity in terms of playing strength. So while NSW are not as successful within Australia, they have achieved some truly outstanding results, the most stunning of which remains the 71–8 humiliation of Wales in 1991. Most recently, NSW have had mixed results in the Super 12 competition, starting strongly but fading to the point where ACT is now considered the strongest state side in Australia.

NIFC
IRELAND

FOUNDED: *1859*
STADIUM: *Shaftesbury Avenue, Belfast*
COLOURS: *Red, Black and Blue*
MOST CAPPED PLAYER: *Mike Gibson (69 caps for Ireland)*
RECENT HONOURS: *None*

One of the great clubs of Ireland, NIFC (North of Ireland Football Club) have provided over 70 international players since the first Ireland side played England at the Oval in 1875 containing six NIFC players. In the first 100 years after its formation in 1874, the Northern stronghold won the Ulster Cup no less than 18 times in 77 starts, the best period coming in the decade between 1893 and 1902 when the club won the Cup nine times. Although they have been gradually on the wane since the War, NIFC have still managed to keep up the tradition of turning out wonderful backs, a fact which has much to do with their proximity to Queen's University. It was through Queen's that Jack Kyle, that magical 46-times capped fly-half, came to join George Stephenson, Fred Gardiner and Noel Henderson at NIFC. The last of the great backs to come out of NIFC was the incomparable Mike Gibson, whose international career spanned 15 years and 81 caps, including the British Lions between 1964–79. The gifted back was a Belfast man who did not come to NIFC via Queen's, but he remains virtually the last

player of any note to have come out of the club. Since his retirement only two players have represented Ireland: John Hewitt as a replacement twice in 1981 and Gordon Hamilton, the open-side flanker who scored Ireland's dramatic "winner that never

was" against Australia in the 1991 World Cup quarter-final at Lansdowne Road. Since that date NIFC's failure to produce quality players has matched a general decline in the club's standing. At least one thing hasn't changed though – the club's Ormagh ground in Belfast also houses one of the finest cricket wickets in Ireland. Regularly used by the national side down the years, the pitch has been graced by teams as far apart in talent and location as Scotland and the West Indies.

SAINT *Tim Rodber of Northampton*

NORTHAMPTON
ENGLAND

FOUNDED: *1880*
STADIUM: *Franklins Gardens*
COLOURS:
Black, Green and Gold
MOST CAPPED PLAYER: *Gary Pearce (36 caps for England)*
RECENT HONOURS: *English Divison Two Champions 1995-6*

One of the greatest of English clubs, Northampton have fought Coventry and Leicester for East Midlands supremacy for well over a century. In the process the Saints, as the club are universally known, have produced some of the most exciting backs ever to have played for England, including three Greats in Dickie Jeeps, Jeff Butterfield and Lewis Cannell (see pages 000). Yet the emphasis in its early years was based more on forward power than three-quarter guile, with the first superstar of Saints rugby being Arthur Blakiston, the flanker who along with Wavell Wakefield and Tom Voyce formed a part of the best back row in the world in the 1920s. Most of the pre-War stars were forwards, with the Westons and Ray Longland the most prominent, although of all Saints internationals wing Edgar Mobbs probably remains the best known today because his name has been given to the annual Mobbs Memorial Match is contested between the Barbarians and the East Midlands. A popular player and local hero, Mobbs was too old for a commission in the First World War but raised a company of 268 local sportsmen, only for 183 of them to perish alongside him in the trenches.

Since 1945, Northampton have produced a wealth of internationals, and given the sort of total-rugby they have long attempted to play it is surprising that as many of them are backs as forwards. David Powell, Peter Larter, Bob Taylor, Martin Bayfield and Tim Rodber are all Saints forward who have gone on Lions tours, while props Ron Jacobs and Gary Pearce have represented England with much distinction. In recent years, the trend of producing internation-

OFS *Free style from the Free State.*

als out of Franklins Gardens has been accelerated by a new, more aggressive administration concerned at the club's low League ranking. First of all it brought in former All Black captain Buck Shelford, who has a catalytic effect on club aspirations and playing standards. His good work was built upon by coach Ian McGeechan and of the 1997 Lions party to South Africa, four backs came from Northampton, including both fly-halves, Gregor Townsend and Paul Grayson.

NORTHERN TRANSVAAL
SOUTH AFRICA

FOUNDED: *1938*
STADIUM: *Loftus Versfeld, Pretoria*
COLOURS: *Sky Blue*
MOST CAPPED PLAYER: *Frik Du Preez (38 caps for South Africa)*
RECENT HONOURS: *Winners of the 1991 Currie Cup*

The Blue Bulls of Northern Transvaal have long been one of the formidable units in South African rugby, and their Loftus Versfeld fortress one of the most impregnable. Based in Pretoria on the oxygen-depleted High Veldt, the rock hard conditions are perfect for the strength-sapping forward-based game that Northerns have played since the Union was formed in 1938. This was allied to the phenomenal kicking talents of Naas Botha from 1976 until his retirement in 1992, a period during which Northern Transvaal dominated the Currie Cup with Botha contesting eleven finals and winning nine of them. But even without Botha's boot, Northerns quickly managed to establish themselves as one of the top Unions, losing to Sam Walker's 1938 Lions by only eight points and soon claiming the scalps of the Wallabies (1953), the Lions (1962), the Welsh (1962), French (1967), England (1972) and finally the All Blacks in a game decided by a controversial piece of refereeing by the home official (1976).

As Northerns have stacked up victories against the best in the world, so their Springbok representation has

burgeoned, with scrum-half Danie Craven just one of five Blue Bulls to face the 1938 British Lions. When South Africa toured Britain in 1951, their brilliant half-back pairing of Hannes Brewis and Fonny du Toit came from Northern Transvaal as did the key forwards, Rhodesian Salty du Rand and Jaap Bekker. After the lifting of the boycott in 1992 Northerns have picked up where they left off. In the first year of readmittance, eleven Blue Bulls pulled on Springbok colours. That was the foundation for the Northern Transvaal side which is today one of the leading challengers for Super 12 honours and which boasts in scrum-half Joost van der Westhuizen and flanker Ruben Kruger two of the most dynamic and exciting players in world rugby.

ORANGE FREE STATE
SOUTH AFRICA

FOUNDED: *1895*
STADIUM: *Springbok Park, Bloemfontein*
COLOURS: *White and Orange*
MOST CAPPED PLAYER: *Andre Joubert (30 caps for South Africa)*
RECENT HONOURS: *None*

With conditions very similar to those at Loftus Versfeld, Orange Free State (OFS) are a side in the same mould as Northerns, even if they have been conspicuously less successful. Many of the reasons for this come down to force of circumstance: Bloemfontein may be a pretty town, but it has neither the population nor the wealth of Pretoria, and has consequently suffered from having its best players poached. If anything, this trend has intensified in recent years as professionalism has become increasingly prevalent, resulting in a continual flow of players away from Vrystaat – and generally to Louis Luyt's Transvaal. That said, not only have OFS been able to hang on to Springbok prop Oz du Randt and flanker Andre Venter, but they have managed to bring in several other Springboks, albeit ones generally reckoned to be well past their sell-by dates. It is this, plus OFS's strong base of local talent and sense of cohesion that enabled the province to make the semi-final of the Currie Cup in 1996, thus ensuring qualification for the Super 12 in 1997. Although OFS had to wait until 1976 for its first Currie Cup success, the province has a long and distinguished history of putting the wind up touring sides. Not only have they

beaten the Lions twice in the space of two months (in 1924), but they also did the double to Australia in one year (28–3 and 23–13 in 1953) and have one of the best provincial records against the All Blacks, following up a draw in 1949 with wins in 1960 and 1976.

OTAGO
NEW ZEALAND

FOUNDED: *1881*
STADIUM: *Carisbrook, Dunedin*
COLOURS: *Blue, Gold and Red*
MOST CAPPED PLAYER: *Mike Brewer (32 caps for New Zealand)*
RECENT HONOURS: *National Championship Runners-up 1996*

In the seasons immediately after the Second World War, Otago went virtually overnight from being a mediocre outfit to the dominant force in New Zealand. Not just that, but the fierce rucking game they developed changed the course of All Black rugby when it was to all intents and purposes adopted as a national style on the 1949 tour to South Africa. That style, in which ball was quickly recycled via vigorous rucking, also went on to become the national style of

RUCTIONS *Otago crashed through a wall of mediocrity with its world-stunning rucking style of play.*

Scotland, so struck was Borders coaching genius Jim Telfer by the efficiency and good sense it made when he encountered it as a British Lion in 1966. It may be coincidental, but Otago was settled heavily by Scots in the nineteenth century, hence the province's nickname of "The Highlanders" and the interesting aside that the streetplan of the Province's captial, Dunedin, is based on Edinburgh's.

Otago's no-nonsense style was based around the concept that in order to create gaps for the backs, the forwards first had to win the ball and then be able to keep it and control the game with it. So it seems natural that the greatest Otago players of the post-war era would be hard, uncompromising but skillful forwards, and that was certainly the case. Kevin Skinner, the hardman prop credited with single-handedly subduing the Springboks in the Second and Third Tests of 1956 to bring a victory the whole of New Zealand yearned for, is typical of the forwards Otago produced in those years and others to feature highly in this era include 1980s' All Black Lester Harvey, Ray Dalton (father of Andy) and prop Mark Irwin. At that time backs like Ron Elvidge, the Haig brothers and Ernie Diack were able to work off bountiful possession and prospered.

Although Otago defeated the British Lions of 1950, '59 and '66, the province underwent something of a slump in the 1970s and early 1980s. Yet it was always likely that Otago would rise again given that it had a continual pool of talent provided by the students who attend New Zealand's famous rugby nursery, Dunedin University. So when coach Laurie Mains, himself a famous Otago captain capped four times by the All Blacks, appointed young flanker Mike Brewer as captain of the Province, he started a revival that has seen Otago maintain their status as one of New Zealand's top five provinces. Recently, the Province have produced backs of genuine quality in Jeff Wilson, John Timu and Stephen Bachop, as well as outstanding back row forwards such as Josh Kronfeld, Jamie Joseph and Tane Randell, but have yet to approach the level of dominance they displayed after 1945.

STUDY HARD... *But tackle harder, Oxford and Cambridge get down, with Rob Andrew very much to the fore.*

OXBRIDGE
GREAT BRITAIN

CAMBRIDGE UNIVERSITY
FOUNDED: *1872*
STADIUM: *Grange Road*
COLOURS: *Light Blue and White*
MOST CAPPED CAMBRIDGE BLUE: *Rob Andrew (71 caps for England)*
VARSITY MATCH RECORD: *54 wins, 13 draws*

OXFORD UNIVERSITY
FOUNDED: *1869*
COLOURS: *Dark Blue*
STADIUM: *Iffley Road*
MOST CAPPED OXFORD BLUE: *Brendan Mullin (55 caps for Ireland)*
VARSITY MATCH RECORD: *48 wins, 13 draws*

Even in these professional days when the institutions of Oxford and Cambridge universities (known collectively as "Oxbridge") have receded dramatically in rugby terms, it is possible to see that they have had an almost unparalleled impact upon the game. As well as staging the third oldest continual fixture in the world in the Varsity Match (a 78,000 sell-out these days at Twickenham), both universities have contributed heavily to the development of the game. It was at Oxford, for instance, at the end of the 19th Century that the numbers in a team were first reduced from 20 to 15. While at Cambridge Wavell Wakefield hit upon the idea of giving each member of the forwards a set position, rather than allowing them to pack down in the order at which they arrived at the scrum or lineout, as was then the custom. Later, Wakefield's Cambridge were the first side to use the back row as a unit, as is now the custom.

In the 126 years since the first Varsity match was contested between Oxford and Cambridge, the two universities have remained evenly matched, although five victories out of the last six Varsity matches for Cambridge has opened up a six win advantage over their scholarly rivals. Yet the results are not as important as the fact that the two universities have turned out more internationals than any other two "clubs" in the world. Drawn by the chance to gain a "Blue" (i.e. appear in the Varsity match) and by the opportunity to play unpressurized rugby for a time, Oxbridge still manages to attract top players from the world over. Indeed, so strong have the universities been that it is only with the recent advent of Leagues that they have lost a first class fixture list, and even then both universities normally provide midweek opposition for touring international sides outside the Big Eight. To go through a list of internationals who have played in the Varsity Match would take most of the chapter, but a few names stand out. For Cambridge, England's Rob Andrew, Wales's Wilf Wooller, Ireland's Mike Gibson and Scotland's Gavin Hastings are just some of Cambridge's most influential players. Oxford, if it is possible, have an even more distinguished player list in which the four home nations are represented by England's Harry Vassall (under whom Oxford won 70 matches without defeat), Wales scrum-half Wyn Brace, Scotland's famous Ian Smith-led threequarter line of the mid 1920s and Ireland's Brendan Mullin. Famous overseas Oxford players include All Black scrum-half David Kirk, Queensland founding father Tommy Lawton and Springbok captain Tommy Bedford (who reckoned his Varsity Match win in 1966 one of the highlights of his career).

BACK FOR MORE *Queensland turned their backs on Union from 1908–29, on their return they showed what the rest of Australia had been missing.*

QUEENSLAND
AUSTRALIA

FOUNDED: *1883 (As Northern Rugby Union)*
STADIUM: *Ballymore Oval, Brisbane*
COLOURS: *Maroon*
MOST CAPPED PLAYER: *Michael Lynagh (72 caps for Australia)*
RECENT HONOURS: *1995 Super 10 winners*

The fact that the Union code has flourished in Queensland to the point where the state is every bit as competitive as long-term rivals New South Wales is nothing short of staggering. 80 years ago, after quarter of a century of success (between 1890 and 1900 Queensland beat New South Wales on 11 occasions and also savaged the Reverend Mullineaux's unofficial Lions in 1899), the game went out of existence in Queensland and between 1908–29 there was no rugby union played in Brisbane or the surrounding areas. Instead, with virtually the whole of the national side turning professional, League took over and Brisbane remains a League stronghold even today. Yet Union lived on in private schools such as the famous nursery Brisbane Grammar School and through the efforts of famous administrators such as Carter, Wesley and Brown, restored union to Brisbane, successfully persuading famous old clubs like Brothers and Southern Districts to revert to the 15-man code.

The pace at which Queensland then made up lost ground was truly staggering, and by the mid 1930s, the Reds (as Queensland are known) were back to their turn of the century strength, and were contributing roughly a third of the strength of Wallaby squads in those years.

Much of the credit for that goes to Brisbane's weather, which is one of the most inviting climates in the world and promotes an outdoor life. In the same way that its hard grounds have fostered adventurous running League in Queensland, so the Union team also became known for their "have-a-go" attitude. Queensland's strength built steadily, with the game also becoming well entrenched in outlying areas such as the Darling Downs and Rockhampton, which have provided many outstanding talents, and by the 1970s, they were the best provincial side in Australia. Since then Queensland have produced many of the best rugby players the world has ever seen, whether it is up front with players such as Jules Guerassimoff, John Eales, Garrick Morgan, David Wilson, Stan Pilecki, Tony Shaw and Mark Loane, or in the backs with the likes of Michael Lynagh, Brendan Moon, Jason Little, Tim Horan and Roger Gould. In very recent years, the form of Queensland has been generally outstanding. They won the Super 10 final against Transvaal in 1995 and dominated the early stages of the 1996 Super 12 series before losing to Natal in the semi-final.

RACING CLUB DE FRANCE
FRANCE

FOUNDED: *1882*
STADIUM: *Stade Colombes*
COLOURS: *Sky Blue and White*
MOST CAPPED PLAYER: *Michel Crauste (63 caps for France)*
RECENT HONOURS: *None*

Often seen as the playboys of French rugby, Parisian giants Racing Club de France hold a central role in the history of French rugby. It was in Paris that French rugby really began in the 1890s, and it was Racing and the club's Welsh international Percy Bush which acted as a powerful missionary force to establish the game in the north of the country. The impact of the first French Championship, which Racing won by defeating the only other entrant, Stade Francais, fired the imagination of sportsmen in the South and created the southern-dominated game that France has today. The French equivalent of London club Harlequins, Racing also play at the former national ground, Stade Colombes, and are regarded as the aristocrats of the game in France and play a similarly expansive game. They also make sure not to take the game too seriously, as witnessed during the 1990 French Championship final, when the famous Racing three-quarters led by the charismatic Frank Mesnel and including Jean-Baptiste Lafond's "Le Showbiz" (a select group of Racing players) took the field wearing berets and pink bow ties. As well as their choice of attire for the final, the Racing players ordered a bottle of champagne for half-time refreshment. Quite what their Agen opponents made of it all wasn't known, but the final scoreline in Racing's favour was a welcome fillip to all those who say rugby is a Corinthian sport. However, that was to be the last time Racing supped from the cup of success for a while, and they have recently struggled against the burgeoning power of the Southern French clubs, failing to qualify for the European Cup in both 1995 and 1996.

LE SHOWBIZ *Jean-Baptiste of Racing Club de Paris.*

SWANSEA
WALES

FOUNDED: *1873*
STADIUM: *St Helen's Ground*
COLOURS: *All White*
MOST CAPPED PLAYER: *Robert Jones (54 caps for Wales)*
RECENT HONOURS: *Welsh league Champions 1996-97*

"The Jacks", as Swansea are known have never lost their place at the top of the game in Wales. Since the club's formation in 1874, Swansea have been based at the St. Helen's Ground. As well as being the ground where Wales regularly played rugby internationals before Cardiff Arms Park was built, St Helen's is also one of the principal venues for Glamorgan County Cricket Club, and has the distinction of housing the wicket where Sir Garfield Sobers once famously hit Malcolm Nash for six sixes in an over. The ground has also witnessed some of Welsh rugby's greatest moments, most notably in 1935 when Claude Davey, Haydn Tanner and Willie Davies conspired to defeat Jack Manchester's All Blacks, making them the first British club to do so. It was a famous day and completed the southern hemisphere "triple", coming after a 3–0 win over the 1912 Springboks and a 6–0 victory over the 1907–08 Australians (the Jacks were also to beat the Wallabies in 1966 and again when they were world champion Wallabies in 1992). The saddest moment in the club's history also came against a touring side in 1994 when the Springboks put 78 points past a devastated Swansea side which could only score eight in return.

Over the years Swansea have produced some of the finest rugby players of all time. Jack and Billy Bancroft together won over 50 caps between 1890 and the outbreak of the Great War in 1914, the same period in which scrum-half Dicky Owen won a record 35 caps and fly-half Billy Trew played 14 consecutive seasons for Wales starting in 1900. More recently, players such as Robert Jones, Tony Clement and the Moriarty brothers have made sure Swansea remain at the very top of Welsh rugby, a point underlined when they won the league title in 1997.

TOULOUSE
FRANCE

FOUNDED: *1899*
STADIUM: *Les sept-Deniers*
COLOURS: *Red and Black*
MOST CAPPED PLAYER: *Rob Andrew (71 caps for England)*
RECENT HONOURS: *French Champions and European Champions in 1996*

The greatest of all French sides, Toulouse have a record of sustained success that cannot be equalled even by Agen. They have won the French Championship 13 times since 1912, including five victories in the 1920s and, since 1985, they have added a further six titles to their roll of hon-

NEVER TO LOSE *The southern French of Toulose are passionate winners.*

our. In 1996, the men from Toulouse not only were crowned champions of France but when they defeated Cardiff in the inaugural European Cup competition, they earned the right to call themselves the unofficial kings of Northern Hemisphere rugby.

Although the recent Toulouse record has owed much to a mean and mobile pack, the club has made it a priority to maintain a Barbarian philosophy which makes it the French equivalent of Llanelli. That is why the club's favourite sons are, virtually to a man, backs. The one exception is Jean-Claude Skrela, a phenomenally talented flanker who established himself as one of France's all-time greats in the 1970s. Yet Skrela is so beloved of Toulouse precisely because he was able to play within the club's open game plan. One man to benefit from Skrela's ball-winning abilities was the great Toulouse hero Jacques

Villepreux, an unconventional genius who won 34 caps in the late 1960s and early 1970s and remains a key influence over not just Toulouse rugby, but also France now that he has become assistant coach to the national side. In his first season, Villepreux helped France to win the Grand Slam for the first time in ten years . Toulouse continue to produce backs of world class, in particular wing Emile Ntamack and centre Thomas Castaignede.

TRANSVAAL
SOUTH AFRICA

FOUNDED: *1889*
STADIUM: *Ellis park, Johannesburg*
COLOURS: *Red and White*
MOST CAPPED PLAYER: *James Small (36 caps for South Africa)*
RECENT HONOURS: *Currie Cup winners 1993 and 1994*

Although all the top provinces in

South Africa present daunting opposition, Transvaal and Western Province have historically been the most feared outfits, with the "Blue Bulls" of Northern Transvaal lagging behind after they split from Transvaal in 1938.

Because of this, there is a long history of fierce rivalry between the two provinces, and it is fair to say that it is only in recent years that Transvaal have been in the ascendancy. Based around Johannesburg, Transvaal is the third of the major South African provinces which plays at altitude, currently at the imposing Ellis Park, a huge edifice capable of seating 80,000 people, as it did during the 1995 World Cup final when South Africa beat New Zealand to become world champions.

Transvaal have long been providers of Springboks from the earliest days of international competition when Bill Maclagan's British Isles side turned up in 1891, through to the World Cup final of 1995. In that latter game, the most historic in South African rugby history, the side was

built around the strong mauling Transvaal side which had won the Currie Cup in the previous season and was led by inspirational captain Francois Pienaar. That strength in depth and the forward-based game are both typical of Transvaal, and it is a combination that has sunk many touring sides. Although Maclagan's Lions returned from Johannesburg having won all their games, when Scotsman Mark Morrison took a party down in 1903, shortly after the Boer War, the reception was a might hotter, with Transvaal beating the British twice in a fortnight.

That was to become a familiar story with Tom Smyth's 1910 team also falling twice to Transvaal, while Maurice Brownlie's 1928 All Blacks and Alec Ross's 1933 Australians also succumbed to the might of Transvaal.

In recent years Transvaal have featured strongly in the Currie Cup, winning the title in 1993 and 1994 and losing to Natal in the 1996 final.

WAIKATO
NEW ZEALAND

FOUNDED: *1909 as South Auckland (Changed to Waikato in 1921)*
STADIUM: *Rugby Park, Hamilton*
COLOURS: *Gold, Red and Black*
MOST CAPPED PLAYER: *Ian Jones (57 caps for New Zealand)*
RECENT HONOURS: *1992 National Provincial Champions*

Without doubt the slow starters of the massively competitive New Zealand rugby scene, once Waikato finally managed to struggle out from under Auckland's umbrella in 1921 there was virtually no stopping them.

They had already served

TRANSVAAL *Whether it's provincial or international, their players always excel.*

WESTERN PROVINCE
SOUTH AFRICA

FOUNDED: *1883*
STADIUM: *Newlands, Cape Town*
COLOURS: *Blue and White*
MOST CAPPED PLAYER: *James Small (36 caps for South Africa)*
RECENT HONOURS: *None*

PUT THE WIND UP *Wellington are always hard and never baulk from the maul, but recently their form has faded.*

notice of their intentions by the time they took and held the Ranfurly Shield for almost two years between 1951–53, but in 1956 they really burst into the big league with a stunning win over the touring Springboks on their first game in New Zealand. That match was played on a rain-soaked pitch and because the whole of New Zealand was frantic to remedy the perceived wrongs heaped on Fred Allen's 1949 All Blacks, who were whitewashed in South Africa, the game was one long brawl.

In between the fisticuffs, though, Waikato showed that they were now a force to be reckoned with. Up front prop Ian Clarke and hooker Ron Hemi emerged as players of real class, but it was the eight points into the wind from the boot of full-back Don Clarke which really won the game, and it was around Clarke that Waikato subsequently built their game.

Waikato now have a reputation for producing durable footballers in the mould of All Black captain Wilson Whineray and prop Richard Loe. In 1992 they scored a first when it overwhelmed Otago 40–5 to win the National Provincial Championship, while in 1993 it went one better humiliating the Lions 38–10.

With All Black veteran Ian Jones now leading the side in the Super 12, and the mighty pairing of Walter Little and Frank Bunce in the centre, Waikato are capable of challenging Auckland as New Zealand's strongest Provincial side.

WELLINGTON
NEW ZEALAND

FOUNDED: *1879*
STADIUM: *Athletic Park, Wellington.*
COLOURS: *Gold and Black*
MOST CAPPED PLAYER: *Stu Wilson and Murray Mexted (34 caps for New Zealand)*
RECENT HONOURS: *None*

When Charles John Monro returned to his native Nelson in 1870 after a spell at school in England and introduced rugby to New Zealand, his first step was to persuade the boys of his old school, Nelson College, to play the game.

His second was to take the school on tour to Wellington and once there he formed New Zealand's oldest continuous rugby club, the Wellington Football Club.

The province has been at the heart of New Zealand rugby ever since, playing at the Athletic Park in a city dubbed "windy Wellington". Although Wellington have never been able to put together a lengthy spell of Ranfurly Shield defences in the style of Auckland, Hawke's Bay or Canterbury, it did manage to hold on to the Shield for 15 defences just after the First World War. Indeed it has won it often enough to have a record surpassed only by Auckland and Canterbury.

In the process Wellington have uncovered many fine players, including "Originals" back Billy Wallace, "Invincible" second five eighth Mark Nicholls, Ron Jarden (the man who the Springboks credit with single-handedly beating them during the first Test in 1956).

Also products of the Wellington "academy" are latter-day household names such as Grant Batty, Ken Gray, Murray Mexted, Stu Wilson, Bernie Fraser and John Gallagher.

With such an amazing list of truly great players, it is inevitable that the province has beaten all the major tourists over the years, its finest hour coming in 1965 when Avril Malan's poor Springbok side were well beaten at Athletic Park.

Although a competitor in the inaugural Super 12 series, Wellington have yet to excel in the tournament, although in full-back Christian Cullen they have one of the most exciting players in world rugby.

Western Province have long been one of the two most powerful provinces in South Africa.

Much of the strength its rugby in the early years can be attributed to the influence of two remarkable rugby families: the Morkels and the Luyts. The Morkels were a 16-strong family in which all 16 played for Western Province and 10 went on to play for South Africa between 1903–28, including Duggie Morkel who captained the national side in two Tests. The Luyt brothers of the same era were the same lines except there were only three of them. The Luyts, like many Western Province players, first played at the top level while at South Africa's answer to Oxbridge, Stellenbosch University, and it is the existence of this centre of rugby learning that has helped keep Western Province at the top of the tree. Stellenbosch has turned out hundreds of Springboks and was also home to the two gurus of South African rugby: A.F. Markotter and Danie Craven, whose perception and deep understanding of the game ensured that Western Province and the Springboks produced outstanding sides. Although the 1997 Western Province side suffered the ignominy of failing to make the Super 12 series, down the years they have churned out some great players including a posse of Springbok captains in Paul Roos, Benny Osler, Danie Craven, Jannie Engelbrecht, Morne du Plessis and Boy Louw. The two most significant Western Province players of the 1990s have been Joel Stransky, who kicked the winning drop-goal in extra-time of the 1995 World Cup final, and Chester Williams, the extraordinary black wing who topped the try list at the same World Cup and made multiracial rugby in South Africa seem a reality at last.

SMALL TALK: *Controversial Western Province winger James Small.*

LEGENDS OF RUGBY

Rugby is the ultimate team game and prides itself on the fact that no man is ever indispensable. Yet every so often one man comes along who dominates so much that he changes the nature of the sport from a team game into a one-man performance. These men are "The Legends".

NAAS BOTHA

The most prodigiously talented kicker ever, South African Naas Botha was untouchable in the thin air of the Veldt, where he could kick a ball fully 80 yards. His country's sporting isolation severely limited Test opportunities, but he still proved himself the most effective points-gathering machines in the game's history.

DAVID CAMPESE

The greatest entertainer the game has ever seen. Campese redefined wing play, taking risks that no other wing would have countenanced even if the idea had entered his mind in the first place. His brilliance was tempered only by a lack of tact and a knack of courting controversy by remarks made off the field.

DAVID DUCKHAM

In an era when England were at their lowest ebb but British rugby was in a purple patch, Duckham was an inspirational figure. A big wing with an outrageous side-step and sackfuls of aggression, Duckham was a one-man entertainment machine for Twickenham's faithful in their darkest days.

GAVIN HASTINGS

One of the game's real success stories, inspirational full-back Gavin Hastings has succeeded at all levels of rugby in a career of unparalleled achievement. School, club, university, country and Lions – Hastings captained them all. A rock as a player, he displayed fearsome drive and determination as part of a country that is invariably outgunned.

BARRY JOHN

"King" Barry John was a shooting star who burned brighter than any other player in the game. Despite retiring at 27, having won only 25 Welsh caps, John proved that he was the most complete fly–half of his time when he masterminded the Lions emphatic Test series win in New Zealand in 1971.

WILLIE JOHN MCBRIDE

The most redoubtable of men, Ireland lock Willie John McBride gave British rugby back its pride in three famous years in the early 1970s when his men stormed the fortresses of New Zealand and South Africa. His genial charm off the pitch masked a man with a maniacal will to win at any cost.

COLIN MEADS

The most talented, abrasive and durable forward the world has ever seen, Meads was an All Black for an amazing 14 consecutive years. He had it all: superb footballing skills, mental toughness, a ferocious will to win – and the limitless respect of his peers. Known as the 'Godfather', Meads was the ultimate competitor.

HUGO PORTA

The only player from outside the "Big Eight" to merit a mention in either the "Legends" or "Greats" chapters. Tactically faultless and defensively outstanding, Porta's armoury was capable of blowing the best sides out of the water – and he could either kick them to death or run them ragged. He turned Argentina into a major world force.

JEAN-PIERRE RIVES

The vision of the blond warrior with streaks of crimson staining his hair and flowing down his face is one that will live with a whole rugby generation for ever. Fearless, reckless and totally devoid of any instincts of self-preservation, French flanker Jean-Pierre Rives was the ultimate competitor.

BOTHA

THE KICKING SPRINGBOK

HIGH KICKING *Naas Botha lets fly-half and legend to boot.*

There is a joke beloved of South African rugby folk and it goes something like this. Naas Botha, the greatest kicking fly-half the world has ever seen, is on a plane home from Cape Town after he has kicked his province, Northern Transvaal, to a dour 3–0 victory. Used to being recognized and idolized wherever he goes, he is puzzled by the fact that the familiar-looking man in the seat next to him is paying him no attention whatsoever and has made no effort to strike up a conversation with him. "Don't you know who I am" says Botha eventually to the man. "Yes" says the man, "you're Naas Botha, the famous rugby player." After a long pause, the man says "And do you know who I am?" A puzzled Botha says no, he has no idea who the man is, although he does look familiar. "That," says the man "is because I was playing at inside-centre for Northern Transvaal this afternoon!"

Naas Botha is the most gifted kicker of a rugby ball the world has ever seen, the most recognized man in South Africa and a peerless match-winner. He was the most prolific re-writer of the Springbok record books, accumulating the fastest ever century of points on tour in New Zealand in 1981 when he passed the 100-mark in six matches, while he totally dominated South African rugby between 1980 and 1992, a period in which he scored 312 points in 28 Tests. It was a sad end when his captaincy of the ill-fated 1992 tour to Britain and France finished his career. On the domestic front, Botha dominated the Currie Cup as he kicked Northern Transvaal to one Currie Cup triumph after another.

Yet despite the fact that the prodigy Botha bestrode the South African rugby scene like a colossus, the feelings of South Africans towards

him remained ambivalent. While they respected the match-winning capabilities of his right boot, even Northern's own fans gradually tired of his endless punting and Botha was consequently held in relatively little affection. The Currie Cup final of 1987, in which Botha scored all of victorious Northern's points through four penalties and four drop-goals, was typical of the entertainment-free fare Botha had to offer.

Botha's legacy, however, as a kicker is an entirely misleading one, for he pursued the kicking game simply because it was the most sure-fire way of winning, a concept that appealed to one of the great competitors. Although there were deficiencies in his game – at times his tackling was non-existent – he was more than able to vary his game when he wished to do so. As a teenage prodigy who broke into the Northern Transvaal side aged just 19, Botha was as well known for his running game as for his kicking. So much so, that when he was still playing for South Africa Under-20s, the All Blacks trekked along to see him play and asked whether he could turn out against them for the South African Barbarians. They even offered to guarantee his safety, an offer that the Springboks wisely did not take them up on.

Botha became Northern's captain at the age of 22, the same year in which he became a Springbok. One of the

Fact File

Born: 27 February 1958
Birthplace: Breyten, Transvaal
Height: 5ft 10in (1.78m)
Weight: 12st (78 kg)
Debut for South Africa: 1980 vs. South America at Ellis Park, Johannesburg
Caps: 28
Points for South Africa: 2t, 50c, 50p, 18dg = 312pts
Club: Northern Transvaal
Honours: As well as contesting 11 Currie Cup finals, of which he was on the winning side nine times, when Botha retired he was South Africa's most capped fly-half; highest points scorer; had kicked the most conversions (50), dropped the most goals in an international (3); kicked the most penalty goals (50). Longest Test career of a Springbok (13 seasons).

quickest three-quarters in the national side at that stage, he masterminded the 26–22 First Test victory over the 1980 Lions in which he didn't kick any penalties or attempt any of his trademark drop-goals as the Springboks scored five tries, thanks in no small measure to artful running of Naas Botha.

Although Botha's best years were lost to the isolation imposed on South Africa by the rest of the sporting world, he exuded enough skill and class on his limited opportunities to demonstrate that he was the greatest fly-half in the world during the early 1980s. Such was his talent that in 1983 the Dallas Cowboys US football team invited him over to the States for trials as their goal-kicker, although Botha failed to adapt to his new challenge and quickly returned home to resume his rugby career.

Botha's international days came to an end in rather ignominious fashion in 1992 following the Springboks unsuccessful tour to France and England. South Africa had been welcomed back into the fold earlier in the season, but losses to both Australia and New Zealand were compounded by defeat at the hands of the French and English. Following his 28th cap against at Twickenham, Botha retired at the age of 34.

> **❝I've played with and against Botha and regard him as extremely overrated ... his poor defence and inability to get involved physically often made him the weak link in the Test games we played together.❞**
>
> *Springbok flanker Rob Louw*

CAMPESE

GOOSE-STEPPING TO GLORY

Fact File

Born:
21 October 1962
Birthplace:
Queanbeyan, Australia
Weight:
14st 2lb (90kg)
Height:
5ft 10in (1.77m)
Debut for Australia:
1982 vs. New Zealand at Lancaster Park, Christchurch
Caps:
101
Points for Australia:
63t, 5c, 6p, 2dg = 301pts
Clubs:
Randwick (Australia); Milan (Italy).
Career milestones:
Most capped Australian player (101); longest Test career (16 seasons); most tries in internationals (63); second most capped player of all-time behind Philippe Sella

David Campese is the most exciting rugby player the world has ever seen. He could win games with moments of sublime genius, or he could lose them through equally unbelievable aberrations or crass stupidity. Either way, the Queanbeyan boy didn't do it quietly – the one guarantee was a running commentary on the thoughts of Chairman Campese that was not for the faint hearted.

No player in the world has divided opinion like David Campese. A one-in-a-generation talent, the winger scored tries at the unprecedented rate of two every three games during his 101 test-career. Yet Campese was such a controversial figure not just because of his pronouncements on all matters rugby, but because he was the ultimate individual player in a team game. As Campese was first to admit: "My first responsibility is to myself. I want to satisfy myself by going out there and doing something that you know no other player in the world has managed to pull off. The spectators are important, but only as a secondary consideration. I don't care if there are seven or 70,000 watching, once I get the ball I'm on my own."

And there lies the nub of the debate. For while Campese steadily stacked up try after try, helping Australia to win the 1991 World Cup in the process, he was also guilty of some spectacular *faux pas*.

The most notorious of those was in 1989 when in the crucial third Test against the Lions he threw a speculative pass to full-back Greg Martin in his own 22 rather than kick to touch. The pass went astray and Ieuan Evans pounced to score a try which swung the series the tourists' way. The lapse sent Campese's detractors in paroxysms, a state not helped by Campese's: "you win some, you lose some" demeanour after the game.

"You do not play Mickey Mouse rugby like that in the Green and Gold of Australia," stormed former Wallaby captain Andy Slack. "This free spirit drivel that is brought up in his defence is just that – drivel. He's part of a team and if he can't act that way he's better off playing tennis."

Throughout his international career, Campese participated in a running verbal battle with some of the English players. He ridiculed them for their boring and uninventive play, accusing them of stifling the game with their reliance on the boot. When Australia beat England 12–6 to win the 1991 World Cup final at Twickenham, it was noticeable that the cause of England's downfall was their last-minute change of tactics; gone were the artillery boot of Rob Andrew and the rolling maul of the forwards, replaced instead by a more expansive game plan. If they changed their tactics because of the criticism emanating from Campese and the Australian camp, then they played right into their rival's hands.

Despite his love of playing Devil's advocate, Campese remained one of the most popular figures in the game, a status due in no small part to the fact that he was consistently able to unlock even the tightest of defences, entertaining countless thousands of spectators in the process. That ability led to Campese being in demand, and lengthy stints playing for Milan in Italy meant that he was able to declare himself: "rugby's first millionaire" several years before the game went professional!

Although his pace diminished over

EASY CAMPESE *The most exciting player ever.*

the years, Campese more than made up for it by grafting a high degree of cunning onto his game. Where once he could beat opponents with sheer pace or his trademark "goose-step" – an exaggerated step which made opponents think he was slowing down when he was in fact speeding up – towards the end of his career he could just as easily fool an opponent with a deft reverse pass or a change in his angle of running.

His defence was always competent, if at times a little unorthodox, while his kicking to touch improved steadily throughout his career. Yet his greatest asset was his sheer unpredictability. Former Wallaby team-mate Nick Farr-Jones summed it up best when he said: "Sometimes even Campo's brain doesn't know where his feet are taking him." But then that was the genius of the man – he could spot an opportunity that would never occur to any other player and then turn that opportunity into a try. And no matter what the detractors say, it is tries that win games, and no player has ever been more successful at scoring them than New South Wales flier David Campese.

> **"Campese tries things – that is part of his genius. Remove the risk and he would be half the player"**
>
> *Jeremy Guscott, Bath, England and Lions' centre*

DUCKHAM

THE BLOND BOMBSHELL

Every country needs it heroes, and in dashing wing David Duckham England found a role model for a new generation. A player of such overwhelming flair and force that he was able to overcome a chronic lack of possession and inspire the covey of talented backs who were to emerge in the late 1970s as Duckham's own international career drew to a close.

As with Ireland's Willie John McBride, Duckham may not have been the single best player ever to pull on a jersey for his country, yet the status of a legend entails more than mere excellence in a player's own position. It is a status that is bestowed only through the ability to inspire others, be they team-mates or supporters, and to leave an indelible impression on the imagination of all rugby folk. If all of that is the mark of a true legend, there is little doubt that no English player deserves his entry to the Rugby Hall of Fame more than Coventry, England and British Lions three-quarter David Duckham.

Never was his star quality more amply demonstrated than in the famous 23–11 Barbarians' victory over the All Blacks at Twickenham in 1973. In an extravaganza of free-running rugby, Duckham was in his element and showed what he could do with quick ball (it was always his gripe that the England forwards: "*never gave me quick ball*"). Despite playing alongside greats such as Mike Gibson, Phil Bennett, Gareth Edwards and J.P.R. Williams in the most talented back division to be assembled outside a Lions tour, it was Duckham who emerged as the most incisive and exciting runner on show that day. Then at the height of his powers, the Englishman was too much even for the great Bryan Williams to contain – not that Duckham confined himself to his wing as he cut inside looking for any opportunity to get involved. It was fitting that it was Duckham who, with the score at 17–11, delivered the final body blow when he jinked and side-stepped his way round five All Blacks before off loading the ball to J.P.R. Williams for the winning try.

That Barbarians side was, as far as was possible, a recreation of the 1971 Lions' side which won a series in New Zealand and in which Duckham excelled on the wing in the final three Tests, having replaced Welshman John Bevan after the opening match. Indeed, with ample ball the Coventry flier was outstanding for the Lions and scored six tries against Buller at Greymouth, a Lions' record that has still to be beaten.

Duckham's appearances for the Barbarians and the Lions demonstrated just how fine a player he was, even if his ball-starved, 36-cap career

Fact File

Born: 28 June 1946
Birthplace: Coventry, England
Height: 6ft 1in (1.86m)
Weight: 14st (89kg)
Debut for England: 1969 vs. Ireland at Lansdowne Road, Dublin
Caps: 36
Points for England: 10t = 40pts
Clubs: Coventry
Honours: 3 caps for the British Lions (1971)

with England never showed him in his best light. Indeed, Duckham registered only ten wins in those 36 internationals between 1969–76, and received an average of less than three passes per match! Even with horrendously poor possession, Duckham made a huge impression upon teammates, supporters and the opposition. At 6ft 1in and weighing in at well over 14 stone, it would have been no surprise had Duckham allied his searing pace with his strong physique to try and run over opponents, *a la* Lomu. But the enduring image is of Duckham's blond mop-head bobbing to and fro as he jinked, feinted, side-stepped and generally tricked his way inside and outside opponents.

Forceful, strong and quick-witted, trying to tie the hyperactive Duckham down was virtually impossible, and his lack of possession was the one consolation for opposing wings. But if the ball didn't come to Duckham, he would go looking for it, and he was often to be found popping up in the centres – his original international position – intent on finding the ball and the action. Not that the indefatigable Duckham was ever given much breathing space, it's just that his duties tended to be defensive ones. Even then he was as forceful, enthusiastic and aggressive in defence as he was in attack – never-say-die qualities that make him the single most inspiring player in English rugby history.

Duckham played his rugby in an era when all the talk was off the magical power of the Welsh backs. It is testament to his own skills that he is remembered by friend and foe as one of the very best of players.

> **"David's approach to rugby was almost too Welsh, and his skills were certainly recognized on our side of Offa's Dyke — big, aggressive and with a chilling side-step, he was one of the great attacking wings of my day."**
> *Gareth Edwards*

BLOND FURY *David Duckham rips through yet another hapless defence.*

HASTINGS

SCOTLAND'S RUGBY BRAVEHEART

Fact File

Born: 3 January 1962
Birthplace: Edinburgh, Scotland
Height: 6ft 2in (1.90m)
Weight: 14st 8lb (92kg)
Debut for Scotland: 1986 vs. France at Murrayfield
Caps: 61
Points for Scotland: 17t, 86c, 140p = 667pts
Clubs: London Scottish, Watsonians
Honours: Scotland 1990 Grand Slam; British Lions victory in 1989 and captain in 1993; captained Scotland in one World Cup and played in two others; World XV vs. NZ; top British points-scorer (733 for Scotland and Lions); 6 caps for the British Lions.

Caps alone do not make the man, but a quick look at Gavin Hastings' battle honours should be more than enough to establish his credentials as the finest player ever to wear the dark blue of Scotland. Indeed, it is difficult to know where to start, or where the honours finish.

For the record though, here is an abridged version of one of the most impressive curriculum vitae in British rugby: Hastings captained the first Scotland schoolboys' side to win on English soil; he captained the victorious 1985 Cambridge University side; he won the Gallacher Shield with Auckland University during his sabbatical year; he was a central figure in Scotland's 1990 Grand Slam and the British Lions' series victory in

Australia in 1989; he captained Scotland in one World Cup and played in two others, including a semi-final; he captained his country and scored the winning try when Scotland registered their first win at the Parc des Princes; he captained the Lions to New Zealand in 1993; he played for the World XV in the New Zealand Centenary Celebrations; and he holds the British points-scoring record with 733 points in Tests for Scotland and the Lions.

Yet even those phenomenal statistics do not really begin to uncover much about the softly-spoken Edinburgh man who was such a dominant, constant force in British rugby for a full decade after he made his debut in the 18–17 victory over France at Murrayfield in 1986.

Success was the hallmark of Hastings' career both at club and international level, yet he was never a driven personality in the same way as the two Scottish captains before him, forwards David Sole and Finlay Calder.

They were men with a point to prove, a mark to make, and they let everybody know it. Their currency was passion and commitment, their language fire and brimstone, yet they could scarcely be more different to the languid Hastings.

Despite consistently being asked to skipper sides from his youth until his retirement after the 1995 World Cup, Hastings was never a natural leader in the way that Sole or Calder proved to be. Never particularly fond of training, Hastings found

BATTLER HASTINGS
Scotland's greatest.

it tough enough to get himself on to the practice park, let alone drag 14 other men with him.

Yet his undoubted abundance of natural talent meant that the laid-back and ever popular Hastings possessed an inner confidence in his own substantial abilities that enable him to lead from the front while simultaneously coaxing the best out of less able or less committed team-mates.

Although a superb captain because of those qualities, his low-key manner ensures that it is as an inspirational full-back of great class that Gavin Hastings will be best remembered. An imposing figure at 6ft 2in and almost 15 stones, Hastings burst onto the scene in 1986 at the age of 24, displacing Peter Dods to claim a place in the Scotland side alongside younger brother Scott, an uncompromising centre

Solid under the high ball, an outstanding goal-kicker and with a siege-gun boot that would almost inevitably find touch, Hastings was defensively strong and came into the line with an impact which perhaps owed more to his stocky frame than great pace, but which was still extremely effective and served any team he played for in any conditions.

A gritty player whose solidity reassured players in front of him and whose huge boot sapped opposition confidence, Gavin Hastings was also a player of immense spirit who invariably led the rearguard action or initiated the fight back. There was no better example of his mental toughness and resilience than his debut performance when, after putting the kick-off out on the full only for the French to run back at Scotland and score without a single Scot touching the ball, Hastings knocked over a record six penalties to give Scotland an 18–17 win.

> " **Gavin is a big man in every sense of the word ... His greatest asset was his ability to engender confidence in those around him and to lead by example when the opposition had to be taken on. In New Zealand they considered him simply the best full-back in the world.** "
>
> *Ian McGeechan*
> *Scotland & Lions' coach*

JOHN

HAIL TO THE KING

THE KING *Not even the mighty All Blacks could master Barry John.*

Fact File

Born: 6 January 1946
Birthplace: Cefneithin, Wales
Height: 5ft 9in (1.79m)
Weight: 11st 11lb (75kg)
Debut for Wales: 1966 vs. Australia at Cardiff Arms Park
Caps: 25
Points for Wales: 5t, 6c, 8dg, 13p = 90pts
Clubs: Llanelli, Cardiff
Honours: 1971 and 1968 Lions' tours of New Zealand

Between 1970 and 1972, Barry John was the greatest rugby player in the world. For Cardiff, Wales and the British Lions, the fly-half tormented and teased teams with his sublime range of unique skills. His premature retirement from the game in 1972, at the age of 27, stunned not only the Welsh fans, but all those rugby followers who appreciated the exceptional talents John had to offer.

It would be tempting to conclude that the willowy maestro retired so young because by 1972 he had achieved everything he could ever hope to in rugby and that he realized the only way from such a giddy height was downwards.

The truth, however, is that John never contemplated personal failure. Great men rarely do, and few are as great or as natural a talent as John, the fly-half who dominated British rugby at a time when British rugby dominated the world.

Even the New Zealanders, the harshest of rugby judges, recognized John's once-in-a-lifetime genius when they crowned him "The King" in 1971, a sobriquet that has stayed with him to this day. It was an alias well earned, for John was majestic on the 1971 Lions' tour Down Under, driving the British side to an unprecedented series victory over an All Blacks side on its own patch. That tour was the pinnacle of John's career, two virtually faultless months in which his supreme play coincided with the first extensive television coverage of a Lions' tour, etching the vision of a peerless John into the British rugby psyche in the process.

But if the image of John looms large in the minds and dreams of rugby fans everywhere, for players who suffered at his hands the image is of a more nightmarish kind. One player who will never forget John, or the very public humiliation he suffered at the Welshman's hands, is the distinguished All Black full-back Fergie McCormick. Coming into the First Test in 1971, McCormick was the player the Lions feared most and John was given the task of holding him in check. Through eighty minutes of steepling garryowens and touch finders that seemed to roll just beyond McCormick's grasp, John tormented the veteran. Following the game, a distraught McCormick was discarded, never again to be chosen to play for New Zealand.

John dominated the tempo and course of every game during the 1971 tour with consummate skills exaggerated by the amount of time afforded him by his forwards. Not that John ever looked rushed in his career, even when scrappy ball came to him with the opposition back-row attached. As with the very greatest of players, John had the ability to sum up the options almost as he was in the action of distributing the ball or deciding to speed through the smallest of half gaps.

While the timing, pace and handling skills were all natural talents refined over the years, John was also born with a vision that was beyond the scope of his peers. It was a package that made for an irresistible talent, and one that still captivates a nation. Not that John was faultless. He didn't like to tackle any more than he had to and if there was a ball loose at his feet, he was rarely the first to fall on it.

For all that, though, John remains a legend in Wales, in whose colours he won 25 caps to go with the five he won for the Lions, the four in 1971 being augmented by the solitary cap he won in South Africa in 1968 in the First Test before he was stretchered off with a broken collar bone. Although his first caps were not unmitigated successes – his first three were on the losing side and by the time he was chosen for the '68 Lions he had only tasted international success once – John was clearly an immense talent whose style endeared him to the ultra-critical Welsh crowds. A laconic runner whose laid-back demeanour cloaked astonishing pace and an elusive running style, the young John was a running fly-half in the classic Welsh mould. Yet he also grafted a match-winning boot onto that game, pinning back opposing teams with his tactical kicking, dropping goals seemingly at will and kicking penalties with a round-the-corner kicking style that brought him a record 180 points on the '71 Lions tour. It was a style that also bore domestic dividends, and in 1969 Wales chalked up a Triple Crown as they topped the Five Nations before going on to win their first Grand Slam for 20 seasons in 1971 thanks largely to John's boot and tactical acumen.

During the Lions' tour of 1971, his imperious runs prompted one journalist to write: "John was the dragonfly on the anvil of destruction."

> **King John was a one-off genius. He had an arrogance which put him in a class apart from his contemporaries, but it was arrogance in the right manner, a self-belief that gave him the confidence to try things that other players simply would not imagine.**
>
> *Phil Bennett, John's Wales and British Lions successor*

McBRIDE

THE ENFORCER

Willie John McBride is the most capped forward in the history of the British Lions. His fellow forwards loved him, because he was the rock in the middle of it all. If something was going down it was usually an opponent on the end of one of McBride's hits. He left behind him a number of beaten bodies during those 17 caps for the Lions.

Colin Meads, the ultimate enforcer, reckoned that McBride hit him with the hardest punch he ever received. He cracked him so hard in the rib cage that it was a while before Meads could get up. McBride, whose

> **He was mentally tough, physically hard and disciplined. He prepared like a professional and was ready to die on the field for victory. He was a rugged, even ruthless, competitor who played to win and was not squeamish about resorting to obstruction, gamesmanship and even the use of his fists or boots to achieve that end.**
>
> *John Gainsford, Springbok*

other talents include his ability as a raconteur, reckoned that he could only die once, so why not hit Meads?

If this appears to found McBride's reputation on his strengths as a hard man that is because therein lie the facts. He was a strong scrummager, a powerful mauler, a bodyguard. But as a line-out jumper or ball-carrying athlete he was no better than mediocre. Scotland's Alastair McHarg, who was never taken on a Lions' tour, skinned McBride every time they met in the line-out. McHarg was the very antithesis of McBride because he was also extraordinarily prominent around the pitch. That created the theory that he couldn't be putting it in in the tight. McBride was the tightest of tight forwards.

The fulfilment of McBride's reputation depends on his captaincy of the unbeaten Lions' tour to South Africa in 1974. McBride had been on two previous losing tours of South Africa and knew the Springbok mentality: crush the opposition physically and psychologically. He decided, therefore, that the Lions would be the intimidators this time around. He had had enough.

Two tales illustrate the extreme of the conviction. The Lions were playing a provincial game and McBride was being cleaned out in the line-out by a man named Johann de Bruyn. De Bruyn was not your average-looking guy. He only had one good eye and before each game he used to remove his glass eye and fill the hole with Vaseline. Mike Burton, who was propping in that game, said: "Vaseline was dripping down his face out of this hole. It was a horrible sight, you could hardly bear to look at him." At half-time McBride decided that something had to be done about the line-out deficit, so he says to Burton: "We're going to have to

do something absolutely despicable. We're going to have to hit him in his good eye." So, under orders, Burton did as he was told.

The more notorious feature of the tour was the call of "99". McBride knew there would be trouble, so on a call of "99" all the forwards were to join in the fight. That way the referee would have to send off everyone or no one. The first time it was used to any great effect was during the brutal third test at Port Elizabeth. The "99" call came and McBride led by example advancing 20 yards through the very heart of the opposition throwing lefts and rights, his shoulders forward, stepping into each punch. J.P.R. Williams ran 30 yards to join in. It was brutal. It was effective. Half way through the match the South African forwards were frightened. One of their supposed hard men actually ran away from a fight.

Under McBride's captaincy the Lions ducked nothing and nobody, which is why the South Africans regarded them as the greatest team to tour their country. The Boer mentality understand and respect might, power, brutality, physical coercion, intimidation. So the '74 Lions are credited with busting the image of South African physical superiority.

On the field McBride had respect

Fact File

Born: 6 June 1940
Birthplace: Toomebridge, Co. Antrim, Northern Ireland
Height: 6ft 3in (1.91m)
Weight: 17st (107kg)
Debut for Ireland: 1962 vs. England at Twickenham
Caps: 63
Points for Ireland: 2t = 8 points
Club: Ballymena
Career milestones: Most capped Irish lock (63 caps); most capped British Lion (17 Tests); captain of 1974 Lions; captain of Ireland.

because he never let anyone else fight his wars. Off the field the soft voice embroidered by cardigan and pipe disarmed many a livid hotel manager upset at the antics of the players under McBride's command. As a player his strength was strength. No great jumper, no great footballer, not a man who grovelled on the floor too much although he shoed plenty an opponent who had the temerity to scrabble in the dirt. But, if he said it was Friday, then it was Friday. As a lock forward he would not stand comparison with someone like Benoit Dauga who won 63 caps for France at around the same time. But as a man he was a cut above the rest.

COMING THROUGH *Willie John McBride, hard but fair... well hard anyway.*

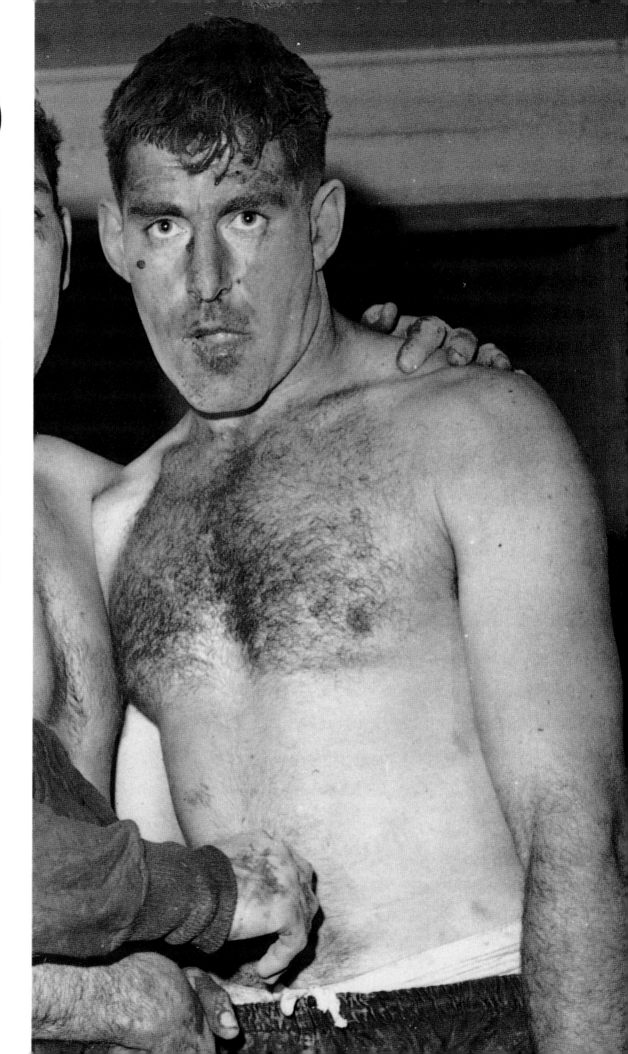

MEADS

MIGHTIEST OF ALL BLACKS

Fact File

Born: 3 June 1936
Birthplace: Auckland, New Zealand
Height: 6ft 4in (193cm)
Weight: 16st 6lb (104kg)
Debut for New Zealand: 1957 vs. Australia at Sydney
Caps: 55
Int. points: 7t = 21pts
Club: King Country
Career milestones: Longest international career as All Black (15 seasons). Most capped lock when he retired (55 caps).

By the modern measurement standards applied to second row forwards Colin Meads was a small man. Despite his nickname of "Pine Tree", he stood only 6ft. 4in., not big compared to the frequent 6ft. 8in. monsters of the 1990s. By other standards, however, he was a giant of a man, a national institution in New Zealand and the most influential forward of his or any generation.

Meads was a farmer from King Country, the rural heartland of New Zealand, and he had all the strength of a man who earned his living working off the land. The popular story about Meads is that he trained for his rugby by running up hills near his home with a sheep tucked under each arm.

As well as having all the right physical attributes for the game, Meads possessed in abundance the requisite mental requirements for the international second row. Put in a nutshell, he was mentally impregnable. There was no intimidating Colin Meads. No one touched him, some players were foolish enough to try but none succeeded. In a series against South Africa in the 1960s, John Gainsford, the Springbok centre, took offence to a piece of Mead's skulduggery. He chased after him, jumping on top of Meads, and letting fly with a barrage of blows. Gainsford recalls clearly what happened next: "He grabbed hold of both of my wrists. It was like being held by a band of steel. I couldn't move. He looked up and said, 'Don't bother, son. Now you know what international rugby is all about'."

The doyen of rugby writers, John Reason, once wrote of Meads: "He was frightened of no one. He revelled in taking on opposing forwards to find out how hard they were. He only respected those who could stand up to him. He truly was the Godfa-

ther, an analogy to the Mafia made even more compelling by the black uniform worn by his country."

Meads started life as a Number Eight. In addition to his menace he was a wonderfully shrewd footballer and immensely mobile. In the modern game he would probably play on the blind-side flank, but the New Zealanders wanted his resolution and power in the heart of the pack. Having made his debut in 1957, Meads was a regular throughout the 1960s, going into battle along such greats as Ken Gray, Wilson Whineray, Brian Lochore and Kel Tremain. For 14 internationals, Meads also played alongside his brother, Stan, who was two years his junior and a fine forward in his own right.

The Meads boys played together in the four Tests against the 1966 Lions, a series which the All Blacks won 4–0. This was the first time the British Lions had been on the receiving end of a series whitewash, and the contribution of Colin and Stan played no small part in the humiliation of Britain's finest 15.

If that was one of the undoubted highlights of Meads' 55-cap career, then the lowest point was the following season when he became only

> ## What does the best forward in the world mean? Is it applicable to anyone? The answer to both is probably Colin Meads.
>
> *Former Ireland player Andy Mulligan*

the second player to be sent off during an international (the first was Cyril Brownlie for New Zealand against England in 1925). Meads was dismissed at Murrayfield during the 1967 tour of Britain for lashing out at a Scottish player with his boot.)

If Meads' aggression and commitment did sometimes border on the very fringes of legality, it was only because of his enormous pride in wearing the silver-ferned jersey of the All Blacks. In turn, Meads was respected throughout the rugby world for his dedication to the cause. Indeed, ken Kelleher, the Irish referee who sent him off against Scotland, continued to exchange Christmas cards with him some 20 years after their initial contretemps. J.P.R. Williams, the former British Lions and Wales full-back, also has fond memories of Meads. In his autobiography, Williams remembers the magnanimity of Meads after the 1971 Lions had avenged their 1966 predecessors by becoming the first ever British Lions' side to win a series against New Zealand. The series defeat brought Meads' career to a close but he still found time to congratulate the Lions on their triumph: " You have won the Test series and you have gone around our provinces unbeaten. This is a great achievement and it will probably never be equalled."

After his retirement from top-class

rugby, Meads remained in the New Zealand public eye, and in 1986 he was at the centre of much controversy when he coached the rebel New Zealand Cavaliers to South Africa. The decision by the squad outraged many liberals in the country and openly defied the NZRFU who opposed the tour. Meads went because of his passion for rugby — politics had no right to interfere with his beloved game. What does matter to him, however, is the continuation of New Zealand supremacy throughout the rugby world. The latest version of the All Blacks, spearheaded by the likes of Christian Cullen and Jeff Wilson, may be anathema to the forward power personified by Meads during his heyday, but as long as they keep winning, that's enough for him.

BRASS MAULS *Meads ensured that the All Blacks won… all the time.*

PORTA

ARGENTINA'S MAN OF MANY TALENTS

Fact File

Born: 11 September 1951
Birthplace: Buenos Aires
Height: 5ft 9in (1.77m)
Weight: 13st 4lb (85kg)
Debut for Argentina:
1973 vs. Romania at Bucharest
Caps: 49 for Argentina; 8 for South America
Points for Argentina/South America: 5t, 54c, 109p, 25dg = 530pts
Club: Banco Nacion
Career milestones:
Played in only South American side ever to beat Springboks; highest points scorer for Argentina (530); most capped player (57); longest Test career (19 years); Argentine ambassador to South Africa; longest Test career of a Puma (20 seasons); Argentine captain

In some ways Hugo Porta is the CB Fry of Argentina — the consumate all-rounder. There is little doubt that Porta, who was later to become his country's ambassador to South Africa, and minister of sport, could have been anything he chose when he started out. He was educated at the De la Salle monastery school in Buenos Aires where he also played soccer. Many people advised him to turn professional, including top soccer side Boca Juniors who tried to sign him as a youngster, but he preferred his father's advice and studied law. This choice determined that he became a rugby player. He started out as a scrum-half in which position he was selected as fourth choice for national training in 1970.

Carwyn James, the visionary coach of the '71 Lions and a former fly-half himself, saw Porta play in South Africa in 1980, he cabled back to London: "To study the craftsmanship of a great player is a privilege. On Wednesday afternoon against the Lions – Porta had been selected for a South African Barbarians XV – everything that happened around Hugo Porta was contested at a much lower level of skill

> **" To see Hugo Porta play was to have my faith in the possibilities of fly-half play completely restored. Rarely have I ever seen such a talent. "**
>
> *Carwyn James, Llanelli and the British Lions*

and intellectual awareness. For a critic or coach or ex fly-half, it was a question of having one's faith restored in the aesthetic and artistic possibilities of back play."

Porta has been compared to Clint Eastwood waiting to erupt from under his sombrero. Perhaps he was the high plains drifter. He was certainly as untouchable and influential. Only he did not strike the opposition down with terrible vengeance, nor did he work the ball to death by greed. He included all with his immaculate distribution.

Ever since Porta stormed onto the scene in the late 1960s, he has been the linchpin of Argentine rugby. Multi-

talented, he was equally adept at dropping goals as he was at making a clean break through a half-gap. Short and stocky, Porta was like lightning over 15 yards and had a wonderful sense of balance that made him deceptively hard to bring down in the tackle. Even in his later years, when age began to catch up with him, Porta adapted his game, relying more on crafty handling skills and tactical kicking. Unquestionably, it was Porta who did more than any other Argentine to usher the Pumas onto the world stage. Against France in 1977, he kicked all 18 points in a drawn match, and he did the same when the All Blacks were held 21–21 in 1985. In between those two stalemates, Porta helped defeat Australia in Brisbane in 1983 and the French in 1985, as well as leading the Jaguars, a South American combination which toured

SUPERB! *The Maradona of rugby. Porta was also good with his hands.*

South Africa and amazed the rugby world by convincingly winning the Second Test in Bloemfontain in 1982 by 21–12.

Yet it wasn't until 1987 and the inaugural World Cup in Australasia, that Argentina had their first real opportunity to demonstrate to the rugby world what they were capable of. Unfortunately, the Pumas underperformed and failed to qualify for the quarter-finals despite being widely tipped to do so before the tournament began. An opening defeat to Fiji proved costly and although they recovered to beat Italy and put up a creditable showing against the All Blacks the damage had been done. Disappointed with the outcome, Porta announced his retirement shortly afterwards, but was tempted back for his swansong three years later when Argentina made their first major tour to the UK. Despite his advanced age of 38, Porta showed glimpses of his old magic and even though his side was comfortably beaten by both England and Scotland, they came within two points of defeating the Irish. The match against Scotland was Porta's last international, but his role as ambassador to South Africa means that at every major rugby occasion in the republic, the smiling face of one of the world's greatest ever players is never far away.

RIVES

GALLIC FLAIR PERSONIFIED

Fact File

Born: 31 December 1952
Birthplace: Toulouse, France
Height: 5ft 10in (1.75m)
Weight: 13st (83kg)
Debut for France: 1975 vs. England at Twickenham
Caps: 59
Points for France: 5t = 20pts
Clubs: Toulouse, Racing Club de France
Career milestones: Two Grand Slams (one as captain); France's most capped captain (34) and flanker (59)

Talk to any Frenchman about rugby and before long the conversation will invariably turn to the: "romance" of the game, a recurring theme in the French notion of what makes up the essence of rugby football. It may seem odd, therefore, to choose a flanker as *The Ultimate Encyclopedia's* 'Legend' of French rugby, yet few figures in French rugby have encapsulated the romance of the game better than Jean-Pierre Rives, the livewire open-side who won 59 caps for France between 1975 and 1984.

As a player Rives contained all the elements that make French rugby so exciting. On the one hand he represented the dash and verve of the outstanding three-quarters that seem to grow on trees in France, while on

the other he was as teak hard and uncompromising a forward as France has ever produced – and for a country which puts its forwards through the most brutal school of domestic rugby in the world, that makes him pretty tough. The French love the silky skills of the three-quarters and they revel in the no-holds-barred close-quarter combat of the forwards – stick them together in one man and it is easy to see why Rives was so revered throughout France.

The most visible player on the pitch thanks to his long blond hair, the diminutive Rives was a triumph of mind over matter. Standing only 5ft 10in and weighting in at under 13 stones, he was a veritable midget in the world of international forward

play, particularly as France were fielding gargantuan packs throughout his career. Rives had an almost fanatical determination to excel in the big league though, and never allowed his lack of inches or pounds to stand in his way as he displayed a recklessness and complete disregard for personal safety that bordered on the masochistic. Mention the name of Jean-Pierre Rives to virtually any rugby supporter and the picture that is sure to be conjured up is one of the flanker with his blond mop streaked with blood, a legacy of his ferocious tackling and complete unwillingness to give an inch to far bigger men.

While Rives was small by the standards of the day, his electrifying pace more than made up for his relative lack of inches. Working in tandem with the blind-side flanker Jean-Claude Skrela and the bearlike No. 8 Jean-Pierre Bastiat, Rives led the most competitive and well balanced back row of the late 1970s and early 1980s. Rives would arrive at the breakdown first, followed shortly by Skrela and then Bastiat would finally lumber along, using his immense upper body strength to reclaim the ball.

Not that Rives was there merely for his pace. He had great distributive skills, was courageous in defence and possessed a highly developed tactical sense. More importantly, as Gareth Edwards explained in his book *100 Great Rugby Players*, the sheer will to win and naked aggression of the super-charged French flanker was enough to put opposing players off their stride. Edwards was not the only scrum-half to think: "I was never taken in by Jean-Pierre's warmth, charm and flashing smile off the field, for once the whistle went he was a hard-faced enemy with a will of steel, an opponent who went all out to win. At set-pieces in the four internationals I played against him, we were never more than a yard or two apart and I could feel the hostility radiating from his berth."

Rives' international career started with a 27–20 win at Twickenham against England, and in his next 13 matches for France he was on the losing side only twice. Such was his drive and ability to read the game that

he succeeded Bastiat as captain in 1978, going on to captain France a record 34 times. The little man with a big heart inspired his sides to such a degree that France enjoyed an unprecedented degree of success, with Rives leading his charges to a 24–19 victory over New Zealand in 1979 before going on to claim the Grand Slam in 1981. Fittingly for France's most charismatic leader, he remains his country's most capped flanker. After his retirement in 1984, Rives published his autobiography 'A Modern Corinthian', an appropriate title, not only in a rugby context, but in a broader context as well. As if to perpetuate the image of the last rugby romantic, Rives now earns a living as a sculptor in Paris.

> **❝He was a phenomenon, quite unlike any other player in France or indeed the world at that time. He was so fast, so courageous — there will never be another quite like him.❞**
>
> *Jean-Claude Skrela, French flanker of 1970s*

RIVES NOT GAUCHE *Fast, accurate, full of flair. Jean-Pierre Rive, voila!*

THE GREAT PLAYERS

Which rugby fan has never passed a few moments in a barroom arguing about the selection of the national team, moving almost inevitably on to memories of yesteryear and a comparison of past and present. "Greatest Ever XVs" are invariably compiled and arguments ensue because judging greatness across the ages is a tricky matter, a process without hope of conclusion but a rewarding one for all that.

There are no guarantees that George Nepia would wipe the floor with Christian Cullen for instance, or that Wavell Wakefield would be a colossus of the game were he playing today. Differences in the laws, physique and styles of play make such comparisons virtually impossible, if hugely enjoyable. Yet every era has its greats, those players with an indefinable edge who send a tingle down the spine of opponents and spectators whose feats are remembered long after the games they played in have faded into history.

Some countries are blessed with more greats than others most notably the two southern hemispher giants: New Zealand and South Africa, these are nations who seem capable of conjuring up sublimely gifted players almost at will. The number of greats selected for each of the original eight rugby-playing nations has therefore been restricted with much difficulty to 25, bringing the total number of players profiled to 200 of the 7,000 capped players to choose from. Although there are many players of great note to have worn the colours of an "emerging" nation, none of these have been included because so few have been exposed to all of the top sides over many years.

CARL AARVOLD

England 1928–33
(centre and wing)

One of the great English centre three-quarters of the 1920s, the straight-running Carl Aarvold was first identified as a precocious talent while still a schoolboy at Durham. Aarvold won his first Blue for Cambridge in 1925 while still 17, and went on play in and win a record four Varsity Matches before his 21st birthday. Taken on the British tour of Argentina in 1927, Aarvold proved himself a wonderful attacking player with an ability to unlock even the tightest defences and was capped the following year in the 18–11 win over the touring Waratahs, essentially the Australian national side. The centre's international career went from strength to strength, the highlight coming in 1930 when he captained the Lions in three of the four Tests against the All Blacks, winning the First Test in Dunedin 6–3 and scoring ten tries on the tour. Genuinely quick, Aarvold was switched to the wing during the Lions' tour, an experiment that was so successful it was repeated by England, and six of his 16 caps were won in that position. In 1932 he was called to the Bar, Inner Temple, and thus his international rugby career, in true amateur style, almost immediately an end. He was knighted in 1968.

PIERRE ALBALADEJO

France 1954–64 (fly-half)

The tall, elegant Albaladejo commenced his international career at full-back against England in 1954 aged

21. It was an auspicious start in which the young fly-half hardly put a foot wrong to chalk up an 11–3 win that secured France joint-top billing in the Five Nations (shared with Wales and England) for the first time in their history. Despite also impressing while winning his second cap in the 39–12 win over Italy a month later, Albaladejo was dropped and lay discarded until a dramatic return six years later when an injury to Roger Martine saw him recalled for the game against Wales in Cardiff. Under the captaincy of Francois Moncla, France scored four tries to win a memorable game 16–8. It was the chance Albaladejo had craved, and in the next Five Nations game against Ireland he knocked over three drop-goals, a record which is still unbeaten. The fly-half well and truly lived up to his 'Monsieur Drop' nickname when he landed four drop-goals to help his club to a dramatic 12–11 victory in the Du Manoir final against Pau. It was always his greatest regret that, despite appearing in four Championship finals with Dax, he failed to add the famous 'Le Bouclier de Brennus' to his impressive collection of trophies. He announced his decision to retire before the Five Nations game against Ireland in Paris in 1964, but made a reluctant comeback at the prompting of the selectors for the one-off international in South Africa. He eventually retired after winning his 30th cap against Fiji in October 1964.

TREVOR ALLAN
Australia 1946–49
(centre)

Trevor Allan was one of Australia's greatest post-war centres. Making his debut on the 1946 tour to New Zealand aged 20, after just 12 first-class games, the stocky three-quarter immediately impressed and went from strength to strength before being chosen as the vice-captain for the 1947–48 tour of Britain. That was to prove a momentous tour for Allan, who assumed the captaincy when tour leader Bill McLean broke his leg in an early game against the Combined Services. From then on, "Tubby" could do no wrong, and his Wallaby party returned to Australia as its most successful tourists ever. Although beaten by Wales, Allan's Wallabies won 35 of their 41 games, scoring 712 points and conceding just 276 on the way. After a career in which he played 14 times for Australia, captaining the side in ten of them, a hard-up Allan finally succumbed to the blandishments of Rugby League and signed for English club Leigh in 1950 for the massive fee of £6,250. Although later rescinded, so allowing him to return to coach his beloved Gordon, Allan's immediate expulsion from the game was a sad way to end a great career, and one that created uproar among a sizeable proportion of Australian rugby followers disgusted at the shabby treatment afforded one of their country's genuine all-time living Greats.

MARK ANDREWS
South Africa 1994– (lock)

Mark Andrews has followed a long line of outstanding Springbok lock forwards. At 6ft. 7in., the Natal player is not particularly tall by the standards of the day, yet has become one of the truly great line-out jumpers of his generation, at a time when Springbok jumpers are in short supply. Helped by his remarkably big hands and an agility that comes from the intensive training he underwent while winning Junior Springbok water polo colours, Andrews is also an extremely versatile player who reacted well when asked by coach Kitch Christie to make the switch from second row to No. 8 against the French in the 1995 World Cup semi-final. A quiet man by nature, Andrews learned his rugby in Durban and had his first taste of touring in Argentina in 1993 – as intimidating a destination as any in world rugby. Never one to dish out punishment, Andrews is none too keen on receiving it either and soon learned to look after himself at any flare-up, to the point where the All Blacks reckoned him South Africa's best tight-forward of the post-isolation era. Still only 25, Andrews has already played almost 30 Tests and, with the increased number of internationals being played in the modern era, seems certain to overtake the great Frik du Preez's record mark of 38 second-row caps.

ROB ANDREW
England 1985–97 (fly-half)

When Rob Andrew came on as a replacement for the last ten minutes of England's 1997 Five Nations match against Wales, he added one more cap to his previous total of 70, and prolonged an international career that most assumed had ended in 1995. Andrew was first capped against Romania in 1985 and for much of his career was pigeonholed as a kicking fly-half. Indeed, he carried on an often intense rivalry for the England fly-half spot with Stuart Barnes, a player perceived as an apostle of the running game, throughout his England career. Rather than the cause of England's conservative ten-man game, however, the trusty Andrew was merely its cipher as he turned forward power, possession and pressure into position and points.

Already well ensconced as the England fly-half by 1988, Andrew nevertheless benefited from manager Geoff Cooke's policy of continuity in selection and developed a new confidence which saw him dominate the crucial second and third Lions' Tests in Australia in 1989 after being called out as a replacement. Late in his career, Andrew added top class goal-kicking to his tactical kicking repertoire, notching up an England record of 30 points with the boot against Canada in 1994. An intelligent, gritty, consistent footballer who was exceptionally strong defensively, for some reason Andrew never quite received the recognition he deserved for a 13-year career which encompassed 396 points for England, three World Cups and two Lions tours.

GARY ARMSTRONG
Scotland 1988– (scrum-half)

Armstrong made his international debut in 1988 in the 32–13 home loss to Australia, but the Jed Forest scrum-half still managed to shine in his first taste of the big time. That would have come as no surprise to those who knew him best, because despite his apparently painful shyness, Armstrong has proved throughout his career to be almost obsessively focused once out on the pitch. A relatively small man, Armstrong tackles way over his weight and combines this with quick service to his

MR DEPENDABLE
England's Rob Andrew.

BORDER TERRIER *Scottish scrum-half Gary Armstrong against England.*

backs and an uncanny ability to break around the fringes just as easily from the first-phase as from ruck or maul. Although Armstrong failed to shine on the victorious 1989 Lions tour of Australia, his gritty nature stood him in good stead when the chips were down in 1990, that famous year for Scotland. Not only was Armstrong a central figure as the Scots pushed the All Blacks to the wire on tour in New Zealand, but he, more perhaps than any other player, was the on-field catalyst for Scotland's 13–7 win in the Grand Slam decider against the *Auld Enemy* England at Murrayfield. Since then, however, Armstrong has been plagued by injury, missing the entire 1992 and 1995 seasons. But in 1996, following a move to Newcastle, Armstrong was back in the Scotland side.

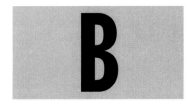

MAX BARRAU

France 1971–74 (scrum-half)

Born just outside Agen, Max Barrau was only 20 when he made his international debut against Scotland in the 1971 Five Nations. He remains the youngest scrum-half ever to have played for France and, despite win-

ning only 16 caps, is still regarded as one of the finest No. 9s ever to have represented his country. However, disaster struck during the 1971 tour of South Africa when he sustained a serious injury in an early game and he was forced to return home before the First Test. He recovered in time to face England at Stade Colombes the next year, relaunching a scintillating career through his masterly control behind the pack as France scored six tries in a 37–12 humbling of the English. Barrau, by now with toulouse, consolidated his reputation as a key member of the French side during the 1972 tour to Australia. In a thrilling two-Test series, the first international was drawn 14-14, before teh decider was won by France 16-15, a victory that gave the French their one and only series win in Australia. Despite the challenge of gifted youngsters Richard Astre and Jacques Fouroux, Barrau was appointed captain of France in October 1973 only to suffer a career-ending injury in the unofficial international against Brazil at the beginning of the 1974 tour to Argentina. It was a sad end to the best scrum-half France has ever had.

JEAN BARTHE

France 1954–59 (No. 8)

Jean Barthe made his international debut in the back row at the age of 22 against Argentina in the First Test in Buenos Aires in 1954 and played

his first Five Nations game against Scotland at lock-forward the following year. The French selectors were not overwhelmed, however, and Barthe spent a year in the wilderness before returning to international duty against Ireland at No. 8. This time, Barthe made more of an impression and he was not to be dropped through loss of form until his career ended prematurely four years later in 1959. A member of the all-conquering Lourdes side of the 1950s, Barthe formed a spectacular partnership with French great Jean Prat, and won the French Championship three times in 1956, 1957 and 1958. The highlight of his career was undoubtedly the South African tour of 1958, during which the French became the first tourists to win a test series on South African soil since the British Lions in 1896. Barthe returned to captain France to a 3–3 draw agianst England at Twickenham, but such were the reviews of his form in South Africa that he was swamped with offers from French clubs, South African provincial outfits and from Rugby League, enjoying a late upsurge in fortunes in France. Barthe found the last option the most appealing and he departed to French Rugby League. As if to emphasize what a good player he was, Barthe soon became a dual-international, and was eventually recognized as one of the all time greats of the professional code.

GUY BASQUET

France 1945–52 (No. 8)

Barnstorming French No. 8 Guy Basquet, the winner of 33 caps in the seven years after the Second World War, started his rugby career by accident. Born in Layrac, a picturesque village near Agen, he was sent by his father to Paris in 1938, seven years after the French had been expelled from the Five Nations for blatant breaches of the amateur code. Basquet, then 17, approached Racing Club de France, to join the basketball section. He had never played rugby before, but the club sent the teenager to the rugby section at Stade Colombes. The young Basquet did not argue and the following week

made his first appearance at centre for Racing's third team. By the end of the year, still aged 17, he had broken into the first team. In 1939 war broke out and Basquet returned to Layrac to help his family. His brother left for the front while the youngster was registered as a farmer, an occupation which saved him from conscription and also provided the local cell of the Resistance with an eager recruit. He joined Agen, where he was moved from centre to No. 8, a position to which he adapted brilliantly. France's first game after the war was against the Army, a hardy combination of Union and League internationals at Parc des Princes, on January 1st, 1945.

With Twickenham still requisitioned by the military, the return game against the British Empire Forces, captained by Welsh international Captain Haydn Tanner, was played at the Richmond Athletic Ground in April. In 1948 Basquet led France, by now fully reintegrated in the Five Nations structure, to one of the sweetest landmarks in French rugby history; a Welsh scalp in Swansea, followed in 1951 by the first ever win against England at Twickenham.

JEAN-PIERRE BASTIAT

France 1969–78 (No. 8)

Born in Pouillon, the giant back-row forward was earmarked for greatness from his days with Dax Youth and France Under-19. Initially selected as a second row, the Dax player's speed about the field, handling ability and exceptional rugby brain convinced the selectors to move him to the back row where he was an instant success. Bastiat made his international debut as one of the five newcomers in the French team that beat Romania 14–9 in 1969. With greats such as Walter and Claude Spanghero, Elie Cester, Alain Esteve and Benoit Dauga all contesting back row places, it took Bastiat until the First Test against Argentina in 1974, to break into the national side at No. 8, with Boffelli and Skrela partnering him in the back row. International action was intermittent in 1974 and early '75, but in October 1975 the Bastiat-Rives-Skrela trio made its debut against the visiting Pumas on Argentina's first ever tour to France. The combination proved successful and was retained for the next 14 internationals, including the 1977 Grand Slam. Appointed captain against England in 1978, Bastiat retired at the end of the season, following defeat in the Grand Slam decider in Cardiff.

GEORGE BEAMISH

Ireland 1925–33 (No. 8)

Recognized as the greatest Northern Hemisphere forward of his generation, No. 8 George Beamish came from a famous rugby family, and was succeeded in the Ireland team by his younger brother Charles, who won 12 caps in the three years following George's retirement. Beamish was the driving force behind the Irish pack for almost ten years after he made his debut as a 19-year-old in the famous draw against the English at Twickenham. A mighty fellow, the Ulsterman stood at a little over 6ft. and weighed in at over 16st. at his heaviest – huge proportions for the time. No matter how heavy Beamish became, however, he remained a great ball player – he was one of the great dribblers of his age – and his inbuilt strategic sense allowed him to dominate proceedings during a period in which Irish teams were fiercely competitive. A natural leader of men, Beamish was quick, fit, immensely strong and led from the front, most notably in 1931 when he led Ireland to their first win at Cardiff Arms Park; and skippered the East Midlands to a win over Bennie Osler's famous Springbok side which was otherwise unbeaten on tour. A distinguished servant of the RAF (he later became Air Marshal Sir George Beamish), Leicester, Ireland and the British Lions, for whom he was the driving force on the 1930 tour to New Zealand, Beamish won 30 caps.

BILL BEAUMONT

England 1975–82 (lock)

Of all the legendary figures in English rugby, none is held in more esteem or more fondly remembered than the 1980 Grand Slam captain, William Blackledge Beaumont (or "Bubble

LIONHEART *Bill Beaumont.*

Bum" to his close friends). A stocky, four-square lock who played for Fylde and his beloved Lancashire until his retirement on medical grounds in 1982, Beaumont won a place in all English hearts when he led his country to their first clean sweep for 23 years in 1980, the highlight being a 9-8 victory over Wales courtesy of Dusty Hare's injury-time penalty in a match of sustained and savage commitment. Beaumont won the first of his 34 caps for England in 1975 and when, in 1977, Moseley lock Nigel Horton had to return from the Lions' party in New Zealand, Beaumont was flown out as a replacement. A robust lock who was safe on his own ball at the front of the line-out, Beaumont hit rucks and mauls with huge impact and was, according to team-mate Fran Cotton: "a colossal scrummager". A modest and quietly spoken man, Beaumont had the respect of all the top British players and in 1980 was made the first Englishman to captain the Lions since Doug Prentice in 1930. Although that tour to South Africa was not a successful one, it did little to diminish the reputation of big Bill Beaumont, a loveable bear who characterized all that is good in English rugby football.

ANDRÉ BEHOTEGUY

France 1923–29 (centre)

Born in Bayonne on October 19, 1900, André was two years and one day younger than his brother Henri.

Between them, the virtually indistinguishable brothers represented France on 25 occasions, pulling on the blue jersey together on five occasions. André, a French champion in rowing and track and field, played 19 times for his country between 1923-1929, while Henri represented France in six internationals. André, in particular, was an exceptionally gifted player, although it is fair to say that both brothers had trouble fulfilling their potential at the top level due to the weakness of the French packs of the period. Andre commenced his career in 1923 in a 12–3 defeat at the hands of an England side in the process of notching up four Grand Slams, it was some six weeks after younger brother Henri made his international debut at centre in the 16–8 defeat by Wales. While Henri was destined not to play again until 1928, André became a regular in the French team. Captaining his country on four occasions between 1927-'29. André retired from international rugby after a 16–6 defeat by England brought France its fifth wooden spoon in six seasons. André can also claim a silver medal as a member of the French rugby team defeated 17–3 by the USA in the final of the 1924 Olympics.

ABDELATIF BENAZZI

France 1990– (No. 8)

A Moroccan by birth and upbringing, gifted utility forward Abdel Benazzi was first capped by his native country for which he played 14 times at lock forward and No. 8. As a teenager he set a number of junior Moroccan records in track and field before he was talked into playing rugby by a friend. During a tour of Czechoslovakia in 1988, a French talent scout spotted his unusual athleticism and convinced the youngster to give France a try. He arrived in Cahor in the autumn of 1988 and a year later was installed as national coach Jacques Fouroux's Agen club. In 1990, much to the annoyance of the Moroccans, he gave his native country's campaign in the qualifying rounds of the 1991 World Cup a miss – his absence almost certainly cost the Moroccans a spot among the last 16 – for a French cap. However, Benazzi's

first international outing ended in disgrace when, in an out-of-character display, he was sent off for stamping against Australia. It was only a minor hitch, though, as Benazzi quickly established himself as the pick of the French packs of the 1990s. At 6ft. 6in., with a startling turn of pace, acute rugby brain and immense durability, he soon became an automatic selection. His cause was also helped by a versatility which meant that, of his first 46 caps, 25 were as a flanker, ten as a No. 8 and 11 were as a second row. It also says much of the regard in which Benazzi is held that, despite French being his second language, he was appointed captain of France by coach Jean-Claude Skrela in 1996. The following season he lead the French to their first Grand Slam in ten years.

PHIL BENNETT

Wales 1969–78 (Fly-half)

There could be no more daunting task in rugby than that facing Llanelli fly-half Phil Bennett when he stepped into Barry John's boots upon the great man's retirement in 1972. However, Bennett went on to win 37 caps in his decade-long career. Perversely, it is not necessarily in a Welsh shirt that Bennett is best remembered. His display for the 1973 Barbarians against New Zealand is one of the great performances of all time, while he confirmed his status as a player of genuine world class on the 1974 Lions tour to South Africa. A quiet and immensely modest man by nature,

WIZARD *Phil Bennett, 1970s' star.*

Bennett was a proud Welsh speaker who was able to convey his passion and *hwyl* to fellow players if required. One of the best known stories about Bennett is the pre-match talk he gave his troops before they ran out to beat England 14-9 at Cardiff Arms Park in 1977 on the way to a Triple Crown. "Look at what these f*****s have done to Wales," he ranted. "They've taken our coal, our water and our steel. What have they given us – absolutely nothing. We've been exploited, raped, controlled and punished by the English – and that's who you're playing this afternoon!"

A brilliant attacking player capable of unlocking even the tightest defences with his pace and innate genius, there were virtually no gaps in Bennett's game.

PIERRE BERBIZIER

France 1981–91 (scrum-half)

Pierre Berbizier's evolution from a talented yet undersized centre-cum-full-back into an international class scrum-half was a major factor in France's dominanation of European rugby in the 1980s. He played centre for the French Juniors alongside Didier Codorniou and after his transfer from his native Lanemezan to Lourdes he played full-back. Coach Jacques Fouroux convinced the talented and unusually serious youngster that he had a future at scrum-half and so, in 1981, he made his debut against Scotland, helping France win not only that match but also the Grand Slam that year. In a career that

spanned 11 seasons and included 56 caps, 1987 was undoubtedly the finest year for Berbizier as he helped France to another Grand Slam and then played a leading role as they reached the final of the inaugral World Cup. As so often in French rugby, however, a personality clash effectively finished Berbizier's playing career when a public disagreement with former teammate Daniel Dubroca, then France's coach, led to him being dropped for good in 1991.

SERGE BLANCO

France 1980–91 (full-back)

Venezuelan-born Serge Blanco is undoubtedly one of the most entertaining players the sport has ever produced. Where Gareth Edward's try for the 1973 Barbarians against New Zealand thrilled a generation of rugby enthusiasts, Blanco's last-minute winner against Australia in the 1987 World Cup semi-final sent shivers of excitement down the spines of a new generation. A running full-back of unshakeable elan and panache, Blanco delighted crowds with his sudden changes of pace and direction, and his laid-back *joie de vivre*. Above all, Blanco was a natural (after all, how many top athletes smoke 40 cigarettes a day and rarely bother to train?). The Biarritz player made his international debut at full-back in a controversial match against South Africa during the sporting boycott in 1980, but it was a 15–0 defeat by Romania three weeks later (the first time France had failed to score in an

THE NATURAL *France's Serge Blanco*

international since 1964) that threatened to put his career on the back-burner. Blanco survived though but was shifted to the wing, from where he played all four games in the 1981 Grand Slam. After dominating the Five Nations for much of the 1980s as a full-back, collecting another Grand Slam in 1987 and winning a World Cup runners-up medal in 1987, Blanco's remaining ambitions centred around the 1991 World Cup. However, following a highly-charged quarter-final against England in Paris in which the French were knocked out, Blanco decided to hang up his boots for good after winning a total of 93 caps.

ANDRÉ BONIFACE

France 1954–66 (centre)

Between them the Boniface brothers – André and Guy – won 81 caps for France, 16 of them together. André, the older brother, is still regarded by French pundits as the greatest centre produced by French rugby – and that in a country that has thrown up players of the calibre of Sella, Codorniou, Trillo and Maso. Athletic, intelligent and skillful, he

made his international debut on the wing against Ireland in 1954 in France's first win against the Irish since 1931. His second international was even more spectacular, André making history as a member of Jean Prat's team which became the first French side ever to beat the All Blacks. In 1959, after picking up 21 successive caps, André was dropped for his alleged timidity. After an absence of two years, he re-launched his international career against the All Blacks in Auckland when he partnered Guy at centre for the first time in his career. Between July 1961 and March 1966 the two brothers proved an irresistible centre partnering in 16 Tests for France. In 1966, however, the party ended when the brothers were dropped after they were caught having a night on the town on the eve of a game. They were never to play for France together again, and less than 18 months later the partnership was finished forever when Guy was killed in a car crash.

NAAS BOTHA

South Africa 1980–92 (fly-half)
(*See **The Legends of Rugby** pages 104–05*)

ZINZAN BROOKE

New Zealand 1987– (No. 8)

It was only relatively late in his long career that Brooke became established in the All Black team and acknowledged as one of the best all-round forwards to have played for New Zealand. If confirmation of his uncanny ball skills was needed, it was provided in the 1995 World Cup semi-final when he dropped an outrageous goal in the 45–29 thrashing of England. First capped against Argentina in the 1987 World Cup, for much of his early career, Brooke was a stand-in utility loose forward, filling in for established back-rowers such as Wayne Shelford, Alan Whetton and Michael Jones. Even when Shelford was dropped in 1990 and replaced by Brooke at No. 8, he did not become an automatic choice and as late as 1994, Brooke was still spending almost as much time on the reserves bench as he was on the field. Yet Brooke revelled in the new-look

QUICK GETAWAY *French scrum-half Pierre Berbizier releases his backs.*

GORDON *"Broon Frae Troon"*

All Black side of 1995, as New Zealand thrilled the world with their exciting brand of total rugby. He continued as No. 8 during the 1996 Tri-Nations series winning his 47th cap against South Africa in August, alongside brother Robin, the lock forward.

GORDON BROWN

Scotland 1969–76 (lock)

Despite the fact that his older brother Peter was capped for Scotland before him, "Broon Frae Troon", became Scotland's greatest second row. Brown was first introduced to rugby at the age of 12 and, after graduating through Marr FP, he moved onto West of Scotland, and quickly came to the attention of first the divisional and then the national selectors, making his debut on the 1969 tour to Argentina. A buoyant, larger-than-life figure, Brown was an abrasive streamroller of a lock. Unmoveable in the scrum and unfailingly sure on his own ball at the line-out, he also displayed a dynamism in the loose and an ability to look after himself when the going got tough. At 6ft. 5in. and over 17 stone, Brown had trouble maintaining peak fitness so it was hardly surprising that his greatest moments came on tour. Indeed, although Brown was a part of Carwyn James's 1971 Lions' tour to New Zealand – often referred to by experts as the best touring party ever to leave Britain – it was as a cornerstone of the 1974 Lions side that beat South Africa that he really made his name. Also selected to tour New Zealand with the 1977 Lions, Brown thus became the only forward to win selec-

tion for all three British Lions' tours in the 1970s.

MAURICE BROWNLIE

New Zealand 1924–28 (No. 8)

Nicknamed the "moving tree trunk" by Wavell Wakefield, the English captain, Brownlie was the New Zealand rugby colossus of his day, a dominant figure in Hawke's Bay when that province had the first of the great Ranfurly Shield eras and the prime New Zealand forward on their tour of Britain and France in 1924–25. Although Brownlie toured Australia with the All Blacks in 1922, it wasn't until the 1924–25 tour to Britain and France that the back-rower won the first of his eight caps. So successful was that New Zealand side, they defeated Wales, Ireland, England and France (they didn't play Scotland), that they have been immortalized in rugby folklore as 'The Invincibles'. Ironically, Brownlie was said to have played his finest match on that tour when he helped defeat England 17–11 at Twickenham. Perhaps his storming performance was due in part to a desire to avenge his brother, Cyril, who, early on in the match had kicked a player on the groun and became the first player to be sent off in an international match.

CYRIL BURKE

Australia 1946–56 (scrum-half)

A country boy from Newcastle, New South Wales, Cyril Burke was one of the most extraordinary players ever to represent Australia. At 5ft. 6in. and weighing in at around 9 stone, he was minute for a scrum-half even in the 1940s, yet he was as pugnacious a No. 9 as ever laced up a pair of boots and pulled on a Wallaby shirt. A member of the Bledisloe Cup-winning side of 1949, and a key player during the Tubby Allan-led tour of Britain in 1947–48, the brave Burke nevertheless had more than his fair share of playing rugby the tough way – going backwards with little or no ball. Yet despite this and despite his lack of inches or pounds, Burke particularly relished the chance to take on the massive Springbok and All Black back rows of the time, and it

was not always the little Wallaby who came off worst. Burke was also an astute attacker who possessed a glorious side-step and a tidy turn of pace when needed. The one great regret in Burke's phenomenal career – one which encompassed a then record total of 26 Tests – was the manner in which he was finally dropped before the 1957–58 tour to England after an unintentional insult to Harry Crow, a member of a ARU.

MATT BURKE

Australia 1993 – (full-back)

A comparatively new addition to Wallaby ranks, Eastwood and New South Wales full-back Matt Burke has already done enough to reserve his place in the Australian Hall of Fame after breaking into the world champion side in 1993 during the series win over South Africa. After making a decisive contribution in New South Wales' one-point defeat of the Springboks, he was immediately drafted in to add some attacking bite to the Wallaby back division in the final Test. The full-back, described by Bob Dwyer as: "one of the greatest young full-backs it's ever been my pleasure to witness" fulfilled his role admirably as Australia ran out 19–12 winners in front of a packed Sydney Cricket Ground. All this when he was still only 20. Rock-solid under the high ball and one of the best cover defenders in world rugby, Burke is also a firm exponent of the "have-a-go" school of thought as witnessed during the 1996 Bledisloe Cup against New Zealand. When collecting the ball in his own 22, Burke ran through eight All Blacks to score an amazing try under the posts. Burke also has application and, with the help of English kicking guru Dave Alred, has laboured to improve the weakest part of his game, his kicking. The result is a punt in excess of 50m with either foot and an 80 per cent success rate when kicking for goal in 1996 Tests. But then Burke is a worker; a gung-ho, free-running full-back, an ultra-sensible young man with his feet on the ground who seems destined – one day – to captain Australia.

JEFF BUTTERFIELD

England 1953–59 (centre)

England and British Lions' star Jeff Butterfield is widely remembered as the most gifted British centre of his generation. A player who always made an immediate impact, Butterfield scored on both his England and Lions debuts, a distinction he shares with England's other outstanding post-war centre, Jeremy Guscott. And if Butterfield's international career started well, it was to continue at the same impressive pace for the next seven seasons, the only down-side being the recurring thigh muscle injury which eventually sidelined him during the 1959 Lions' tour and caused his retirement shortly afterwards. That said, although hampered by injury, Butterfield played through the pain barrier to win 28 consecutive caps for England. It was as a Lion in 1955, however, that Butterfield was truly outstanding. Working in conjunction with fellow England centre Phil Davies, the lithe Yorkshireman gave a virtuoso display as he tore through the Springboks' three-quarters to score in three of the four Tests in the drawn series.

Butterfield, however, was more than just a superb attacking player. He recognized the importance of fitness and subjected himself to a punishing training routine – he once said that: "In rugby football if two minutes go by and the whistle is not blown the game is devastatingly fatiguing, so you must be fit".

FINLAY CALDER

Scotland 1986–91 (flanker)

As with the Brown brothers before him and the Hastings and Milnes later on, it was sibling rivalry that provided a keen motivation for uncompromising Heriot's FP open-side Finlay Calder. Brother Jim, capped at blind-side before Finlay, was every bit as dogged and determined as his slightly smaller but quicker brother. Yet while Jim was the first Calder to come to the attention of the national selectors – and the most high profile after scoring a decisive try in Scotland's 1984 Grand Slam triumph – it was Finlay who was eventually to eclipse his brother's achievements as captain of the victorious Lions who toured Australia in 1989, and as a vital component of the side which so shocked England with their emotion-fuelled win in the Grand Slam showdown at Murrayfield in 1990. Calder's ability to use his drive, determination and innate knowledge of the game to overcome his undoubted shortcomings – in particular, he was always a bit slow for an out-and-out open-side – helped him become one of the most effective back-row operators of the modern era. If he and the other two members of the Grand Slam back row, John Jeffrey and Derek White, could not impose their own game, they certainly would make sure the opposition could not impose theirs. He retired after the 1991 World Cup having won 34 caps.

OLLIE CAMPBELL

Ireland 1976–84 (fly-half)

Every era has its memories. If the late 1970s were the days when the Welsh were invincible, and 1980 was the year when Bill Beaumont's England triumphed at last, then the next three years was the era when a willowy Irish fly-half called Ollie Campbell kicked himself into the record books. And Campbell could surely kick. On his first major outing with Ireland, on the 1979 tour to Australia, Campbell established a record by amassing a half-century in just four Tests, and throughout the next five years the sight of Campbell smacking the ball

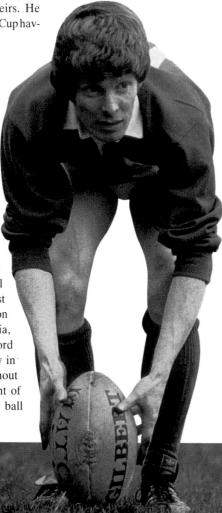

OLLIE CAMPBELL *First he kicked into the record books, then - inspired by his rivalry with Tony War, he learned the running game as well.*

between European uprights was a familiar feature of the Five Nations. Campbell's finest season came during the Triple Crown-winning season of 1982, when he underlined his dominance by scoring 52 of Ireland's 72 points. It would not be fair, however, for Campbell to be remembered simply as a remarkable goal-kicker. Not only could he also kick well from the hand, but once he established himself over long-time rival and silky-smooth runner Tony Ward in the national side, Campbell began to show a penchant and talent for running at opposition defences. A gritty defender, Campbell was also an able orchestrator of his back line, although his failure to do so adequately on either the 1980 Lions tour to South Africa (he was injured) or their 1983 tour to New Zealand means the bulk

of his claim to greatness throughout his 22-cap career rests with his right boot.

MIKE CAMPBELL-LAMERTON

Scotland 1961–66 (lock)

There are some players to whom history is particularly unkind, and none more so than Mike Campbell-Lamerton. Had the giant second row stopped playing after the 1962 Lions tour, when he excelled as a No. 8 in all four Tests, he would undoubtedly be remembered more fondly by his countrymen. However, his disappointing record as captain of the whitewashed 1966 Lions tour to New Zealand – he was playing so poorly that he dropped himself and handed over the captaincy to Welshman David Watkins – has tainted the memory of a fine playing career. A captain in the Army, the London Scottish player was one of the biggest players of his day at 6ft. 5in. and just under 18 stone. A strong scrummager, who held his own at the line-out and was a considerable presence in the loose, Campbell-Lamerton excelled in the second row for Scotland from his first cap in 1961 until his 23rd in 1966, and would have been equally as effective for the Lions had the selectors picked him in his right position in 1966. But because he had performed very well at No. 8 on the 1962 Lions tour to South Africa, the selectors persisted with him out of position on that fateful tour. Although Campbell-Lamerton handled the painful fall-out of the '66 Lions tour with great stoicism and dignity, he never again played for either the Lions or Scotland. His son, Jeremy won two caps in 1986-87.

DAVID CAMPESE

Australia 1982–91 (wing)
*(See **The Legends of Rugby**, pages 106–07)*

LEWIS CANNELL

England 1948–57 (centre)
Lewis Cannell was a prodigious talent who started his international career in 1948 as a 21-year-old and ended it ten seasons and 19 caps later in 1957. Well-balanced, artful and accomplished, Cannell nevertheless

suffered from the selectorial chaos that was de rigueur at the time and found himself in and out of the England side, being dropped for whole seasons at a time and not playing in 1951, 1954 or 1955. Astute technically, Cannell was a great straightener of the line who was at his best alongside Jeff Butterfield, with whom he formed a very effective partnership after Butterfield's debut in 1953. Despite setting up two tries for his centre partner, Cannell found himself dropped for the bulkier Phil Davies, and it was three more years until they played together again. Although the high points of Cannell's career were his glorious match-winning tries against France in 1949 and Wales in 1953, he also had two other important landmarks. The first was a run of three consecutive Varsity Match wins in the dark blue of Oxford (1948–50), while the second was fronting up to the 1951–2 touring Springboks three times in a week, being on the receiving end for Midlands Counties, England and the Barbarians in Cardiff.

WILL CARLING

England 1988–97 (centre)

England centre Will Carling shall always be remembered as the man who led English rugby's startling revival in the late 1980s. In tandem with coach Geoff Cooke, who appointed Carling to lead England when the then army captain was still a youthful 22, he quickly identified the two pillars that were to make England the dominant force in Northern Hemisphere rugby for the next seven years: consistency of selection and a willingness to play a game based around strong-mauling forwards such as Dean Richards, Wade Dooley and Mike Teague. From the time that Carling made his debut as England captain in the 28–19 win over Australia at Twickenham in 1988 until his retirement as captain in 1996, Carling led his country to an unprecedented period of success, albeit predominantly against Northern Hemisphere opposition, with Grand Slams coming in 1991, 1992 and 1995. Although notable wins were scored against the All Blacks (once), the Australians

GOLDEN BOY *Will Carling.*

(twice) and the South Africans (twice), Carling's England were never really a match for the best of the Southern Hemisphere.

A powerful runner and a gritty tackler, Carling was one of the mainstays of the English back division alongside Rob Andrew, Jeremy Guscott, Jon Webb and Rory Underwood. The most recognisable and high profile player in rugby, Carling became headline news after a dalliance with the Princess of Wales.

SANDY CARMICHAEL
Scotland 1967–78 (prop)

First capped by Scotland in 1967 against Ireland, Carmichael's second cap was against the touring All Blacks the same year, an experience that stood him in good stead for the 1971 Lions' tour to New Zealand. It was on that tour that Carmichael was battered into rugby history during a savage match against Canterbury in Christchurch. Carmichael suffered five fractures of his cheekbone in the violence that ensued, yet still played until the final whistle. Photos of his disfigured face sent shockwaves round the rugby world. For all that heroism, though, Carmichael was far more than a player who could tough it out. A solid scrummager, he was a superb minder at the line-out and, surprisingly for a prop, was well known as a great cover tackler.

CHRISTIAN CARRERE
France 1966–1971 (flanker)

Christian Carrere grew up in Morocco where he played handball. On his fam-

ily's return to Tarbes, he took up rugby at the junior section of the local club before joining Toulon, where his athleticism, rugby brain and leadership quickly made the young flanker a household name. A leader of men, fast, fearless and outrageously athletic, Carrere had it all and was clearly destined for great things. In 1966, eight days after his 18th birthday – making him the youngest player ever to represent France – Carrere made his debut against Romania alongside Claude Dourthe and Jean Salut, one of the most talented wing forwards of his generation. The next year, he became the youngest captain of France when he led his men against the visiting All Blacks, and the year after that, he captained France to its first Grand Slam after missing out by one point against Scotland the year before. Carrere, true to the God-like status he enjoyed in French rugby circles, scored the winning try in that 1968 Grand Slam decider against Wales. Carrere went on to win 28 caps until his international career was terminated in strange circumstances in 1971 when he was alleged to have requested an illegal transfer from Toulon to his first club, Tarbes.

KEN CATCHPOLE
Australia 1961–68 (scrum-half)

The memory of outrageously gifted scrum-half Ken Catchpole is all too often obscured by the horrific manner in which his Test career was prematurely finished in the 1968 Bledisloe Cup clash in Sydney. With Australia, and Catchpole in particu-

TOUCH OF CLASS *Ken Catchpole.*

lar, frustrating the All Blacks, the diminutive scrum-half was caught in a ruck and driven into the splits position by All Black legend Colin Meads. When play moved away Catchpole remained prone, his leg tendons and muscles so badly damaged that his career was over. After making his New South Wales debut aged 19 against a 1959 Lions side containing men such as Tony O'Reilly and Peter Jackson – and ending up on the winning side in the only Lions' defeat in Australia that tour – Catchpole made his international debut against Fiji in 1961 before being given the job of coach and captain of Australia for the tour to South Africa the next year. Catchpole's finest hour came on the 1966–67 tour to Britain, however, when he was in superlative form as he masterminded the 23–11 destruction of England at Twickenham, before inspiring his forwards to a 14–11 win in front of 50,000 screaming Welshmen at the Cardiff Arms Park – the first time Australia had ever beaten Wales. Catchpole won 27 caps, 13 as captain.

BILL CERUTTI
Australia 1928–37 (prop)

Somehow the time-honoured phrase "larger than life" doesn't quite do justice to Bill Cerutti. The ever popular prop was more of a "huger than life" sort of man. A man who lived life to the full, Cerutti has provided a template for generations of bad boy props; a slugger who got his retaliation in first in the darker recesses of the forward confrontation and then drank his way to eternal friendship with his fellow combatant afterwards. An immensely popular man, Cerutti wrung every last bit out of his life and only gave up playing when dismissed as a 43-year-old while also doubling as an Australian selector. For all his attributes off the pitch, however, it was on the pitch where "Wild Bill" Cerutti really did his talking. A huge man, his technique was also faultless, and he was never bettered in the set-piece. Cerutti began his career against the All Blacks in 1928, but it was his seven Tests against the South Africans – and the legendary prop Boy Louw in particular – which

really tested him; a test he passed when Louw insisted on moving sides to get away from the mad Italian-Australian. Indeed, the only regret Cerutti ever expressed about his rugby career, in which he won 21 caps, was that he missed out on tours to Britain in 1927 (too young) and 1939 (too old).

DON CLARKE
New Zealand 1956–64 (full-back)

To a generation of New Zealanders, Clarke was known simply as "The Boot", the full-back who would kick the goals to win the Test matches. Introduced into Test rugby halfway through the tempestuous 1956 series against South Africa, Clarke had the sort of impact that continued throughout his 31-Test career. In his first Test, the third against the Springboks, he scored eight points in New Zealand's 17–10 victory. From then until his retirement in 1964, Clarke missed only one Test, and that was because of injury. His most celebrated kicking display was in the First Test against the Lions in Dunedin in 1959 when the Lions scored four tries, but Clarke, with his straight-line, toe-kicking style, kicked a world record six penalties to ensure an All Black win. Clarke was more than just a kicking machine, however. He was big for a full-back and strong in the tackle or on forays into the backline, and he also had uncanny ball skills honed from his many years as a first-class cricketer. Colin Meads once remarked that Clarke had "unworldly" hands and was, without doubt, the best full-back of his generation. Clarke's brother Ian was a durable prop for New Zealand on both the 1953–54 and 1963–64 tours of the UK, Ireland and France and won three caps. Three other brothers all played rugby for Waikato, the five of them appearing in one game in 1961.

BERT COOKE
New Zealand 1924–30 (centre)

It was instructive that when the New Zealand Sports Hall of Fame was formed in 1990, one of the first rugby players to be inducted was Bert Cooke, even though few of the selectors had seen him play and none had the benefit of video archives to assess his undoubted brilliance. Cooke is still regarded as one of the finest backs to have played for New Zealand, though his career was brief by modern standards. On the 1924–25 Invincibles' tour of Britain and France, Cooke played in 25 of the 30 games and scored 23 tries, the highest tally. He continued that sort of form against New South Wales in 1926 but was unavailable for the All Blacks' tour of South Africa in 1928. The last of his eight appearances for New Zealand came in the Fourth Test against the British Isles in 1930, scoring two tries in the final Test. Cooke turned to Rugby League in 1932 and played for New Zealand against Great Britain and Australia. After the Invincibles' tour, Cooke was described in a booklet as the most brilliant back in the team: "As swift as a hare, as elusive as a shadow, strikes like lightning, flashes with brilliancy, Cooke is the shining star of the side."

GREG CORNELSON

Australia 1974–82 (No. 8)

Along with Mark Loane and Tony Shaw, Greg Cornelson formed one of the most outstanding back-rows in the history of Australian rugby. A tall rangy 6ft. 5in. No. 8, who was unstoppable at the back of the line-out, Cornelson had the ability to break tackles and make ground as he pinned his ears back – "they just used to bounce off me," he said of his early days. Generally regarded as one of the greatest natural athletes ever to pull on a Wallaby shirt, towards the end of his career Cornelson managed to add raw strength to the incredible fitness that had been his hallmark since he first emerged as a durable and hyperactive livewire back-rower in the early 1970s. From a sporting family (his father also played for Randwick), and with an impeccable sporting background himself – he excelled at athletics, cricket and swimming – Cornelson's promise was spotted early and, at the age of 17, he toured South Africa with his Wallaby representative age group. A member of the New South Wales Country side that beat both Sydney and Queensland in 1973, Cornelson

made his debut against the All Blacks in 1974 after Mark Loane broke his hand in the First Test. The Second Test was drawn and the Third lost as the All Blacks retained the Bledisloe Cup, but Cornelson achieved a unique feat four years later against the New Zealanders, when he scored an unprecedented four tries in Australia's 30–16 win over Auckland.

FRAN COTTON

England 1971–81 (prop)

Born and raised in Wigan, the heart of Rugby League country, Cotton's father and brother were noted professionals with Warrington, and Cotton's boyhood heroes were Rugby League legends Billy Boston and Bev Risman. Yet Cotton become a major force in Union as a player with England and the Lions, and as a businessman (he owned Cotton Traders, who at one stage supplied kit to half of the world's top national sides). He was also chosen to be the 1997 manager of the British Lions' tour to South Africa. At 6ft. 2in. and over 17stones, he had all the raw materials for a prop, but it was his innate strength, inner drive and technical appreciation that helped him accumulate 31 caps. One of the fittest play-

ers of his generation, Cotton was also one of the most versatile and because of his technical acumen became as proficient on the tight-head as he was on his more accustomed loose-head. Cotton's top-level career began as a 23-year-old when he led the North to a famous victory over the 1972 All Blacks at Otley – the first time an English province had beaten the All Blacks. Over the next decade, until his retirement in 1981 after an on-field heart attack, Cotton was a central figure in British rugby. The first choice Lions tight-head in South Africa in 1974, Cotton also played three of the four Tests in New Zealand in 1977 as a loose-head, andd returned to South Africa with the 1980 Lions' tour.

D

BENOIT DAUGA

France 1964–72 (No. 8)

Nicknamed the "Big Brother" and once described by Jean Prat as the best forward produced by French

BENOIT DAUGA *"Big Brother"*

rugby, Benoit Dauga governed the aerial battles of the 1960s and early 1970s with an iron hand, both figuratively and literally. The rugby writers had run out of metaphors to describe the 6ft. 5in. colossus: the strongest, most gifted, fastest, most astute, hardest, most perceptive, meanest. All were true. A uniquely talented player, and one that the peerless Mervyn Davies described as the best No. 8 he ever played against, the Mont de Marsan utility forward won the first of his 63 caps against Scotland in 1964. Despite losing 10–0 in Edinburgh, Dauga retained his position in the side right through until the 1968 Grand Slam. After that, however, while still in the side, the French hit a mini-trough, a 2–0 series defeat against the All Blacks starting an undreamt-of run of seven consecutive losses. Dauga became captain of France in the Second Test in South Africa in 1971 and skippered his country in six consecutive Tests before his last international selection, against Wales in Cardiff in 1972, brought to an end one of the most remarkable careers in international rugby. Having played in every position in the second row and back row, Dauga would have gone on to win more caps had it not been for a running row with incoming captain and No. 8, Walter Spanghero, who immediately dispensed with Dauga's services.

GERALD DAVIES

Wales 1966–78 (wing)

Gerald Davies was unquestionably the finest Welsh wing of the modern era, a player of such style, verve and potency that he was one of the main-

MUD MAN *England and Lions' prop Fran Cotton.*

GERALD DAVIES *Poetry in motion.*

into Welsh rugby just as it began to enter a prolonged period of darkness. With expectations still high from the successes of the 1970s and early 1980s, results became increasingly hard to fashion out. Third place in the 1987 World Cup erroneously convinced many in Wales that the game was in a healthy state. A semi-final 49–6 thrashing by the eventual winners New Zealand was repeated the following year when the touring Welsh were humiliated 52–3 and 54–9 in a two-Test whitewash. With constant carping and finger-pointing by top andminstrators, Davies became increasingly disillusioned and left for Widnes Rugby League club at the end of 1988. Once in League, Davies prospered. His creativity, good hands,

pace and wonderfully accurate kicking stood him in good stead for both Widnes and Great Britain, and once he bulked up to become a better defender he became one of League's greats. With the move to professionalism in 1995, Davies was lured back to Cardiff RFC, seven years after his switch. Despite his advanced age of 33, he won three more caps and played against England in 1997 in the last major international to be staged at Cardiff Arm's Park.

MERVYN DAVIES
Wales 1969–76 (No. 8)

Although he later became quite possibly the best No. 8 Britain has ever produced, Mervyn Davies started his career in inauspicious circumstances

MERYVN DAVIES *Merv-the-Swerve*

stays of the outstanding Welsh sides of the 1970s. Along with Gareth Edwards, Phil Bennett, J.J. Williams and J.P.R. Williams, Davies formed the backbone of one of the most outstanding back divisions ever seen as the men in red dominated the British rugby scene in the 1970s. Blessed with outstanding pace and a lethal sidestep, Davies began international life as a centre before switching to wing during the 1969 tour of New Zealand. The effect was mesmerizing. Given extra space and time, Davies gave full rein to his creativity and sheer speed becoming one of the most effective and feared finishers in world rugby. By the time he retired in 1978, he had scored 20 tries in 46 internationals. At the his peak, with the British Lions in 1971, Davies destroyed New Zealand defences, and was one of the most impressive components of the best back line ever to leave Britain. Had he not declined to tour in 1974 or '77, he would undoubtedly have become the Lions' most capped winger. A quiet, thoughtful academic, Davies is now a rugby correspondent for *The Times*.

JONATHAN DAVIES
Wales 1985–97 (fly-half)

A gifted young fly-half in the classic Welsh mould, Jonathan Davies came

PRODIGAL SON *Welsh fly-half Jonathan Davies returned to the Union fold in 1997 after almost a decade as a League star.*

as a 22-year-old when he arrived at London Welsh unheralded and with no rugby pedigree. Quality will out, however, and within three months, "Merv the Swerve" was in the Wales side which defeated Scotland 17–3 at Murrayfield. He went on to win 38 caps for Wales - captaining them to a Grand Slam in 1976 - and eight for the Lions, before a brain haemorrhage in a 1976 Schweppes Cup semi-final tie put him out of rugby forever and almost killed him. By modern standards Davies' 6ft. 4in. physique wasn't awe-inspiring, but his strength and athleticism compensated for his lack of bulk. Moreover, Davies was a Great precisely because he allied his incredible physical talents with an almost unprecedented degree of foresight which allowed him to overcome virtually the only flaw in his make-up, a lack of really top gear acceleration. As effective in attack as in defence, Davies added an extra dimension to the line-out play of both Wales and the British Lions. In fact, both New Zealand's Colin Meads and South Africa's Morné du Plessis identified Davies' contribution at the back of the line-out as one of the biggest single reasons why the Lions' backs received such a limitless amount of quality ball from the set-piece in 1971 and 1974.

TERRY DAVIES
Wales 1953–61 (full-back)

A natural footballer who was technically superb, Davies was safe under the high ball, a sure tackler, positionally faultless and a touch-finder of prodigious length and reliability. In addition, he was also a goal-kicker of much repute, and throughout a nine-year international career he was a consistent scorer for Wales. He started off as he meant to continue, stroking over a penalty on his debut against England at Twickenham in 1953, and scoring in each of the remaining Five Nations games that season. A big player for his time and position (Davies was almost 6ft. and weighed over 14 stone), the Llanelli man was nevertheless very prone to injury and as soon as he had established himself in the Wales side disaster struck when he picked up a career-threatening shoulder injury in Bucharest as he was tackled into a concrete support. After a rehabilitation of four years and several operations to pin the joint, Davies rejoined the fray, almost inspiring Wales to a famous victory at Twickenham in 1958 when a 50-yard kick into the wind bounced back off the crossbar. The pre-eminent full-back of the 1950s, Davies was also an inspirational captain and revelled in that role for Wales in 1960 and 1961. A winner of 21 caps for Wales, Davies also won two Lions' caps on the 1959 tour of New Zealand.

WILLIAM DAVIES

Wales 1936–39 (full-back)

William Thomas Harcourt Davies made a sensational start to top class rugby when, at fly-half outside his cousin Haydn Tanner, he orchestrated Swansea's defeat of the 1935 All Blacks. The pair were just 19-years-old at the time, provoking New Zealand captain Jack Manchester to write home, saying "You can say we lost, but just don't say we were beaten by two schoolboys." The Gowerton Grammar School pair created two tries for Wales skipper Claude Davey as New Zealand's defence was split by what a visiting journalist called "sensation-making runs." Unfortunately for Davies, his Union career coincided with that of Cliff Jones and he was selected for only six matches from 1936 until 1939, with one at centre and the rest at fly-half. Though his international appearances

came mainly when Jones or Davey were either injured or taking exams, Davies did score the try and drop goal that beat Ireland 7–0 in the final match before the War and service in the RAF intervened. Davies turned professional with Bradford Northern in August 1939 and continued to play until 1950, appearing in Challenge Cup finals in 1944, 45, 47, 48 and 49, being on the winning side three times. Honours continued for this quiet but elusive runner as he won three caps for Great Britain on the 1947 tour of Australasia and played on nine occasions for Wales.

W.J.A. DAVIES

England 1913–23 (fly-half)

W.J.A. (widely known as "Dave") Davies won 22 caps as an outside half and was only once on the losing side (against South Africa in 1913). Born in Wales in Pembroke, he played on eight occasions before World War One interrupted his progress. During the war, Davies served with distinction in the Navy before resuming his career at the conclusion of hostilities. He played club rugby for RNEC Keyham, RNC Greenwich and United Services Portsmouth, and county matches for Hampshire; he appeared for England/Wales in the 1923 Centenary Match at Rugby School. Davies had begun as a dockyard apprentice in his home town of Pembroke but turned his back on Wales soon afterwards and at Greenwich won the Champions Cup as the best athlete of the year. An unselfish player adept at getting the best out of his three-quarters, he also scored four international tries and dropped three goals, the last coming left-footed against France in the closing moments of his final appearance. Renowned for his touchfinding, Davies was a clever runner with room to move thanks to the length of scrum-half Cyril Kershaw's passes in one of the greatest partnerships in English history. Davies wrote *"Rugby Football"* and *"Rugby Football – How to play it"* in 1922 and 1923 respectively and after retirement became the president of the Civil Service RFC. A teetotaller and fine athlete who always kept in the best of shape, he later

received an OBE.

CLAUDE DAVEY

Wales 1930–38 (centre)

One of the finest tacklers of his or any other era, Swansea centre Claude Davey was one of the mainstays for Wales throughout the 1930s, and proved himself an inspirational captain for both club and country. In fact, Davey shares a unique distinction with Cardiff's Bleddyn Williams: that of having beaten the All Blacks for both club and country. The 11–3 defeat at the hands of Davey's Swansea in 1935 was the first time that the All Blacks had ever been beaten by a club side, and Davey was a major contributory factor, scoring two tries and spreading panic in the All Black ranks with several crushing tackles. It was a combination which Davey was to use to great effect when the full international dawned. In tandem with the great Wilf Wooller, Davey launched himself at the All Blacks in defence, and ran straight and hard in attack, again being rewarded with a try as Wales ran out 13–12 victors. Davey had a justifiable reputation as a try-scorer with 22 for Swansea in the season when he made his international debut against France in 1930. He even managed to score in Swansea's narrow 10–3 defeat at the hands of Bennie Osler's unbeaten Springbok tourists of 1931–32 (a match described by Danie Craven as the dirtiest game of rugby he ever played in). By the time Davey retired aged 29 after winning 23 caps, he had undoutedly established himself as one of the Greats of Welsh rugby.

EUGENE DAVY

Ireland 1925–34 (fly-half)

In the days before crash ball centres had even appeared on the horizon, chunky Lansdowne fly-half Eugene Davy was lighting a way for the crash ball fly-half. From the time that Davy made his first appearance in an Ireland shirt in the 19–3 win over Wales at Ravenhill in 1925, he became one of the most feared opponents in international rugby. Davy was not just physically intimidating, but he was

also surprisingly fast and would launch himself into his opposite fly-half during a time when there was no drift defence and before it was assumed that the back-row would cover. With his strong physique, acute sense of timing and total commitment, Davy was also a good man to have alongside you if your team was on the back foot. Equally effective in the centre where he played many of his 34 Tests, Davy was as expert in setting up team-mates as he was in running up his personal try tally (which probably explains why fellow Lansdowne and Ireland centre Jack Arigho still holds the Irish record for the most tries scored in an international season, five – from three matches – during the 1927–28 Championship winning season).

RONNIE DAWSON

Ireland 1958–64 (hooker)

As a player Ronnie Dawson was a perfectionist. A fine footballer, Dawson was fast in the loose, a spot-on line-out thrower and a formidable scrummager. A relative latecomer to Test rugby at 26, the hooker had to wait in line behind the great Karl Mullen and Robin Roe until he finally made his Test debut in the 9–6 victory over Australia at Lansdowne Road in 1958, but he went on to collect 27 caps. For good measure, Dawson scored the winning try in this win, Ireland's first over a touring side. Dawson enjoyed the finest moments of his career against the Australians and the next time he met the Wallabies it was as captain of the 1959 British Lions touring party; an amazingly rapid promotion given that he had made his international debut a year earlier. With the all-Irish front-row of Dawson, Syd Millar and Gordon Wood (father of current Ireland hooker Keith) dominant, Australia were overwhelmed 17–6 and 24–3 in two torrid Tests. The Lions could not keep up the momentum when they moved on to New Zealand, winning only one of the four Tests. Dawson himself was a tremendous success both on and off the pitch, gaining the trust of both his players and the New Zealand public, while also performing miracles on the pitch – par-

HAWICK HOOKER *Colin Deans, one of Scotland's 1984 Grand Slam winners.*

ticularly in the tight, where he reportedly took over 30 strikes against the head in his 19 games on tour.

HENRY OSWALD DE VILLIERS

South Africa 1967–70 (full-back)

Henry Oswald de Villiers, or "HO" to his hordes of admirers, would probably have established himself as the greatest in a long line of marvellous Springbok full-backs but for a serious knee injury that ended his career aged 25. Even despite the setback, though, the dark-haired De Villiers did enough in 14 Tests to vie for that accolade, scoring tries that were unbelievable for stunning strength and vision from deep-lying defence. He was brave and immovable under the high ball and a fearless tackler. An added goal-kicking gift made him the complete footballer. Rugby skills came easily to this product of famous Dale College in King Williams Town, a conveyor belt for many fine South African sportsmen. De Villiers crowned his Test debut against the French in 1967 with a sparkling display in a 26–3 victory. He was one of seven new Springbok caps that day and one of the nucleus of the team which was to carry South Africa into an exciting era in the 1970s prior to Apartheid-induced world sports isolation. Blessed with a desire to attack from anywhere, De Villiers never neglected his defensive work and some of his finger tip catches under fierce pressure during the UK tour of 1969–70 made him the individual star. Then came the knee calamity and it was all over by 25.

COLIN DEANS

Scotland 1978–87 (hooker)

In the Border town of Hawick, where hooker Colin Deans played rugby from the time he cut his teeth as a pupil of famous commentator Bill McLaren's at the local primary school, to the day he eventually hung up his boots up 52 caps later, he was always considered a bit on the slight side. Yet as the prototype for the faster hooker, acting as an extra flanker that has since emerged, Deans has few equals. Superb in the loose and a wonderfully quick striker of the ball at the scrum, the rugged Deans was also a pinpoint line-out thrower (despite the fact that Derrick Grant tried to persuade the young Deans that he should leave throwing-in to the wingers). But if Deans was to enjoy numerous highs with Scotland – the pinnacle being the 1984 Grand Slam – then it was with the Lions who toured New Zealand in 1983 that he endured his greatest low. To almost universal surprise, new Irish hooker Ciaran Fitzgerald was selected as tour captain, and Deans, despite playing the better rugby, had to sit out the series on the replacements' bench as the Lions were whitewashed 4-0..

AMÉDÉE DOMENECH

France 1954–63 (prop)

Identified when a young player, Domenech played prop for the French Juniors and then graduated to became a regular of the French teams in the mid-1950s. Nicknamed "The Duke", Domenech won a total of 52 caps in his career and has the unique distinction of appearing as a wing three-quarter against England in 1961. With Dupuy carried off injured – at the time no replacements were allowed – French captain Francois Moncla summoned Domenech to take over the right wing berth and keep an eye on Harlequins speedster JRC Young. Despite a barrage of up-and-unders from England fly-half Richard Sharp, the veteran prop did not flinch. He fielded every ball, cleared to touch and tackled like a demon. Celaya and Bourgoyn took turns at loose-head prop and France drew 5–5 to win the Five Nations. Domenech commenced his club career with Narbonne, but was playing for RC Vichy when he was selected to win his first cap against Wales in 1954. In Domenech's first season France won three of the four Championship matches under the captaincy of Jean Prat and shared the Five Nations with Wales and England for the first time ever. He missed the early games in 1963 due to a shoulder injury, and returned to international action in the last game of the season against Wales on March 23. The following game, in which the French pack was completely dominated by a formidable set of Italian forwards, with France scraping home to a lucky 14–12 win, convinced him to call it a day.

CAREL DU PLESSIS

South Africa 1982–89 (wing)

Carel du Plessis was one of three Springbok brothers to play for South Africa. In fact he played his first two Tests with brother Willie and his last six with brother Michael, the third time that three brothers have represented South Africa on the rugby field. The others were the Luyts of 1910–13 (Freddie, Dick, John) and the Bekkers of 1951–60 (Jaap, Dolf, Martiens). An attacking wing of pace and subtlety, Carel Du Plessis made his international debut against the South American Jaguars in 1982 and became one of the backline giants of his time. Most of his rugby was played for Western Province apart from one unhappy season without their wing wizard. In a career of 12 Tests his contemporaries rated Du Plessis as the "most complete footballer" and it was one of the great sadnesses that he had such a limited span (1982–89) because of South Africa's isolation. If Jannie Engelbrecht had earlier won the title of "Prince of Wings", Carel du Plessis was equally a rugby blue-blood, a remarkable footballer in a remarkable family. In February 1997, Du Plessis renewed his commection with the Springboks when he took over as coach replacing Andre Markgraaf who had resigned in disgrace following alleged rascist comments.

MORNÉ DU PLESSIS

South Africa 1971–80 (No. 8)

Western Province No.8 Morné du Plessis comes from good sporting stock. His father Felix captained the Springboks against the 1949 All Blacks, his mother was a hockey international and his uncle, Horace Smethurst, led the South African soccer team on a tour of Australia soon after WWII. So it was hardly surprising that the rangy No.8 would follow in his father's footsteps. He won the first of his 22 caps against Australia in 1971 before being handed the captaincy and leading South Africa to a 3–1 series win against New Zealand in 1976. His finest hour came in 1980 as the Springboks trounced the touring British Lions. A wise, thoughtful and committed player whose 6ft. 5in. frame was immensely valuable at the back of the line-out, Du Plessis's retirement from the game at all levels just as he seemed set to lead South Africa on the turbulent New Zealand tour of 1981, left a huge void, Since his playing days in Springbok rugby, Du Plessis has made an impact as manager of the Springboks, notably during the 1995 World Cup when worked alongside coach Kitch Christie.

FRIK DU PREEZ

South Africa 1960–71 (lock)

Big Frik du Preez was a larger than life figure whose legend looms large among South Africa's rugby followers even now. The second row amassed 38 Test appearances in his international career, beating the 1968 Lions almost single-handedly and setting a record for appearances since equalled only by flanker Jan Ellis. His total of six overseas tours, which started in 1961 and stretched for the next twelve seasons, is also a record and he wore the famous jersey an unprecedented 87 times. Yet while Du Preez set impressive statistics and records, they never matched the impressiveness of the man himself. One of the most cherished images in Springbok rugby is of Du Preez bursting through, ball in one hand, his giant strides carrying his powerful frame at a deceptively fast pace, a mop of black hair flopping in the wind. His greatness has been established beyond all doubt, though a few detractors would point to a lazy streak in his make-up that hinted at his marvel-

lous sense of humour and relaxed attitude to life off the pitch. It is frightening to imagine what heights he might have scaled had he possessed the dour uncompromising attitude to rugby of some of the other giants of the game. He eventually sought fulfilment in a farming life in the semi-desert of the Kalahari.

DAVID DUCKHAM

England 1969-76 (wing)
*(See **The Legends of Rugby**, pages 108-09)*

WILLIE DUGGAN

Ireland 1975–84 (No. 8)

Rarely can one man have spawned more anecdotes than the back-rower from Kilkenny, Willie Duggan. Every contemporary to have laced up boots in the Emerald Isle seems to have a stock of stories about this legend-in-his-lifetime, a man whose off-field feats appear as famous as those on it. That is some going, for Duggan was one of the most fearless, passionate players ever to play for Ireland. From the time that he pulled on the Ireland shirt in the famous win over England in 1975, Duggan careered around world rugby fields with a wanton abandon that made him one of the least popular opponents of all time.

A large man with famously huge hands – his nickname was "spade hands" – Duggan was noted for his storming runs and committed tackling. A useful line-out forward, Duggan had a quick temper is remembered for his role in a punch-up between the Welsh and Irish packs in 1977 that saw both him and Geoff Wheel dismissed. In tandem with the lightning-quick Fergus Slattery and the more cerebral talents of the great blind-side John O'Driscoll, Duggan completed an extremely effective back-row trio. In 41 caps for Ireland and four for the 1977 Lions in New Zealand, the "Blackrock bomber" established himself as the epitome of the Irish back-rower. As wholehearted as Bill McKay, Duggan was also as skilful as Jimmy Farrell. Almost as famously, he was also notoriously genial and popular when the after-match festivities began.

JOHN EALES

Australia 1991– (lock)

One of the most complete second-rowers of all time, John Eales burst onto the international scene in 1991 and later that year had a World Cup winner's medal to show for his efforts. Since then, despite a break for a shoulder injury in 1993, Eales has continued to develop into the best lock in the world. At 6ft. 7in., he is not particularly tall for an international level lock, yet combines sublime timing with an impressive standing jump to dominate taller opponents at the line-out – England's Martin Bayfield, for instance, was completely outplayed when the two first met in 1991 despite the fact that Bayfield stands 6ft. 10in. tall, while Eales counts New Zealand's Ian Jones his trickiest opponent. Hugely mobile in the loose, Eales is also a genuinely talented footballer who has taken to acting as a stand-in place-kicker at Test level with a remarkable degree of accuracy (he boasted a 100 per cent success rate during the 1991 World Cup, making two conversions from the touchline). Now firmly in place as the Wallaby captain, Eales will be only 29 at the

1999 World Cup and when World Cup 2003 comes around don't bet against the Queensland lock being present.

GARETH EDWARDS

Wales 1967–78 (scrum-half)

In his 53 caps for Wales over 12 years and ten Lions caps over three tours, Edwards proved himself the best scrum-half ever to play in the northern hemisphere and only Australian Ken Catchpole has ever been referred to in the same breath as Edwards by contemporaries. An accomplished gymnast and sprinter, Edwards had great upper body strength and pace to burn off a standing start, as he showed when scoring *that* memorable try for the Barbarians against the 1973 All Blacks. A Welsh cap at 19, a Lion and captain of Wales at the tender age of 20, by the time Edwards came of age he had already established himself as a world-class No. 9, even if many of his Lions team-mates on the 1968 tour of South Africa considered him "selfish and inclined to keep the good ball for himself" in the words of South African writer Chris Greyvenstein. Yet Edwards was nothing if not eager to learn and soon became the complete player, whether in the colours of Cardiff, the Lions or Wales. In 1971 he was outstanding in New Zealand alongside Barry John, while in 1974 he was at his imperious best in South Africa partnering Phil Bennett. Edwards combined

WHO CAN STOP A MAN LIKE THIS? *Gareth Edwards taunts the Blue Bulls.*

MARK ELLA *Aussie master fly-half.*

remarkable strength with incredible physical resilience – he won all 53 of his Welsh caps without missing a game. Robust in defence, Edwards had superb balance, remarkable hands and was a master of the grubber kick. His tally of 20 tries has only been bettered by Ieuan Evans.

MARK ELLA
Australia 1980–84 (fly-half)

It is perhaps one of rugby's greatest tragedies that Mark Ella retired aged just 25 after winning only 25 caps. Probably the most naturally gifted fly-half the game has ever seen, Ella had just reached the peak of his powers, leading the hugely entertaining Wallaby side of 1984 on an unbeaten Grand Slam tour of Britain. Had Ella carried on playing, he may well have become the most accomplished player the game has ever seen, and his decision to retire prematurely caused widespread consternation throughout the rugby world. One of three Aboriginal brothers to play for the Wallabies, Mark Ella was discovered by Randwick coach Bob Dwyer – now in charge at Leicester – and drafted into the first grade – along with his twin Glen and younger brother Gary – at just 17. Using looping moves they had perfected as schoolboys, the three brothers revo-

lutionized back play at the top Sydney club, introducing the flat back line that has since been adopted by the Wallabies as something akin to a national style. Standing unusually close to the scrum-half and moving the ball quickly, Ella developed a style of playing virtually on the gain line that brought results at Test level as spectacular as when he first used them in the Under-15s.

JAN ELLIS
South Africa 1965–76 (flanker)

Raised in the vast emptiness of South West Africa (now Namibia), flame-haired flanker Jan Ellis was a highly individualistic loner who preferred to sit with a book or write a letter home while on tour. An aloof man who alienated many in South West Africa for his perceived brusque manner, the social side of rugby, after-match functions and partying, were not for the man they called "Red Devil". A rangy flanker best remembered for his surprisingly fast loping run, ball held arrogantly in one hand, mowing a path through would-be-tacklers, Ellis is regarded as one of the best flankers ever to play for South Africa. Ellis played hard, and he played to win: to a man as focused as he was, everything except winning was superfluous. Ellis was lucky in that through-

JAN ELLIS *The "Red Devil".*

out his 12 straight years as a Springbok regular after his debut against the All Blacks in 1965, his two usual back-row partners shared his playing philosophy, making the loose forward trio of Ellis, Piet Greyling and Tommy Bedford an outstanding one. Ellis worked in marvellous tandem in 24 Tests with Greyling on the blindside, twelve of those with Bedford at No. 8 and won 38 Test caps, a record he still holds with Frik du Preez

JANNIE ENGELBRECHT
South Africa 1960–69 (wing)

The "Prince of Wings", in full flight Jannie Engelbrecht was a truly awesome sight to behold, running with the ball tucked under his right arm with his head tilted at a slight angle, a high-knee action eating up the ground. As if mesmerizing would-be tacklers, the pacy swerve took him to the bulk of his eight tries in 33 Tests, although his detractors always suggested this was too sparse a return for a player of his undoubted pedigree. Seldom, however, did they pay more than lip service to the brilliant corner-flagging cover defence that prevented as many tries as he scored. Engelbrecht played all his rugby at Stellenbosch, in the country's hotbed of backline play, where he came under the wing of his lifelong mentor, Dr Danie Craven. His record of 33 Tests for a wing has only recently been equalled by James Small. After being a permanent right wing fixture, unless injured, Engelbrecht played his last Test against the touring Australians in 1969 and missed the demonstration-marred tour to Britain later that year. He turned successfully to administration and is currently president of the Stellenbosch club. His sojourn as a successful Springbok team manager, however, ended in acrimony after a messy public dispute with SARFU president Dr Louis Luyt.

ERIC EVANS
England 1948–58 (hooker)

Eric Evans was a late starter who won his first cap as a hooker against Australia in 1948 at the age of 26, but failed to impress and only managed to regain his place in the England

starting line-up – this time back in his proper position of hooker – for a solitary Test against Wales in 1950, before becoming a fixture from 1951 until his retirement in 1958. As a player, Evans was extremely fit and his shock of blond hair was a regular feature of three-quarter movements and the early stages of any breakdown. Yet he was also one of the finest hookers England have ever possessed, particularly in the days when suppleness and flexibility were vital as the props went nose to ground as often as possible. An exuberant man both on and off the pitch, Evan's leadership style was to expect every man to follow his example or expect a tongue-lashing if they didn't. It was not always popular, but it was effective: as early as 1948 Evans led Lancashire to a 5–0 victory in the County Championship final, while his record as England captain in 13 of his 30 internationals was outstanding and included a Grand Slam in 1957.

IEUAN EVANS
Wales 1987– (wing)

It is a measure of the class of Llanelli, Wales and British Lions wing Ieuan Evans that he has been able to prove his undoubted quality despite his international career coinciding with the worst period Wales have ever had to endure. Indeed, Evans' career started in 1987, the year when a crushing World Cup defeat at the hands of the All Blacks brought Wales's decline into stark relief, and it con-

THE SURVIVOR *Ieuan Evans.*

135

tinued through horror spots such as the 1988 whitewash tour to New Zealand, the 1991 drubbings in Australia and the World Cups of 1991 and 1995. Worse still, injuries – particularly one to his shoulder – hampered his progress, yet Evans is Wales's most devoted servants, its longest-serving captain and most capped player. Modest and ever pleasant, Evans has been as constant off the pitch as he has been on it. A solid defender, the Llanelli wing is outstandingly quick, and possesses a shimmy that has helped him score a record 32 tries in his 71-Test career, another Welsh record. Evans has a hat-trick of Lion's tours.

NICK FARR-JONES
Australia 1984–93 (scrum-half)

During the decade between his first and last caps, Sydney University scrum-half Nick Farr-Jones dominated the world of scrum-halves. Australia's most capped scrum-half with 63 caps, Farr-Jones was also a natural leader, who took a young Wallaby side to the World Cup final in 1991 where they beat hosts England. By the time Farr-Jones arrived at Sydney University as a law student, it

was obvious that he had all the attributes needed by the modern scrum-half. Tall and exceptionally strong, Farr-Jones played in attack and defence like an extra back-row forward. Alan Jones recognized Farr-Jones's potential and drafted him into the national squad in 1984, at the age of 22. He was impressive on that year's Grand Slam tour of Britain; his quick brain, slick service and ability to take the pressure off Mark Ella were major contributors to the whitewash, and he remained a fixture in the Wallaby side until his retirement in 1993. Controversially made captain in 1988, Farr-Jones formed an inspirational management team off the pitch, alongside coach Bob Dwyer, and he played a major part in the radical reshaping of the Wallaby pack following the physical battering and series defeat inflicted by the all-conquering Lions in 1989.

JIMMY FARRELL
Ireland 1926–32 (second row)

Dublin strongman Jimmy Farrell built up a reputation as a bit of a crazed bull let loose in a porcelain shop during the six years and 34 caps he careered around the Test venues of the world as a fierce Robin to George Beamish's Batman. Yet that reputation belied an immensely skilled footballer who was marked by an intense, single-minded pursuit of victory. A second-row of vision, Farrell was part of the formidable Irish pack of the late 1920s, where he toiled alongside men such as Beamish, the teak tough Jim McVicker and the great Jammie Clinch, and took a key part in the great dribbling rushes common at the time. A fine line-out operator, Farrell's supply of ball was one of the main reasons behind Ireland topping the Five Nations back-to-back in 1926 and 1927. A unstintingly abrasive yet talented player, Farrell gained much of his strength from manual labour on his Leinster farm, but could also claim to be one of the first truly conscientious trainers. Well-liked and laid back off the pitch, Farrell was a popular tourist with the 1930 Lions to New Zealand and Australia, a tour on which he played in all five Tests.

DRIVING FORCE *Sean Fitzpatrick, the most capped All Black of all time.*

SEAN FITZPATRICK
New Zealand 1986– (hooker)

New Zealand rugby's most durable forward who, by the end of the 1996 season, had played in 83 Tests, a record for New Zealand. But more significant than the statistics is his competitiveness, a dedication to fitness and his technical skills that keep younger challengers and opponents at bay. Fitzpatrick, the son of 1953–54 All Black Brian Fitzpatrick, had a fortuitous All Black debut in 1986. Most of the leading All Blacks had been suspended for their rebel tour to South Africa and the original choice for the Test against France was injured, so he was called in as a late replacement. It was the beginning of an extraordinary career and there was more luck for Fitzpatrick, when the All Blacks' World Cup captain in 1987, hooker Andy Dalton, was injured and Fitzpatrick went from the prospect of a Cup as understudy to playing in every match. Fitzpatrick took over the captaincy of New Zealand in 1992 and, despite leading them to the 1995 World Cup final, considered the effort a failure such is his desire to be a

winner. Driven by an ambition to become the first New Zealander to win a Test series in South Africa, Fitzpatrick stayed on as captain for the 1996 season and achieved his dream in August of that year when the All Blacks took the series 2–1.

GRANT FOX
New Zealand 1985–93 (fly-half)

Grant Fox was a scoring machine for New Zealand in his 46 Tests in the 1980s and 1990s and the All Blacks

SCRUM-HALF KING *Nick Farr-Jones*

DEAD-EYE *All Black Grant Fox.*

many times had reason to be grateful for his presence. For all the goal-kicking records Fox holds it would be a mistake to dismiss him as just a goalkicker, however gifted. He was a perfectionist and a tactician, advising and cajoling the backs, planning moves and then ensuring their accurate execution; and he was seen as the brains of the All Black backline. New Zealand coaches found they could not do without him. John Hart, when he first coached the All Blacks on a tour of Japan in 1987, dropped Fox and Laurie Mains, when he took over in 1992, also tried other fly-halves, but Fox proved to be as indispensible as it's possible for a rugby player to be. Fox made his All Black debut on the 1985 Argentina tour and became the regular fly-half in the 1987 World Cup, remaining one of the dominant figures for the All Blacks.

JEAN GACHASSIN
France 1961–69 (utility back)

Jean Gachassin was one of the most gifted and versatile three-quarters of the 1960s. He made his international debut at the age of 20 against Scotland and retired somewhat prematurely at the age of 28 after winning 32 caps. His devastating pace and brisk side-step, combined with a high level of skill and unusual intuition, made him one of France's trump cards during this decade. However, it took him a while to establish his credentials in the highly competitive French set-up, and he never fully established himself in any one position, playing at wing as well as fly-half, centre and full-back in his eight-year international career. Gachassin started his club career with Vichy, and after a spell with Bagnerre, he joined Lourdes with whom he won the French Championship in 1968. Throughout his playing days, Gachassin was known as "Peter Pan", a reference to his diminutive physique; he stood 5ft. 4in. tall and tipped the scales at

a modest 10stone. Yet what he lacked in physical presence he more than made up for in courage. On retirement he became coach of the Stade de Bagneres club.

JOHN GAINSFORD
South Africa 1960–67 (centre)

Call it the killer instinct, call it what you will: John Gainsford had that controlled fury and deep burning desire to win, and carried them into big matches like a boxing champion stepping into the ring. Those qualities turned the big thrusting centre into the best in the world in his heyday, which was to stretch for seven years from his debut in 1960 against Scotland. He notched up eight scorching tries, two of them in the miracle of Christchurch in 1965 when Gainsford helped turn a 16–5 half-time deficit into an unlikely 19–16 South African win over the All Blacks, until the selectors decided he had lost his cutting edge and dropped him for the final Test of the winning series against the French in 1967. After playing 71 matches for South Africa, scoring 31 tries, 17 of those on the tour of Britain and France in 1960–61, the heavily-built 6ft. 1in. wing felt embittered about being discarded mid-series and never played for the Springboks again. He continued to captain Western Province, and later went on to be a successful wine producer on the Cape.

JEAN GALIA
France 1927–31 (lock)

One of the most talented players of his era, Jean Galia had also been the amateur heavyweight champion of France before turning his pugilistic bent to better use in French club rugby. A teak-hard second row who won 20 caps and a Championship medal with Quillan, Galia failed to fulfil his immense potential after he joined the Villeneuve club in 1932 and was suspended for life for allegedly offering a financial inducement to a player to join Villeneuve. Bitter for being made a scapegoat for what was the current practice in French rugby, he joined the Rugby League and became a dual international, winning five international caps

for France. In 1934 Galia was instrumental in bringing the French Rugby League team on tour to England where he revelled in his role as selector, trainer and captain. The French rugby union authorities, however, never forgave him for what they perceived to be an act of treachery.

TIM GAVIN
Australia 1988– (No. 8)

Tim Gavin will long be remembered as one of the most effective Wallaby forwards of the modern era, a workhorse No. 8 who learned his trade the hard way, playing lock in his early internationals. Although already a Wallaby by the time the 1989 Lions came to town, Gavin was yet another player to benefit from the series defeat which effectively marked the end of rival back rower Steve Tuynman's Test career. After that Gavin was a regular fixture with both New South Wales and Australia, becoming as much of a talisman for the Wallabies as Dean Richards became for England. In fact, Gavin rates his much-vaunted performance in the 40–15 defeat of England shortly before the 1991 World Cup as his greatest moment, because it saw him eclipse the great Englishman who had been the hammer of the Wallabies two years earlier while wearing a Lions shirt. The accolades for that game – and indeed for his monumental effort against the Springboks in 1993 – are perhaps all the more significant 1991 because Gavin missed out on a World Cup winners medal through injury. At 6ft. 5in., Gavin was always a threat at the line-out, while his huge upper-body strength always made him a presence at breakdown.

SIMON GEOGHEGAN
Ireland 1991– (wing)

Once memorably described as "Bambi on Benzedrine", London Irish and Bath wing Simon Geoghegan became celebrated for the manic energy he oozed as he waited in vain for the ball. However, it came infrequently during Ireland's dismally barren patch in the early 1990s when it seemed that Geoghegan was lucky to receive the ball more than once a

BAMBI *Ireland's Simon Geoghegan*

game. Yet that only served to make him all the keener to go and find it, and one of the familiar sights of the Five Nations in recent years has been the blond winger piling into a breakdown looking for the ball. Big, quick and extremely aggressive, the young Geoghegan had an appetite for work that marked him out as a winger in the mould of Tony O'Reilly 30 years before. Defensively suspect – he missed out on selection for the Lions to New Zealand in 1993 after Scotland's Derek Stark cruised round him for a dramatic score that led to Scotland's 15–3 win – Geoghegan has been one of the great folk heroes of Irish rugby in an age when it desperately needs them.

DANIE GERBER
South Africa 1980–92 (centre)

From the time he made an impression on Bill Beaumont's 1980 touring British Lions as a 22-year-old Junior Springbok, Daniel Mattheus Gerber, better known to the rugby world simply as Danie, was destined to make his mark. After 24 Tests and a South African record 19 tries, Gerber was regarded as one of the great-

BOK BOMBER *Centre Danie Gerber.*

est backs of the modern era, scoring tries that few others could emulate. His blistering speed, allied to huge piston-like thighs, made him hard to tackle and there were many memorable efforts among his tally for the Springboks. He scored a hat-trick of tries in the 35–9 Second Test win over John Scott's England side at Ellis Park in 1984, exhibiting the startling quickness off the mark, magnificent co-ordination and ability to maintain speed over a distance which made him such a feared opponent. Gerber's Test career was marked by his partnerships in midfield with two brothers, Willie and Michael du Plessis. He played in eight Tests with the former and six with youngest brother Michael. A natural athlete, Gerber turned, on his rugby retirement, to working as a sports organizer and coach among the disadvantaged peoples of Port Elizabeth and retains his keen interest in all sports.

SCOTT GIBBS
Wales 1991– (centre)

A formidably abrasive powerhouse centre with a crunching tackle and an ability to consistently cross the gainline, Scott Gibbs is one of the finest backs to have come out of Wales since the halcyon days of the late 1970s. Although Gibbs came into a side demoralized by a poor run of results which culminated in the shock dismissal from the 1991 World Cup, he immediately stood out as a young centre of immense promise. Quick, committed and with good hands,

Gibbs quickly established himself as one of Britain's finest centre three-quarters, a position he confirmed when he toured New Zealand with the 1993 Lions and displaced Englishman Will Carling. However, the very qualities that made the young Swansea centre one of the unmitigated successes of that tour were also those which made him so tempting for League scouts and later in 1993 Gibbs switched to Warrington RLFC. A success at the League code, Gibbs followed the path forged by Jonathan Davies in 1996 and returned to Wales to play for Swansea. If anything, the years in League made Gibbs an even stronger defensive player and his destructive tackling was a major feature of Wales's encouraging campaign on Gibbs' return to Five Nations action in 1997. He capped a remarkable return by touring South Africa with the 1997 Lions.

MIKE GIBSON
Ireland 1964–79 (centre)

Although Barry John is often thought of today as the most feted back ever to issue from the British Isles, many of his contemporaries are equally adamant that the greatest British three-quarter of the post-war years was Ireland's Mike Gibson. He possessed fierce mental and physical resilience, allied to a brilliant play-making mind. A rather singular man and strict teetotaller who has kept a determinedly low profile since retiring, Gibson was noted for his rigorous, structured approach to fitness, and for intensive pre-match planning in an era before this became the norm. A model of consistency throughout his 69 caps for Ireland and 12 for the Lions over five tours between 1966 and '77, Gibson actually started his Test career at fly-half

in the famous 18–5 win at Twickenham in 1964. The qualities that made the Ulsterman a fine fly-half made him a great centre, particularly outside Barry John on the 1971 Lions tour to New Zealand, when he was at his peak. Strong in the tackle and quick to spot a gap, it was Gibson's mindset that really gave him the edge. His perception always put him in the right place at the right time, while his quick hands and wonderful passing frustrated opponents and gave team-mates valuable time and space in which to work. Gibson always looked good himself, but one of his great skills was to make every player around him look good too.

SID GOING
New Zealand 1967–77 (scrum-half)

Going was regarded as an unorthodox player and a great improviser, who often played as if he was a one-man tactical band. He was a master of the dummy, feint and slight of hand and, at times, passing the ball to his fly-half seemed the option of last resort. He was also a goalkicker during his 29-Test-career, often used when the kicks required were of prodigious length. Much of the jiggery-pokery that was a hallmark of Going's game was developed at his club, Mid-Northern, and his province, North Auckland, with brothers Brian, who was a fly-half, and Ken, an All Black full-back on the centenary tour of Ireland in 1974. The trio developed a series of cut-outs and scissors, double-scissors and triple-scissors that mesmerized opponents and often confounded their team-mates as well. Going's early All Black career was as understudy to Chris Laidlaw and his Test appearances came only when Laidlaw was either unavailable through exams or injured. But by 1971 Going was the incumbent No.8.

KEN GOODALL
Ireland 1967–70 (No. 8)

Picked from obscurity as a 19-year-old City of Derry player in 1967, No.§8 Ken Goodall was a player whose flame burned brightly in his four years with Ireland. Economic circumstances cut

A MODEL OF CONSISTENCY *Ireland's Mike Gibson, more than simply fit.*

short the teacher's career by persuading the popular Ulsterman to take an offer from Workington Rugby League club in 1970 yet, despite winning only 19 caps, Goodall had comfortably established himself as one of Ireland's all-time greatest No. 8s. Making his debut under Noel Murphy in the 15–8 win over Australia, the tall, athletic Goodall immediately impressed watchers with a natural talent and ball-handling ability that was akin to the rising Welsh star of the time, Mervyn Davies. Goodall left for League immediately after perhaps his finest moment, when Ireland beat Wales 14–0 at Lansdowne Road in the final match of the 1970 Five Nations to stop the Welsh winning the Triple Crown. Goodall was immense in that game, inspiring Ireland with an outrageous try that set the scene for the famous victory. Fielding the ball deep in his own half, Goodall beat three tackles before kicking ahead and gathering, eluding two more would-be tacklers to dot down under the Welsh posts. When he went to League, Ireland's loss was Rugby Union's loss.

JULES GUERASSIMOFF

Australia 1963–67 (flanker)

One of the fittest players ever to pull on a Wallaby shirt, flanker Jules Guerassimoff was also one of the fastest and hardest. It was a lethal combination, and throughout his heyday the Queenslander scalped more fly-halves than perhaps any other breakaway in world rugby. Guerassimoff made his debut in the drawn four-Test tour to South Africa in 1963. The gritty qualities displayed by Guerassimoff on that tour came to the fore again during the 20–5 defeat of the All Blacks in Wellington in 1964 – New Zealand's heaviest ever defeat. Despite facing All Black legend Kel Tremain, so dominant was Guerassimoff in that series that he gained the unique distinction of being voted one of the players of the year by the almanacs of South Africa, Australia and New Zealand. Destined to be one of the game's greats, Guerassimoff's career was cut short when politics intervened on the 1966–67 tour to Britain and France. A straight-

talking man, the flanker was incensed when hooker Ross Cullen was sent home early for biting and, after consuming a skinful that night, told captain John Thornett and manager Bill McLaughlin so in forthright terms. After that tour, Guerassimoff was essentially blackballed and never invited to wear the green and gold again. After a distinguished career of 12 Tests, Guerassimoff turned his considerable energies to making Queensland into the top side they are today.

JEREMY GUSCOTT

England 1989– (centre)

Jeremy Guscott has dominated English three-quarter play since his debut for England and the Lions in 1989 and remains indisputably the finest English centre of the modern era. Indeed, there are virtually no weaknesses in Guscott's game; he is so quick that Jack Rowell was able to play him on the wing to great effect in 1997, while he remains one of the most technically outstanding tacklers in the game, a fact he demonstrated most effectively against Canterbury in 1993 when a performance of immense grit single-handedly secured a much-needed win for the beleaguered Lions. In addition, his exceptional acceleration mark him out as the one English back consistently able to prise open tight drift defences from first phase possession, a useful skill in a period dominated by forward-orientated tactics. Guscott's skills were also complementary to those of his long-term England centre partner Will Carling. Carling provided the brawn, Guscott provided the pace and the tries. Despite being a proven try-scorer, Guscott's talents have remained largely under-utilized by England in an age when muscle and the direct route were often the favoured approach. However, Guscott has been one of the major influences in Bath's dominance of English league rugby in the 1990s, that has seen the West Country club win five league titles and five Pilkington Cups. Capped five times by the Lions prior to the 1997 tour to South Africa, Guscott won his 48th English cap against Wales in 1997.

ANDY HADEN

New Zealand 1977–85 (lock)

One of the ironies of Haden's All Black career is that he is remembered as much for events off the field as for those on it, and even the match memories include the controversial. Haden served an apprenticeship on the All Blacks' tour of the UK, Ireland and France in 1972–73 but was not picked for the All Blacks again until 1976, finally making his Test debut against Phil Bennett's Lions in 1977. He went on to win a total of 41 caps before his retirement in 1985. Often controversial and always colourful, Haden was one of the pioneers among New Zealanders playing the off-season overseas, initially in France, and then in Italy and Britain. For a time, he played on Saturdays for Harlequins in Britain and on Sundays for a club in Italy, actions which did not endear him to officialdom. His alleged dive in an effort to earn the All Blacks a last-minute penalty against Wales in 1978 ensured him an enduring notoriety in Britain. Though the All Blacks won the match 13–12 because of a last-minute penalty, English referee Roger Quit-

CONTROVERSIAL *Kiwi Andy Haden.*

tenton always maintained it was against Welsh lock Geoff Wheel who was marking Frank Oliver, and had nothing to do with Haden's theatrics. Haden's amateur status was often questioned and once investigated by the NZRFU, but in an ironic twist, the poacher became the gamekeeper in the late 1980s when Haden was appointed the NZRFU's first marketing agent.

ROWE HARDING

Wales 1923–28 (wing)

A superbly balanced runner, West Walian wing Rowe Harding was the pick of the Welsh crop in an age where the national side were struggling to live with the power of the England sides of the time. Making his debut at the age of 21 against England in 1923, Harding displayed a maturity well beyond his years as he put in tackle after tackle as Wales struggled to impose themselves. A courageous tackler who never shirked his defensive duties when Wales were on the back foot, Harding was at his best going forward where his marvellous side-step and ability to deceive opponents with a slight feint or swerve gave him the space which he was frequently able to exploit through his searing change of pace. A bright, intelligent player who was later to become a judge, Harding honed his game at Cambridge University before joining Swansea. A victim of some eccentric selection decisions, Harding's tally of 17 caps for Wales does not do justice to his undoubted skills, while playing behind beaten packs during his international career limited the impact he could make. Harding did, however, give a glimpse of his full potential on the Lions tour to South Africa in 1924 despite playing for a losing side in his two Tests.

GAVIN HASTINGS

Scotland 1986–95 (full-back)
*(See **The Legends of Rugby**, pages 110-11)*

SCOTT HASTINGS

Scotland 1986– (centre)

Scott Hastings is remembered by those present when he first entered the Scottish squad set-up in 1986 as one of the most cocksure personalities they had ever met. And while that wild joie de vivre and natural ebullience has sometimes since overspilled off the pitch, on it they have been a positive boon. In his early days Scott Hastings was most notable for his searing pace, straight-running and ability to break the gain line virtually every time he received the ball. It was not long, however, before his bullocking runs from centre were complemented by the stonewall defensive qualities which were to remain the salient quality in his game as his pace faded later on. Hastings's finest moments came early on during his career specifically while on tour with the Lions in 1989, if

there is one moment for which he will long be remembered it was during the 1990 Grand Slam decider, the proudest day in Scottish rugby history. English winger Rory Underwood had scythed through the Scottish defence when Hastings managed to drag him down short of the line when a try had seemed inevitable. Scott won his 62nd cap on tour against New Zealand in June 1996, thereby overtaking brother Gavin's record of 61 appearances and becoming Scotland's most capped player.

FULL STEAM AHEAD
Scottish centre Scott Hastings.

DAVID HEWITT
Ireland 1958–65 (fly-half)

A barnstorming centre, David Hewitt is yet another Ulsterman to make the cut as an Irish Great. Although sometimes an erratic decision-maker, Hewitt more than made up for it with the ball in hand when he displayed natural pace and power, allied to an eye for a half-chance which often turned tight games. A natural talent who was elevated to the full Ulster side while still a schoolboy, Hewitt was one of six members of his immediate family, including father Tom, to wear the green of Ireland. A sturdy defender with good positional sense, Hewitt was also a dangerous strike runner who ran deadly straight in attack. For all that, though, the Instonian will be best remembered as a phenomenal kicker who scored 112 points on his first Lions tour to New Zealand in 1959, running in 13 tries, kicking ten penalties and 20 conversions and dropping one goal to make him one of the few players to have scored more than 100 points on a Lions tour. An injury sustained on the 1962 Lions tour curtailed Hewitt's career, and he only played once more at international level thereafter, brought back in 1965 for the 14–8 loss to Wales in Cardiff, where he won his 24th cap.

JOHN HIPWELL
Australia 1968–82 (scrum-half)

Although a scrum-half out of the top draw in virtually every department, if John Hipwell had one defining feature it was his tremendous coverdefence. He needed to be of the highest order because the Australian packs of the 1970s were not known for their solidity, and it's ironic htat Hipwell\s retirement coincided with the rise of the stronger Australian forwards. In such circumstances, his unrivalled durability and tenacity were valuable commodities indeed. Yet Hipwell was not just an outstanding defender, as his surprising speed off the mark and frequent scuttling breaks down the short side showed. Although he had gone on the unhappy tour to Britain in 1966–67, Hipwell started his Test career in the furnace of Bledisloe Cup competition, coming on as

a replacement for Wallaby great Ken Catchpole after the little scrum-half's career had been tragically ended. Over the next 14 years, the stocky little New South Wales Country scrum-half, with the no-nonsense service and an appetite for the rough stuff round the fringes, went on to win 36 caps, becoming one of the legends of Australian rugby in the process.

TERRY HOLMES
Wales 1978–85 (scrum-half)

A mighty man determined to take on all back row adversaries no matter what the circumstances, the muscular, bludgeoning approach of Wales scrum-half Terry Holmes could not have been more at odds with the rapier thrusts of his predecessor, Gareth Edwards. For all that, though, Holmes was one of the most effective scrumhalves ever to play for Wales and was certainly a man suited to a period when Wales's forward power was beginning to wane. A thick-set man of 6 ft., Holmes could easily have been a flanker and often played like one, running back to his forwards as often as he span out a pass to club and country fly-half Gareth Davies. It was not that Holmes was a poor passer, far from it. It was simply that the Cardiff man had an endless thirst for physical confrontation. Holmes was a regular try-scorer throughout his 25-cap international career, most of the scores coming from powerful drives from close in. Unfortunately, the demands he heaped upon his sturdy frame were too much and in two Lions tours a string of injuries meant that he managed just one Test on the 1983 tour to New Zealand. Towards the end of his career, the injuries became more frequent and more damaging, and after a painful knock on his shoulder against England in 1985, Holmes finally accepted the League dollar and signed with Bradford.

DOUG HOPWOOD
South Africa 1960–65 (No. 8)

Doug Hopwood was denied the great honour of captaining the Springboks on the 1965 tour of Scotland and Ireland when the executive of the South Africa Rugby Board vetoed the national selectors' choice. The controversy raged all the harder because no satisfactory explanation was ever made public and although Hopwood kept a dignified silence apart from expressing his regret, the sad chapter may have had much to do with the plunge in morale and the seven straight Test defeats suffered at the time of the notorious Hopwood affair. Avril Malan and later Dawie de Villiers took over the captaincy, but Hopwood remained a member of both touring parties and played a major role in the Third Test win in Christchurch which ended the poor run of results. Hopwood's fame spread through Britain. Qualities which stamped him as a leader and a remarkably gifted No. 8 in a long line of great Springbok back rowers, came to the fore in the 1961 Test at Twickenham when he scored the winning try against England. Rugby League talent scouts were ready with the then handsome fee of £20,000, but Hopwood heeded his wife's suggestion and stayed at home in Cape Town where he was a diesel mechanic. "No amount of money can repay the pleasure rugby union has given me," he said of his 22-cap career.

TIM HORAN

Like so many of Australia's current greats, Queensland centre Tim Horan entered the international fray in the fallout that followed the 1989 series defeat by the British Lions. The stocky centre was joined that year by Jason Little, a lithe Queenslander who had

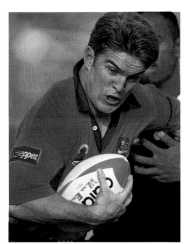

TEENAGE PRODIGY *Tim Horan*

grown up alongside Horan as a schoolboy on the Darling Downs, and together the two formed one of the most enduring centre partnerships of all time, with both winning the majority of their 50-odd caps alongside each other. An untried teenager when Bob Dwyer elevated him to Wallaby status against the All Blacks in 1989, Horan soon justified the faith shown in him and by 1991 was one of the main reasons behind Australia's World Cup triumph. A bustling centre who is rock solid in defence and has the speed to exploit any half gap in attack, Horan has proved a consistent try-scorer, grabbing 16 tries in his first 30 Tests. Horan sustained a potentially career-ending knee injury in the 1994 Super 10 final against Natal which sidelined him for a year. Yet by 1996 Horan was back to his best in the Australian side as he demonstrated in victories against Scotland and Ireland.

ANDY IRVINE
Scotland 1972–82 (full-back)

Looking back at the history of the game, there is a temptation to view world-class attacking full-backs in the same way as the local bus: you wait for ages and then two arrive at the same time! Yet if Andy Irvine MBE, one of the first real superstars of the game North of the Border, spent much of his rugby career in competition with that great Welsh full-back JPR Williams, that does little to diminish the impact he had upon Scottish rugby throughout the 1970s. First capped against the All Blacks in 1972, Irvine played 52 times for his country in a career that spanned ten seasons. Yet despite his many caps, Irvine was notoriously frail under the high ball, and even his staunchest supporters could not pretend that he was the most defensively sound of Scotland's recent full-backs. For all that, though, the Heriot's FP star was a potential match-winner for club or country, espe-

EASY DOES IT *Scottish full-back, Andy Irvine "runner of great invention"*

cially after the unbeaten 1974 Lions tour to South Africa, when he absorbed many of the moves and patterns of play and grafted them onto his own natural flair and love of counter-attacking from deep.

PETER JACKSON
England 1956–63 (wing)

Once described as "the old dancing master a cross between Nijinsky and Stanley Matthews", Coventry wing Peter Jackson was one of the great entertainers in a career that spanned eight seasons, 25 caps and three of the best tries ever seen in internationals. A charismatic player, Jackson was a cult figure at Twickenham from the moment he made his debut in the narrow 8-3 defeat at the hands of Wales in 1956. With an amazing sleight of hand, a wonderful side-step and divine sense of balance, the speedy Jackson was a confirmed crowd pleaser throughout his career,

with his finest hour coming when he ran through seven tackles in the dying seconds to score a try in the corner and snatch an unlikely win over the 1958 Wallabies. That try was never bettered by Jackson, although his spectacular efforts for the Lions in the First and Fourth Tests in New Zealand in 1959 must come close. Indeed, Jackson's driven performances on that tour – where he finished as the second highest scorer behind prolific Irishman Tony O'Reilly, crossing the line 19 times in 18 games – confirmed him as a player of the highest calibre.

Slight and pallid due to a childhood kidney complaint, Jackson's combination with fly-half Richard Sharp was at the heart of England's Championship triumph of 1963 when only a 0-0 draw in Dublin prevented them from winning the Grand Slam.

ADOLPHE JAUREGUY
France 1920–29 (centre)

One of the all-time greats of French rugby, Basque-born centre Adolphe Jaureguy won 31 caps in an international career spanning ten seasons. He captained France on 12 occasions, the first time against Wales in 1926, and oversaw the national side's transformation from perennial wooden spoon recipients to a genuinely challenging Five Nations outfit. He made his international debut against Scotland in 1920 and retired after the game against England in 1929. A sprinter of class, Jaureguy was introduced to the game by his brother Pierre, who represented France in 1913. He saw action in an artillery regiment during the Great War, when he also played for the French Services alongside Rene Crabos, returning afterwards to his school in Tarbes, where he played with Francois Borde for the Tarbes team which won the French Championship in 1919. A nomadic player who played for nine different clubs, he also helped Toulouse win the National Championship title in 1922 and 1923.

DICKIE JEEPS
England 1956–62 (scrum-half)

Courageous, gritty and with remarkable physical resilience for a small man, Dickie Jeeps was the perfect scrum-half during seven years in which he was generally reckoned the best No. 9 in the world. His rise to prominence was remarkably swift after his debut for the British Lions against South Africa in 1955 as an uncapped 24-year-old. During the drawn series, Jeeps provided fly-half Cliff Morgan with inch-perfect service while also halting the Springbok forwards in full charge to help the tourists to a famous victory in the First Test. That was to be the first of Jeeps' 13 appearances for the Lions (he also toured New Zealand in 1959 and South Africa in 1962), a record bettered only by Willie John McBride. A great thinker on the game, Jeeps possessed an ebullience and inner strength that earned the undying respect of team-mates and commentators by consistently proving himself willing to take enormous punishment rather than pass on bad ball to his fly-half. In addition, Jeeps was blessed with outstanding leadership qualities which saw him captain England 13 times out of his 24 caps. The key member of England's 1957 Grand Slam side, Jeeps retired in 1962 and became President of the RFU in 1976–77.

GREAT WHITE SHARK *John Jeffrey*

JOHN JEFFREY
Scotland 1984–91 (flanker)

No matter how much the average Scotsman enjoys beating England – and every red-blooded kilt-wearer loves nothing better – there are few to whom it means more than John Jeffrey, the Borders farmer whose one regret about his farm is that "If I stand on a hill I can see England". To Jeffrey, giving the Auld Enemy a stuffing was everything, and he in turn became synonymous with cross-border raids against England, whether it be as a vital cog in the 1990 Grand Slam winning side or as the man who famously dented the Calcutta Cup after an impromptu game of Tag after the 1988 post-match dinner! A lean blind-side flanker of 6ft 4in who lived more on guile and guts than sheer speed, the blond thatch belonging to "The Great White Shark", as Jeffrey is universally known, was one of the most galvanizing sights in Five Nations rugby throughout the 1980s and early 1990s. When he retired in 1991, Jeffrey had won a record 40 caps for Scotland as well as touring Australia with the 1989 British Lions.

VIVIAN JENKINS
Wales 1933–39 (full-back)

When Vivian Jenkins retired prematurely in 1939 at the age of just 28, the game in Wales lost a deep thinker with an unrivalled feel for the nuances of full-back play. As with everything else in his life, however,

Jenkins made a huge success of his new career and rugby's loss was also its gain as he went on to establish himself as one of the world's most respected rugby journalists. In many ways, that transformation was symptomatic of the rest of Jenkins's life. He was a naturally gifted athlete who also kept wicket for Glamorgan, yet who brought quiet and thoughtful efficiency to everything he did. The finest British full-back of his generation, the speedy Jenkins was resolute under the high ball, a ferocious and technically perfect timer of the tackle and a sound punter to touch. A goal-kicker of prodigious length, in the first Lions Test of 1938 against South Africa at Ellis Park, Jenkins kicked three huge penalties, one of which was from inside his own half with the other two not much shorter. After winning his first cap against England at 21, Jenkins spent seven seasons as a Welsh regular, amassing a total of 14 caps for his country and two for the 1938 Lions.

BARRY JOHN
Wales 1966–72 (Fly-half)
*(See **The Legends of Rugby**,*
pages 112–13)

ROY JOHN
Wales 1950–54 (lock)

Roy John was widely regarded as the best line-out forward in the world

during the first part of the 1950s. At 6ft. 4in. he was already large for his time, but John was also blessed with outstanding timing, spring heels and sure handling, the latter ensuring that not only was the supply of ball plentiful but of good quality. It is said that John had such a good standing jump that he could leap up and grab the crossbar in both hands without a run-up (the crossbar is 10ft. 6in.). Roy John was far more than an outstanding line-out jumper, however. Multi-skilled and fast over the ground, he was also capable of switching position if necessary and played at No.8, blind-side flanker and second row for the Lions in New Zealand in 1950. It was with the Lions that John really came into his own against All Black forwards who regularly overwhelmed the tourists with their sheer strength. Not only was he rated the best line-out jumper ever to have toured New Zealand, but he was also feted for his abrasiveness and all-round input outside the set-piece. If that were not enough, the Springboks in 1951–52 rated him by far the best line-out forward in the country. John started his career against England at the age of 24, and was surprisingly put out to grass by the Welsh selectors aged just 29 after winning 19 Welsh caps and six for the 1950 Lions.

MARTIN JOHNSON
England 1993– (lock)

Captain of the 1997 Lions to South Africa, Leicester lock Martin Johnson established himself as a great player after his strong performances as a tyro replacement for Wade Dooley on the 1993 Lions tour to New Zealand. With only one cap to his name Johnson came into the Lions'

LEADER OF THE PACK *Martin Johnson, 1997 Lions' captain.*

side and along with Martin Bayfield dominated the line-out in the Second Test, sending the British to a much deserved victory. Since then, Johnson has gone on to establish himself as the dominant front five forward in Northern Hemisphere rugby, winning 30 caps at the relatively tender age of 27. Possessing a startling standing jump and wonderful timing, Johnson is most conspicuous as a ball winner at the line-out yet he is a far more complete player than that. Fast for a big man at 6ft. 7in. and 18 stone, and with sure hands, Johnson is as adept at playing the mauling game as he is playing in a looser rucking role. Rugged, well-co-ordinated and athletic, the only weakness in his game remains a short fuse: two off-the-ball incidents in separate 1997 Five Nations games resulted in two England tries being disallowed. Nevertheless, he is now managing to graft a greater contribution in the loose onto his outstanding set-piece and mauling game.

CLIFF JONES

Wales 1934–38 (fly-half)

An inventive and highly dangerous runner, it is often said by veteran Welshmen that had Cliff Jones been as adept with the boot as Barry John, then there would have been nothing to choose between the two fly-halves. That Jones was never a great kicker is not surprising. Not only was the kicking game alien to a man who lived to tease back rows with his dancing runs from fly-half, but he had been taught as a schoolboy by Llandovery College's T.P. Williams, a man who rammed home the message that kicking was an option of last resort. Born in the Rhondda, the diminutive Jones was just one of a clutch of outstanding players who came together in the pre-War Welsh sides. A precocious talent in his own right, with backs such as Claude Davey, Vivian Jenkins, Haydn Tanner and Wilf Wooller in the same side, Jones looked like the world beater he was – particularly in the famous one-point win over the 1935 All Blacks. Whether it was for Cardiff, Cambridge University – who he and Wooller memorably inspired to a six-try demolition of Oxford in

the 29–4 Varsity Match of 1934 – or Wales, Cliff Jones was an outstanding influence. Only the outbreak of war and a series of injuries restricted him to 13 caps and prevented him from testing himself at the very highest level with the 1938 Lions in South Africa.

KEN JONES

Wales 1947–57 (wing)

The only Welsh winger who could hold a candle to Gerald Davies, Newport flier Ken Jones combined his rugby career with life as an international athlete. A sprint champion in the Far East during the war years, Jones also won the Wales 100 yd. sprint title seven times, and collected a silver medal at the 1948 London Olympics. Yet Jones had far more to offer than scintillating pace. He was also supremely competent in all the basic skills and was well-known for his ability to catch poorly directed passes while travelling at top pace. Never a side-stepper, Jones was the possessor of a frightening swerve which he combined with his sheer pace to ease himself around hapless opponents, even at international level. It was this elusive quality which brought him 17 tries for Wales in 44 Test matches, 43 of which were played consecutively. Many of the tries he scored were at crucial moments, such as the famous instance when he latched onto captain Clem Thomas's hack out of defence to score the try which beat the 1953 All Blacks. However, it was as a wing for the 1950 Lions to New Zealand that Jones proved his ability to live with the best. So outstanding were his displays that he was named as one of the New Zealand Rugby Almanack's five players of the year, an honour which was a fitting tribute to a man who tackled like a madman and scored 16 tries in 17 games.

LEWIS JONES

Wales 1950–52 (utility back)

The autobiography of Benjamin Lewis Jones in 1958 was entitled "King of Rugger", and that was certainly what this prematurely bald-headed genius could claim to have been. Jones

BELIEVE THE HYPE *Micheal Jones is rated as the best forward in the world.*

was so versatile that he won his ten caps in three different positions as an integral member of the Grand Slam winning sides of 1950 and 1952. Unfathomably omitted from the original Lions party to tour Australasia in 1950, he was called up when George Norton broke his arm and went on to be the find of the tour. In 14 matches he notched 114 points, including a record 16 in the First Test against Australia; and he amazed Bleddyn Williams when he picked off a pass destined for Williams in the final Test against the All Blacks and sent Ken Jones away to score at the other end. Just as he seemed set to become a Welsh immortal, Jones followed a well worn path North and signed for Leeds Rugby League club for £6,000 in 1952. As the scorer of a record 496 points in Leeds' Wembley Cup-winning season of 1957, and as the collector of 15 Great Britain caps, Jones went on to become one of the most successful dual internationals both codes have ever seen.

MICHAEL JONES

New Zealand 1987– (flanker)

When two coaches as different in outlook as Laurie Mains and John Hart describe Michael Jones as the best forward in the world, it has to be some-

thing more than coach's hyperbole. Jones has had an extraordinary international career that started in 1986 when he represented Western Samoa, the county of his birth, against Wales. His performance in that match so impressed the New Zealand selectors that they persuaded the 22-year-old flanker, who had lived in Aucklan since childhood, to play for the All Blacks in the 1987 World Cup. That was the start of a magnificent career, interrupted for a year in 1989 by a serious knee injury, that took in the 1991 World Cup and has to date earned Jones 50 caps. Respected on the pitch by both friend and foe, Jones has achieved legendary status off the pitch as well for his refusal to play on Sundays because of religious beliefs. His insistence on observing the Sabbath cost him his place in the 1995 World Cup squad such were the number of games scheduled for Sundays, but he forced his way back into the side and played a prominent part in the historic series win against South Africa in August 1996.

ANDRE JOUBERT

South Africa 1989– (full-back)

Andre Joubert's silky skills have earned him the accolade as the Rolls-Royce of full-backs. Quietly spoken

COMPLETE PLAYER *Andre Joubert*

and now in his 1930s, he was something of a late bloomer in international rugby, due mainly to South Africa's isolation. Joubert won the first of his official Test caps against Australia in 1993, when he was already aged 29, although he had played for South Africa in the rebel Tests against the World XV in 1989. It took Joubert several post-isolation seasons to establish himself ahead of other talented full-backs such as Gavin Johnson and Theo van Rensburg, but consistently impressive performances during the 1995 World Cup consolidated his reputation as one of South Africa's most influential players. There is little doubt that Joubert would have been a colossus in any era but the recent law changes which have added such a new dimension to an attacking full-back running from deep defensive positions have enhanced Joubert's contributions to the Springbok cause. A strong runner and prolific try-scorer, Joubert is the complete footballer.

KEN KENNEDY
Ireland 1965–75 (hooker)

Back in the days when it was a ques-

tion of "how low can you go?" in the front-row, Ulster hooker Ken Kennedy was an undisputed king of the limbo routine. So much so, in fact, that many of his contemporaries swore he could hook a ball with his nose if he needed to! Supple, strong and incredibly fit, the CIYMS dynamo was an ever-present in the loose for Ireland for 11 seasons. He made his debut as a 24-year-old in 1965 and finally retired in 1975 after winning his 49th cap in the 32–4 humiliation by Wales at Cardiff Arms Park. A deadly accurate line-out thrower who profited from the presence of "Wiggs" Mulcahy and Willie John McBride at various stages in his career, Kennedy was nevertheless a bit on the small side, even for hookers of that era. Although this meant added mobility in the loose – and Kennedy could often have been mistaken for a back-rower – it also meant problems for him when the game was a very tight one. Although Kennedy thrived in the Five Nations, he never made much impact for the Lions when faced by the huge maul-based New Zealand pack in 1966, while by 1974 he was forced to play second fiddle to Welshman Bobby Windsor in South Africa.

TOM KIERNAN
Ireland 1960–73 (full-back)

There was little reason to presume that Tom Kiernan would go on to become Ireland's most capped full-back of all time when he made his debut against England at Twickenham in 1960. Yet, 14 seasons later, with 54 Irish caps and two Lions tours under his belt, the quiet and self-effacing Munsterman had established himself as one of the most efficient and dependable Test players in the history of Irish rugby. An outstanding place-kicker who scored over 150 points for his country, Kiernan was also an astute kicker from the hand and had shrewd positional sense. A natural footballer with an even temperament well suited to international rugby, Kiernan tackled well and came into the line with real purpose, even if his slight lack of pace was a handicap in this area. Kiernan's influence continued well after his retirement

in 1973. Not only was he a mentor to his nephew Michael, an accomplished Irish back who won 44 caps as a kicking centre with a penchant for attack in the 1980s, but Kiernan has remained a mover and shaker in the game's halls of power. Now one of the main driving forces behind the burgeoning World Cup organization, Kiernan became president of the Irish Rugby Union in 1989.

DAVID KIRK
New Zealand 1985–87 (scrum-half)

As Rhodes scholar, medical doctor, business executive and would-be politician, Kirk did not fit the All Black imagery, yet he led New Zealand to one of its finest rugby triumphs, victory in the first World Cup in 1987. Kirk's career was also relatively brief. He was first an All Black, as the No.2 scrum-half on the tour of England and Scotland in 1983, a ranking he retained in Australia the following year. He won the first of his 17 caps in 1985 against England, the same year that he opted out of the rebel tour to South Africa. Kirk was made captain of the "Baby Blacks", the team that beat France when the Cavaliers were unavailable, and he retained the job when they returned for a series against Australia. He was replaced as captain by Jock Hobbs for an end-of-year tour of France and then by Andy Dalton as leader of the inaugural World Cup squad. Fate intervened, however, and when Dalton pulled a hamstring before the first cup match Kirk took over the captaincy. He led the team throughout the Cup campaign, coach Brian Lochore deciding against reintroducing Dalton for the later matches when he had regained fitness. One of the enduring images of the World Cup, and of New Zealand rugby generally, is of Kirk holding aloft the Webb Ellis Trophy, then drawing in Dalton to share the moment with him.

IAN KIRKPATRICK
New Zealand 1967–77 (flanker)

One of the greatest flankers to have played for New Zealand, Kirkpatrick's place in history suffers because he was captain on the 1972–73

tour of the UK, Ireland and France, a tour rooted in the controversy over the banishment of prop Keith Murdoch after a fracas with a security guard in a Cardiff hotel. That is a harsh judgment, especially since Kirkpatrick played no part in the decision to send Murdoch home. For happier reasons, Kirkpatrick is remembered not only for his 39 caps but for displacing the great Kel Tremain in the Test team in France in 1967, for scoring three tries when he went on as a replacement against Australia in 1968 and for a 60-metre solo try against the Lions in Christchurch in 1971, the only Test of that series the All Blacks won. Kirkpatrick was controversially dropped as captain (and replaced by Andy Leslie) for the 1974 tour of Australia and responded by playing what many observers regarded as his finest Test, the first against the Wallabies in Sydney, in strong winds and driving rain. His final Test series was against the Lions in 1977 and despite continuing fine form, he was left out of the team to tour France later that year. Kirkpatrick added another controversial chapter to his career when in 1986 he managed the rebel All Black team in South Africa, the Cavaliers.

JOHN KIRWAN
New Zealand 1984–94 (wing)

New Zealand's leading try-scorer in Tests with 35 from 63 matches, his try total is almost double that of the previous record-holder, Stu Wilson. Kirwan was 19 when the Auckland coach, John Hart, spotted him and placed him in the side with immediate, stunning effect, prompting comparisons with another electric Auckland wing of a decade earlier, Bryan Williams. Kirwan was first chosen for the All Blacks for a series against France in 1984 and went to Australia with New Zealand later that season, but a shoulder injury cut short his tour. He returned to the All Blacks in 1985 for the two-match series against England and was chosen for the aborted tour of South Africa. He and scrum-half David Kirk were the only two members of that team not to go on the rebel tour the following year. Kirwan's speed and strength,

allied with sidesteps off either foot, body swerves and a fiendish fend, made him a devastating attacking wing, perhaps best exemplified by a 90-metre try against Italy in the opening match of the 1987 World Cup. Injuries, including a ruptured achilles tendon on the tour of Wales and Ireland in 1989, were all that kept Kirwan out of the All Blacks until 1993 when coach Laurie Mains, in a controversial decision, left him out of the team to tour England and Scotland, promoting Kirwan to say publicly that Mains "had lost the plot". Kirwan retired from Rugby in 1994 and played Rugby League in 1995 and 1996 for the Auckland Warriors

RUBEN KRUGER
South Africa 1993– (flanker)

Great loose forwards hunt in pairs and Ruben Kruger is no exception. Fast and dynamic but at 6ft. 2in. smallish in build by modern flanker standards, the Springbok won plaudits for his World Cup displays in tandem with Francois Pienaar. Kruger established his Test place after moving to Northern Transvaal and has become an integral part of the current Springbok set-up having graduated through the South Africa Schools, South Africa Under-20 and South Africa Sevens ranks. With pace and good hands, an uncanny sense of sniffing out where the ball is going and an

ability to finish off with telling effect, Kruger has proved outstanding since making his debut against Argentina in 1993. A shy man off the field, Kruger's role on the field matches his personality off it: an unflashy team player who works best out of sight of the crowd, setting up his more dynamic colleagues. Even so, after making his debut against Argentina in 1993, he still managed to score eleven tries in his first Test season. With a World Cup winner's medal under his belt at the age of just 24, Kruger seems certain to be at his prime during the 1999 World Cup, and is already being touted as a future Springbok captain.

JACK KYLE
Ireland 1947–58 (fly-half)

It would not be over-egging the pudding to say that only Barry John stands comparison with Jack Kyle in the history of fly-half play since the end of the Second World War. A diminutive genius, he dominated Irish back play from the time that he sliced through the French defences in 1947 until he hung up his boots after beating Scotland 12–6 a record 52 caps later. Under Kyle, Ireland achieved a level of dominance in Europe which they have never threatened to repeat since his retirement. He brought Ireland their only Grand Slam in 1948, while the next year only a 16–9 defeat by France denied back-to-back clean sweeps. Kyle was perceptive in attack,

quick to spot a gap and even quicker to zip through it. He seemed to be able to turn matches with moments of brilliance plucked out of the ether, yet he was also able to dictate the course of tight matches with raking punts that landed inches short of the touchline. Kyle endeared himself to those around him by making the ball work to give them space, and he was certainly no shirker – he was a lightweight who packed a heavyweight tackle. The Belfast doctor even won the admiration of the Kiwis, who rated him one of the best players ever to tour New Zealand, even though his Lions side failed to win any of the four Tests there in 1950.

CHRIS LAIDLAW
New Zealand 1964–70 (scrum-half)

An outstanding scrum-half for New Zealand in the 1960s, Laidlaw played for his province, Otago, for South Island and for New Zealand Universities in his first year out of school. He was the youngest player on the All Blacks' 1963–64 tour of the UK, Ireland and France and played his first Test on that tour, against France. Barely 20, the tour established him as New Zealand's first-choice scrum-

half, a standing he retained for the rest of his career, including full series against South Africa in 1965, the Lions in 1966 and the tour of Britain in 1967. He captained the All Blacks against Australia in 1968 when regular leader Brian Lochore was injured. After completing a Rhodes Scholarship at Oxford University, Laidlaw returned to New Zealand and won the last of his 20 caps on the 1970 tour to South Africa. Laidlaw was a scrum-half of the classic mould, with a long, quick pass, a deft kick over the top of forwards and brought a tactical vision of the game. In an age when it wasn't the done thing to do, Laidlaw wrote a book *Mud In Your Eye*, which was critical of Rugby administration. He also condemned South Africa's Apartheid system though he himself was criticized for playing against South Africa for Oxford and for touring there. Laidlaw was later a diplomat as New Zealand high commissioner to Zimbabwe and had a prominent role in the multi-racial talks that led to the formation of the South African Rugby Football Union. He was also, for a term, a Labour member of New Zealand Parliament.

ROY LAIDLAW
Scotland 1980–88 (scrum-half)

Every country has, at some stage, a double-act which sees two players, through sheer longevity, become mentioned in the same breath. England had Dooley and Ackford, Wales had the Viet Gwent (the Pontypool front row of Faulkner, Windsor and Price) and Australia had Lynagh and Farr-Jones. One of the most enduring partnerships of all was that of Jed Forest's Roy Laidlaw and Selkirk fly-half John Rutherford. For nigh on a decade, the two were immovable at half back for Scotland. Unlike most of the other famous pairings, however, it was Laidlaw and Rutherford's differences, rather than their similarities, that melded them into an outstanding partnership. On the one hand, there was the peerless Rutherford, all grace and poise, who could glide through tackles and drill a ball onto a sixpence in the opposition's 22. On the other, there was Laidlaw, a gutsy little fighter in the classic Borders mould. The pair

played together on 35 occasions, a world record for a half-back partnership. They also teamed up for the British Lions in the Third Test against New Zealand in 1983.

TOMMY LAWTON

Australia 1983–89 (hooker)

The grandson of Wallaby captain Tom Lawton, a Rhodes Scholar and outstanding fly-half who won 13 caps between 1925 and 1932, hooker Tommy Lawton will nevertheless be best remembered by Rugby aficionados for his sheer bulk. The Wallaby front row in the mid-1980s was so powerful that when Australia achieved perhaps its greatest win by twice outplaying the All Blacks in New Zealand to claim the Bledisloe Cup in 1986, much of the credit was laid at their door. Lawton, however, was more than just an immense presence at the scrum. A line-out thrower-in of incredible accuracy, he also contributed through his unerring ability to hit lock and giant jumper Steve Cutler. Not only that, but Lawton made a surprisingly robust presence in the loose and was the author of some crunching tackles in his time. Even were it not for the Bledisloe Cup triumph, the Queenslander will also go down in history as one of the Wallaby greats through his integral role in the 1984 Grand Slam side that defeated all four Home Union countries. His career finished on something of a low, however, when the Australian pack was physically overwhelmed by the British Lions during the 1989 series defeat

SILVER SERVICE *Scottish scrum-half Roy Laidlaw feeds the ball out.*

HENNIE LE ROUX

South Africa 1993– (fly-half)

Hennie le Roux is one of life's thinkers on Rugby and perspectives in and around the game. Not always in favour with those who control and influence the game, the diminutive utility back has already stamped his mark on Springbok Rugby after 24 Tests. An individualist in his approach but a good team man despite what his detractors say, Le Roux has played international Rugby effectively at both fly-half and centre. After moving to Transvaal from Port Elizabeth where he was schooled in nearby Grahamstown, adding communications and marketing degrees from University of Port Elizabeth and Rand Afrikaans University to his CV, Le Roux has brought a refreshing touch to South Africa's outside backs, never afraid to operate in the furnace heat close to the advantage line and predatory loose forwards. While Le Roux prefers fly-half, national coach Kitch Christie was quick to recognize his midfield qualities and he was switched to become, in partnership with Japie Mulder, one of the Springboks' trump cards in the World Cup. Le Roux should stay at centre after Joel Stransky was seamlessly replaced by Henry Honiball. Le Roux has had his share of injuries but, this versatile 29-year-old will be carrying the banner for the Springboks in Wales in 1999.

DAVID LESLIE

Scotland 1975–85 (flanker)

Every team needs a nutcase, a player who – no matter how urbane and civilized off the field – cares so little for his own physical well-being that he is prepared to sacrifice himself every time he laces up his boots. David Leslie was such a man. Throughout his career, he was consistently the most focused and fearless player in a Scottish squad which had far more than its fair share of fearless breakaways. One story is instructive. So uncompromising was Leslie that shortly after his retirement when he returned to his alma mater, Glenalmond College near Perth, to play in an old boys match alongside David Sole, the body count was so high that the College's Master-in-Charge had to appeal to his guest's better nature – difficult for a man who knew no way other than full bore until full-time. For all his intensity, Leslie found it hard to establish himself in the Scottish side until late on in his career. First capped against Ireland in 1975, he didn't become a regular in the side until 1981. When he finally decided to hang up his boots in 1985 he had won 32 caps.

BRIAN LOCHORE

New Zealand 1964–71 (No. 8)

Lochore first gained national acknowledgement in 1963 when he was on the shortlist for a home series against England and he made his debut at the end of the year on the tour of the UK, Ireland and France, playing in the England and Scotland internationals. A No. 8 of power and perception, he had a tigerish strength in rucks and mauls and was

blessed with deceptive speed. Lochore became All Black captain in 1966, after Wilson Whineray's retirement, and continued to lead with dignity and success, retiring after the tour of South Africa in 1970. But he was persuaded to come back in 1971 and play, at lock, in the Third Test against the Lions when he won his 25th and last All Black cap. Lochore turned to coaching and was an immediate success with his Masterton club team before doing the improbable when he coached his province, Wairarapa-Bush, into the first division. He was fast-tracked onto the national selection panel and was coach of the 1985 All Black team that was stopped from going to South Africa. He coached a team of All Black newcomers to beat France in 1986 when most of the established All Blacks were under suspension for their rebel tour of South Africa, and in 1987 he coached the first team to win the World Cup. Lochore continued to serve Rugby in a variety of less high-profile roles and in 1995 he was brought back as campaign manager for the World Cup and was widely regarded as being one of the main reasons for that team's outstanding play.

RECORD BREAKER *Wallaby Micheal Lynagh, Rugby's top scorer.*

MICHAEL LYNAGH

Australia 1984–95 (fly-half)

Australia's most capped fly-half, with 72 Tests to his name, Lynagh is also the most prolific points-scorer in international Rugby, amassing 911 points before his retirement after the 1995 World Cup. Although he made his debut in 1984 against Fiji as a 21-year-old, it was later in that year on the Grand Slam tour of Britain that Lynagh came of age. Despite being unable to shift the great Mark Ella from the No.10 spot, he demonstrated his versatility by playing at inside centre. Lynagh will be best remembered working in tandem with scrum-half Nick Farr-Jones, who also first made his mark in 1984 before going on to play in 47 Tests alongside Lynagh. Farr-Jones's efficient service and attacking ability took a good deal of pressure off his fly-half, allowing him to stand virtually on the gain line in attack. Although Lynagh could take on opposition defences one-on-one, as he brilliantly proved when scoring a famous injury-time winning try against Ireland in the 1991 World Cup quarter-final, he was better as a player who gave the dynamic runners such as David Campese the space and time in which to work. In the summer of 1996 "Noddy" announced his shock move to London club Saracens where he linked up with Phillipe Sella, one of his former adversaries.

WILLIE JOHN McBRIDE

Ireland 1962–75 (lock)
*(See **The Legends of Rugby**, pages 114–15)*

IAN McGEECHAN

Scotland 1972–79 (centre)
*(See **The Famous Coaches**, page 174)*

ALISTAIR McHARG

Scotland 1968–79 (lock)

At just over 15 stone and just 6ft. 4in., Alistair McHarg was hardly the identikit second row forward, even in the days when they didn't exactly breed 'em huge. Yet as a testament to the powers of athleticism and a good dose of getting your retaliation in first, 44-times capped McHarg was a marvel. A tough and notoriously abrasive Glaswegian, McHarg once joked that his whole playing career was shrouded "in red mist". McHarg, though, fails to do himself justice with that remark. As a counterbalance to the slower and heavier Gordon Brown, McHarg could not have been a better choice. His speed around the park was perfectly suited to the mobile rucking game played by the Scots, while his timing and nous made him a safe bet at the line-out and one of the best number two jumpers of his generation. Despite his chestful of Scottish caps, McHarg never won selection for a Lions' tour, missing out on trips to New Zealand in 1971 and South Africa in 1974 because of injury and stiff competition from the likes of Gordon Brown and Willie John McBride and Delme Thomas.

IAN McLAUCHLAN

Scotland 1969–79 (prop)

As the richly deserved epithet "Mighty Mouse" would indicate, Ian McLauchlan was both small for a prop, but also remarkably strong. Certainly, McLauchlan was not the conventional size and shape for a loose-head prop in the 1970s, but in many ways it was precisely the combination of an amazing power to weight ratio plus his ability to get under his opposing tighthead that made him such an effective performer in the tight. McLauchlan, however, was also outstanding in the loose and prospered as a member of the Lions party which tore across the hard grounds of the South African Veldt in 1974. As a larger than life character, he played best in the most intimidating circumstances, which is why he was so effective in Paris, Cardiff and on the 1971 Lions tour of New Zealand where he played all four Tests. During his ten-year career, McLauchlan won 43 caps, captaining his country in 19 of those matches and recording ten victories, making him Scotland's most successful captain. After his retirement the Scottish Rugby Union showed their gratitude by banning him for publishing a his autobiography.

PAUL McLEAN

Australia 1974–82 (fly-half)

A member of the famous McLean clan, Paul came from a sporting dynasty as powerful as any in Australian Rugby union: his grandfather won his first cap on tour with the 1904 Wallabies; his uncles Doug, Jack and Bill all played for Australia, with Bill captaining the side; cousin Peter followed the family business when he played in his first Test; and brother Jeff racked up 13 Wallaby caps. Yet of all the McLeans, the self-effacing Paul was undoubtedly the most talented. Although perceived as a safety-first type of player, McLean was in fact magically gifted in all areas: he could kick from hand and for goal, break through opposition defences almost at will, had superb hands and was a brilliant cover defender. Not that he needed to be up to much when he made his Test debut in the 1974 Bledisloe Cup – the Aussies were so bad that they had just been beaten at home by the Tongans, humiliated by the All Blacks and dubbed the "Awful Aussies". His career finished in controversial circumstances, at the comparatively young age of 28 when, after winning 31 caps, Queenslander McLean was dropped by Bob Dwyer in favour of the young Mark Ella. The resulting fallout – when the Ellas were booed by fans while being beaten by the touring Scots in Brisbane – saw McLean brought back for one final Test. Brilliant in that match, McLean scored a record 21 points, signing off in style as Australia racked up an emphatic 33–9 victory.

HUGH McLEOD
Scotland 1954–62 (prop)

In his 40-Test career tight-head prop Hugh McLeod proved himself one of the best tight-forwards Scotland has ever produced. Despite being only 5ft. 9in. tall and weighing in at around 14 stone – miniscule for a prop then and now – McLeod was a fitness fanatic and mighty scrummager as well as a player of surprising pace who made a huge contribution in the loose. After beginning his Rugby career at the age of 16, it was less than a year before McLeod was drafted into the Hawick first-team pack, then one of the mightiest forward units in Britain. Within four years, and only just out of his teens, he made his Test debut against the 1954 All Blacks in Scotland's closest game against the New Zealanders – a 3–0 defeat at Murrayfield. Although McLeod went on to become one of Scotland's finest players, he found himself confined to the midweek dirt-trackers side on the 1955 Lions tour of South Africa, but he played in all six Tests on the 1959 tour to Australia and New Zealand, once memorably taking four strikes against the head in the 25–13 win over New Zealand Universities.

RAY McLOUGHLIN
Ireland 1962–75 (prop)

Few men have had a more profound and lasting effect on Irish Rugby than loose-head prop Ray McLoughlin. The UCD engineering graduate applied the same principles to Rugby that he did to his academic disciplines. This meant that, in addition to being an extremely competent prop, McLoughlin was one of the first players to understand and apply a full

HAWICK HARDMAN *Hugh McLeod.*

range of pre-match preparations. McLoughlin's organizational talent, and the results that could follow from it, first surfaced when he became captain of his province, the small and unfancied Connacht. Instead of meeting at lunchtime before provincial games, he insisted on the team training the day before a game and staying together in a hotel to go through the game plan. His emphasis on fitness training and working on the technical basics of the game found favour, and in 1965 McLoughlin was made captain of the national side, revolutionizing the outlook of Irish Rugby at the top level. It was a formula that also worked well for the Lions in 1966 and, more particularly, in 1971 when McLoughlin was left to run the forwards very successfully by coach Carwyn James. As a player, the technically outstanding McLoughlin was as tough as nails and a fierce competitor who won 40 caps for Ireland and three for the Lions in a career spanning 13 years. Yet it is for his intelligent, thoughtful approach to the game and emphasis on fitness that he will be most remembered.

HUGO MacNEILL
Ireland 1981–88 (full-back)

Hugo MacNeill probably ranks as Ireland's greatest attacking full-back. Never one to hide his light under a bushel, by the time he made his international debut at 22, he had already achieved the unprecedented feat of

captaining Blackrock College, Leinster Schools and Ireland Schools for two years in succession. A beautifully balanced runner, MacNeill played an adventurous brand of attacking Rugby and was always at his best when running from deep. Although an efficient place-kicker and a more than competent defender, it was his speed and sheer willingness to have a go that marked him out and brought him an Irish full-back record of eight tries. A scholar who captained Oxford University in two Varsity matches, MacNeill was always game for a laugh and was either the instigator or butt of many a team prank. Yet there was also a serious side to the Dubliner, such as his response to the IRFU's questionnaire to players in 1981, asking whether they would be willing to tour South Africa later that year. Despite having won only one cap, MacNeill was quick to return his form, stating that he did not wish to tour the country. Fortunately for MacNeill and Ireland, the tour was called off and the reluctant players continued their careers – which in MacNeill's case meant two Triple Crowns and another 39 caps, three of which he won with the Lions on the 1983 tour to New Zealand.

JO MASO
France 1966–73 (centre)

Perpignan and Narbonne centre Jo Maso won his 25 caps in spite of the system rather than because of it. Arguably the most gifted centre of his era, Maso was regarded by the connoisseurs as heir apparent to Andre Boniface, the legendary French centre of the late 1950s and early 1960s. Nevertheless, Maso had a chequered international career in a time when the French panel of selectors was dominated by safety-first former forwards. Dropped for a variety of ridiculous reasons, some of which including donning long hair and being too concerned with his attire both on and off the field, Maso's long absences were a mystery to every other Rugby playing country. A formidable footballer with a sizzling turn of foot, fine hands and a dangerous outside break, Maso also displayed a languid character when faced with

the incomprehensible selection criteria of the national panel. Only 22 when he made his debut against Italy in 1966, Maso's Test career spanned eleven seasons, yet saw him win only 26 caps before he finally called it a day at the end of the 1973 season.

COLIN MEADS
New Zealand 1957-71 (wing)
(*See **The Legends of Rugby**, pages 116-17*)

BRYN MEREDITH
Wales 1954–62 (hooker)

Byrn Meredith was the perfect exponent of front row play throughout his nine seasons and 42 caps for Wales and the British Lions. A precocious talent, Meredith went straight from school into the Newport side and by the age of 23 had forced his way into the Wales side, displacing Dai Davies to make his debut in the 1954 12–9 win over Ireland. Often working in tandem with props Courtenay Meredith and Billy Williams – with whom he starred for the 1955 Lions to South Africa – Meredith was a handful in both tight and loose and quickly established himself as the best hooker in the British Isles. Fearsomely fit, fast and rugged, Meredith made an unheard-of contribution in the loose, regularly popping up on the wing to round off a movement. If Meredith's outstanding form for the 1955 Lions helped him attain cult status in South Africa, by the time of his third Lions' tour, again to South Africa in 1962, he was regarded as a living legend. Meredith played superbly in all four Tests despite being part of an outgunned and outclassed Lions side. An immensely modest man who inspired confidence in all around him, Meredith remains the best hooker to have played for Wales, collecting 34 caps in eight years and being voted Welsh Sportsman of the Year on his retirement in 1962.

CLIFF MORGAN
Wales 1951–58 (fly-half)

The star attraction for Cardiff, Wales and the British Lions, Cliff Morgan was a fly-half capable of sparkling genius in attack and dogged resistance in defence. In tandem with Cardiff and Wales immortals Clem Thomas and Bleddyn Williams, he helped Cardiff become the dominant force in Welsh Rugby, and was a key factor in both Cardiff and Wales's win over Bob Thomas's All Blacks in 1953. Morgan was also a member of the Welsh Grand Slam side of 1952, and went on to lead his country to the Five Nations crown in 1956. For all the plaudits he won for his displays on British soil, however, it was as a British Lion that Morgan will be best remembered, not least because he remains the only Welshman to have captained a side to victory over the Springboks on South African soil. That 9–6 Third Test win in Cape Town came against all the odds, and put the Lions 2–1 up in a four-Test series that was eventually drawn. His feats in 1955 led the 'Boks of the time to label him the best fly-half ever to have visited the Republic, and it is certainly true that South Africa was the perfect environment for the quicksilver Morgan. With 29 Welsh caps to go alongside the four he won for the Lions, Morgan retired from Rugby in 1958 to enter the world of media. He proved as successful in the world of broadcasting as he was on the rug by field, eventually becoming the BBC's head of Outside Broadcasts.

TWINKLE TOES *Cliff Morgan.*

GROUND BREAKER *Murray Mexted.*

MURRAY MEXTED
New Zealand 1979–85 (No. 8)

In the process of winning 34 caps as an All Black, Mexted brought a new dimension to the play of the No. 8, his style never better demonstrated than in his First Test, against Scotland at Murrayfield in 1979. He won the ball toward the back of a line-out, then broke through the line, ball in one hand, and with long strides and side-steps, scored a try without the Scottish defence laying a hand on him. Mexted's height of 6ft. 5in. made him an ideal line-out ball-winner but he also had a fitness level and athleticism that made him seem, at times, to be an extra back. Playing Rugby was his joy and his vocation and at a time when many All Blacks complained of too much touring, Mexted was always available and always picked, playing series against Australia (1980, 1984), the tempestuous series against South Africa in 1981, the 4–0 series win over the Lions in 1983 and the tour to England and Scotland in 1983. Mexted was picked for the 1985 tour of South Africa and when that tour was abandoned, he went instead on the rebel Cavaliers tour in 1986, retiring after it. He also played club Rugby in France and was one of the first New Zealanders to play club Rugby in

South Africa. Mexted married a Miss Universe, Lorraine Downes, in 1986. His father Graham had been an All Black in 1950 and 1951.

LUCIEN MIAS
France 1951–59 (second row)

Although he captained France in only six internationals, Mias is regarded as one of the greatest captains in French Rugby history. His playing feats, passion, pride and his uncompromising style of leadership helped the under-rated French win the Test series against the Springboks in 1958 and set the scene for the development of French Rugby for the following decades. Mias made his debut against Scotland in 1951 in a re-shuffled French team following the previous season's 21–0 stuffing in Cardiff. In a dramatic reversal of fortunes, Mias and a rejuvenated French side came within a whisker of claiming France's first Grand Slam when they beat England, Wales and Scotland before being edged out 9–8 in Dublin. Lucien Mias won 17 caps between 1951 and 1954, when he abandoned Rugby to concentrate on his medical studies. At 25 he had left his teaching job to pursue his medical vocation, a break which helped him crystallize a new playing philosophy that he applied with ruthless efficiency during his second spell with the national team between 1958 and 1959. He returned to international action against Romania at the back end of 1957 and was immediately appointed tour captain for South Africa. Winning the series by drawing the First Test and then outmuscling the Springboks 9–5 in a Second Test trial of strength at Ellis Park has ensured Mias's place in France's Rugby Hall of Fame.

SYD MILLAR
Ireland 1958–70 (prop)

Through three Lions tours and 13 years at the top with Ireland, powerful prop Syd Millar earned entrance to Irish Rugby's Hall of Fame through his rugged play and the sheer consistency he displayed in a long and distinguished international career. Such was the esteem in which Millar was held that his involvement with

club, country and Lions was extended to a coaching and management role long after he retired as a player. A huge man for his time – he stood 6ft. 1in. tall and weighed over 16st – the intelligent Millar, a fly-half in his schoolboy days, was far more than a big bruiser. Fit, highly mobile, abrasive and technically astute, the Ballymena man was also able to switch to the loose-head at the highest level if necessary. Despite being discarded by Ireland for four years after a 27–6 drubbing by France in Paris in 1964 (in 1965 he was dropped from the Ulster pack), Millar came back stronger than ever in 1968 to win a further 14 Ireland caps and two Lions' caps on the 1968 tour to South Africa. It brought his caps tally to 37 for Ireland and nine for the Lions.

IAIN MILNE
Scotland 1979–90 (prop)

In many ways, "The Bear", as Iain Milne was affectionately known, was one of the great anomalies of Scottish forward play, a lumbering bull of a man whose greatest strength lay in his sheer strength. Although a capable footballer, it was Milne's destiny to build up a reputation as a formidable scrummager; the type of man even the Paparembordes of the world thought twice about taking issue with. But then, as Milne himself says, it was his ability to provide a solid tight platform that would allow Scotland to play No. 8s such as Derek White and Iain Paxton in the second row so that they could play a more fluid style and get away with it. Milne, who played for Heriots FP and Harlequins, won a total of 44 caps before he retired following the 1990 tour to New Zealand. His younger brother Kenny, with whom he scrummed down with in his last Test appearance, won 39 caps as a hooker.

HERBERT H. MORAN
Australia 1908 (flanker)

The captain of the 1908 Wallaby side which toured Britain, Dr Herbert H. Moran ("Paddy" to his many friends) is unique in that his first Test, a 9–3 loss against Wales at the Cardiff Arms Park, was also his last. Moran, though, was far, far more than a one-cap wonder. Injured for most of the tour of Britain – hence the single cap – Moran gave up international Rugby to concentrate on medicine and then pursued an alternative lifestyle as an itinerant Rugby player roaming the towns of Europe. The son of Irish immigrants, Moran became continually preoccupied with Catholicism and spent the rest of his life musing in France, Germany and Italy. An intensely subdued and contemplative soul, Moran was an outrageously talented player with the on-field aggression to match.

RAY MORDT

South Africa 1980–84 (wing)

Powerfully built Rhodesian right wing Ray Mordt ran his way into Rugby folklore when he scored back-to-back hat-tricks of Test tries, crossing three times in the Third Test against the All Blacks in Auckland in 1981 and against the US Eagles a week later. However, at the time his amazing record was overshadowed by wider political events. The Auckland Test became known as the "crazy Biggles" Test because an anti-Apartheid activist circled Eden Park in a light aircraft dropping flour bombs on the players and threatening to crash the plane into the crowd if the New Zealand Air Force tried to force him down, while the Test against the Eagles was held in virtual seclusion on a polo field after the date and venue were changed to avoid anti-Apartheid campaigners. As powerful as John Kirwan and as difficult to stop as Jonah Lomu, the stocky Mordt is still a legend in South Africa, where he was once memorably referred to as a "rhino in a man's body." Yet while he certainly possessed his fabled strength in abundance, it was speed, fearlessness and wonderful sense of balance that marked him out, allowing him to play in 18 Tests and score a total of 12 tries for South Africa. Those qualities were also much in demand elsewhere, and when South Africa's growing isolation reached the point of no return, Mordt packed his bags and joined Wigan Rugby League Club 1984.

MARK MORRISON

Scotland 1896–1904 (utility forward)

A rugged farmer, Mark Morrison won 23 caps and led Scotland 15 times, a record that stood until Arthur Smith's era, 60 years later. Morrison was one of the first stars of Scottish Rugby; a man who Jimmy Sinclair, the Springbok forward who doubled as a cricket international and opposed Morrison during the British Lions' tour of South Africa in 1903, described as "a real roughouse of a man, and a great leader". Morrison, who won his first cap in 1896 while a teenager playing for Royal HSFP, captained Scotland to Triple Crowns in 1901 and 1903, and also led the Lions to a 1–0 series defeat in South Africa in 1903. That series saw one of the more bizarre moments in international Rugby when, in the First Test, Morrison found that the South African captain was Alex Frew, who had played in Morrison's Triple Crown-winning side of 1901, while the referee was William Donaldson, with whom Morrison had played for Scotland against England and Ireland during the 1896 international campaign!

GRAHAM MOURIE

New Zealand 1977–82 (flanker)

A flanker with a cool, analytical brain and an astute captain on and off the field, Mourie led New Zealand successfully through a period when the All Blacks' dominance was under severe threat. He was first picked to lead a New Zealand 'B' team to Argentina in 1976 and won the first of his 21 caps against Phil Bennett's 1977 Lions. At the end of that year, he took over the captaincy for a tour of Italy and France and the following year was again leader when the All Blacks achieved the Grand Slam in Britain and Ireland for the first time. Injury and farming commitments interrupted Mourie's career, but he returned to Britain in 1979 to lead the All Blacks on a tour of England, Scotland and Wales. In 1981, he caused a storm in New Zealand Rugby when he refused to play against South Africa on its contro-

versial tour, but he returned for an end-of-year tour of Romania and France. In his last season, 1982, he led the All Blacks to a series win over Australia. Mourie wrote a book at the end of that year and, unusually for the time, told the NZRFU he was keeping the profits. He was therefore banned and was only reinstated in 1994 when he publicly advocated the appointment of John Hart as All Black coach. Mourie's tireless play, his inspiring leadership and his moral stance on South Africa ensured his place in New Zealand Rugby history.

BILL MULCAHY

Ireland 1958–65 (lock)

There can be no better testament to a player than being lauded by the best of his generation. On that basis, lock Bill "Wiggs" Mulcahy must rank alongside the best Ireland have ever produced, for none other than Willie-John McBride described his play in South Africa for the 1962 Lions as "among the best performances I have ever seen". Modest and stoical off the pitch, Mulcahy was a raging bull on it, proving one of the most adept tight mauling forwards of his time. Not very tall for a second-row, the Limerick man was nevertheless an extremely adept line-out jumper who comfortably held his own against both Colin Meads and Avril Malan, two of the greatest Southern Hemisphere locks of that (and any other) time. A player of remarkably few frills and incredible consistency, although Mulcahy captained Ireland seven times during his 41-cap career, he was by common consent at his best during his second Lions' tour in 1962. His first Lions outing, to Australasia in 1959, had been severely disrupted by a serious shoulder injury that restricted him to two Tests, but three years later he came of age as a player, being described by the Springboks at the time as the finest player forward to have visited South Africa since the war. A player who led by example and was never intimidated, Mulcahy's powers of motivation became so apparent that he was frequently made captain for midweek Lions games in South Africa.

KARL MULLEN

Ireland 1947–52 (hooker)

In a country that has sent forth more British Lions captains than any other, Old Belvedere hooker Karl Mullen remains the best and most successful captain Ireland have ever produced. In a career spanning just six seasons and 25 caps, Mullen took Ireland to their solitary Grand Slam in 1948, the Triple Crown in 1949 and led the 1950 Lions in in the shared series against Australia and New Zealand. While the legendary Ireland fly-half Jack Kyle marshalled the backs for Ireland and the Lions, the indefatigable Mullen spurred his forwards onto ever greater efforts. Unfortunately, the Lions pack available to Mullen, while strong enough to dispatch the Wallabies in both Tests, lacked the mettle to live with an All Black side that had revolutionized loose play by adopting the rucking game as coached by Vic Cavanagh and practised by Otago. The result was a 3–0 whitewash on the Lions' visit across the Tasman Sea. A shrewd tactician, Mullen was a step away from the traditional blood and thunder, up and at 'em approach to captaincy generally favoured by the Irish. Although thick-set and technically outstanding at the set-piece, Mullen's own ability to keep up with a running game played at a frantic pace tended to influence the style of play he advocated, and for most of his representative career his main concern was unleashing the creativity of Jack Kyle and his talented back-line.

HENNIE MULLER

South Africa 1949–53 (No. 8)

Known as the "Whippet", Hennie Muller was arguably one of the fastest forwards to have played for the Springboks. As a dynamic No. 8 he was the scourge of the 1949 All Blacks, who were whitewashed 4–0 in the series. Muller's whipcord physique and hardness were moulded in his job in a gold mine near Boksburg, and his speed, big-hit tackling and relentless pursuit made playing against him a harrowing experience. He was the only player to figure in all thirteen Tests after the Second World War during which the Springboks, then regarded as the best side in the world, lost only to the Wallabies in 1953 in Cape Town. Muller inherited the captaincy following a serious eye injury to Basil Kenyon during the 1951–52 tour of Britain when he further established his reputation as a fine leader and No. 8. The Springboks won all four Tests on that tour, thrashing Scotland 44–0 when Muller displayed his full repertoire of skills. He was a kind, compassionate man, very different to the steely-eyed destroyer on the pitch. On Muller's premature death aged 55, South Africa's Rugby doyen, Dr Danie Craven, described him thus: "He was finely strung and emotional, a strong man, who, nevertheless, could and did cry tears of sorrow and joy".

BRENDAN MULLIN

Ireland 1984–95 (centre)

A schoolboy prodigy, Blackrock flier Brendan Mullin was one of the most complete centres to have played for Ireland. A dual international, Mullin excelled at athletics in his early years and for a while combined his sprinting and Rugby careers, breaking the 30-year-old Irish 110 metres hurdles record in 1986, two years after he made his debut in the Irish side beaten by the 1984 Grand Slam Wallabies. Eventually, though, the demands of working as a stockbroker meant that the well-heeled Dubliner was forced to choose between Rugby and athletics, and fortunately chose the oval ball above the spikes. Although Mullin was sometimes accused of floating in and out of games late in his career, he was for the most part a wonderfully committed player who matched his pace with his timing in the tackle. Indeed, timing was another one of Mullin's main assets, and his slick handling meant that, despite notching up an Irish record of 17 international tries, he was as much a try provider as a try scorer.

Incredibly quick, Mullin also had a wiry strength that was allied to sound technique and perception to make him a formidable defender. A fine all-round player who also played at full-back, wing and fly-half for Ireland, Mullin remains Ireland's most capped specialist centre with a half-century of caps to his name.

NOEL MURPHY

Ireland 1958–69 (flanker)

A flanker of fire and incredible persistence, Cork Constitution battler Noel Murphy was almost an ever-present for Ireland through 12 seasons, during which time he won 49 caps for Ireland and the Lions. From the time that Murphy made his debut, aged just 20, in the famous 9–6 win over the touring Wallabies in 1958, he quickly established himself as one of the most consistent performers of his generation. A fiery character, Murphy was also a naturally gifted footballer who could play either openside or blind-side with equal alacrity. An intelligent player who rarely took a wrong option, Murphy was a canny and strong defender who also excelled as an outstanding runner in attack. Although Murphy never managed to win a Triple Crown, he did prove that he could make the step up to a higher level when he toured with the 1959 and 1966 Lions to Australasia, excelling on the successful tour of '59 before being part of a side eclipsed by All Black forward power seven years later. Murphy retired in 1969, after he was famously decked by a Welsh forward in Ireland's disappointing 24–11 loss. He retains a keen interest in Rugby administration and has worked in a coaching or managerial capacity for Ireland and the Lions as recently as 1995.

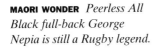

MAORI WONDER *Peerless All Black full-back George Nepia is still a Rugby legend.*

GEORGE NEPIA

New Zealand 1924–30 (full-back)

Although he only won nine caps Nepia is one of the most revered figures in All Black history. A member of the 1924–25 "Invincibles" tour to Britain and France, he played in all 30 matches on the tour plus another two in Canada on the way home. He also played in four matches in Australia and two in New Zealand as a warm-up for the tour. As a 19-year-old Nepia won much praise for his kicking, tackling and fielding of the ball. In the 13 months after his debut, Nepia played 39 consecutive matches for New Zealand but he played only another seven for the rest of his career. He couldn't go on the All Blacks' tour of South Africa in 1928 because he was a Maori, while injury restricted his appearances in Australia in 1929, but he was back to play all four of the Tests against the British Isles in 1930. He tried unsuccessfully to make the 1935–36 team for Britain and captained a New Zealand Maori team to Australia. He switched to Rugby League with Halifax in 1936 and played for New Zealand at League in 1937. He returned to Rugby Union in 1947, at the age of 42, and in 1950 he became the oldest man to play in a New Zealand first-class match when he led the Olympians club against Poverty Bay

GWYN NICHOLLS

Wales 1896–1906 (centre)

The man who helped usher Wales into their first "golden era" of 1900–1911, when they won the Triple Crown six times, and the first Welshman ever to represent the British Isles, Gwyn Nicholls remains one of the founding fathers of Welsh Rugby. A strong-running three-quarter who was capped 28 times for Wales and the Lions, Nicholls was brave in the tackle and had outstanding on-field judgement. He was also a potent attacking weapon and an intelligent captain for both Cardiff and Wales. After making his debut against Scotland in 1896, he established himself as one of the best backs in Britain, touring New Zealand with the British Isles side in 1899 and playing in all four Tests as well as ending the tour as top-scorer. Already a member of the Triple Crown-winning sides of 1900 and 1902, Nicholls led Wales to a Triple Crown in 1905 and then onto a famous 3–0 win over the All Blacks, a feat he almost repeated with Cardiff before the visitors eventually triumphed 10–8. Despite Nicholls' continuing brilliance for Cardiff, the following season saw his international demise when an 11–6 defeat by Ireland was followed by an 11–0 defeat at the hands of the first Springbok touring party, led by Paul Roos. Despite masterminding Cardiff's emphatic 17–0 thrashing of the same Springboks,

Nicholls was deemed to have passed his sell-by date and was never again selected for Wales.

BOB NORSTER
Wales 1982–89 (lock)

One of the great forward confrontations in the Northern Hemisphere throughout the late 1980s was between Wales's lock Bob Norster and England's Wade Dooley. Only 6ft. 5in. tall, Norster was the perfect technician, a spring-heeled line-out jumper with immaculate timing who ensured Wales a constant supply of quality line-out ball. In the opposite corner was 6ft. 8in. Dooley, a streetwise bruiser who ruled the line-out jungle through a mixture of brute force and determination. Despite his prodigious talent, Norster was in many ways atypical of Welsh tight forwards during the 1980s. A mobile lock who preferred a fast rucking game to the more static mauling game favoured by the Gwent forwards, Norster was also a scrupulously fair player who shied away from niggle and confrontation. After serving as understudy to Allan Martin, the Cardiff man made his debut in the 34–18 home humiliation at the hands of an Andy Irvine-inspired Scotland. Although Welsh defeats became depressingly regular throughout the 1980s, Norster was still able to provide Wales with a lifeline to possession, and was to prove his credentials independently when he emerged as the single most important Lions' forward on the 1983 tour to New Zealand. In all, Norster won 34 caps for Wales, equalling his mentor Allan Martin's record number of caps, and three Lions' caps (two against New Zealand in 1983 and one against Australia in 1989).

JOHN O'DRISCOLL
Ireland 1978–84 (flanker)

London Irish captain John O'Driscoll was big, intelligent and gritty – the

HIGH ROLLER *Tony O'Reilly.*

perfect qualities in a blind-side flanker for Ireland as well as the Lions that toured South Africa in 1980. A great thinker on the game, even when the red mist had descended in the heat of international combat, O'Driscoll was very astute and had the leadership qualities to take his back-row with him. The second O'Driscoll to play for Ireland in the 1970s – older brother Barry won four caps in the 1971 Five Nations championship – John won his first cap in the 12–8 win over Scotland at Lansdowne Road in 1978. Within a season of establishing himself as an Ireland regular, in 1980 – the year in which he also distinguished himself with the Lions in South Africa, winning a Test berth in all four internationals – the erudite doctor had become the rallying point for his countrymen. His intelligent, determined performances culminated in a series of outstandingly dogged displays in 1982 and '83, when he was widely acknowledged as the forward who helped shape Ireland's Triple Crown campaign of 1982.

TONY O'REILLY
Ireland 1955–70 (wing)

One of the most colourful characters ever to play for Ireland (an accolade in itself), Tony O'Reilly also ranks – alongside Mike Gibson and Jackie Kyle – as one of the three best backs Ireland has ever produced. By the tender age of 18, O'Reilly had made his international debut and arrived in South Africa as first-choice wing for the 1955 Lions. At 6ft. 2in., 15 stone, and with a blistering turn of speed, O'Reilly's impact was similar to John Kirwan in 1987 or Jonah

Lomu in 1995. Difficult to put down and fiercely determined, he proved the sensation of the tour, returning with two tries in four internationals and the undying admiration of the Springboks. O'Reilly's outside career boomed, but business and Rugby were incompatible, limiting him to 29 Irish caps, and he was never at his best on the European stage. Further proof of O'Reilly's greatness came in 1959, on the Lions tour to Australasia, when he scored four tries in six Tests. All told, O'Reilly scored 38 tries for the Lions, a record unlikely to be beaten. His Test career ended in off-beat fashion, seven years after his last cap. On a business trip to London in 1970, he was called up after right-wing Bill Brown was injured in training before the Twickenham game. Overweight and nowhere near match fit, O'Reilly's main contribution to the game was to raise Irish morale by pitching up in his chauffeur-driven Rolls Royce!

WILLIE OFAHENGAUE
Australia 1990– (flanker)

From the time that "Willie-O" made his first huge hit on All Black flanker Alan Whetton during the opening play of the first Bledisloe Cup Test in 1990, Australia knew it had unearthed a real gem. But if Ofahengaue was to become one of the greats of Australian Rugby, it owed as much to luck as judgement. Tongan-born and raised, the 6ft. 4in. Ofahengaue toured Australia as a New Zealand Colt in 1988 only to find himself denied entry back into New Zealand by customs officials. The All Blacks' loss was the Wallabies' gain, however, as the ARFU successfully petitioned the government to allow Willie-O to be allowed to stay in Sydney with his uncle. From that moment on, with the exception of an injury-plagued 1993, Ofahengaue became central to Bob Dwyer's plans, providing him with a dynamic breakaway who could be relied upon to cross the gain line every time he took the ball on, while also acting as an extremely effective stopper on the blind-side. Ofahengaue also did much unseen work, and Australia's try in the 1991 World Cup Final was typical. At a line-out ten metres from the England line, Phil Kearns threw the ball over the fourth man in the

PILE DRIVER *Wille Ofahengaue demonstrates the "Tongan Sidestep"!*

line to Ofahengaue, who was then rolled round into midfield towards the England try-line, from where prop Tony Daly emerged as the try-scorer, the only one of that final. Injury prevented Ofahenagaue from taking part in the 1996 Tri-Nations series and, with a fresh crop of talent installed in the Australian back-row, his international days look numbered.

PHIL ORR
Ireland 1976–87 (prop)

One of the key players in Ireland's Triple Crown campaign of 1983 was gargantuan loose-head prop Phil Orr, a rock in the Ireland front-row for 12 seasons after coming on as a replacement in Paris to win his first cap in 1976. While fly-half Ollie Campbell provided the finishing touches during that 1983 campaign, it was generally recognized that it was a series of gutsy performances from an adrenaline-fuelled Irish pack that turned the screws throughout that season. Few forwards were more adept at applying telling pressure than Orr; his contribution in the loose was never overwhelming, but his scrummaging ability was legendary. A phenomenally bright man, Orr shared many of the attributes and the technical excellence of his predecessor Ray McLoughlin, but tended to have a more laid-back demeanour, and he lacked McLoughlin's obsessive tendencies. Not that Orr was not dedicated, quite the reverse. His thick mop was always in the thick of the action, and throughout his 58 caps for Ireland he displayed a consistent fervour and desire to win that made him one of the great Irish props.

ROBERT PAPAREMBORDE
France 1975–83 (prop)

One of the all-time great scrummagers, Robert Paparemborde had a fearsome reputation as a tough man to get to grips with. This was due, in large part,

PAPA! *Robert Paparemborde.*

to the fact that his shoulders seemed to come all the way up to meet his head – as England prop Mike Burton once said, if he had a neck, then there was certainly no way of telling. A big man, although not quite in the same weight class as monsters such as his long-time international tight-head partner Gerard Cholley, Paparemborde allied a supreme technique at the set-piece with a fierce determination and surprising agility. That many opponents were surpised by his agility, however, is more down to their lack of homework: as a top class handball player and judo black belt, Paparemborde's athletic qualities were hardly well hidden. Paparemborde began his international career the hard way, on the whitewashed tour to South African in 1975, but soon established himself as the cornerstone of the feared French pack of the late 1970s, playing in all four internationals as France won their second ever Grand Slam in 1977. An ability to bore in at the hooker was an invaluable part of his repertoire, yet the Pau hardman was never a dirty player. Having won a record 55 caps including a second Grand Slam in 1981 when he announced his retirement, Paparemborde remains France's most capped prop forward.

IAIN PAXTON
Scotland 1981–88 (No. 8)

Iain Paxton's international Rugby career started in 1981 when he toured New Zealand playing in both Test matches against the All Blacks. From then until his retirement in 1988, Paxton was a major force in the Scottish pack either as No.8 or lock. He played in all four matches in the 1984 Grand Slam season, relegating his long-time rival John Beattie to a spot on the replacements' bench. Paxton's inclusion on the 1983 British Lions' tour to New Zealand owed a great deal to his outstanding form during the previous season's Five Nations. Against Wales in particular, Paxton was in superb form, scoring one of the greatest tries ever seen at Cardiff Arms Park as Scotland beat Wales at home for the first time since 1962. Paxton duly repaid the selectors' faith by playing some of his best Rugby. When he finished his career in 1988 Paxton was Scotland's most capped No. 8 with 36 caps.

FRANCOIS PIENAAR
South Africa 1993– (flanker)

Francois Pienaar is a strange Rugby player: a man almost as important for what he represents as for how he plays the game. Pienaar is the exciting new Afrikaner face of South African Rugby which profited from the country's democracy both during and after its wonderful World Cup triumph of 1995. As the most identifiable face of the tournament, Pienaar's massive contribution as captain on and off the field, stretched into homes of all colours and cultures. He became a role model for young, disadvantaged blacks and helped enormously to spread the game into the townships and non-white areas. After 29 Tests as captain from his debut against France in 1993 – a record eclips-

ing the previous best held by Dawie de Villiers – his controversial axing by new national coach Andre Markgraaff before the 1996 tour to Argentina and France caused a national uproar. Upset at his treatment, Pienaar took advantage of the new professional era and made a lucrative move to London club Saracens where he is now coach, acknowledging in the process that his international days could well have come to a premature end.

SIMON POIDEVIN
Australia 1980–91 (flanker)

Australia's most capped flanker with 59 caps, New South Wales flanker Simon Poidevin was also one of the fittest players ever to wear the green and gold. An urbane, sophisticated stockbroker off the pitch, Poidevin

WORLD BEATER *Francois Pienaar.*

PERFECTIONIST *Simon Poidevin.*

was the original "100 per center" on it, yet he wasn't a selfish player and never lost sight of his belief that his role was to help others play the game. This attitude, combined with his incredible levels of fitness and speed to the breakdown, created a flanker who snaffled countless tries out wide, while also acting as a linkman to provide endless quick ball to his backs. In other words, he was the perfect flanker for the game Australia have played in modern times. Captain of the ill-fated tour to Argentina in 1987, after which he temporarily retired, Poidevin rates winning the World Cup in 1991 and winning the Bledisloe Cup on New Zealand soil in 1986 as the high points of his career. The best summary of Poidevin was that by Mark Ella in his autobiography *Path to Victory*: "Simon is such a perfectionist, it's almost a disease. Not only is he the best Rugby player in Australia, he's the most determined."

HUGO PORTA

Argentina 1974-91 (fly-half)
*(See **The Legends of Rugby**, pages 118-19)*

JEAN PRAT

France 1945–55 (flanker)

Jean Prat was the man who finally put French Rugby on the map. A wing forward and captain emeritus, Prat missed only three games in an illustrious international career during which he played 51 Tests for France over an eleven-year period. Born in 1923 on his father's farm, within sight of the Lourdes Rugby club, the man nicknamed "Monsieur Rugby" became the catalyst of a revolution in French Rugby, largely described as the "Lourdes Phenomenon". Under his visionary leadership, the Lourdes club won six Championship titles in ten years, the last three with him as player-coach after his retirement from international Rugby in 1955. Prat was first capped on the New Year's day in 1945 against the British Army team at Parc des Princes. The game was a watershed in French Rugby history, hence the decision to award caps against a Services side. It was France's first game since matches were suspended in 1940, and it was against the same opponents at Parc des Princes), 13 new caps were awarded on the day and it heralded the resumption of the relations with the Home Unions severed in 1931. Jean Prat became captain in 1953 against Scotland and he scored a then record 146 points for France before his retirement in 1955.

GRAHAM PRICE

Wales 1975–83 (prop)

If Fran Cotton ranks as the greatest British loose-head of the modern era, then Welshman Graham Price certainly ranks as the greatest tight-head. In 41 caps for Wales and 12 consecutive Tests for the Lions on tours in 1977, '80 and '83, Price proved himself the strongest and most formidable scrummager in international Rugby against the best the Southern Hemisphere had to offer. Perfect technique, a huge reservoir of natural strength and a grimly determined mindset were the tools of the trade for Wales's most capped prop. In tandem with his two Pontypool front row teammates – fellow Lions Bobby Windsor and Charlie Faulkner, or the "Viet Gwent" as Max Boyce christened the threesome – the softly-spoken Gwent strongman dominated Welsh front row play in the late 1970s and early 1980s. Not that the Price was just a scrummager, as he showed in his debut at the Parc des Princes when French No. 8 Jean-Pierre Bastiat spilled the ball just outside the Welsh '22 and Price seized it before running 75 yards for a try that sealed a 25–10 win. Some would argue that his decision to retire in 1983 at the age of 32 was premature, but Price continued to play for his beloved Pontypool as late as 1989 when he packed down against the touring All Blacks.

JOHN PULLIN

England 1966–76 (hooker)

A quiet man, Bristol farmer and hooker John Pullin was the sort of unsung hero who inspires respect and admiration from team-mates and opponents alike. Certainly, as England captain during the worst period in the country's Rugby history, Pullin was able to work miracles as he drew the team together to chalk up unlikely victories over every one of the major nations – with New Zealand and South Africa being beaten in their own back yards in two of international Rugby's greatest upsets. Impressive statistics certainly, but they do not explain the impact of a man who won 42 caps for England and seven for the Lions in a career that spanned eleven seasons. Not a big man by modern standards, Pullin was nevertheless an immensely rugged customer who allied natural strength with a rigorous training regime and a profound technical grasp of his trade. A quick-footed striker of the ball at the scrum, Pullin was also guaranteed to steal at least one ball against the head no matter the quality of the opposition. A player who poured every ounce of his energies into perfecting the science of set-piece play, Pullin was never a huge presence in the loose, but was a stalwart for England and as first choice hooker for the '68 Lions to South Africa and the '71 Lions to New Zealand he proved himself one of the best tight-forwards in the world.

JIM RENWICK

Scotland 1972–84 (centre)

The bald pate of Hawick's Jim Renwick was one of the most familiar sights of the 1970s. Although the Borderer's lack of hair made him look a deal older, and at times he was overshadowed by the genius of John Rutherford, Renwick was no journeyman. Staunch in defence, it was in attack where he was at his most effective. A short man, he had the ability to wriggle through tackles and to consistently break the gain line. Renwick announced his presence on the international stage with a try on his debut against France in 1972. He went on to score another seven in a career that won him 52 caps and a place on the British Lions' tour to South Africa in 1980. Renwick played in the First Test against the Springboks but was subsequently dropped in favour of England's Clive Woodward. On his return to Britain, Renwick continued to play for Scotland until he retired at the beginning of the 1984 season. Somwhat unfortunately for Renwick, Scotland went on to win the Grand Slam that season!

DEAN RICHARDS

England 1986–96 (No. 8)

"Deano", as No. 8 Dean Richards is widely known, was the single most influential forward in the Northern Hemisphere from his debut in 1986 until the last of his 48 caps against Ireland a decade later. A huge bear of a man whose lumbering gait belied a shrewd Rugby brain and a determination to win at all costs, Richards' preference for the rolling maul coincided perfectly with England's priorities and strengths in the late 1980s as the Leicester man became the driving force behind England's gargantuan and unstoppable pack. Despite his less than athletic frame, Richards always seemed to be in the right place at the right time because of his knack of knowing where the ball would end up. He regularly took games by the scruff of the neck as he drew the ball into his mighty mitts and dragged team-mates along with him. Never happier than when engaged in a war of attrition, as England looked to play a more expansive game Richards' lack of speed was perceived as a deficiency rather than a virtue. It was this atti-

OLD CONTEMPTABLE *Dean Richards.*

tude that led Richards to be dropped for the 1991 World Cup campaign where he was replaced by Mick Skinner. A marvellously intuitive player and a cult hero wherever he played, the shy and retiring Richards also won six caps for the British Lions.

TOM RICHARDS

Australia 1908–12 (flanker)

The younger brother of distinguished Wallaby second row Billy Richards, Tom Richards became one of the greatest and most-travelled breakaway forwards ever seen. Hailing from the tough, Rugby-obsessed Queens-

land gold town of Charters Towers, he followed brother Billy's example by winning three caps (compared to his brother's five), yet there can surely be no better example of statistics failing to tell the full story than in the case of Tom Richards. When the Richards's father migrated towards the gold fields of South Africa's High Veldt in 1906 and the brothers worked their way into the Transvaal team, Tom suddenly realized the opportunities that Rugby afforded for travel and became the game's first – and finest – Rugby nomad. Over the years, he represented most of the giants of international Rugby, including: Queensland, Transvaal, Bristol, Gloucestershire, Australia (winning an Olympic Gold medal in 1908), the British Lions (he played two Tests against South Africa in 1910), and Toulouse (with whom he won the French Championship). As The Times said in 1908, when Richards had again proved the scourge of the English: "If ever the Earth had to select a team to play Mars, Tom Richards would be the first player chosen."

BEV RISMAN

England 1959–61 (fly-half)

The son of the legendary Gus Risman, who won 17 caps for Great Britain at Rugby League, Bev was a brilliant fly-half in the Union game before switching to his father's code and joining Leigh RLFC aged 25 after just eight caps for England. Yet in those three short years Risman did more than enough to establish himself as one of the all-time greats, displaying a consistent ability to breach the gain-line in a time of sterile attacking play. Indeed, it was only Risman's immense misfortune in becoming injured in 1960 and being replaced by Richard Sharp – the only back of the time who could hold a candle to Risman – that thwarted a long and successful union career after the experiment of playing Risman at centre in 1961 failed. A running fly-half capable of tearing sides apart and with perfect timing, exquisite hands and a fine tactical boot, the young Mancunian showed what could have been on the Lions tour of 1959 in his first season of international Rugby.

Although injured for the middle two Tests in New Zealand, Risman was the driving force behind convincing wins in Australia and gave a virtuoso performance in the final Test, scoring a dazzling late try to give the Lions a much-deserved victory. Predictably, Risman was a major success in League, playing for Great Britain and kicking seven goals against New Zealand in his final Test.

JEAN-PIERRE RIVES

France 1975-84 (centre)
(See **The Legends of Rugby***, pages 120-1)*

PETER ROBBINS

England 1956–62 (flanker)

Peter Robbins was the prototype of the modern open-side flanker: strong, fast and very fit. Yet Robbins was also one of the great thinkers, and memorably led Oxford University to victory in 1955 against a exceptionally talented Cambridge side. Ever the pragmatist, Robbins worked out that Cambridge's back division could not play without the ball and so kept it in the Dark Blues' front five all game – Oxford eventually won 3–0! One incident illustrates better than any other the calibre of Robbins' game. In the 1958 match against Australia, an early injury meant that centre Jeff Butterfield moved to fly-half and Robbins was asked to play in the centres. Rather than become a weakness, so refined were the Coventry man's distributive skills that he dominated the game, his quick hands setting up the late try-scoring opportunity through which Peter Jackson turned the game.

A naturally witty man who lived life to the full, Robbins' antics often backfired upon him. As well as upsetting some of the stuffier members of the RFU with his forthright views and constant lampooning of officials, Robbins also missed out on the 1959 Lions tour when he broke his leg larking about in a bath after a game on the Barbarians Easter tour to Wales. The best flanker in the world at that time, it was a cruel blow, but one from which the 16-times capped Robbins bounced back with characteristic charm.

KEITH ROBERSTON

Scotland 1978–89 (wing)

A legend down Melrose way, Keith Robertson never possessed the acceleration which usually marks out the great wings. Yet what he lacked in out-and-out pace he more than made up for in guile and sheer footballing ability. An accomplished Sevens player, the willowy Melrose wing – he was a shade under 11 stone – was also a prolific try-scorer at every level except international. During his Scotland career, which spanned 11 years, Robertson only managed to score eight tries. Comfortable either as a centre, where he won 20 of his 44 caps, or on the wing, he won his last cap against France in 1989 at the ripe old age of 34. Much like John Rutherford, Robertson had a languid look to him, an aristocrat of the back division – a complete footballer who could and did play in several positions. Although Roberston never made a Lions' tour, he did scoop a Grand Slam in 1984 when Scotland beat France at Murrayfield in the first-ever Grand Slam decider. Now involved with the Border's Rugby, he has long been an advocate of professionalism in the Scottish game.

FLYING SCOTSMAN *Keith Robertson*

LAURENT RODRIGUEZ

France 1981–90 (No. 8)

A durable, robust bruiser, Rodriguez was a man of huge strength whose charges from the back of the scrum would take three or four players to stop. Although particularly in vogue during the time when coach Jacques Fouroux was obsessed with fielding gargantuan packs, the "Bull of Dax" was always far more than just a big man. A skilled ball player, he showed an acute tactical sense during a career that brought him 56 caps. Although never an instigator of the rough stuff, Rodriguez was more than able to hold his own as the Wallabies first found out during the bad-tempered series of 1981 in which he made his debut. Drafted into the side immediately after the 1981 Grand Slam, Rodriguez was to win the ultimate European prize in 1987, which turned out to cap a magnificent 12 months for the Dax player. First, in 1986, Rodriguez had been outstanding when the French beat the All Blacks 16–3 in a frenzied assault during the Second Test. So gruelling was the Rugby that New Zealand legend Buck Shelford, who required 22 stitches in his scrotum after the match, called it the hardest match he had ever played in, adding that he was convinced the French must have been

DAX BULL *Laurent Rodriguez.*

"on something" to play with such sustained savagery. A year later, another Rodriguez crowning moment occured when he was again instrumental in France's injury-time 1987 World Cup semi-final win over Australia in one of the great contests of all time.

ALFRED ROQUES

France 1958–63 (prop)

Arguably one of the most formidable forwards of the 20th century and an eccentric of class, the larger than life Alfred Roques played his first game of Rugby aged 26 and made his international debut at the tender age of 33 against Australia. He was an instant success, his formidable strength, mobility and all-round ability securing him a further 27 selections. A player with local side, the Stade Cadurcien club, offered him a contract and he became the axle of a fearsome pack which won promotion to the first division in 1955.

In 1958, after an infamous match against the then mighty Lourdes, he was spotted by the selectors and made his debut shortly afterwards in the 19–0 win against Australia.

OLIVIER ROUMAT

France 1989– (lock)

Up until the age of 18 Olivier Roumat channelled all his sporting energies into basketball. Then one day his father – a former player with Mont de Marsan and now an official at the famous Dax club – persuaded him to take up the game. At 6ft. 7in., weighing over 17 stone and with a basketball player's hands, Roumat took to the game with alacrity and, at the age of 22, made his debut against the All Blacks. The most consistent line-out jumper in France for many years, Roumat soon became a regular feature of the second row, although he did miss the 1992 tour to Argentina after being sent-off for stamping whilst playing for the World XV against the All Blacks in the 1992 Centenary Celebrations. Roumat has had his share of periods out of favour – such as when he played for Natal for a season against the wishes of the French Federation – but has also had some glorious successes against the

cream of the Southern Hemisphere. Those finest moment include leading France to a series win over South Africa (the first on South African soil since 1958), captaining France during the shock win over the world champion Wallabies in Bordeaux in 1993, and then in 1994 the awesome achievement of being part of the only side except the 1937 Springboks to win two Tests in a row in New Zealand.

MANNETJIES ROUX

South Africa 1960–1974 (centre)

Mannetjies Roux, the popular name of Francois du Toit Roux, was a brilliant individualist and yet another product of the celebrated Stellenbosch factory line where Danie Craven rolled out world class backs with almost indecent speed. A small, agile man and a darting, nippy runner, Roux was also a killer tackler with a big heart, often taking on and bringing down forwards twice his size. But it was an infamous tackle on British Lions' star Richard Sharp which won him international notoriety because of the fractured cheekbone suffered by the England fly-half in the incident during the 1962 tour match against Northern Transvaal. Putting Sharp – the only British back capable of unlocking the Springbok defences – out of commission earned him the label in the Fleet Street press as the "Monster", a sobriquet hardly fitting a man standing 5ft. 8in. and 13 stone in a dripping wet shirt. Roux was to go on to a distinguished career of 27 Tests, 21 at centre and six on the wing, his less preferred position. An accomplished try-scorer, the pick of his bunch was try against the Lions in the Fourth Test in 1962 when he sidestepped and waltzed through six tackles to score. Mannetjies ended his career on a high note as a star of the 3–1 series win over the powerful 1970 All Blacks.

JOHN RUTHERFORD

Scotland 1979–87 (fly-half)

Outside Wales, perhaps only the Irish pair of Tony Ward and Ollie Campbell were able to hold a candle to fly-half John Rutherford, the man who dominated Scottish back play for

STAR TURN *John Rutherford.*

most of the 1980s. Rutherford was peerless when halfback partner Roy Laidlaw dogged it out in front of him and gave the Selkirk man time by providing quick ruck and maul ball as the Scots tried to play a fast-moving game. Deceptively quick and a natural athlete, he was able to hoof the ball prodigious distances or beat a man one-on-one, seemingly at will. Allied to a keen Rugby intellect, Rutherford was Scotland's star turn throughout the 1980s. Surprisingly durable for a slender man, Rutherford was an ever present from his first cap in 1979 – the year when Scotland lost five Tests – until injury finally finished him off during the 1987 World Cup opener against France. His high points were a Grand Slam in 1984 and playing for the 1983 Lions in New Zealand, even if it was at centre outside Ollie Campbell in a whitewashed side.

ULI SCHMIDT

South Africa 1986–94 (hooker)

Uli Schmidt was the cult hero of the

Loftus Versfeld faithful in Northern Transvaal's Pretoria. They chanted his name – U-li, U-li, U-li – in passionate adoration until he moved to rivals Transvaal. Then they booed him. But when he played in the green and gold of South Africa, Schmidt was still a favourite son, like his Springbok father Louis, who played two Tests on the flank against the French in 1958. Arguably the world's best hooker until a neck injury forced his retirement only five months before the 1995 World Cup, Schmidt and controversy have never been far apart. A doctor, he spoke his mind and stood firm on his principles, once making himself unavailable for a tour because he felt aggrieved that South Africa had to play Test matches without a national anthem being played. A part-time triathlete, Schmidt was fearsomely fit and fast. Outstanding in both tight and loose, he regularly turned up on the wing when he was expected to be in the heat of the action. He was viewed by some as a traitor and the political overtones surrounding him put his career on hold for a while in 1992, the year of politically acceptable unity in South African Rugby. But for injury, the Springbok's isolation and his self-imposed periods on the sidelines, the charismatic Schmidt would have won many more than the 17 caps he claimed and scored many more than five tries, the best of them against the New Zealand Cavaliers at Loftus in 1986.

KEN SCOTLAND

Scotland 1957–65 (full-back)

Like Gavin Hastings against France nearly three decades later, Ken Scotland started his international career on a high note, scoring all six points in his country's win over France. Yet although Scotland made a huge impact as he won his first cap aged 19, it could all have been so different. Until circumstances caused his selection at full-back for the Scottish Trial earlier that year, Scotland had always played fly-half. That experience of playing fly-half added another dimension to his game, and he soon emerged as the first true attacking full-back in an age where a safety-first atti-

PROTOTYPE *Ken Scotland.*

tude and a large boot were the most important attributes for any No.15. Although he struggled to establish himself at Cambridge University, it did give him a chance to work in tandem with Scotland's visionary fly-half Gordon Waddell, also at Cambridge, on the move where the full-back came into the line at speed between fly-half and inside centre. Novel at the time, it is now the staple diet of attacking full-backs the world over. Scotland made the cut for the 1959 Lions tour to New Zealand, playing five of the six Tests despite going as second choice to Welshman Terry Davies. The Fourth Test win is still regarded as the high point of an outstanding career in which one man redefined the role of full-back, winning 27 caps in the process.

PHILIPPE SELLA

France 1982–95 (centre)

Agen centre Philippe Sella retired from international Rugby in 1995 as the most capped player in the history of the game after wearing the French jersey in a total of 106 full Tests. A stocky player whose prodigious strength in defence was allied to a blistering turn of pace in attack, Sella was also remarkably consis-

tent, his durability leading to a run of 45 consecutive Tests at one stage, while he scored tries at a steady rate throughout his career, finishing with a tally of 30. Sella made his international debut, aged 20, on the wing in a rare defeat by Romania in 1982, although he was not in any state to care after being concussed and spending the night in a Bucharest hospital. Sella also played a number of games at full-back. The milestones in an unparalleled career are too numerous to all be listed, but scoring a try in each of the four matches of the 1986 Five Nations and playing in every game of the 1987 Grand Slam would certainly be among them. Sella also took part in the first three World Cups, finished runner-up in 1987, was knocked out by England in the quarter-finals in 1991 and avenged the misfortunes of 1991 by beating the English in the play-off for the bronze medal in 1995. Except for the very early years of his career when he played amateur Rugby League in Clairac and a couple of formative seasons with Valance D'Agen, Sella remained faithful to the Agen club until 1996 when, with the game now fully professional and having made the decision to retire from international Rugby, Sella joined the north London club Saracens.

RICHARD SHARP

England 1960–67 (fly-half)

Although Richard Sharp was given his international debut only because of an injury to incumbent fly-half

TON-UP *Centurion Philippe Sella*

Bev Risman, the Cornishman did not need to be asked twice and delivered a mesmeric performance full of poise and menace to destroy Wales 14–6. Given his imperious form and the understanding he had clearly developed with Dickie Jeeps, Sharp retained his place even when Risman was ready to return and was considered one of the key figures in England's 1960 Triple Crown. When Risman switched codes the next season, Sharp assumed the mantle of the saviour of English back play, and when the Lions side was selected for the 1962 tour to South Africa, the rugged former Commando's name was the first on the teamsheet. Yet a head-high tackle by Springbok centre Mannatjies Roux in an early match of the tour smashed Sharp's cheekbone and the Bristol player had to wait for the chance to show the South Africans his elusive running or ability to shift up a gear and squeeze through the smallest of gaps. Although Sharp recovered to play in the final two Tests, the Lions back play was pedestrian without him and the tourists failed to win a Test. Sharp led England to the Five Nations Championship in 1963, including the historic 13–6 win in Cardiff, but that effectively marked the end of his career apart from his 14th and final cap in the 23–11 trouncing by Australia at Twickenham in 1967.

GEOFF SHAW

Australia 1969–79 (centre)

"Bunter" Shaw was the original crash-ball centre. Weighing in at around 16 stones, and with ability to scuttle over the ground at a fair old pace, the New South Wales Country boy who won 28 caps and nine as captain in his ten-year Test career, virtually invented the concept of a player deliberately taking out two tacklers in midfield to create more space in the second phase. Immensely strong, Shaw would attempt to remain standing as he off-loaded the ball, but such was the impact as he ran into his opposite inside centre that ball would invariably come back through a quick ruck. Being type-cast as a crash-ball merchant didn't please Shaw, who was also a sublime kicker and a great planner on the hoof, but he was happy to subdue his own preferences in the interests of the team. An intelligent man who verged on the extrovert, Shaw's game and personality were well suited to League, and he received many offers during his long career, but turned them all down.

WILSON SHAW

Scotland 1934–39 (fly-half)

Seasoned player and journalist J.B.G. Thomas once wrote of free-running Glasgow High School FP fly-half Wilson Shaw: "I cannot ever remember seeing an outside half with greater speed off the mark than Shaw." Ironically, this was Shaw's main problem in his early international career because, despite outstanding games against both England and the All Blacks in 1935 (the latter was for the Combined Edinburgh & Glasgow XV, in which Shaw scored one of the best individual tries ever seen in Britain), it allowed the Scottish selectors to pick him on the wing. Nevertheless, Shaw was so consistently outstanding at fly-half that he became Scotland's regular No.10, eventually becoming captain and leading Scotland to the Triple Crown in 1938 (France were still banned from the competition at this stage). Shaw had the opportunity to test himself against the South Africans in 1938, but turned down the invitation to tour with the Lions because of work commitments.

DAVID SHEDDEN

Scotland 1972–78 (wing)

As with most great players, their greatness comes in part from their ability to combine with other great players of the era. David Shedden, a flier from Glasgow's West of Scotland club, was lucky to be playing at the same time as Andy Irvine, one of the great attacking full-backs of all time. A classic speed merchant, Shedden profited from Irvine's ability to slice through opposing defences, and would regularly pop up on the full-back's shoulder to take a final scoring pass. Shedden, who was limited to only 15 caps because his career overlapped with another of Scotland's great wingers Billy Steele, was also defensively sound and astute in providing cover when Irvine went on his charging runs upfield. He played his last game for Scotland in 1978, and it was not until Tony Stanger won his first cap eleven years later that Scotland had another out-and-out flier to rely on.

SIR NICHOLAS SHEHADIE

Australia 1947–58 (utility forward)

Despite not taking up Rugby until three years after he left school, Nick Shehadie turned into one of the greatest players Australia has ever produced. After a debut against the All Blacks in 1947, Shehadie made his mark on the 1947–48 tour of Britain during which the Wallaby line was never crossed by an international side. As well as being a hugely amusing and effervescent personality, Shehadie was also a very versatile player who, after the First Test in South Africa in 1953, was switched to the front row to counteract the fearsome prop Jaap Bekker. The Springbok was quietened and Australia gained a famous victory in the Second Test. In his 30 Tests for Australia, Shehadie had the unique record of playing in every position except hooker. After retiring, Sir Nicholas (as he later became) retained a interest in the game, first refereeing before becoming president of the ARFU for eight years. In his time as ARFU president, he came up with the idea for a World Cup and successfully sold it to the other nations of the world.

WAYNE SHELFORD

New Zealand 1986–90 (No. 8)

"Buck" Shelford was one of the All Blacks who had a long wait for his Test debut. He was first chosen for New Zealand on the tour that never was, the 1985 visit to South Africa that was cancelled because of court action. He made his debut on the replacement tour to Argentina but had to wait for a Test debut until the retirement of Murray Mexted. His first Test was in France in 1986 and he thereafter became one of the most popular Rugby players in New Zealand, crowds loving his no-nonsense style and his utter commitment. He played in all but one match when New Zealand won the World Cup in 1987 and when David Kirk retired,

THE HARDEST OF THEM ALL *Buck Shelford lifts the Bledisloe Cup.*

Shelford took over as captain, leading New Zealand through its unbeaten run in the late 1980s under coach Alex Wyllie. He was controversially dropped after a successful but hard-fought home series against Scotland in 1990, prompting a wave of "Bring back Buck" sentiment throughout New Zealand that was unprecedented. But the selectors decided 22 caps were enough for Shelford and so, disillusioned, he moved to England to coach Northampton.

KEVIN SKINNER

New Zealand 1949–56 (prop)

Kevin Skinner played in only 20 Tests for New Zealand between 1949 and 1956, but for all the stories and legends that have followed the prop's name and his fame, he might have played in 60. Skinner, who was also the New Zealand amateur heavyweight boxing champion, was introduced for the All Blacks' 1949 tour of South Africa and played in each of the four Tests, all won by South Africa in one of New Zealand Rugby's darkest years. Skinner was retained for the following year when he played in each of the four Tests against the British Isles. Having announced his retirement following the 1953–54 tour to the UK, Skinner made a return to club Rugby in 1955, and he was recalled to the All Black front row, which was being battered and bowed by the South Africans. The series stood at one each when Skinner was recalled for the Third Test, apparently with orders to "sort out" the troublesome Springbok props, Chris Koch and Jaap Bekker. Skinner has been remarkably reticent about explaining exactly what happened in the first few scrums in the Third Test, but it is indisputable that he played half the game at tight-head and half at loose-head, and that the South African front row was sorted out. The method used is unclear, some historians said it was with his fists, others suggested it was his technique, possibly his tongue and or just simply with his strength.

JEAN-CLAUDE SKRELA

France 1971–78 (flanker)

THE PRODIGY *Jean-Claude Skrela.*

Skrela made his international debut in 1971 in the Second Test against South Africa in Durban. Skrela replaced Walter Spanghero, who had been dropped after a disappointing First Test. The Toulouse prodigy managed to hold his Test berth through the two-Test autumn series against the Wallabies, before he was replaced by Beziers's Olivier Saïsset. From then until the 1975 Five Nations, Skrela's performances for France were intermittent as he fought a four-way competition for an international berth with Biémouret, Boffelli and Saïsset. By 1975 Skrela had established himself in the French side and in 1977 played no small part in helping France win the Grand Slam. Yet he retired prematurely at the end of the 1978 season when he was twice overlooked for the captaincy of France. Although leaving on a losing note when Wales denied France their second Grand Slam in a row, Skrela scored his only international try of a 46-cap career that day.

ANDREW SLACK

Australia 1978–87 (centre)

One of the Rugby's thinkers, as a player Slack was a talented playmaker whose intuitive knowledge of the game helped him dictate the pace of the proceedings. He was lucky to have gifted individuals such as Mark Ella, Nick Farr-Jones and Michael Lynagh around him, for they fed off his organizational skills and sheer will-to-win as he lived off their creativity. That was one of the reasons that Slack became one of Australia's best captains: he knew what made players tick, who gelled with whom, and worked accordingly. An intelligent, straight-down-the-line man, Slack enjoyed the respect and trust of his team-mates, which impacted upon the way he led the side. He never shouted, he never screamed and he never had to raise his voice – he was the sort of man whose quiet instructions were listened to and then followed. A man who once said he would rather win a game 3–0 than lose 60–59, Slack was also dedicated to winning and managed to pass that on to his charges – it obviously worked because, under his leadership, the Wallabies completed a Grand Slam tour of Britain and wrested the Bledisloe Cup from the All Blacks on New Zealand soil in 1986. It was disappointing that after winning 39 caps, Slack retired on a low note following Australia's 22–21 bronze medal play-off defeat against Wales in the 1987 World Cup.

FERGUS SLATTERY

Ireland 1970–84 (flanker)

Over the years, Ireland have produced many barnstorming forwards, men like George Beamish, Bill McKay, Ken Goodall and Jim McCarthy. But no Irish back-rower ever managed to fuse speed, fire and commitment quite as successfully as open-side flanker Fergus Slattery. At his peak, only Frenchman Jean-Pierre Rives of his contemporaries occupied the same stratosphere as the Blackrock flier. A fitness fanatic and doggedly determined tackler, Slattery's keen Rugby brain ensured perfect lines of running and an extremely high count of hits on fly-halves. In an international career spanning 14 years, Slattery captained his country 17 times – including the victorious 1979 tour to Australia – and won 61 caps for Ireland, a record for a flanker, yet it is as a Lion that Slattery will be best remembered. In 1971, as a 21-year-old, injury and the dominance of Welshman John Taylor meant that Slattery did not face the All Blacks in a Test. Three years later, though, Slattery was at his phenomenal best as the Lions stormed through South Africa unbeaten. Much of the credit for that success was down to the forwards who, for virtually the first time since the 1890s were able to dominate the mighty Springbok forwards on their own soil in South Africa. On the hard grounds of the High Veldt, Slattery was outstanding, playing a central role in all four Tests. He threatened to have the final say when he touched down just before the whistle went in the drawn Fourth Test, but the referee controversially ruled no try.

JAMES SMALL

South Africa 1992– (wing)

James Small has been the object of both praise and condemnation. From the time the feisty wing made his international debut in 1992, trouble has never been far away. Banned after

BARN STORMER *Fergus Slattery.*

being sent off for verbal abuse of the referee in Australia in 1993, he found himself in the doghouse once again following a pre-Test scrap in a beach bar that was splashed all over the next day's newspapers. A temperament which seems to resist most forms of convention, has, however, failed to dim the brilliance of a Rugby career which still continues to shine. His tally of 33 Tests, with more to come, which will take him past the record for a Springbok back, underpins his value to the current South Africa team. Highly individualistic, fiercely patriotic and a rebel to the end, Small's contribution to the side was best typified by the way in which he coped with the much-vaunted All Black wing Jonah Lomu in the 1995 World Cup final. Yet only 12 months after his heroics in the World Cup, Small landed himself in more trouble when, during the 1996 Tri-Nations series, he was spotted in a South African nightclub a couple of days before a major international. Coach Andre Markgraaf dropped him from the side as punishment, but later recalled him when the Springboks toured France and Wales.

ARTHUR SMITH

Scotland 1955–62 (wing)

Arthur Smith made his international debut in 1955, at a most unfortunate time for Scottish Rugby as 17 Tests in a row had been lost. Yet on his first appearance he scored a try as Scotland broke the losing sequence with a 35–10 defeat of Wales at Inverleith in possibly the biggest upset in post-war Rugby. Smith was picked for the 1955 Lions' tour to South Africa, and would probably have played on the opposite wing to Tony O'Reilly had he not injured a hand at the beginning of the tour. He did return to South Africa, however, first as captain of the 1960 Scotland tour (the first major tour undertaken by a Home Union) when he scored eight points in Scotland's 18–10 defeat, and then as captain of the unsuccessful 1962 Lions. As well as possessing searing pace, the farmer's son from Castle Douglas in Galloway also possessed great intellect and gained a first-class degree in maths from Glasgow University before completing his PhD at Cambridge – and all that while winning 33 caps for Scotland and captaining the Lions. Smith was a seasoned Rugby traveller who played for Glasgow University, Cambridge University, Gosforth, Ebbw Vale, Edinburgh Wanderers and the Barbarians (the latter on the famous 1957 Easter tour of Wales when they beat mighty Cardiff 40–0). Sadly, Smith died of cancer less than ten years after playing his last competitive game of international Rugby.

GEORGE SMITH

New Zealand 1905 (utility back)

Without doubt, George Smith was the most versatile All Black ever to take the field and quite possibly the most versatile Rugby player anywhere at any time. In an extraordinary career, Smith played Union and League for New Zealand, was a national sprint and hurdles champion in New Zealand, Australia and England, and was a champion jockey, winning the New Zealand Cup in 1894. Smith first played Rugby for New Zealand in 1897 on a tour of Australia, during which he scored 11 tries. He didn't play Rugby again until 1901 when he played just two matches, then disappeared again until trials were held for the team to tour Britain in 1905. He scored 19 tries in as many games on the Originals' tour, including two against Scotland. Back in New Zealand, he was one of the two organizers of the first New Zealand Rugby League team, the All Golds, which introduced League to Australia and then toured Britain. Smith signed with Oldham while in England and continued playing until 1916. His athletics prowess included the New Zealand 100 yards title and the 250 yards national title. In 1904, he set an unofficial world record of 58.5 seconds in the 440 yards hurdles.

IAN SMITH

Scotland 1924–33 (wing)

A member of the famous Oxford-Scottish quartet of Wallace, Aitkin, Macpherson and Smith, the lithe Australian-born wing made his mark as an integral member of the outstand-

ing sides of the 1920s which won the Grand Slam in 1925, the year when he scored an astonishing eight tries in the first two internationals of the season against France and Wales. The previous season he had marked his international debut with three tries against Wales as Scotland won 35–10 The fastest of the Scottish three-quarters, Smith also won the Triple Crown in 1933, his last international season, and retired after winning 32 caps for Scotland and two for the Lions on their tour of South Africa in 1924. An exuberant young man, who once famously drove his car down an Edinburgh pavement after a post-international drinking binge, Smith held the record for tries scored (24), until he was overtaken by Australia's David Campese 55 years after Smith hung up his boots to concentrate on his career as a solictor.

DAVID SOLE

Scotland 1986–92 (prop)

Loose-head prop David Sole is another of those players who is remembered and virtually defined by

one moment: in this case it was when he made the decision for his side to take the now famous walk onto the pitch for the Grand Slam decider against England at Murrayfield in 1990. As a statement of resolve, it was a masterstroke from which the English never recovered as they lost the most high-profile game in Five Nations Rugby history. It also cemented Sole's name in Scottish folklore. But if Sole if remembered for that day, it was only a snapshot in an illustrious career that brought him 44 caps. As well as captaining a Scotland Grand Slam side, Sole was also a key component of the British Lions side which stormed through Australia in 1989. That tour, in particular, was one suited to Sole, who remains probably the greatest ball-handling prop of the modern era. Relatively small for his position, there was a constant question-mark over Sole's scrummaging ability, especially after England's pack destroyed Scotland in the tight during the 1991 World Cup quarter-final. Sole, though, makes the point that he never conceded a pushover try in his career. It is a point of

EDINBURGH ROCK *Steely-eyed Scottish prop David Sole.*

honour for Sole, one of the game's most softly-spoken and considered men off the field and one of the most inspirational and thoughtful captains and players on it.

WALTER SPANGHERO

France 1964–73 (No. 8)

The most famous member of a Rugby dynasty who dominated French Rugby during the 1960s and 1970s, Walter Spanghero represented France 51 times in the decade between 1964 and his retirement in 1973. Despite being only 6ft. 1in. tall, Spanghero was a bull of a man; immensely strong, frighteningly committed and one of the most physically intimidating forwards of his generation. The Narbonne bruiser made his debut in France's memorable 8–6 win over South Africa in Springs during a one-off Test in 1964. During that match, Spanghero formed a second row pairing with another outstanding converted No. 8 of the time, Benoit Dauga, which lasted until March 1967 when Spanghero was injured and pulled out of the Italian game. They resumed their partnership in the Second Test of the 1967 South African tour, but this was going to be Spanghero's penultimate game at lock forward. In the Third Test he joined the back row, to become one of the best and most influential No.8s in the game. He played in all four matches of the 1968 Grand Slam and became captain of France in February 1972. His younger brother Claude won 22 caps between 1971 and '75 while the senior Spanghero, Jean-Marie, and the youngest, Gilles, were useful club players who represented the two family clubs of Narbonne and Castelnaudary.

JOE STANLEY

New Zealand 1986–90 (centre)

Joe Stanley was one of the most underestimated yet effective achievers of the great All Blacks team of the late 1980s that went, under coach Alex Wyllie, 20 test matches without defeat. A dependable centre with outstanding peripheral vision, he was introduced to the All Blacks in 1986 for the Test against France, when most of the leading All Blacks were ineligible following the rebel Cavaliers tour to South Africa. He retained his place with marked effect, giving the All Blacks a midfield solidity that had previously been questionable and giving his wings welcome opportunities. A quiet, unassuming man, Stanley never gave interviews reputedly because in the early stages of his career he had been misquoted by a journalist. "Smokin' Joe" Stanley was one of the outstanding players in New Zealand's World Cup win in 1987 and remained an essential cog in the All Black game plan for the rest of the 1980s. Like his captain and close friend, Buck Shelford, Stanley was dropped after the 1990 series against Scotland. Capped 27 times by the All Blacks, the hole left by his his departure was plain to see during the 1991 World Cup when the New Zealand backs looked a sorry sight as they were comprehensively beaten by Australia in the semi-final.

BILLY STEELE
Scotland 1969–77 (wing)

Although Billy Steele, who won 23 caps as a winger, hailed from Langholm in the Scottish borders, his job in the RAF took him away from his homeland and into deepest enemy territory, the Bedford club in England! Never the quickest of wingers, Steele's gritty defensive qualities and combative nature combined perfectly with some of the more attacking Scottish internationals of his day, particularly Andy Irvine and David Shedden. Selected on the right wing for the 1974 British Lions' tour to South Africa, Steele was considered lucky to have been picked having missed the preceding Five Nations due to injury. Yet once in South Africa, Steele showed his gritty Border qualities playing in the first two Tests of what turned out to be an unbeaten tour for the Lions.

GEORGE STEPHENSON
Ireland 1920–30 (centre)

The tall, lithe Ulsterman vies with Mike Gibson for the title of greatest Irish centre of all time and would certainly make it into any all-time greatest Ireland XV. For a player of genius, Stephenson looked surprisingly fragile, yet if appearances were ever deceptive it was in Stephenson's case. A wonderful cover tackler who was astute in defence, he had a superb running style which he used to glide past bewitched defenders. Tactically clever, with safe hands and a great boot, Stephenson won 42 caps – 14 of them alongside his brother Harry, who played on the wing – in an era when the Five Nations represented virtually the only route to caps. The only down-side to Stephenson's career was that by the time the 1930 Lions' tour to New Zealand came round, his considerable powers were on the wane.

ADRIAN STOOP
England 1905–12 (centre)

As a man who lived for the game of Rugby, it is fitting that Harlequins centre Adrian Stoop left an indelible mark on the game when his club named their ground the Stoop Memorial Ground after their favourite son. Stoop followed a well-worn path to England honours: starting at Dover College, passing through Rugby School and Oxford University (where he won three Blues in 1902–4, scoring a solo 60-yard try as captain in 1904) and ending up at Harlequins, where he played 15 times for England in the years leading up to World War One (during which he won the Military Cross after being wounded in action in Mesopotamia). A man with a Barbarian attitude towards the game, Stoop's balanced running and high-speed swerve were a joy to behold unless you happened to be an opponent. From the moment he won his first cap in the 8–0 defeat by Scotland to his last appearance in 1912, Stoop played alongside some of the finest players of the era; men such as Ronnie Poulton-Palmer, John King and Cherry Pillman who, like Stoop, won the MC during the First World War. After his retirement from Rugby, Stoop became President of the RFU in 1932–33.

MARK SUGDEN
Ireland 1925–31 (scrum-half)

One of the most natural athletes ever to have played for Ireland, the lithe Wanderers No. 9 Mark Sugden remains probably the best scrum-half Irish Rugby has produced. Yet it could all have been so different had Sugden not made the move from centre, where he was a competent if unspectacular club player, to the hothouse of scrum-half. Once he had made the switch, though, Sugden proved to be an inspired choice. A deceptively lazy-looking player with a long wind-up and sure service, Sugden possessed a divine side-step and dummy, as well as being blessed with a most precious quality at international level, the ability to make time for himself through his immaculate reading of the game. He earned 28 caps for Ireland, and by far the most memorable of these games was the famous 1929 match when Sugden scored a classic blind-side try from a scrum to win the game 6–5 and give Ireland their first win over England at Twickenham in seven previous attempts.

HAYDN TANNER
Wales 1935–49 (scrum-half)

A teenage sensation who played in the Swansea and Wales sides which beat the 1935 All Blacks while still a schoolboy, Haydn Tanner was a scrum-half more in the mould of Terry Holmes than Gareth Edwards. Enormously strong and weighing in at over 14 stones, Tanner made muscular breaks around the fringes, tackled like an extra back row forward and was capable of flinging the heavy leather balls of the day up to 30 yards with pinpoint accuracy – all important attributes at a time when Welsh packs were regularly struggling to be competitive at international level. In an international career of 15 years that straddled the Second World War, Tanner won 25 caps and played alongside some of the most talented backs ever to pull on a Welsh jersey, including his cousin and Wales full-back

WTH Davies. Yet it was his pre-War partnership with Cliff Jones that was possibly the most fruitful period of a long career – an era in which Tanner and Jones established themselves as the John and Edwards of their own time. Tanner played once for the British Lions, in the Second Test against South Africa in 1938, but a 19–3 defeat led to him and three other backs being dropped for the final match of the series.

JOHN THORNETT
Australia 1955–67 (utility forward)

One of three brothers to play Rugby for Australia (brother Ken played Rugby League for the Kangaroos while Dick played for both the Kangaroos and Wallabies), prop-cum-lock John Thornett was stoical in his belief that the amateur game of Rugby Union was the maker of men. A huge bull of a man, Thornett had some of the greatest battles of his 37-cap international career with the Springboks and All Blacks, and became universally popular in both countries. Adept at doing much of the unseen work, Thornett was very much a team player, but was also a grand footballer who possessed a surprisingly good pair of hands. During his 12-year service with the Wallabies, the affable and modest Thornett captained his country 16 times, the most trying episode being the ill-tempered and unsuccessful tour to Britain in 1966–67 which was disrupted by the sending home of hooker Ross Cullen for biting. Thornett played once more for Australia against France before retiring in 1967.

BERT TOFT
England 1936–39 (hooker)

Despite having his career curtailed by the outbreak of the Second World War, hooker Bert Toft is still regarded as the greatest of England's pre-War captains. A born leader of men whose ability to inspire his players was legendary, even though he only captained England four times in his ten internationals, his influence was such that contemporaries rated him the key decision-maker in the other six internationals as well. Although the influential writer EHD Sewell regarded him as in the wrong position to lead, the famous "Dromio" in his book entitled *Rugby Recollections* reckoned Toft a clever hooker, greater leader and fine captain – an opinion shared by most. An energetic and thoughtful player, Toft began his career at Manchester Grammar School and • Manchester University and whilst a schoolmaster he played 64 times for Lancashire, more often than not as captain. His astute captaincy of the combined Lancashire-Cheshire side that met New Zealand at Birkenhead Park in 1935 led straight onto his England debut in 1936 during which his speedy striking helped England defeat Scotland. Of his ten caps, only three of England's matches ended in defeat for the Waterloo man, with his international career concluding with the final match before World War Two,

though he appeared in a 1944 Services international against Wales.

GREGOR TOWNSEND
Scotland 1993– (fly-half)

The contrast between Northampton fly-half Gregor Townsend and his great rival, Melrose's Craig Chalmers, could not be greater. When the youthful prodigy Townsend was first drafted into a Scotland side dominated by the boot of Chalmers since 1989, his brief was to instill a running game more suited to the mobile rucking style the Scots were determined to pursue under coaching guru Jim Telfer. Although a true flair merchant, Townsend certainly struggled to fulfil that brief, most notably in 1993 at Twickenham when England's Stuart Barnes exposed the full

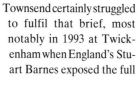

FLAIR MERCHANT
Scotland fly-half Gregor Townsend.

extent of his defensive frailties. Yet class will out, and Townsend's ability to find a gap and use his extraordinary pace off the mark to glide through it were always likely to see him through. Indeed, it was Townsend's ability to read a game and the remarkable sleight of hand which produced his inside pass to Gavin Hastings for the try that saw Scotland win for the first and only time at the Parc des Princes in 1995. Townsend showed his maturity in late 1996 when he was given the role of captain following an injury to Rob Wainwright.

KEL TREMAIN
New Zealand 1959–68 (flanker)

Kel Tremain was one of the finest flankers in world Rugby in the 1960s and seemed to epitomize the New Zealand spirit of unflagging energy and unwillingness to compromise. He made his debut against the 1959 Lions and for the next decade, the All Blacks seldom took the field for an international without him. Though not regarded as a big forward, he was an asset in line-outs for New Zealand and especially in the driving move that came to be known as the "Willie away", named after his first captain Wilson Whineray. Tremain scored ten tries in 38 Tests, which was then an All Black record. He captained New Zealand once in a Test, against France in 1968, but that was his last series. It was a major surprise the following year when he was omitted from the All Black side to play Wales and by the end of the year he announced his retirement. Tremain turned to administration and became chairman of the successful and innovative Hawke's Bay union and a member of the NZRFU council. He was being touted as a future NZRFU chairman when he died suddenly in 1992.

JEAN TRILLO
France 1967–73 (centre)

Accomplished and creative in attack, opportunist and very physical in defence, 23-year-old Begles centre Jean Trillo sky-rocketed to international fame when he made a telling

contribution during his international debut, an historic 19–14 win over South Africa at Ellis Park in 1967. With South Africa leading 11–9, he intercepted a hesitant pass from Dawie de Villiers and scored between the posts, a win sealed by Guy Camberabero's late drop-goal. Whether in partnership with Claude Dourthe, the speedy Jean-Pierre Lux, or his all-time favourite and friend Jo Maso, Trillo proved himself startlingly consistent throughout his 23-cap career. He also helped his club, Begles-Bordeaux, to their first Championship final win in 1968.

JOCK TURNER
Scotland 1966–1971 (fly-half)

Although he was at his height a decade before John Rutherford appeared on the scene, Gala's Jock Turner shared many similarities with the Selkirk legend, not least the Borders school of hard knocks in which they plied their trade on a domestic level. A regular with the great Gala Sevens sides of the 1960s, Turner had a huge boot on him, but was equally at home running at opposition defences, as he did to such effect in Scotland's 14–3 loss to the touring All Blacks in 1967. In 1968 Turner toured South Africa with the Lions playing in all four Test matches. The Lions lost the series 3–0 and although he was criticized in some quarters for an over-reliance on the boot, Turner was one of the few British backs to shine on what was a turbulent tour. In 11 games he dropped two goals and scored three tries. He won the last of his 20 caps in 1971, guiding the Scots to their first victory at Twickenham for 33 years.

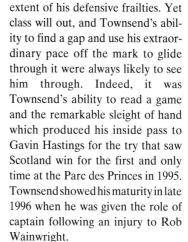

RORY UNDERWOOD
England 1984–95 (wing)

With 85 caps, Rory Underwood is the fourth most-capped player of all-time and the English record holder, not only for caps won, but for tries scored. His total of 49, including five against Fiji in 1989, a feat that equalled Dan Lambert's 1907 record, is unsurpassed in English Rugby. Underwood was first capped as a 20-year old against Ireland in 1984. Since then he has managed to juggle his life as an international Rugby star with his career as a fighter pilot in the RAF. Indeed, were it not for his flying commitments that prevented him touring with England to South Africa in 1984 and Argentina in 1990, Underwood would have more caps in his collection. Although justifiably criticized in the past for defensive aberrations - Wales have made him look inept on a couple of occasions - Underwood is devastatingly quick once the ball is in his hands. Two Lions' tours (Australia in 1989 and New Zealand in 1993) bear testimony to the quality of his try-scoring ability. His younger brother, Tony, has also played on the wing for England and when, in 1993, they lined up against Scotland in the Five Nations, they became the first brothers to appear in an England Championship side since the Wheatleys in 1938.

ROGER UTTLEY
England 1973–80 (utility forward)

A player who earned his spurs as a young lock in 1973 and 1974, Roger Uttley will be best remembered as a blind-side flanker after winning four caps in that position for the victorious 1974 Lions in South Africa. Originally selected as a lock for the 1974 series, as the tour progressed it became clear that Uttley was ideally suited to play the blind-side stopper role that Derek Quinnell and Peter Dixon had so admirably performed three years earlier in New Zealand. Tall at 6ft. 5in., raw-boned and utterly committed, Uttley was also superbly fit and strong, making up for a lack of genuine pace with a shrewd Rugby brain, unstinting effort and an ability to make a difference when he did arrive at the breakdown. Sound in defence, Uttley was perfect material for the Lions adding the necessary physical edge to Fergus Slattery's pace and Mervyn Davies' ball-handling excellence. After 1974, however, Uttley's

career was blighted by injury, and he was never to tour with the Lions again. He eventually retired in 1980 after he had helped England to their first Grand Slam for 23 years. The final 30–18 win over Scotland at Murrayfield was his 23rd cap for his country, of which 11 were won at second row, seven at No. 8 and just five caps on the blind-side.

JOOST VAN DER WESTHUIZEN
South Africa 1993– (scrum-half)

Joost van der Westhuizen quickly established himself as the highest profile Springbok of the modern era after a spectacular 18 months in which he came from second grade university Rugby to become one of the most sought-after players in the world. Van der Westhuizen burst spectacularly onto the scene as part of the impressive class of '93 given its head in Argentina, and went on to have a spectacular year as first Scotland and then England were treated to outrageous individual scores. Yet if Van der Westhuizen became famous for

his audacious tries, it was for his defence that his team-mates valued him every bit as much. Never was this more true than in the 1995 World Cup final against New Zealand, when the Northern Transvaal man was conspicuously quickest and most effective at bringing down the raging All Black giant wing Jonah Lomu. Van der Westhuizen may not have the finest pass in the world, and his options were certainly wild in his early years, but as a scrum-half prepared to spot a gap and accelerate through it he has no equal. Added to his good looks and star quality, it was a combination which drew Rugby League agents like bees to honey. In another era, Van der Westhuizen may well have been lost to the Union code, but with the Rugby union professional era ready to explode into being, the 24-year-old with the Midas touch decided he could stay at home in Pretoria and have the best of both worlds.

TOM VAN VOLLENHOVEN
South Africa 1955–56 (wing)

Despite playing only seven Tests for the Springboks before defecting to St Helens Rugby League club in 1957, signing for the huge fee of £4,000, Northern Transvaal wing Tom van Vollenhoven became a household name in both League and Union

codes. Known simply as "The Von", his move to the north of England with his new bride cut short a Springbok career which had started so brilliantly with a hat-trick of tries in the Second Test at Newlands against the talented 1955 British Lions touring team. Van Vollenhoven played in all four Test matches against the Lions, a series that ended in a two-all draw. Slim, shy with closely-cropped blond hair, the willowy wing was breathtakingly quick and, with an elusive quality to his running, was a born try-scorer. If proof was ever needed of his popularity, it was provided by the fact that his exploits with St Helens were said to have sold more newspapers than any other personality of his time.

MICHEL VANNIER
France 1953–61 (full-back)

Legendary full-back Michel Vannier was identified as a potential international at an early age, and when Racing Club de France talent scouts spotted him while on national service in Paris, he was immediately signed up and remained with RCP until 1960, when he joined Chalon. As the French Army sprint champion, Vannier undoubtedly possessed sizzling speed, but he was also blessed with a near-perfect sense of timing and an incredible kicking prowess. He won the first of his 43 caps against Wales in the last game of the 1953 Five Nations in Paris. The Welsh, captained by Bleddyn Williams, scored two tries to France's solitary penalty to win 6–3 and Vannier, who had an indifferent game, lost his place to the previous incumbent Georges Brun. Vannier re-emerged against Scotland and Ireland in the 1954 Five Nations, but injury prevented him from completing the season. His international career dramatically took off during the summer tour of Argentina, when he scored the first eight points of his career in front of 30,000 spectators. He never looked back and went on playing for France until a devastating knee injury sustained during the 1958 South African tour sidelined him for over a year. He made his comeback during the 1960 Five Nations when France won the Championship.

THE JUICE *Voost Van Der Westhuizen clears his lines for the RSA.*

The following year he made what was described as a "heroic" contribution to the scoreless draw with South Africa in Paris before finishing off his international career in style with a hard fought 15–8 win against the Wallabies in Sydney.

ROBERT VIGIER

France 1956–59 (hooker)

Robert Vigier began life as a scrum-half, and only moved into the front row when he joined Montferrand after the war. He won 24 caps at hooker between 1955 and 1959, but his unusual strength and wide range of positional skills enabled Vigier to play for his club either at scrum-half, in the back row, or in any position among the front three. He made his international debut against Scotland in 1956, when the young and inexperienced French team (containing six new caps) got thrashed 12–0. It was France's first game without the great Jean Prat, who had pulled out at the end of the previous season, and the French had yet to learn to live without "Monsieur Rugby". They proved their coming of age, however, in style in South Africa in 1958, their first-ever tour to one of the International Board founder-members, when the French captained by Lucien Mias won the Test series. It was the first foreign team to win a Test series on South African soil since 1896. Robert Vigier, a fine Rugby brain and a knowledgeable front-row operator, was Mias's closest ally during the bruising battles with the Springboks. Together with Aldo Quaglio and Alfred Roques, he formed a formidable front row which is still regarded by South Africans as probably the toughest and most skillful front-row trio to have toured the Republic.

PIERRE VILLEPREUX

France 1967–72 (fly-half)

One of the finest exponents of the attacking game in his playing days, following his retirement Pierre Villepreux became the leading advocate of total Rugby, the new game involving all 15 players in both attack and defence. An unconventional and passionate man, Villepreux has ded-

GALLIC FLAIR *Pierre Villepreux*

icated himself ever since to spreading the gospel of running Rugby, and in 1997 was finally employed by France in an official capacity after already working with both the Italian and English national sides. Villepreux started his career at his local club, Brive, but became best known as a long-striding full-back for Toulouse. He succeeded Claude Lacaze in the French team in 1967, but was replaced by Jean Gachassin for the Welsh game in the Five Nations. The two-match experiment with Gachassin at full-back was deemed a failure, and the selectors brought Villepreux back for his first Five Nations match in Ireland two weeks later. Until the retirement of Angouleme's Lacaze in 1969, Villepreux was never able to claim a regular spot in the French side and missed the 14–9 win over Wales at Cardiff Arms Park, when France claimed its first Grand Slam. However, by the time Villepreux won the last of his 35 caps in 1972, beating Australia 16–15 to take the series at the same time, he had already assured his position as one of the greatest French backs ever.

PIET VISAGIE

South Africa 1967–71 (fly-half)

Piet Visagie seldom received rightful acclaim as an international fly-half of repute. Somehow the freckle-faced player from unfashionable province Griqualand West always seemed to have to achieve the impossible before general acceptance of his

talents, although a cursory glance at his Springbok record proves the doubters wrong. Until Naas Botha came along, his tally of 130 points in 25 Tests and a total of 240 in 44 matches for his country, was a record. Essentially regarded as a defensive, kicking fly-half – as opposed to his main rival of the day, Transvaal's mercurial Jannie Barnard – the Griquas' pivot kicked well with either foot and was a drop-goal expert who slotted five in Tests. Visagie could also make clean breaks as he proved in the 1969 series against the Wallabies when he scored tries in the Second and Third Tests of the series. On three occasions he topped 12 points in internationals, with his best all-round display coming in the series-clinching final Test in 1970 against the All Blacks when his solo try launched the Springboks to a 20-17 victory.

TOM VOYCE

England 1920–26 (flanker)

Gloucester wing forward Tom Voyce was an integral member of what was reckoned far and away the best pack in the world in its time and was a key component in the England side which won three Grand Slams in four years in the early 1920s. Along with prop Ronald Cove-Smith, fellow wing forward Arthur Blakiston and inspirational captain Wavell Wakefield, Voyce was at the heart of a pack which took on and dispatched all-comers. A rugged footballer of enormous heart, speed and tactical acumen, despite being relatively small even for that time, the ginger-headed Gloucester tearaway was strong and durable, collecting an unprecedented 27 caps for England plus two with the 1924 Lions. That tally for the Lions would have been even bigger but for injury, yet Voyce was still the top points scorer on tour and, in a testimony to his basic skills and versatility, he also covered at full-back in the days when specialist positions had just become a widespread part of the game. Voyce remained involved with Rugby until his death in 1980, becoming president of both Gloucestershire and the RFU, and receiving the OBE in 1962.

ROB WAINWRIGHT

Scotland 1992– (No. 8)

It is difficult to know exactly how to define Rob Wainwright, the army doctor whose quiet and urbane manner belies a steely resolve that led Jim Telfer to eventually appoint the utility back-row man as skipper after Gavin Hastings's retirement in 1995. Earmarked early as a natural leader of men, he was first capped in 1992 as a reserve against Ireland, after he was forced to wait until the famous back row of Jeffrey, Calder and White called it a day after the 1991 World Cup before he could force his way into the Scottish squad. An athletic player of 6ft. 4in., he is a versatile big match performer who has played in all positions in the back row, although he is at his most effective when in the pivotal No. 8 position. An unshowy player who does much of the unseen work, Wainwright is a useful tail of the line jumper and a consistently good tackler – Despite Scotland's poor 1997 season when they won only one Five Nations' match, Wainwright was selected to tour South Africa with the Lions.

WAVELL WAKEFIELD

England 1920-27 (utility forward)
*(See **The Famous Coaches**, page 175)*

BILLY WALLACE

New Zealand 1903–08 (utility back)

Billy Wallace was one of the pioneers of New Zealand Rugby. Records he set in the early years of this century were not broken until 50 or more years later. Wallace could play on the wing, at centre or at full-back and it was in the latter position that Wallace made his debut in New Zealand's first official Test, against Australia in 1903. He was on the wing the following year against a British team in New Zealand and on the groundbreaking 1905–06 tour to the UK and France he played three Tests on the wing, one at centre and one at full-back. Two years later he was on the wing for all three Tests against Australia in 1907 and his last match for New Zealand, against the Anglo-Welsh side of 1908, was at full-back. Wallace was the first New Zealander to score 500 points – his total of 527 was achieved in 112 first-class matches. The 28 points he scored against Devon in the opening match of the 1905 tour was an individual record for an All Black match until 1951. He also set an improbable record, one that still stands and is likely to remain for ever, as the only All Black to score a try while wearing a sunhat (against Cornwall in 1905).

TONY WARD
Ireland 1978–87 (fly-half)

There have been famous fly-half rivalries, such as that between England's quicksilver Stuart Barnes and metronomic kicker Rob Andrew, or that between Scotland's equivalents Craig Chalmers and Gregor Townsend, but the very public rivalry between Tony Ward and Ollie Campbell was probably the most intense contest for a No.10 shirt ever. It was a rivalry which has seemed to define Ward's career, the enterprising artist who lost out to Campbell, but never quite faded away. Nevertheless he earned but 19 caps in a decade-long international career. Ward burst on to the scene against Scotland in 1978, and for two years lorded it over European Rugby, being widely described as the best fly-half in the world, as he thrilled crowds with searing breaks and spontaneous brilliance. Yet for all that, the Irish selectors had him marked down as an individualist and, on the 1979 tour to Australia, dropped him in favour of the more reliable Campbell. Ward was stunned, the Wallabies were stunned and Irish Rugby was in uproar, with every bar-room divided in a debate that raged for the next seven years. Yet campbell was an unmitigated success on that tour, leaving Ward in the international wilderness. The high point of Ward's career came in 1980, during the Lions' First Test against the Springboks – he had been flown out as a replacement for the injured Campbell – when he scored a record 18 points. Yet for one of Ireland's most naturally gifted footballers, his career yielded scant reward for so much talent.

PETER WHEELER
England 1975–84 (hooker)

Capped 41 times by England, Peter Wheeler had all the mental attributes which go to make up a superb hooker. But he also managed to combine his fire and determination with a technical excellence that made him a truly outstanding competitor. His line-out throwing, in particular, was peerless and he was a solid scrummager who more than pushed his weight and who had lightning reflexes at the strike (in only his third international he took four strikes against the head in England's 23–6 victory over Australia). Wheeler won seven caps for the Lions in the 1977 and 1980 tours. Unfortunately both were dogged by controversy and the Lions' performances suffered as a result. As captain of the Leicester Tigers, Wheeler led them to a hat-trick of national cup victories between 1979–81 and it was said that only his outspoken nature stopped him being awarded the captaincy of his country. That was an omission remedied in 1983 when just one week short of his 35th birthday he led England against the touring All Blacks, a match which an inspired England won 15–9. Wheeler is now president of top Midland's outfir Leicester and has been largely responsible for helping the club make such a successful transition from amateurism to professionalism.

WILSON WHINERAY
New Zealand 1957–65 (prop)

Whineray was a loose-head prop who won the first of 32 caps for New Zealand in 1957 and was made captain the following year for a series against Australia. He was then 23 and the youngest All Black captain for 30 years. He subsequently captained New Zealand against the Lions (1959), South Africa (1960), France (1961), Australia (1961–62), England (1963) and South Africa (1965) in addition to the 1963–64 British tour. When he scored the last of the All Blacks' eight tries against the Barbarians at the end of that tour, he was carried from the Arms Park and the crowd spontaneously sang, "For He's A Jolly Good Fellow". Whineray played for several New Zealand provinces but mostly for Auckland. Though a prop, he played successfully toward the end of his career as a No. 8 for Auckland and the All Blacks. Whineray became a successful businessman and director of several companies and was appointed by the government to chair various committees, including the Hillary Commission, the overall funding body for New Zealand sport.

BLEDDYN WILLIAMS
Wales 1947–55 (centre)

Bleddyn Williams left a lasting impression on opponents from Cardiff to Canterbury, scoring tries by the bucketload wherever and whenever he laced up his boots. A teenage prodigy who was coming up for 17 when war broke out, Williams had broken into the Cardiff 1st XV by the time he left school and while just 20 he scored three tries in the Welsh Services' 34–7 victory over the English Services in 1943. Williams made his debut against

ENTERPRISE ZONE *Mercurial Irish fly-half Tony Ward on the hoof against Scotland.*

England in 1947 after having already made his mark in the Victory Internationals of 1945–6, and became a permanent fixture for Wales until his retirement in 1955 at the age of 33. Williams' stock in trade was an outrageous sidestep, which he seemed to employ without slowing his progress. Floating past opponents, the ethereal Williams was a prolific try-scorer and still holds the Cardiff record of 41 tries scored during the 1947–8 season. Williams' robust physique stood him in good stead, particularly on the 1950 Lions tour to Australasia, where he played in 20 of the 29 matches despite missing the First Test through injury. He was made captain in three Tests when Karl Mullen was injured, and proved to be an astute and popular leader. A Rugby journalist after his retirement, the modest 27-times capped Williams is still fondly remembered in Wales as one of his country's true superstars.

BRYAN WILLIAMS
New Zealand 1970–78 (wing)

Bryan Williams was a 19-year-old sensation on his first tour to South Africa in 1970. The tour was a breakthrough because it was the first on which New Zealand included Polynesian players, and Williams, Auckland-born but of Western Samoan ancestry, was the star of the show. His strong running and powerful sidestep earned him 14 tries in 13 matches and he played in each of the four Tests. Williams was a dominant figure in New Zealand Rugby throughout the 1970s, adding to his credentials when it was discovered he was also a goalkicker of prodigious length. He was a first-choice wing throughout the tours of the 1970s, including the long tour of the UK, Ireland and France in 1972–73 and the Irish Centenary tour of 1974. A dislocated hip and torn adductor muscle in France in 1977 could have ended his career, but he was on tour again the following year to share in the All Blacks' first Grand Slam in Britain and Ireland, winning the last of his 38 caps against Scotland. When his Auckland career finally ended in 1982, Williams turned his attention to developing Western Samoan Rugby and when the Samoans proved

to be such a hit at the 1991 World Cup, Williams was the side's technical adviser, a position he retained until he became coach in 1996.

CHESTER WILLIAMS
South Africa 1993– (wing)

Next to Francois Pienaar and State president Nelson Mandela, the face of Chester Williams was the most visible of the 1995 World Cup and arguably its most marketable. After making his debut alongside a new crop of young players such as Ruben Kruger on the 1993 tour to Argentina, the black flash on the Springboks' left wing scored 13 tries in his first 16 Tests and, but for a serious knee injury in a Super 12 match against Canterbury which sidelined him for the whole of the 1996 Southern Hemisphere season, Williams would have been an automatic choice for the Tri-Nations Tests and the series against the All Blacks. Before the World Cup in 1995, it was a common theory outside the Republic that Chester Williams was a token selection designed to forestall some unpleasant questions on the lack of black players in South African Rugby. That perception soon faded, however, as Williams proved himself a wing of real class during the tournament, and particularly during the ultra-physical game against the West-

ern Samoans, where he scored four tries. Yet, for all Williams' try-scoring heroics, it is outstanding defence that makes the Western Province wing a player of genuine greatness. A media-shy, quiet man with a disarmingly humble view of the world, Williams is a devout Christian who has consistently steered away from becoming enmeshed in the politics of colour which are now an open part of South African Rugby.

J.P.R. WILLIAMS
Wales 1969–81 (full-back)

John Peter Rhys Williams, universally known by the acronym J.P.R., became the identikit attacking full-back in the 1970s. Big, fast, fearless and utterly committed, Williams was first spotted as a 19-year-old full-back on tour with a Wales development side in Argentina in 1969; he was quickly drafted into the senior side to make his debut in the 17–3 win at Murrayfield. Williams's 15 stone frame, allied to strong running, was

DOCTOR DYNAMIC *J.P.R. Williams.*

enough to unsettle any defence and he quickly became one of the most potent threats in Wales's attacking armoury. Yet there was far more to Williams than attacking prowess. Famous for his aggressive tackling, he was also rock-solid under the high ball and positionally immaculate. Williams was fortunate to be a part of Welsh

BLACK PEARL *Chester Williams proved more than a politcal token.*

back divisions that were truly gifted. He remains Wales's most capped fullback with 55 caps and eight for the Lions. In a 12-year career he won the Triple Crown six times, the Grand Slam three times and was only on a beaten Lions Test team once in eight starts (Second Test against New Zealand in 1971). Almost as importantly to a Welshman, he played England 11 times and was never on the losing side!

RHYS WILLIAMS

Wales 1954–60 (lock)

Rhys Williams won 23 caps for Wales and ten for the Lions – and it was to be the Lions by which his playing career was defined. Although a fiery and uncompromising lock who won more than his own fair share of ball at the front of the line-out, Williams finished his life as a Welsh international without ever actually winning either a Triple Crown or Grand Slam. Yet put Williams on a plane and send him to South Africa or Australasia and the man seemed to step into a different class. Williams gained the status of an immortal in the First Test of the 1955 tour to South Africa. Down to 14 men and with the Springboks scenting victory in front of a packed Ellis Park, it was Williams's mighty efforts at the line-out which secured the tourists enough possession to keep the Boks at bay and hold on for a famous 23–22 victory. Even better was to come in New Zealand and Australia in 1959, when Williams went head-to-head with All Blacks RA White and Colin Meads as he had done four years before with Springboks Johann Claassen and Salty Du Rand.

In the Fourth Test in Auckland, the strong-mauling, spring-heeled Williams was the key forward as the British Lions, who had lost the first three Tests on the New Zealand tour, came through a match of sustained savagery and ferocious commitment with a 9–6 win in Auckland to avoid a whitewash.

Even now, knowledgeable New Zealanders remember 6ft. 4in. Williams as one of the best locks ever to have toured Down Under.

STU WILSON

New Zealand 1977–83 (wing)

One of the fastest and most explosive backs New Zealand Rugby has seen, Wilson played for the All Blacks between 1976 and 1983 and when he retired was the country's leading Test try-scorer with 19 in 34 Tests, a record subsequently broken by John Kirwan. Wilson made his debut on a New Zealand second team tour of Argentina in 1976 and made his Test debut in France the following year. He was a crucial figure on the All Blacks' Grand Slam tour of Britain and Ireland in 1978 and scored New Zealand's only try in the Welsh Test. His position in the All Blacks was unchallenged throughout his career and in the latter part of it, he was joined on the left wing by his Wellington teammate Bernie Fraser, with whom he later combined in a joint biography, *Ebony and Ivory*. Wilson's finest series was the 4–0 blackwash of the 1983 Lions, during which he broke Ian Kirkpatrick's Test try-scoring record. Regular captain Andy Dalton was unavailable for the tour of England and Scotland at the end of 1983 and Wilson was made captain, an experience he acknowledged he didn't enjoy. The Scottish Test was drawn and the England Test lost. Wilson, an extrovert and a natural comic, was regarded as too much of an individual to be a good captain and wing.

PETER WINTERBOTTOM

England 1982–93 (flanker)

Few players in the world have been held in such high esteem either during their playing days or after their retirement as Peter Winterbottom, England's most capped flanker. From 1982, a vision of the Yorkshireman's blond shock of hair screaming towards them ready to deliver one of his telling, heavy tackles dominated the nightmares of fly-halves the world over, for Winterbottom was a Rugby nomad who plied his trade wherever he felt most comfortable. By the time he retired in 1993 with 58 England caps and seven Lions appearances to his name, the Straw Man had spent time in New Zealand with Hawke's Bay and, more spectacularly, with Trans-

STRAW MAN *Peter Winterbottom.*

vaal in South Africa, where the man is regarded as a living legend. At 6ft. 2in. and 15 stone, Winterbottom was the perfect build for open-side and although he lacked the handling skills of the naturally gifted footballer, he gradually learnt how to mitigate these faults in his game and he became one of the core members of the outstanding England pack of the late 1980s and early 1990s. Although bedevilled by injuries throughout the late 1980s, Winterbottom's England career spanned 12 years and he was as effective on his last Lions' tour to New Zealand in 1993, as he had been on his first in 1983.

WILF WOOLLER

Wales 1933–39 (centre)

A long-striding centre, the much-travelled Wilf Wooller was a member of an extravagantly talented back division which saw him line up alongside scrum-half Haydn Tanner, fly-half Cliff Jones and fellow centre and captain Claude Davey. He shares with those players two special moments in Welsh Rugby history as part of the first Wales side to win at Twickenham (7–3 in 1933 on Wooller's debut), and as a key player in the side that beat New Zealand

13–12 in 1935. Indeed, if Davey was the defensive hammer that dented the All Blacks' armour, it was Wooller who acted the role of the rapier, cutting the Kiwis apart with two defence-splitting runs. A marvellously gifted sportsman, Wooller hailed from the football-playing North Wales town of Rhos-on-Sea, where as a young man he concentrated on soccer and cricket. As Wooller says, they were not wasted years: "As well as utilizing my soccer skills to become a prodigious kicker of the Rugby ball, I developed a party trick where I could drop from my hand any ball, ranging in size from a tiny squash ball to a large heavy football, and place it perfectly into a basket with a drop kick." Wooller returned from a Japanese POW camp in 1945, and lead Glamorgan CC to the County Championship in 1948

Wooler died in 1997 but his memory will live on through his excellent autobiography, *The Skipper*.

THE SKIPPER *Wales' Wilf Wooller*

THE FAMOUS COACHES

Carwyn James once memorably defined the coach's role as follows: "The coach must resolve all that is difficult to resolve into something simple." Stunningly simple, yet stunningly true. Coaching has long been about the art of the possible, so the best coaches have invariably proved to be men who empathize with players and who understand their potential while also understanding their deficiencies.

As well as being a visionary with the ability to analyse and communicate, the great coaches have acted as mentors. The two are not synonymous. The great Danie Craven of South Africa, for instance, was a mentor to generations of players, but not a coach in the way that we understand it. But it is not possible to be a truly great coach without being a mentor, a man who players respect and have faith in. Welshman Carwyn James was just such a man. Although he never coached Wales, as coach of the 1971 Lions to New Zealand and the great Llanelli side of the 1970s, he had a level of success unprecedented in British coaching – and the players at the time place a good deal of the credit for their success in his coaching methods and quiet powers of motivation.

Another man of the same ilk was South African Izak van Heerden. Like James, his genius was never rewarded with the stewardship of his national side, but his intuitive analysis of the game and the principles he laid down are as valid today as they were in his heyday of the 1960s. Indeed, Springbok coach Kitch Christie openly acknowledged that his game-plan for the 1995 World Cup campaign was based on the principles laid down by Van Heerden 30 years before.

As the great thinkers of rugby football, New Zealanders have made a huge contribution to the development of the game, and none more so than Vic Cavanagh in the 1930s and 1940s. A rugged loose-forward with Otago in his day, where Van Heerden later developed a game with mauling at its centre, Cavanagh laid down the foundations for the intense rucking game that has been the model for New Zealand rugby ever since. In that, he shares much with Ian McGeechan, the recent Scotland and British Lions coach, who qualifies as a great through his ability to develop a similar pattern of play which has seen Scotland make the most of meagre resources. That in itself is enough for McGeechan to make the cut, yet his versatility in taking the 1989 to a series win in Australia – and adapting his ideas so that he centred his approach around the strong mauling English forwards of that time – assures him of his place.

Lastly, New Zealand's John Hart, the man who engineered Auckland's record Ranfurly Shield run and coached the All Blacks to an unprecedented series whitewash of the Springboks in South Africa, deserves his place among coaching's greats.

There have been many other great coaches who do not feature here. Australia's Grand Slam coach Alan Jones and World Cup-winning coach Bob Dwyer both merit consideration, as do New Zealand's Charlie Saxton and Maurice Trapp. Geoff Cooke, who did so much to revive English rugby in recent times, the Ireland duo of Ray McLoughlin and Syd Millar, Scotland's Jim Telfer and South Africa's Kitch Christie all also deserve a place in the coaching hall of fame.

FROM THE HART *New Zealand coach John Hart lays down the law to the All Blacks.*

VIC CAVANAGH
FATHER OF THE RUCKING GAME

Vic Cavanagh, the founder of the modern rucking game, is recognized as the best New Zealand coach never to coach the All Blacks and one who laid down principles generally followed in New Zealand rugby since the Second World War. Cavanagh, who played in the old position of wing-forward for Otago in the early 1930s, also played cricket for Otago and was 12th man for New Zealand against MCC in 1933. His father, Vic Senior, coached the University and Southern clubs in Dunedin as well as Otago and was coaching University while his son coached Southern.

Cavanagh's greatest period was as Otago coach in the immediate post-war period when the province successfully defended the Ranfurly Shield in 17 matches and New Zealand rugby argued about whether: "the Otago game", as developed by Cavanagh, was good or bad. The New Zealand selectors must have thought it was good because when the All Blacks went to South Africa in 1949, 11 Otago players were in the side.

Although considered the best man to coach the All Blacks on that tour, Cavanagh was passed over in favour of Alex McDonald, a 1905 All Black who was then in his sixties. The All Blacks lost all four Tests to the Springboks, and Cavanagh thereafter refused to have anything to do with national rugby, remaining a trenchant critic of the New Zealand Rugby Union until his death in 1980.

His coaching method was founded on the simple basis of forwards gaining and retaining possession, then bringing backs into play. Under him, forwards' body positions were crucial and Otago was renowned for its rugged, fierce rucking.

With the grounds in the South Island wetter than other parts of the country, Cavanagh's rucking concept was ideal. Otago forwards bulldozed over the top of the ball as soon as the opposition came into view. The physical momentum of teh tactic overwhelemed all Otago\s adversaries.

It was used to great effect against the 1950 British Lions who were beaten 23-9 by Otago, an experience they admitted to finding "humiliating and discouraging".

Name: VIC CAVANAGH
Born: June 19, 1909, in Dunedin
Died: July 20, 1980, Dunedin
Nationality: New Zealander
Teams coached: Southern, Otago
Teams played for: Otago (wing-forward)
Honours won: Ranfurly Shield

> **❝It was a pity some of those team talks weren't kept for posterity. They were classics for their clear, logical rugby thinking.❞**
>
> *Ron Elvidge, Otago and New Zealand midfield-back, on Cavanagh's preparation.*

After his retirement from coaching, Cavanagh wrote a series of articles about his beliefs and principles, and even now they could serve as a textbook for any coach. "I believe it is impossible for a team to be successful over a long period unless it is able to build up, by a series of attacks, such unrelenting pressure that the opponents wilt sooner or later and allow the attackers in for tries," he wrote.

"Although the Otago forwards have had a large part in the tactics recently, the backs have scored the tries. I believe this is a sound method as the backs are faster and better handlers and, broadly speaking, it is their function to score tries. Give me an orderly and organized team, working in unison, helping one another, and I think they would score tries which would bring any crowd anywhere to its feet."

Ron Elvidge, the Otago and New Zealand midfield back, recalled Cavanagh's team talks as being models of clarity and recall. "He had a photographic memory, total recall of almost entire matches," he said.

Cavanagh became general manager of the *Evening Star* newspaper in Dunedin and the newspaper's boardroom often became a rugby forum when visiting rugby teams were in town. Among the coaches to seek him out was Carwyn James, the coach of the 1971 Lions, the first Lions side to take a series from the All Blacks. James and Cavanagh were closeted away in the boardroom for several hours before the Lions' First Test win in Dunedin.

PRESSURE COOKER *Cavanagh understood how to win games by pressure.*

JOHN HART
THE COACH WHO WON IN SOUTH AFRICA

> **"I rate John Hart as the best coach I've come across in any sport."**
>
> *Jim Blair, New Zealand critic*

In New Zealand's rich rugby tradition, there is still one benchmark by which all players and coaches judge themselves: their record against the Springboks. On that score alone, John Hart deserves his place in the All Blacks hall of fame, particularly given the controversial circumstances under which he took a young tour party to South Africa in 1996.

Hart had been selected as coach following the resignation of Laurie Mains in the bitter aftermath of the 1995 World Cup, when tactical naivety had allowed South Africa to snatch an extra-time victory in the final. A three-Test tour to South Africa was hastily arranged, following on the back of the 1996 Tri-Nations Series.

This was not Hart's first experience with the All Blacks. He had been backs coach during the 1991 World Cup, forming an uneasy alliance with Grizz Wyllie, yet the Tri-Nations Series and tour to South Africa was a chance for the prodigal son of New Zealand coaching to show what he could do. In just two months, the All Blacks defeated Australia twice and then beat South Africa five straight times – the last three in South Africa.

TEAM PLAYER *John Hart has proved himself to be an inspirational man-manager.*

But if Hart cemented himself into New Zealand rugby history on that tour, it was an honour that had been brewing for many years. A scrum-half with Otahuhu, Stratford, Waitemata and Auckland, Hart displayed the virtues of shrewdness, thinking on his feet and an ability to inspire those around him that were later to stand him in good stead as a coach. Although Hart never pulled on the black shirt, his experience at Auckland gave him a priceless insight into what was needed to succeed at the top. ce into the most formidable side in New Zealand. By the time he gave way to Maurice Trapp in 1986, he had already established a legacy of success – in his five-year reign, Auckland played 90 games and lost only 11. Although Auckland is the most populous province in New Zealand, Hart's success was down to shrewd man-management and keen eye for talent.

Yet throughout his time with Auckland, New Zealand Colts and then the All Blacks, it was not just Hart's ability to gain results that marked him out, but his manner. An erudite and articulate man who doubled as a successful businessman, Hart successfully managed to draw together New Zealand's rugby public as he forged one of the best All Blacks sides of all time.

A high-flying businessman, Hart's independence and willingness to speak his mind often threatened to see him alienated on a whole range of topics.

His high profile stand on the rebel tour to South Africa and on Buck Shelford's sacking led to him being controversially rejected as All Black coach in 1988 and 1992, but rugby needed John Hart more than John Hart needed rugby and by 1995 he was back at the helm. In his last period of isolation in 1993–94 when a series of losses led to signs being erected in Auckland reading "Another Hart-less Performance", the subject of John Hart was a constant bone of contention between north and south islanders.

But Hart was perfectly suited for the new professional era – as he showed in 1996-97 by guiding New Zealand through what was arguably their toughest ever season. Only one defeat in seven full internationals against the might of both South Africa and Australia tells its own story.

Name: JOHN HART
Born: Auckland
Nationality: New Zealander
Teams coached: Auckland,
New Zealand Colts,
New Zealand
Teams played for: Otahuhu,
Stratford, Waitemata,
Auckland (scrum-half)
Honours won: Tri-Nations
Series (1996), Ranfurly Shield,
World Cup finalists (1995)

IZAK VAN HEERDEN
THE THINKING-MAN'S COACH

> ❝ He was truly light years ahead of the rest. ❞
>
> *Kitch Christie, South Africa's 1995 World Cup-winning coach*

Izak van Heerden was years ahead of his time, yet in terms of national rugby recognition in his own country, the former Natal mastermind was almost a forgotten man. It is true, that during his innovative days at the helm of Natal, then one of South Africa's less powerful provinces, Van Heerden reigned supreme.

It was not unknown for the scholarly-looking coach to arrive at practices straight from his school-mastering duties at Durban High School in tweed jacket or conservative dark suit. If this was considered eccentric, it became one of the many foibles that grew with the reputation. But there is no doubt that Van Heerden suffered at the hands of the crass thinking of the time, unless a coach had played for the Springboks, he should be disqualified from being South Africa's coach.

But if he was a neglected visionary in his own land, Van Heerden became a helping hand greedily grasped by others. He became a mentor for Argentine rugby after he first flew to Buenos Aires to help them prepare for their first trip to South Africa during the 1960s. It was the start of a long and happy relationship, especially as Van Heerden virtually invented what we now term the "tight loose", an area in which the Argentines still excel. The Pumas repaid the initial debt by beating the Junior Springboks at Ellis Park, and their emergence as one of the better modern rugby nations is due largely to the talents of the quiet Durban schoolmaster and rugby tactician.

His celebrated work, Thinking Rugby, has become the game's bible for coaches around the globe. Several strategies devised by Van Heerden during his rise to prominence when he masterminded Natal's win over the touring Australian Wallabies in 1953, to his death some twenty years later, have become part of the high-speed, high-intensity modern game.

Kitch Christie, the man who guided South Africa to their 1995 World Cup triumph, is a committed Van Heerden disciple, having studied and used many of his methods. If Christie is the most prominent of Van Heerden's followers, many others adopted him as a role model and his fame as a rugby coach grew in Britain as reports filtered through about the rugby guru with the golden touch.

Somehow, however, all these acknowledgments worked against him in his native South Africa. Petty jealousies overtook his growing reputation and, apart from one series against the British Lions in 1962 in which the Lions were comprehensivley out-played, losing the series 3-0, Van Heerden's massive input was not required by South Africa. Yet his footsteps laid a path for others, like Christie, to follow.

His unique ability to create scoring opportunities by playing 15-man rugby, even with limited possession from tight phases, made him a formidable adversary. Among the great players who went through Van Heerden's hands were Springboks like Tommy Bedford, Keith Oxlee, Trix Truter and Snowy Suter.

As a player himself, Van Heerden had only moderate success. He was a loose forward, and once he had turned to coaching he brought perhaps the most insight to an appreciation of back-row play.

Kitch Christie reveals that he grafted much of his mentor's thinking on loose forwards onto his World Cup blueprint. "Most of what you hear the modern coaches saying and the phrases they use were first coined by Izak."

NOT WANTED *Van Heerden turned to Argentina to show his international talents.*

Name: IZAK VAN HEERDEN
Born: August 1910 in Durban
Died: June 1973
Nationality: South African
Teams coached: Natal, Argentina

CARWYN JAMES
WELSH VISIONARY

❝Now go and show the world what all of Stradey knows.❞

James's attempt to motivate Llanelli's Phil Bennett before an international

MASTER MIND *Welsh genius, Carwyn James, was the greatest coach never to have been given charge of Wales.*

Many coaches place a firm belief in luck playing a part in their team's progress. Carwyn James did not come into that category. For him preparation for every eventuality would negate the need for good fortune.

James was a very good player, although never in danger of being a great. Capped twice by Wales in 1958, against Australia at centre and France at stand-off, the Llanelli man was to make his indelible mark on rugby history as the coaching mastermind that gave form to the most outrageously talented tour party ever to leave the British Isles, the Lions of 1971 and the finest British side ever to play on home soil, the 1973 Barbarians.

Shy, unprepossessing and noticeably diffident as a young man, by the time James came to accompany Doug Smith on his first Lions tour

Name: CARWYN JAMES
Born: 1929
Died: 1983
Nationality: Welsh
Teams coached: Llanelli, Rovigo, Wales and the Barbarians, British Lions

to New Zealand in 1971, he had developed into an inspirational motivator of men and a shrewd compiler of game plans. With raw material like Barry John, Gareth Edwards, Mervyn Davies, Willie John McBride, Mike Gibson, J.P.R. Williams, J.J. Williams, Phil Bennett, Gordon Brown et al, James was able to produce sides able to compete in the harshest of rugby environments – New Zealand and South Africa.

Always a man who preferred pulling players in the direction he wanted, rather than trying to push them, James became a master not only at motivating players at the peak of their rugby careers but also of adapting game plans around the players available. Of all those players, it was a skinny kid from Cardiff via Llanelli called Barry John who stood out as the player around who James would base his whole game plan. "The King", as the fly-half was later to become crowned, responded in kind to establish himself as the lynchpin around which the 1971 Lions' triumph was forged.

But if James was able to inspire great players with quiet phrases such as his now famous aside to Phil Bennett – "now go and show the world what all of Stradey [Llanelli's home ground] knows" – then he was also capable of being extremely hard-headed when the situation warranted.

Before the second Test against New Zealand in 1971, James took Barry John out for a beer. Over a game of pool, James told John he wanted him to destroy the All Black full-back Fergie McCormick during the impending second Test. John did as he was told with a series of tortuous kicks that broke McCormick. He never played for New Zealand again.

Whether it was dealing with the media, or resisting the NZRFU's desires to appoint a referee who had once raised arms in triumph when the All Blacks had slotted a dropped goal, James could be stoically stubborn. As a street-wise coach, there were few to match a man better known for his fondness for back play. James coined the now infamous phrase "Get your retaliation in first", during the often brutal Lions' tour of 1971, and he was also responsible for unleashing Derek Quinnell at All Black scrum-half Sid Going, a confrontation which was to be a turning point on that same Lions' tour. An ardent Welsh nationalist, James turned down an MBE.

IAN McGEECHAN
MASTER OF PSYCHOLOGY

❝We must encourage players to play, and to do that we must offer them a tactical framework.❞

McGeechan, explaining his coaching philosophy

There is no more graphic an illustration of the flaw in rugby's traditional maxim that a good big 'un will always get the better of a good little 'un than Scotland and Lions centre Ian McGeechan. At 5ft 9in and 11st 7lb, "Geech" was nothing if not little, yet there can be few, if any, opponents who ever really got the better of him.

As a player, the softly-spoken McGeechan was a playmaker par excellence. Not the most physically imposing player in defence, he had very quick hands, skirted the offside line and was a technically outstanding tackler. His greatest on-field achievement was to play in all four Tests as Willie John McBride's unstoppable 1974 Lions rampaged their way around South Africa.

Yet while McGeechan certainly rates as one of the best players ever to pull on a Scottish shirt, it is for his contribution as a coach that he will be best remembered. Although he moved straight into coaching at international level, eschewing an apprenticeship as a club coach, McGeechan was an instant success within the Scotland coaching set-up.

One of the game's most original and innovative thinkers, McGeechan explained his philosophy simply: "The challenge is to merge a group together to play one way and to have an identity. I lay down a tactical framework and say 'this is what I want you to do and this is how I want you to do it'. Then it is up to the players to adjust."

McGeechan's philosophy of "horses for courses" was one which proved spectacularly successful during his time with Scotland. In conjunction with Jim Telfer, McGeechan pioneered the fast-rucking style of play based around an abrasive back-row that has now become his national side's hallmark. McGeechan immediately appreciated that Scotland's small pool of players and lack of muscular front five forwards meant that a style of play had to be developed which would make the most of the fast-flowing style of Scottish club rugby. So effective was the style imposed by McGeechan and Telfer that Scotland were able to prosper while at the same time mask the deficiencies of players struggling to compete at international level.

In 1995, a year after McGeechan retired as national coach, he became Director of Coaching at Northampton. Already destined for relegation from England's first division, the free-running style McGeechan imposed upon the Saints' youthful players saw them sweep all before them on their way back to the first division, where they subsequently consolidated their position in the top flight.

Yet it has not been just the Scots and Northampton who have benefited from McGeechan's coaching ability. During the first of his three Lions tours as a manager, when he coached the party to Australia, his ability to change tack in mid-tour and construct a side based around the strong-mauling English front-five led to a famous series win. McGeechan was back with the Lions in 1993 during the tour to New Zealand where the series was lost 2–1 after the Lions had battled back to level the series having lost the First Test 20–18.

In 1997 came arguably his finest hour when McGeechan coached the Lions to a 2–1 series victory against the Springboks. Asked to explain the reasons behind the Lions' 1997 success, McGeechan said: "We've tried to be positive and bold about everything we've done. We've encouraged the players to play open football."

Name: IAN McGEECHAN
Born: 1946
Nationality: Scottish
Teams coached: Scotland, British Lions (3 tours), Northampton
Teams played for: Headingley Scotland (32 caps), British Lions (8)
Honours won: Grand Slam 1990 (with Scotland) Division 2 (with Northampton); winning tour with the British Lions (1989)

MIND OVER MATTER *McGeechan has proved his ability to produce winners.*

WAVELL WAKEFIELD
THE FIRST TRUE COACH

> **"This man is responsible for the game we have today. We owe it all to him."**
>
> *Carwyn James, 1971 Lions coach*

Sir Wavell Wakefield might have been the man who gave truth to the myth of a rugby superman: the sort of man who could play, think, administer and charm all in the same afternoon. In fact, Wakefield performed all those functions over a lifetime, yet in rugby terms his was the most remarkable lifetime in rugby history. It would be no exaggeration to say that no man since William Webb-Ellis has done as much to give us the game we recognize today.

As a player alone, Wakefield did enough to enter any rugby hall of fame. A breakaway with a breathtaking turn of pace, plus amazing strength and stamina, by the time he retired he had amassed a record 31 caps. Not only that, but he had managed that between 1920–27, during a period of unprecedented England domination of the Five Nations. As well as captaining his country to the Grand Slam in 1924, Wakefield also led two Triple Crown-winning sides. Whether wearing the colours of Harlequins, Cambridge University, RAF, Leicester, the Barbarians or England, Wakefield was probably the outstanding player of his generation.

But as an administrator, Wakefield was also way out of the ordinary. An ebullient and charismatic man, he quickly rose to the top and eventually became President of the Rugby Football Union.

In addition, Wakefield became a Conservative MP shortly after his retirement from the game, entering parliament at the age of 37. In 1963 he became the First Baron Wakefield of Kendall.

Yet it is neither for his on-field contribution or for his administrative genius that Wakefield will be remembered, but for his revolutionary changes that changed forward play forever. Until Wakefield arrived on the scene, the general form was for players to arrive at the scrummage or line-out as soon as possible and prepare for the set-piece in the order in which they arrived. Back row forwards operated on their own, independent of their fellow back-row forwards, in an ad hoc, haphazard manner.

What Wakefield did was to develop forward play into a highly specialized science by allotting each forward a specific function at the scrummage and in loose play. In addition, he also turned the breakaways from three disparate individuals playing games not related to each other into three-pronged tactical team with specific functions both in attack and defence.

Wakefield also reorganized centre play, removing the practice of playing three interchangeable centres and replacing them with a centre pairing – which later became inside centre and outside centre – plus a specific, dedicated fly-half.

When one looks at the other great coaches of all time selected, perhaps the most amazing thing about Wakefield, was that he built up all of his tactical acumen – and applied it – while he was playing. In this, as in virtually every other aspect of his staggering rugby life, he was unique.

THE ONE AND ONLY *Wakefield's legacy is as unique as he was.*

Name: WAVELL WAKEFIELD
Born: 1898
Nationality: English
Teams coached: Cambridge University, RAF, Leicester, Barbarians
Teams played for: England (31 caps), Harlequins, Cambridge University, RAF, Barbarians, Leicester
Honours won: Grand Slam 2, Triple Crown 4 (as player)

THE GREAT MATCHES

Every so often, a match of true greatness comes along. A contest so intense and satisfying that everyone it touches has their faith in the sport restored forever; so gripping that it begs the uninitiated to begin a lifelong love affair with the game; so heart-stopping that huge passages of play remain indelibly etched in the memory. It is rugby's ability to rise above the mundane and throw up contests of spectacular endeavour and unsurpassable drama that makes it the most compulsive sport in the world.

But rugby's splendour can take many forms. First there is the grandstand finish: who can forget Gareth Edward's early charge for the Barbarians against the All Blacks in 1973? Or Serge Blanco's heroic last-ditch try to snatch the 1987 World Cup final place from under the Wallabies' noses?

Not all matches need one defining moment to be forever memorable, though. Nothing is more satisfying than the sight of a triumphant underdog. And which underdogs could have faced greater odds than the Jaguars side that faced South Africa 5,000 miles from home and with only a week to erase the memory of a 50-point Test savaging back in 1982.

The greatest theatre can come when old rivals lock horns. Grand Slam showdowns, that involve rivalries going back well over 100 years and which inevitably have added spice because of the historical connotations: England Vs. Scotland or the perpetually bruising France Vs. England encounters. Lions's tours also bring out the best in the opposition; witness the 1997 tour of South Africa. Clashes between the All Blacks and the Springboks also provide utterly compelling spectacles ; witness Joel Stransky's injury-time drop-goal to win an absorbing World Cup final. High drama, high entertainment.

IN THE NICK OF TIME: *Michael Lynagh dives over to snatch a last-gasp victory for Australia against Ireland in the 1991 World Cup.*

THE BLACK BEATERS *The 1953 Welsh team that defeated the All Blacks in a thrilling encounter at Cardiff Arms Park were the last to do so.*

WALES BLACK OUT NEW ZEALAND

WALES 13
NEW ZEALAND 8

19 December 1953
Cardiff Arms Park

For many of the early years of rugby, one of the fiercest rivalries was between Wales and New Zealand. Of all the rugby-playing countries, only South Africa can come close to matching the passion which these two rugby-mad nations bring to the game.

Although it may seem like a quirk of history today, when New Zealand played Wales at Cardiff Arms Park in 1953, it was the All Blacks who were the underdogs. They had only previously managed to beat Wales once, in 1924, they had already been defeated by Cardiff a month earlier, as well as being held to a 6–6 draw the previous week by Swansea. Moreover, Wales had completed a Grand

Slam in 1952, and only a shock 8–3 loss against England had prevented them winning a second successive Slam in 1953.

Wounded All Black pride is a dangerous enemy, however, and as soon as the match got underway it was clear that the New Zealanders were a far more effective unit than the one that had struggled against Swansea and Cardiff. The tourists dominated the early forward exchanges and looked to be controlling the pattern of the game as the first quarter passed without a score. But against the run of play it was the beleaguered Welsh who drew first blood when fly-half Cliff Morgan hoofed the ball downfield from a collapsed maul in Wales's 22. Full-back Bob Scott fielded the ball, but had no time to work with it as the ultra-fast wing Ken Jones arrived and piled in to Scott. Isolated and running out of options, Scott tried to find wing Ron Jarden, only to spill the ball into the path of the oncoming flanker Clem Thomas who hacked ahead to cre-

ate an easy try for Sid Judd.

The New Zealanders hurled themselves at the desperate Welsh defenders, redoubling their efforts in attempt to get points on the board. Cracks began to appear in the Welsh defensive wall and after Jarden had kicked a touch-line penalty, the All Black forwards took over, applying every ounce of muscle at their disposal. It was a tactic which began to work as the Welsh defence flagged. Finally, with half-time looming, Jarden put up a steepling garryowen which Wales failed to deal with and the first man to the ball was the flanker Clark. The conversion made it 8–5 to the All Blacks at half-time, but even this score failed to show quite how dominant the visitors had become.

In a frenetic second half, the All Blacks laid siege to the Welsh try-line, yet it was the home side who were to score next to level the match at eight points each. For the All Blacks it was more of the same as they launched attack after attack

at the Welsh line. Once again, though, Wales held firm before scoring a try against the run of play.

With five minutes to go, New Zealand lock Alan Elsom failed to control a line-out ball and Thomas pounced on it, swinging his foot in the same instant to send the ball spiralling downfield. Winger Ken Jones raced up as much as in hope as in expectation, but the ball took a wicked bounce to wrong-foot Jarden and Jones gratefully accepted his slice of luck, scoring the try that gave Wales a famous victory against the odds.

WALES: *G. Williams; K. Jones, G. Griffiths, B. Williams (capt), G. Rowlands; C. Morgan, R. Willis; W. Williams, D. Davies, C. Meredith, R. John, J. Gwilliam, S. Judd, J. Stephens, C. Thomas.*
NEW ZEALAND: *B. Scott; A. Elsom, Tanner, R. Jarden, B. Fitzpatrick; L. Haig, K. Davis; K. Skinner, R. Hemi, I. Clarke, G. Dalzell, R. White, R. Stuart (capt), W. Clark, W. McCaw.*

COURAGEOUS LIONS COME ROARING BACK
SOUTH AFRICA 22
BRITISH LIONS 23

First Test. 6 August 1955
Ellis Park, Johannesburg

When Robin Thompson's 1955 Lions arrived in South Africa, they soon established themselves as the best touring side to visit the Republic since the turn of the century, winning ten of the 12 matches in the lead-up to the First Test.

It was a gloriously talented side in general, but six players in particular stood out: the England centre pairing of Phil Davies and Jeff Butterfield, the Welsh outside half Cliff Morgan, the Irish winger Tony O'Reilly, English scrum-half Dickie Jeeps and the formidable Welsh hooker Bryn Meredith.

The Lions' success in the opening games and the controversial appointment of veteran flanker Stephen Fry to lead the Springboks, ensured that interest in the First Test was at fever pitch, with 95,000 spectators cramming into Johannesburg's Ellis Park stadium. What unfolded over the next 80 minutes was a contest that the great South African Danie Craven reckoned was the best he had witnessed in all his years of playing and watching the game.

The Lions drew first blood when Davies made a break in midfield and delivered a wayward pass to the feet of the onrushing Butterfield. Without breaking stride, the Northampton man picked the ball off his bootlaces with one hand and, as he took out two tacklers, flung the ball to flying Irish wing Cecil Pedlow for the opening three points (the value of a try in 1955). Despite being under the cosh, the Springboks staged a mini rally with two penalties from full-back Jack van der Schyff being followed by a Briers try after a storming run by Fry. With the score at 11–3 and the home side in danger of pulling away, the Lions clawed their way back into the game. Morgan was the catalyst,

spearing through a gap in the South African three-quarters before off-loading to Davies, who put the smooth-running Butterfield over for a try which bought the Lions back to 11–8 as the half-time whistle blew.

By the time the two teams resumed battle in the second half the atmosphere was alive with anticipation that grew even more intense three minutes into the second half when outstanding English flanker Reg Higgins was carried off, leaving the Lions with only seven forwards (there were no replacements in 1955).

Yet rather than be overwhelmed by the size of the task facing them, the Lions staged one of the most dramatic come-backs in the history of Test rugby. It was again Morgan who made the breakthrough, rounding the flat-footed Basie van Wyk for one of the greatest individual tries in Lions' history. But rather than shut up shop, the 14-man Lions began to run riot. Morgan was again the prime mover, this time through two garry-owens he put up to test the nerve of fullback Van der Schyff. The Springbok failed to cope, and with the ball taking a wicked bounce on both occasions, first Jim Greenwood and then O'Reilly charged over for tries which gave the Lions a 23–11 lead.

Gradually however, the disadvantage of playing with one man fewer than their oppponents began took its toll and, as the Lions' forwards tired, the home side came storming back with a try of their own from scrum-half Tommy Gentles. When the bulky figure of Chris Koch weaved over for a another try, the crowd erupted. Sensing a famous victory, Fry led the charge deep into the Lions' half. Piercing through the visitors' defence, he fed the ball to wing Theuns Briers for the try that brought South Africa to within a point of the Lions. The conversion, which was to be the last kick of the game, was half way between the posts and touch-line. Ninety-five thousand supporters held their breath as Van der Schyff ran up,

BREAK-NECK SPEED *Lion Cliff Morgan tries to evade 'Bok Thevns Briers.*

kicked and missed by a whisker. The whistle blew, the Lions jumped for joy and Ellis Park knew it had witnessed the greatest of matches.

SOUTH AFRICA: *J. van der Schyff; J. Swart, D. Sinclair, T. van Vollenhoven, T. Briers; C. Ulyate, T. Gentles; A. du Plooy, C. Kroon,* *C. Koch, Salty du Rand, J. Claasen, C. van Wyk, S. Fry (capt), D. Retief.*

BRITISH LIONS: *A. Cameron; T. O'Reilly, J. Butterfield, P. Davies, C. Pedlow; C. Morgan, D. Jeeps; W. Williams, B. Meredith, C. Meredith, R. Williams, R. Thompson, R. Higgins, R. Robins, J. Greenwood.*

FLYING START *Tom David plays his part in the now legendary Gareth Edwards' try that set the scene for a thrilling match.*

A GAME TO END ALL GAMES
BARBARIANS 21
NEW ZEALAND 13

27 January 1973
Cardiff Arms Park

Of all the rugby games staged on British soil, the 1973 Barbarians game against the All Blacks has gone down in history as the most thrilling ever played. A joyous celebration of the Barbarians' ethic of throwing caution to the wind, the match started with a try by Gareth Edwards, a sublime moment unequalled in British rugby.

The try started with an innocuous kick-ahead by the New Zealand's Bryan Williams four minutes into the game. Phil Bennett fielded the ball in front of his own posts and prepared to kick right. Just as the cover closed down on him he changed his mind, throwing two outrageous side-steps to flat foot the oncoming All Blacks. Bennett headed left and, as the third would-be tackler closed in,

the Llanelli man off-loaded to J.P.R. Williams, who was half caught around the neck but managed to ship the ball on to and English hooker John Pullin.

Pullin took a couple of steps before handing on to captain John Dawes, who stepped inside a tackler and stormed up the pitch. The move was now in full flow, with the ball nearing half-way and the crowd on its feet. Flanker Tom David was the next to field a pass, taking it at such pace that he looked as if his own momentum was about to make him fall over. As he stumbled, David flung the ball single-handedly, and fellow back-rower Derek Quinnell stooped to pick the ball off his bootlaces. Realizing he did not possess the pace to make the line, Quinnell looked for wing John Bevan and floated a pass towards the Welshman. It never made it to Bevan. At exactly that moment, scrum-half Gareth Edwards hit the accelerator and picked off the pass from Quinnell. Pinning back his ears he dashed straight for the line,

flinging himself into the corner before the pursuing Grant Batty could get across in cover. The audacious move had covered the length of the pitch and passed through seven pairs of hands to produce the most memorable start ever to a major international.

Rather than an end in itself, the try sparked a game the like of which has not been seen on British soil since.

With David Duckham in supreme form, the Barbarians played enterprising, all-action rugby which the All Blacks did their best to match, but by half-time the visitors trailed 17–0. Through the whole of the second half the All Blacks rallied themselves for a supreme effort, and scrum-half Grant Batty's virtuoso individual try brought them back to 17–11 down with 15 minutes to go. Yet a weaving run by Duckham, leading to a try by J.P.R. Williams, finished off the All Blacks with five minutes remaining. It was a remarkable way to round off the most extraordinary

of games.

For British rugby supporters it was a victory of supreme importance. An outrageously talented Lions party spearheaded by Barry John and Gareth Edwards had gone to New Zealand in 1971 and returned with the prize of a series win. A major event, the confidence from that unprecedented run of success had been gradually eroded throughout the All Blacks' 1972–73 tour to the British Isles.

BARBARIANS: *J.P.R. Williams; J. Bevan, J. Dawes (capt), M. Gibson, D. Duckham; P. Bennett, G. Edwards; S. Carmichael, J. Pullin, R. McLoughlin, W.J. McBride, R. Wilkinson, T. David, F. Slattery, D. Quinnell.*

NEW ZEALAND: *J. Karam; G. Batty, B. Robertson, I. Hurst, B. Williams; R. Burgess, S. Going; G. Whiting, R. Ulrich, K. Lambert, P. Whiting, H. McDonald, I. Kirkpatrick (capt), A. Scown, A. Wyllie.*

MAULED BY THE JAGUARS
SOUTH AFRICA 12
SOUTH AMERICAN
JAGUARS 21

Second Test; 3 April 1982
Bloemfontein, South Africa

This extraordinary game was remarkable for providing one the biggest upsets ever recorded in international rugby. For the Jaguars, an Argentinian touring side in all but name, to beat the mighty Springboks was virtually unthinkable at that time. It was like the British Lions losing to the Cook Islands, or the All Blacks being put to the sword by Hong Kong. Argentina were not a force in world rugby and defeat for the South Africans just wasn't an option that had been seriously considered.

The two-Test tour had been organized by Danie Craven and the SARB, who by 1982 were feeling the anti-Apartheid pressure and were increasingly desperate for as much overseas contact as possible.

As no South American country would have countenanced sending a representative side to play in South Africa, a composite Jaguars side that contained 30 Argentinians, five Uruguayans, five Chileans and two Paraguayans was put together specifically for the 14-match tour. Out-gunned in the provincial games, the Jaguars came a spectacular cropper in the First Test at Loftus Versfeld when the Springbok three-quarters cut them to pieces. Danie Gerber, Carel du Plessis, Willie du Plessis and Ray Mordt scored eight tries between them as the Jaguars were crushed 50 points to 18. After that loss, nobody expected the Jaguars to attain anything other than doormat status in a Second Test that was reckoned a home banker by the rest of the world. Even the Jaguars' captain, the legendary Argentine fly-half Hugo Porta could not conceive that his side might turn the tables. "Morale was at rock-bottom after Pretoria," Porta said later, "and although I have never in my life started a game thinking that I might lose, before the game in

Bloemfontein I told the players that our objective must be to make sure we did not lose by 50 points again."

Arriving at the Free State Stadium in Bloemfontein, the Jaguars were well aware that their only realistic hope of success was over-confidence on the part of the Springboks. The tourists were not to be disappointed.

The Jaguars' well-deserved win was founded on some huge tackles from the back-row of Branca, Allen and Megri, and some stonewall midfield defence from Loffreda and Madero. Knocked back time and time again, the Springboks found that when they lost the ball the Jaguars pack, in which Dengra and Ure were heroic, were capable of shielding the ball as they advanced slowly upfield. What had been expected to turn into a romp turned into a war of attrition in which victory would go to the side with the

most desire – and that battle was won by the Jaguars.

By half-time the realization that the South Americans could win began to dawn on Porta and his players. "I just said to the players 'Yes, we can win, just carry on as you did in the first half.'" And carry on they did. Porta continued to pin back the Springboks with searching kicks into the corners, while the Jaguars pack amazed both the Boks and themselves by gradually shading the battle up front. Halfway through the second half they were winning the forward tussle convincingly, deploying the eight-man shove of the "bajada" scrum to devastating effect. So dominant were the Jaguars that the first score came from a strike against the head, from which lock Ernesto Ure fed Porta, who dummied his way over for a richly deserved try.

The Springbok ill-tempers which had been bubbling under for much

of the match now came to the fore as time and again brawls broke out, with four penalties from Porta's boot the end result. Five minutes from time, Porta put the result beyond doubt with a drop-goal to bring his points total to a match-winning 21. This victory did much to raise the profile of rugby not only in Argentina but throughout South America.

SOUTH AFRICA: *J. Heunis, C. du Plessis, W. du Plessis, D. Gerber, R. Mordt; N. Botha, D. Serfontein; P. du Toit, W. Kahts, O. Oosthuizen, B. Geldenhuys, T. Stofberg, L. Moolman, R. Louw, W. Claasen (capt).*

SOUTH AMERICA: *Sanguinetti; Varone, Loffreda, Madero, A. Puccio; H. Porta (capt), Soares-Gache; S. Dengra, Courreges, Devoto, E. Ure, Bottarini, E. Branca, Allen, M. Negri.*

A LOSING BATTLE *Springbok Rob Louw's spirited charge was ultimately in vain against the Puma's in 1982.*

FRENCH COCKEREL CROWS
FRANCE 30, AUSTRALIA 24

World Cup Semi-Final
13 June 1987
Concord Oval, Sydney

Australia had eased their way through the opening pool of the inaugural 1987 World Cup, dispatching England, the USA and Japan. In just three games they had scored 108 points, but conceded 43. Yet all that was forgotten after Australia overwhelmed Ireland 33–15 to book a place in the semi-final against France. As far as the home media was concerned, the "dream ticket" final of co-hosts Australia playing New Zealand was a virtual certainty.

In many ways, the home confidence was not too surprising. France had stuttered all the way into their semi-finalists berth. They had been held by Scotland and had laboured to beat weak Romanian and Zimbabwean opposition, while in the quarter-final they had only overcome unseeded Fiji by applying forward muscle. More to the point, the Wallabies had totally outplayed the French just a year before at the same venue, and so Australia expected to win at a canter once again.

At no stage of the semi-final was the result ever assured, with the lead changing hands six times in a see-saw game of startling intensity. It was as much a meeting of styles and of cultures as a rugby game, and it provided a fascinating contest. On the one hand were the French, all panache and pace behind the scrum, but with lock Alain Lorieux inspiring an awesome effort from his strong-mauling forwards. By contrast, the huge Wallaby machine, with the faultless tactical play of half-backs Michael Lynagh and Nick Farr-Jones working off a set-piece platform that gave them an immense amount of ball to work with.

Lynagh started the scoring, with a drop-goal after five minutes and then added three more points when the French collapsed a maul. Despite France playing the more attractive rugby, it was again Lynagh who stretched Australia's lead to nine points ten minutes before half-time. This time France's response was instantaneous, with Laurent Rodriguez setting up a number of driving mauls which tore through the heart of the massive Wallaby pack. It was dynamic, pragmatic and it worked, Lorieux driving over the Australian try-line from a line-out for a vital score just before half-time.

When Philippe Sella carved his way through for a try just after the break to make it 12–9 to France, the 17,000 crowd began to stir. Australia hit back through a David Campese try, but the French responded through the long-striding French full-back Serge Blanco who sent winger Patrice Lagisquet over for a try that made it 21–15. The match was reaching boiling point when replacement flanker David Codey latched on to a knock-on and stormed over unopposed for a try that made it 21–21 with five minutes remaining. Such was the tension that when Blanco fielded a ball on his own line, he fumbled and put his centres in trouble before Lynagh was awarded a penalty which he duly kicked, only to see Didier Camberabero slot over a penalty of his own to make it 24–24. Then came a passage of play which will be forever remembered as one of the most inspirational and memorable moments in the game's long history.

The French forwards began a rolling maul deep in their own half, before flanker Eric Champ burst into open space linking with Lagisquet. Suddenly the move gained momentum as first Berbizier, then Mesnel, Charvet, Berbizier again and Lorieux poured deep into Wallaby territory. Just as the move appeared to be breaking down, with injured and exhausted players lying prostrate, Rodriguez fed the hamstrung Blanco. Outstripping the cover defence over 20 metres, the full-back dived past the despairing Tom Lawton, knocking over the corner flag as he touched down to seal a Final place in the most dramatic fashion.

AUSTRALIA: *P. Grigg; M. Burke, A. Slack (capt), B. Papworth, D. Campese; M. Lynagh, N. Farr-Jones; A. McIntyre, T. Lawton, C. Lillicrap, S. Cutler, B. Campbell, J. Miller, S. Poidevin, T. Coker.*

FRANCE: *S. Blanco; D. Camberabero, P. Sella, D. Charvet, P. Lagisquet; F. Mesnel, P. Berbizier; P. Ondarts, D. Dubroca, J-P. Garuet, A. Lorieux, J. Condom, D. Erbani, E. Champ, L. Rodriguez.*

BULL-NECKED *French No.8, Laurent Rodriguez – a.k.a "the Bull of Dax" – brushes aside Michael Lynagh.*

THE MOMENT THAT MATTERED *Scottish scrum-half Gary Armstrong starts the move that led to the winning try and broke English hearts in 1990.*

ENGLISH ROSE WILTS UNDER POWER OF SCOTLAND
SCOTLAND 13 ENGLAND 7

Five Nations; 17 March 1990
Murrayfield, Scotland

When the unbeaten English visited Edinburgh on the final Saturday of the 1990 Five Nations championship to contest the Calcutta Cup, Triple Crown and Grand Slam with unbeaten Scotland, there was more at stake than just mere trophies. This was a meeting of two pround nations determined to show to the other that they were the stronger. It was a match which was to bring the drama and exhilaration of the Five Nations to a whole new audience, so keen had become the e interest throughout both England and Scotland.

England arrived seeking their first Grand Slam since Bill Beaumont's unbeaten season in 1980, and they had every justification in making themselves hot favourites to walk away with the prizes on offer. Their monster pack had steamrollered the French by 20

points in Paris, while their rapier backs had put 30 points on the hapless Welsh at Twickenham, and produced a performance of sublime confidence to beat Ireland 23–0 on their home ground. While England were hitting their most purple of patches, Scotland had stuttered to one unconvincing win after another, eking out victories through sheer willpower and stubborness.

It looked for all the world like a game between two unequals, yet the joy of the Five Nations is that status is as nothing next to the passions that "local derbies" can bring. Scotland used the tag of underdog to work themselves into a frenzy which they unleashed on over-confident England to devastating effect. In a gesture that is now legendary, captain David Sole led his side out onto the pitch at a slow, almost funeral march. As a statement of intent it was a masterstroke. It said to the watching England players that here was a deliberate, focused side ready to do battle in the next 80 minutes.

As soon as the match got underway, the Scottish game-plan became crystal clear. England's big pack had yet to be shifted around

all over the paddock, so the Scots back-row got on the case, disrupting possession wherever possible, switching play wide whenever the chance arose. All the while the Scottish centres were stepping up to the gain-line and making huge tackles that stopped the English in their strides. For an England side used to controlling proceedings the whole effect was profoundly disorientating, and despite scoring the only try of the first half through the skills of centre Jeremy Guscott, it was the home side which went into half-time in front. Better still, Scotland fly-half Craig Chalmers had managed to kick three penalties, and the Scots had withstood the one extended period of pressure the English pack had been able to exert through a punishing series of scrums on their try-line in the minutes leading up to half-time.

In the first few minutes of the second-half, a mistake by Mike Teague, the England No.8, when he fumbled the ball as he tried to pick up from a scrum, led to a Scottish scrum from which Scotland scored what was to be the decisive try of the match. Veteran blind-side John Jeffrey picked up and fed the ball

to Gary Armstrong. The scrum-half took out his marker before firing a pass to full-back Gavin Hastings. Heading towards the touch-line, Hastings managed to put up a perfectly weighted kick ahead. At that moment it became a simple race between the two wingers, Scotland's Tony Stanger and England's Rory Underwood. The Scot was first to the touchdown, and although England clawed their way back to within six points, the defence and sheer resilience of the Scots proved too much for England. When the final whistle went, the whole of Scotland celebrated a famous victory.

SCOTLAND: *G. Hastings; I. Tukalo, S. Hastings, S. Lineen, T. Stanger; C. Chalmers, G. Armstrong; D. Sole (capt), K. Milne, P. Burnell, D. Cronin, A. Gray, F. Calder, J. Jeffrey, D. White.*

ENGLAND: *S. Hodgkinson; R. Underwood, J. Guscott, W. Carling (capt), S. Halliday; R. Andrew, R. Hill; P. Rendall, B. Moore, J. Probyn, W. Dooley, P. Ackford, P. Winterbottom, M. Skinner, M. Teague.*

A WAR OF ATTRITION
FRANCE 10
ENGLAND 19

World Cup Quarter-Final
19 October 1991
Parc des Princes, Paris

The intense rivalry that developed between Europe's top two powers, England and France, during the late 1980s and early 1990s exploded in an autumn afternoon in 1991 when the two sides met in a charged World Cup quarter-final at the Parc des Princes. The match was a culmination of a three-year struggle for domination of Europe which England were winning hands down. In that time, Will Carling's side had won every match between the two sides, although they had only won one game in Paris.

The quarter-final came just six months after England had won their first Grand Slam since 1980 by beating France at Twickenham. Yet that victory over the French was by no means a comfortable one: a youthful France had lost 21–19, but Philippe Saint Andre had scored one of the greatest tries ever seen at Twickenham and the French had generally felt they had the measure of the English at last. In Paris, they reasoned, it would all be different. They didn't just hope to win, they expected to win.

When France and England walked out on to the Parc des Princes turf on a sunny Saturday in October, nothing could have prepared them for the atmosphere that awaited them.

The stadium was a intimidating riot of colour and noise unprecedented in European rugby, and the potential for an explosive game of rugby was there for all to see and feel in those tense moments before the game kicked off.

England hooker Brian Moore, who has played in every major Test venue in world rugby, reckoned that atmosphere by far the most intimidating he had ever come across, anywhere. "The French were psyched up beyond belief," said Moore. "All I can remember now is the whistle going and the whole place going crazy. It was 80 minutes of sheer guts that brought us through."

The pent-up tensions and emotions of the French players became clear as soon as the whistle was blown. The blue pack tore into the English and private battles quickly developed in the heat of the forward exchanges. Within five minutes the pattern for the rest of the game had been set when England wing Nigel Heslop put up a garryowen which French full-back Serge Blanco gathered. Heslop, arriving fractionally late, clattered into Blanco and all hell broke loose as the Englishman was punched to the floor in an uncharacteristic assault by Blanco.

From that moment on, the two sides indulged in an epic confrontation in which one side never truly gained control. The match threatened to descend into violence at several stages, with Philippe Sella laying out England fly-half Rob Andrew, English fists leaving Laurent Cabannes with a bloodied nose and English flanker Peter Winterbottom lucky to escape censure for a flinging his boot at Laurent Cabannes' head.

With the score locked at 10–10 and extra-time looming, French prop Pascal Ondarts was penalized for handling in a ruck and Jonathan Webb kicked a penalty that took his side into the slenderest of leads. The French, who had become increasingly ragged, were finally beaten in the last minute when Carling put up a garryowen and, chasing up, caught Blanco in the act of fielding the ball, dispossessing him in the process and diving over for a try that finally put England out of sight. It was a match of relentless effort and hostility. It had been a war of attrition, and England emerged triumphant.

FRANCE: *S. Blanco (capt); J-B. Lafond, F. Mesnel, P. Sella, P. Saint-Andre; T. Lacroix, F. Galthie; G. Lascube, P. Marocco, P. Ondarts, J-M. Cadieu, O. Roumat, E. Champ, L. Cabannes, M. Cecillon.*
ENGLAND: *J. Webb; N. Heslop, W. Carling (capt), J. Guscott, R. Underwood; R. Andrew, R. Hill; J. Leonard, B. Moore, J. Probyn, P. Ackford, W. Dooley, M. Skinner, P. Winterbottom, M. Teague.*

SAFE HANDS *Paul Ackford wins more possession in the line-out jungle. The English forwards dominance was to win the day.*

LAST-GASP LYNAGH BREAKS IRISH HEARTS

IRELAND 18
AUSTRALIA 19

World Cup Quarter-Final
20 October 1991
Lansdowne Road, Dublin

If the definition of a great match is one that is packed full of drama, then the 1991 World Cup quarter-final between Ireland and Australia must surely qualify as one of the greatest matches ever played. The match was all the more dramatic because its course was so unexpected. Australia had been going like a steam train all year, beating England 40–15, annihilating Wales 63–3, winning the Bledisloe Cup at a canter and coming unbeaten through a difficult pool which included Argentina, Western Samoa and Wales. Ireland, on the other hand, had come in to the tournament on the back of a humiliating series loss in Namibia and a Five Nations in which they failed to win a match. They only managed to make the quarter-finals because they were in the same pool as Zimbabwe and Japan, the two weakest sides in the competition. As far as the world was concerned, they were mere canon fodder for the most exciting Wallaby side since the Grand Slam team of 1984.

Yet as all Ireland's Five Nations opponents could have predicted, nothing is ever straightforward at Lansdowne Road in front of a capacity crowd of 50,000 when the Irish are in their favourite position of complete underdogs. Irish passion is a dangerous emotion when let loose, and even on a beautiful autumn day, perfect for the running rugby so beloved of the Wallabies, Ireland came within a whisker of derailing the side which was to go on and claim the title of world champions within a fortnight.

Not that the game plan which so rattled the Wallabies emerged by chance. If Ireland have one strength, it is their willingness to "have a go"; to get in under the opposition's skin and disrupt everything at source. It was a strength they were determined to deploy.

IRISH EYES A'WEEPING *Wallaby Marty Roebuck feeds Tim Horan during the 1991 World Cup quarter–final.*

Buoyed by the ball won at the set-piece, Ireland's forwards were in rampant form, matching their illustrious Wallaby counterparts in virtually every sphere and completely outperforming them in the area of sheer effort. Ireland were like terriers, snapping at the heels of the Australians every time they moved in an adrenaline-fuelled performance that never allowed the Wallabies the time to settle.

It was certainly the right way to play the game, because as they demonstrated all too graphically when they managed to move the ball wide, Australia's backs were just too slick for the Irish. David Campese rammed home the point with two outstanding scores, the first coming when he scythed through the Irish midfield for a try under the posts. But with their pack applying pressure up front, Ireland managed to doggedly stay in touch through the boot of fly-half Ralph Keyes. Yet with five minutes remaining and the score at 15–12 to

Australia, it seemed as if the Irish had shot their bolt.

But that was when the old stadium witnessed the most amazing scenes in its history. As time ebbed away, the ball ran loose on the left side of the stadium, and wing Jack Clarke picked up and fed flanker Gordon Hamilton. The Ulsterman tore through one tackle and headed toward the Australian line 40 yards away. As the Lansdowne roar grew, Hamilton pinned back his ears as Wallabies Roebuck and Campese gave chase. Campese just managed to get to the flying Irishman, but could not stop him grounding the ball in the corner for a try which bought a mini crowd invasion amidst jubiliant scenes. Keyes' touch-line conversion made it 18–15 to Ireland.

The Wallabies had three minutes to make amends. With the match three minutes into injury time and with Ireland winning a line-out just outside their own 22 they looked to have blown their

chance. But then Irish scrum-half Rob Saunders missed touch with his kick, and Australia, knowing that his was their very last chance to snatch the win, moved the ball infield. Lynagh shipped it on to Horan, and looped behind his centres taking the pass from Campese and going over for a try which shocked Lansdowne Road into silence. Australia had won, leaving the Irish to cry into their Guinness.

IRELAND: *J. Staples; S. Geoghegan, B. Mullin, D. Curtis, J. Clarke; R. Keyes, R. Saunders; N. Popplewell, S. Smith, D. Fitzgerald, D. Lenihan, N. Francis, P. Matthews (capt), G. Hamilton, B. Robinson.*

AUSTRALIA: *M. Roebuck; R. Egerton, J. Little, T. Horan, D. Campese; M. Lynagh, N. Farr-Jones (capt); A. Daly, P. Kearns, E. McKenzie, R. McCall, J. Eales, W. Ofahengaue, J. Miller, S.Poidevin.*

THE TRY FROM THE END OF THE WORLD
NEW ZEALAND 20
FRANCE 23

Second Test
3 July 1994
Eden Park, Auckland

France had arrived in New Zealand in 1994 via North America, where they had been beaten for the first time by Canada in a full Test match. Team talisman Philippe Sella had been sent off and the French, who were touring on the back of a Five Nations in which they had won only two of their four matches, looked to be in disarray. As if to further prove the tourists' weakness, they had been edged out 27–23 when they played North Harbour, the only first class New Zealand province they were scheduled to meet before the First Test in Christchurch.

By the time the First Test dawned in late June, the Kiwi prophets of doom had already written the French off. Yet in an authoritative display the All Blacks were outclassed, out-gunned and plain outplayed by a French side which showed much of the verve and flair that had been missing throughout their poor season. Loose-head prop Laurent Benezech and flanker Philippe Benetton led the charge against a

curiously listless home pack while full-back Jean-Luc Sadourny, wing Emile Ntamack and centre Philippe Sella carved holes through the New Zealand backs almost at will. After 80 minutes France comfortably deserved a 22–8 win for only their second Test victory on New Zealand soil.

Amid a great deal of soul searching, the All Blacks prepared grimly for the Second Test to be held a week later in Auckland. The New Zealand public, already in a froth over the inexplicably dull display by the All Blacks in Christchurch, was whipped up into a frenzy when the French lost 30–25 in midweek to an average Hawke's Bay side. Media comment and a wave of public discontent made it clear that New Zealand expected nothing less than the complete crushing of the tourists.

As soon as the first whistle blew at Eden Park, the All Blacks tore into the French. With hooker and captain Sean Fitzpatrick in no mood to take prisoners, and the home forwards completely dominant, wave upon wave of All Black

attacks smashed into Sella and Thierry Lacroix in the French midfield. But while the French bent, they did not break and just before half-time wing Emile Ntamack ran the length of the field to claim an interception try which gave France an unexpected lead at the interval. That insult, however, only seemed to spur the bullocking All Black forwards on to greater heights and shortly after the interval Fitzpatrick rounded off an irresistible drive by his forwards with a try. Five penalties from Matthew Cooper meant that with normal time about to run out France were trailing 20–16.

Into injury time, the French threw caution to the wind when All Black fly-half Stephen Bachop kicked long towards the French corner flag and failed to find touch. Saint-Andre knew there was time for one last counter-attack. Setting off on a mazy run from behind his own posts, the French captain brushed past three would-be tack-

lers before linking with scrum-half Accoceberry who, in turn, passed to the charging prop Benezech. Ntamack took it on next, injecting pace as he surged into the All Black half. Next in on the act was Laurent Cabannes who made a crucial change of direction, allowing Jean-Luc Sadourny to sprint for the line for the greatest try ever seen at Eden Park. The ball passed through nine pairs of hands for a series-winning try which French captain Philippe Saint Andre rightfuly called: "a counter-attack from the end of the world – a true image of French rugby."

New Zealand: *J. Timu; J. Kirwan, F. Bunce, M. Cooper, J. Lomu; S. Bachop, S. Forster; R. Loe, S. Fitzpatrick (capt), O. Brown, I. Jones, M. Cooksley, B. Larsen, M. Brewer, Z. Brooke.*

France: *J-L. Sadourny; E. Ntamack, P. Sella, T. Lacroix, P. Saint-Andre (capt); C. Deylaud, G. Accoceberry; L. Benezech, J-M. Gonzalez, C. Califano, O. Merle, O. Roumat, A. Benazzi, L. Cabannes, P. Benetton.*

THE COMEBACK CREW *Deep into injury time and looking a Second Test defeat in the face, the French threw caution to the wind, and victory was theirs.*

ALL TOGETHER NOW *The Springboks World Cup victory triggered a spontaneous out-pouring of joy in SA.*

THE RAINBOW NATION RISES TO THE CHALLENGE

SOUTH AFRICA 15 NEW ZEALAND 12

World Cup Final
24 June 1995
Ellis Park, Johannesburg

As a feast of open running rugby, the 1995 World Cup final doesn't even get a mention in dispatches. But if you are looking for drama, intrigue, scandal and a game of unparalleled passion, then look no further. This was a gladiatorial contest that pitted two ancient and fierce rivals against each other.

For rugby-mad South Africa, the All Blacks playing the Springboks was a dream final. New Zealand had swept aside all opposition with contemptuous ease, putting 43 points on Ireland, 34 on Wales and setting a new record when they beat Japan 145–17. Scotland were comfortably beaten in the quarter-final. To cap the run-in to the final, in a riotous semi-final, Jonah Lomu scored four tries as England were utterly annihilated 45–29 in the most outrageous display of running rugby ever seen at the famous Newlands Stadium.

South Africa had beaten world champions Australia in the opening match of the tournament, but looked unconvincing after that. What the South Africans did have was unity and a whole country behind them. President Nelson Mandela embraced the Springbok cause, and for the first time both blacks and whites saw the team as theirs, a process helped by the fact that their top try-scorer was a black wing named Chester Williams.

When the day of the World Cup final dawned, the whole of South Africa had thrown itself behind Francois Pienaar's underdogs, and domestic politics were put on hold as for the first time all South Africans united together in a common cause. It was difficult for the new nation to keep at bay the feeling that winning the 1995 Webb Ellis Trophy was South Africa's rugby destiny.

Into this highly charged atmosphere came the All Blacks. Yet as the match began it became clear that South Africa would present a far tougher proposition than England had in the semi-final. Every time giant wing Jonah Lomu received the ball, he was gang-mugged, with the gritty scrum-half Joost van der Westhuizen to the fore. It was no surprise to hear after the match that the Springboks had been on a bonus for every time they brought down the huge New Zealander.

Not as sharp as they had been in previous matches, the All Blacks allowed themselves to be harried, put off their stride and disrupted at every turn (it transpired later that a stomach bug had laid low many of the side, giving rise to the allegation that the side had been poisoned – see Scandals, pages 214–17). The South Africans smashed into the All Blacks, allowing them no time to dwell on the ball and stopping the supply line to Lomu. For the first time in the World Cup, the New Zealand team began to look vulnerable.

As the match progressed, so close were the two sides that neither managed to get more than three points in front as the lead see-sawed. A match of unrelenting tension and drama was not to see any tries, however, and at full-time, despite the impression that the All Blacks were gradually getting on top through the line-out work of Ian Jones, the frantic Springbok defences had held tight and nine points from the boot of All Black fly-half had been matched by a similar total from Joel Stransky. A missed drop goal attempt from Mehrtens on the stroke of full-time meant that the scores were 9–9 at the close. In that charged atmosphere of extra-time, Mehrtens and Stransky again swapped penalties before Stransky knocked over a drop goal with two minutes remaining to give South Africa a 15–12 lead that they never lost. South Africa had fulfilled their destiny.

SOUTH AFRICA: *A. Joubert; J. Small, J. Mulder, H. le Roux, C. Williams; J. Stransky, J. van der Westhuizen; P. du Randt, C. Rossouw, B. Swart, K. Weise, H. Strydom, F. Pienaar (capt), R. Kruger, M. Andrews.*

NEW ZEALAND: *G. Osborne; J. Wilson, F. Bunce, W. Little, J. Lomu; A. Mehrtens, G. Bachop; C. Dowd, S. Fitzpatrick (capt), O. Brown, I. Jones, R. Brooke, M. Brewer, J. Kronfeld, Z. Brooke.*

THE GREAT STADIUMS

Great sport is great drama, and to be fully savoured every moment of theatre needs to be played out on a fitting stage. Of all the sports in the world, none can boast better stages than the world of Rugby Union. The game is a wide church and its places of worship around the world reflect that tradition marvellously. Which other sport can offer a range of venues as diverse as Billy Williams' stately "Old Cabbage Patch" in suburban London, through to the gleaming splendour of downtown Johannesburg's Ellis Park, and on to Hong Kong's So Kun Po Stadium, Asia's high-tech monument to the game of Sevens.

The great rugby stadia of the world aren't just piles of bricks and mortar where people happen to play the game. And they are more than mere symbols of the game for the wider world. Grounds such as Cardiff Arms Park, Eden Park and Murrayfield represent the living soul of a game which places a premium on tradition. The great grounds of world rugby provide an element of continuity that

provides a bridge between today's professional era and the Corinthian days of the early pioneers. So when the Lions stepped out onto the Newlands turf in the summer of 1997, they knew they were following in the footsteps of Bill Maclagan's first Lions side over a century before. Or when a Welshman strikes up "Land of My Fathers" before a game against England at Cardiff Arms

Park, he knows he is not just one but one of millions to have done so. Rugby now has the biggest and the best stadia in the world – but tradition means that the game's great grounds will always be measured by more than just their seating capacity.

IMPRESSIVE *The imposing structure of Twickenham, arguably the finest of all the rugby grounds in the world.*

BALLYMORE
BRISBANE, AUSTRALIA

Capacity: *30,000*
Opened: *1968*
Hosted: *1987 World Cup semi-final*

The home of Australian giants Queensland, Ballymore is one of the most impressive stadiums in the southern hemisphere. Its opening in 1968 also coincided with the dramatic rise of "The Reds" and of Queensland rugby in general. A bold venture at the time, particularly as Queensland were suffering once again from the incursion of Brisbane's powerful Rugby League clubs (or more specifically from their powerful cheque books), the financial outlay has been more than recouped in the intervening years. Not only do Queensland play at Ballymore, but the ground has become a regular Test venue for the Wallabies.

Ballymore was a radical departure for Australian rugby. Until its conception and construction in the late 1960s, provincial and national level Rugby Union had been played at cricket grounds, whether in Sydney or Brisbane. Tests in

IN THE RED *Ballymore is home turf to the Queensland Reds.*

Queensland had been played at either the famous Gabba, Brisbane Exhibition Ground or, latterly, the Brisbane Cricket Ground. All very good for cricket spectators, but in a land where Rugby League was king, the viewing problems presented by playing at cricket grounds did not help Union's meagre crowds.

As a vehicle for expanding rugby in Queensland, Ballymore has fulfilled its role perfectly. As it has grown steadily, so have the crowds. Interest has received a spur since the launch of the Super Ten, and then the Super 12 tournaments,

with crowds averaging almost 30,000 – which is a full house at Ballymore and a huge support at Australia's provincial level. It is a level of interest that owes something to Rugby League's internal disputes, but even more to the sparkling play from Queensland which culminated in winning the 1995 Super Ten when they beat the much-fancied South African side, Transvaal, 30-16 at Ellis Park. Last season the Reds treated their fans to more of the same when they thrashed Auckland, the eventual winners, 51–13 in the finest

Queensland display Ballymore has ever witnessed. Not that there is a shortage of candidates for the prize of greatest match ever seen at Ballymore: how about Wales's 63–6 annihilation at the hands of Australia in 1991; or Queensland's defeat of the 1971 Lions (one of only two defeats for the Lions during their 26-match tour); or even the tumultuous 19–17 Second Test win over the All Blacks in 1992 which clinched the Bledisloe Cup for Australia ?

Whichever one of those matches is chosen, one thing is for sure – there is no better place to watch rugby than in the warm, temperate climate of Brisbane. Situated in a leafy, middle-class suburb of Brisbane, Ballymore's main pitch (it also has practice areas and a gym) is now flanked by two grandstands, each with the capacity to hold around 10,000 seated spectators. The balance of the 30,000 capacity is made up from two grassy banks where spectators can come and eat food in a relaxed atmosphere. It is from these grassy banks, in particular, that the fierce parochialism of Queensland's supporters is the most vocal.

CARDIFF ARMS PARK
CARDIFF, WALES

Capacity: *54,000*
Opened: *1884*
Hosted: *1991 World Cup final third-place play-off.*

By the time the World Cup final is played there in 1999, Cardiff Arms Park will be one of the best sports stadia in the world. With government grants worth almost £100 million, the total redevelopment of Wales's most famous landmark has already begun in time for the millennium. The new-age bowl design includes a roof which can be moved into place and seating for 72,500 supporters. The stadium has also been pivoted through ninety degrees to ensure sufficient space to develop even further. It's a new stadium for a new century, which is

NEW AGE ARENA *Cardiff's famous old stadium has undergone a radical £100m overhaul ahead of the year 2000.*

why the ground is being renamed The Millennium Stadium.

Yet tradition is an enduring thing and it is virtually certain that the ground will continue to be known as the Cardiff Arms Park. There is a good precedent for believing so, as after the last time the ground was completely rebuilt between 1968 and 1980 it was renamed the National Stadium, only for everyone to continue referring to it as the Arms Park. (The Arms Park is, in fact, the 20,000 capacity ground of the club Cardiff, which currently backs on to the ground where the national side play, a quirk of history left over from the days before 1962 when Wales played on Cardiff's pitch.) Before the turn of the century

Wales played at a variety of venues, including Newport and Llanelli, before finally alternating between Swansea's St Helen's ground and Cardiff's Arms Park (so called because it was built on the site of a pub of that name). That arrangement continued until 1937, and since then, withthe exception of an enforced move during the building work in 1997-98 Cardiff has been the venue for all internationals unless bad weather has intervened.

The first match at Cardiff took place on 12 April 1884, when Wales beat Ireland by a drop goal and two tries to no score, although the most memorable feature of the match was that Ireland had to borrow two Welsh players as two of their number failed to turn up! Since that day

there have been many truly memorable matches on the famous pitch. One epic battle was the controversial 1905 match when Dave Gallaher's New Zealand "Originals" lost the international 3–0, the only defeat of a tour that included 32 matches in Britain and Ireland, after young Kiwi centre Bob Deans was dragged back over the line after grounding the ball in the final minutes of the game. Another game played at the Arms Park was the 1973 Barbarians game against New Zealand which started with Gareth Edwards' amazing try (see page 180) and ended with a 23–11 Barbarians win in one of the most spectacular games of rugby ever played. Yet whether or not the ground is called the Arms Park, the

National Stadium or the Millennium Stadium, the city centre ground has an aura all of its own. With a current capacity of 55,000, it nestles on land that once belonged to the Marquis of Bute and now stands in the middle of a bustling shopping centre.

The last match ever staged at the Arms Park was the 1997 Welsh Cup final when Cardiff beat Swansea in a suitably thrilling contest that included a try from Cardiff wing Nigel Walker. The following day, some of the stadium's memorabilia was auctioned off; among those items that fetched a tidy sum was the seat reserved when the Princess of Wales was a guest (£1,600), while a square yard of the famous old turf was going for £1.50.

CARISBROOK
DUNEDIN, NEW ZEALAND

Capacity: *33,000*
Opened: *1908*
Hosted: *1993 Bledisloe Cup v Australia*

The Test venue in Dunedin in New Zealand's South Island, Carisbrook has the distinction of being perhaps the only major sports ground in the world to be named in memory of a honeymoon. An early colonial administrator in the Otago province, James Macandrew, had honeymooned at Carisbrooke Castle on the Isle of Wight and perpetuated his happy memories by naming his Dunedin home Carisbrook (without the final 'e'). The home overlooked a swamp that was part of land owned by the Presbyterian Church and when cricketers in the 1870s developed the area for their own use, they took the name of Macandrew's home. The name was retained when rugby men became residents more than 20 years later, continuing to lease it from the Presbyterian Church until buying the freehold in in the Otago Rugby Union's Centenary year, 1981. Cricket continues to be the main summer user of Carisbrook and much other

THE HOUSE OF PAIN *Otago's Carisbrook ground on the South Island.*

sport has been played there, including international soccer, hockey and even a trotting meeting, to which the Presbyterian trustees objected until they learned that the totaliser at the meeting would ensure the canny Scots got their rent. But it is for rugby which Carisbrook is most noted, from the first international in 1908, when the All Blacks thrashed a forerunner of the Lions, the Anglo-Welsh, 32-5. The Lions in fact have inflicted the All Blacks' only defeat at Carisbrook – in 1930 when Doug Prentice's side beat New Zealand 6-3 in a game that began when Carisbrook was carpeted with snow, and in the memorable match

in 1971 that set the Lions on the road towards winning a series in New Zealand for the only time. John Dawes' team won 9-3, Ian McLauchlan scoring the only try when he charged down an attempted clearing kick by All Black No.8 Alan Sutherland and flopped on the ball inches from the dead ball line. The All Blacks' only other loss at Carisbrook was in 1973 when they were beaten by a national Under-23 team, the New Zealand Juniors, who were coached by a future All Black coach, Eric Watson, who still lives just around the corner from Carisbrook.

In the opinion of many, one of the All Blacks' most talked-about

wins should, in all justice, have been a loss. That was in 1959 when Ronnie Dawson's Lions scored four tries to none but still lost the Test 18-17 thanks to the prodigious kicking of the All Black fullback Don Clarke, who landed six penalties.

Carisbrook is the home to the Otago provincial side, renowned for its free-flowing approach to the game, even when they're losing, and revered by the Otago University students ("the Scarfies") who pack the terraces. Like any sporting team, Otago's fortunes have waxed and waned and their high point was either side of the Second World War when they and neighbours Southland shared the premier domestic rugby trophy, the Ranfurly Shield, for the best part of a decade.

In the 1990s, when Otago regained their reputation for being long on spirit and attitude if sometimes short on raw talent, Carisbrook became known fondly as the "House of Pain", a phrase coined by an Otago No.8 Brent Pope, after a particularly gruelling training session under Laurie Mains, the Otago coach who was in charge of the All Black's from 1992 to 1995. Of New Zealand's major rugby grounds, Carisbrook is generally regarded as the one with the most distinctive atmosphere.

EDEN PARK
AUCKLAND, NEW ZEALAND

Capacity: *47,000*
Opened: *1921*
Hosted: *Inaugural World Cup in 1987*

Such has been the strength of Auckland and All Black sides down the years that playing at Eden Park has become the ultimate challenge, whether domestically or in a Test match. Most major sides have now triumphed in the stadium's 76-year history, but none has found it easy.

South Africa were the first to try and succeed when the 1921 Springboks, led by "Boy" Morkel beat the All Blacks in one of the most memorable matches of all time. With the scores level in the second half, Springbok full-back Gerhard Morkel (yet another scion of the famous rugby family from which ten boys from the same generation represented Western Province) picked up the ball well inside his own half, ran in-field a few steps and smacked a drop goal between the uprights for the winning score. Pandemonium ensued, and several of the 40,000 supporters on hand rushed on to the pitch to

offer Morkel a drink, which he duly took after toasting the crowd. Matters got even more out of hand in the second half when wing South African Bill Zeller broke clear and was heading towards the line when he found himself surrounded by a pitch invasion!

The Springboks won that match 9–5, and managed to triumph the next time they were in New Zealand in 1937, when they were rated the best 'Boks ever. Since then, however, the All Blacks have triumphed every time at Eden Park, and even the top South African provincial sides have had precious little joy in recent seasons against Auckland in the Super Ten and then Super-12 competitions.

Eden Park itself is a very open ground which has only been used for Test rugby since 1921 and only regularly since the late 1930s. The lushness of its turf means that it has also been put to other uses, and as well as being the venue for the Empire Games of 1950, it has also staged Test cricket matches and one-day Eventing. The ground has also hosted many of rugby's biggest events, with the 1987 World Cup final, in which David Kirk's New Zealand beat France by 29–9 foremost amongst these.

As well as some big Tests, Eden

PARK LIFE *Eden Park is the world's most forbidding venue.*

Park has played host to some outstanding internationals. The Second Test against France in 1994, for instance, rates as one of the ten greatest games of all time (see page 186), while the Tests played against the British Lions at Eden Park comprise one of the most thrilling series of rugby matches ever played, with five of the eight Tests played there won or lost by three points or less.

Perhaps the most bizarre match to have been staged at Eden Park was the 1975 Test against Scotland when a pre-match downpour made conditions treacherous. The pitch was so wet that many considered it extremely dangerous to play on, but the match went ahead and it was the Scots who failed to come to terms with the conditions as they

lost 24-0. Afterwards, Andy Leslie, the All Black captain, was heard to say, "This was one of the greatest moments in New Zealand swimming."

While Eden Park does not have the claustrophobic intensity of an enclosed arena such as Murrayfield or the Parc des Princes, the passionate and vociferous crowd do their best to make up for it. Since starting their record Ranfurly Shield run in 1985, Auckland have become the strongest provincial side in the world. They have dominated New Zealand domestic rugby and have swept through Southern Hemisphere provincial rugby, winning the 1996 and 1997 Super 12s at a canter, and in the process making Eden Park the single most forbidding rugby ground to visit in the world.

ELLIS PARK
JOHANNESBURG, SOUTH AFRICA

Capacity: *80,000*
Opened: *1928*
Hosted: *1995 World Cup final*

When new Ellis Park was reopened in 1982, it was undoubtedly the most impressive monument to the game of rugby the world had ever seen. Indeed, it was the most hi-tech stadium in the world in any sport – even the top American Football venues were not on the same level. Although the capacity had been reduced from 95,000 to 70,000, the ground had been improved immeasurably. All-covered and all-seated, the home of the powerful Transvaal Union

looked to all the world like a potent symbol of the strength of Rugby Union in South Africa and a testament to the financial clout of the Johannesburg rugby community. However, things are rarely what they seem and the reconstruction of Ellis Park brought with it almost as many problems as it solved. So far-reaching were the problems associated with the rebuilding that many of the profound changes that have shaped the game in recent years stem directly or indirectly from that renovation. Turning the ramshackle and extremely dangerous scaffolds of pre-1970 Ellis Park into the gleaming monument to rugby that had been built by 1982 was an expensive business. The final bill, which included factors such as lost gate revenue during rebuilding, is

MONEY PIT *Ellis Park cost £60m.*

estimated to have been the equivalent of £60 million. Twenty years ago, it was more than the union could sustain, and by the mid-Eighties, Transvaal's finances were in crisis as debts of £25 million became public knowledge. The upshot was that the architects of the rebuilding, veteran administrator Jannie le Roux and his committee, were forced to resign and replaced by irascible multi-millionaire Louis Luyt.

Luyt is a formidable man. As well as getting Transvaal's finances in check, he invested heavily in playing personnel, which in turn ensured success on the pitch and full houses at Ellis Park. As Transvaal became more successful and worked their way into the black, Luyt also became head of the South African Rugby Football Union, and from that position he was able to strengthen the already strong voices calling for the World Cup to be held in South Africa. More than that, Luyt was also able to ensure that Ellis Park was the venue for the major showpiece events in rugby in South Africa. When, for instance, isolation ended in 1992 and South Africa re-entered the international fray, it was at Ellis Park where the Springboks met the All Blacks. In 1995, when South Africa was awarded the World Cup, Ellis Park, which had undergone further work to expand the capacity to 80,000, was the venue for the final between South Africa and New Zealand.

With international rugby and the Super 12 now regular features of the South African season, Ellis Park is better used than ever before. As well as the lush grass of its pitch, the stadium is also noted for the large video screen which replays tries. Yet even before it was

redeveloped after 1972, Ellis Park was one of South Africa's premier venues. Built on the site of a disused brick factory in 1928, Ellis Park has played host to some of the greatest games of all time. The All Blacks have always played a Test at Ellis Park, including the 7–6 victory

the year the stadium was built, while the First Test between the Lions and Springboks in 1955, a game which the Lions won 23–22 and which the then coach Danie Craven considered the most exciting ever played, was played in front of a record 95,000 spectators.

HONG KONG STADIUM
HONG KONG, CHINA

Capacity: *40,000*
Opened: *1994*
Hosted: *World's premier Sevens tournament*

The main sports stadium in the tiny former British colony of Hong Kong, the Government Stadium is not one of the biggest venues in world rugby; it has not staged any of the world's most dramatic Test series and it cannot boast a history to rival living shrines such as Twickenham, Ellis Park or Eden Park. Yet for all that, Hong Kong's significance as a missionary centre which has spread the gospel of the game through its annual Sevens tournament, and which has almost single-handedly popularized the abbreviated code outside the Scottish Borders cannot be underestimated.

For many years rugby was alive and well in Hong Kong. There is evidence of rugby being played on the Island almost as soon as it had been wrested from China by the British in the early 1840s, but the game remained the domain of expats and visiting servicemen for over a century. However, with the post-1946 commercial explosion of the Pacific Rim, Hong Kong became a major financial and trading centre and there was a massive influx of professionals from Britain. Many of these found their way into the rugby clubs and a great number were Scots. Hong Kong had joined the Asian Championships in 1969 and played occasional matches against touring nations in the 1960s and 1970s, but the HKRFU felt there was a need for a more regular form of international contact. The

idea of Sevens raised its head at the behest of a Scot called "Tokkie" Smith, who suggested a Sevens tournament on the lines of those held at Borders clubs in his native land and the idea was accepted, not least because it would give the physically smaller Asian nations a chance to compete on a more level playing field (not to mention the indigenous Chinese who the HKRFU were keen to spread the game to).

When the invitations went out in 1975 and the Cantabrians, an invitation side from Canterbury, won the inaugural 1976 tournament, few could have really understood what was underway. The invitation-only competition grew steadily in size and status, with more and more national sides attending, and by the

mid-1980s, the All Blacks, Wallabies, Fijians, Tongans, Argentinians and Samoans were all regular participants, and stars such as Jonah Lomu, Christian Cullen and Waisale Serevi all gained wider recognition through playing in Hong Kong. But it was the inclusion of up and coming nations like Taiwan, Japan, Germany, Holland, Papua New Guinea which made the world take notice.

For many of these smaller nations, the Hong Kong Sevens was a lifeline to the big time and a valuable source of kudos for the game in their country.

But if the rugby at Hong Kong was important, so were the environs. Played in the scenic 30,000-seater Government Stadium overlooking Kowloon Bay, the tourna-

ment is as much a social as a sporting occasion; one in which spectators are as likely to return with as many memories of the famous Joe Bananas bar as they are of events on the pitch. For Asian participants and spectators, the social side of the tournament and the general bonhomie are eye-openers which go some way to showing that rugby can be more than a pursuit restricted to the elite. Although in 1994 the tournament was switched to the sparkling new stadium of the same name, the ethos of sporting excellence allied to drunken excess has continued to this day. It is a combination that started a new rugby era in the Government Stadium in Hong Kong. With China now in charge, one can only hope that the festivities are allowed to continue.

GROUND BREAKING *The venue for the Hong Kong Sevens is the perfect meeting place for sporting excellence.*

LANSDOWNE ROAD
DUBLIN, IRELAND

Capacity: *49,600*
Opened: *1878*
Hosted: *1991 World Cup quarter-final*

HOME OF THE HAVE-A-GO *Landsdowne Road, the world's oldest Test ground.*

Lansdowne Road remains one of the most atmospheric of rugby grounds. With Ireland having played all of their games there since the thumping loss to England by one try and two goals to no score in 1878, it is also the oldest Test ground in the world. Originally bought by Henry William Dunlop, a Trinity College graduate, the site of the ground is on seven acres between the River Dodder and the Lansdowne Road railway station. Initially purchased so that the old boys of Trinity College who were playing for Lansdowne Rugby Club would have a home (the club, which was at one stage nicknamed the "Second Trinity", still play in the Irish first division next door to the national ground), Dunlop also allowed Dublin Wanderers to use the site.

When Ireland played England in 1878, they handed over the princely sum of £5 to Dunlop for the privilege of using the Lansdowne Road ground. For the next three-quarters of a century, Ireland internationals were staged at either Lansdowne Road or at one of three Belfast venues, NIFC's Ormeau ground (which also doubles as the finest cricket ground in Ireland), the Royal Ulster Agricultural Society's Balmoral Exhibition Ground or, after 1924, Ravenshill. The building of the latter venue in the early 1920s coincided with the end of work to upgrade Lansdowne Road, a project into which the bulk of the IRFU's resources had been poured. The Dublin stadium was given a West Stand in February 1908, which was eventually finished in 1955, and work on the East Stand started in 1923, to be finished in 1927. The basic layout of the ground has remained pretty much unchanged ever since, with the East Stand rebuilt in 1982, and the West Stand undergoing major work in 1955 and 1978. The capacity today stands at just under 50,000.

The IRFU planned more work at Lansdowne Road, including North and South Stands, but political considerations were to take a front seat in the early 1920s – the Republic of Ireland and Ulster split in 1922 – and in order to ensure that the IRFU continued to be made up of all four provinces, it was decided to invest heavily into building Ravenhill and to play internationals there. That state of affairs continued until crowds begin to dwindle, with Scotland and Wales in particular playing many of their games in Belfast until 1956, when a terminal lack of interest in Ulster meant that all major games were transferred to Dublin.

Lansdowne Road is now the only major ground in the Home Unions to have terracing. That makes for interesting times at key Five Nations matches when visiting fans turn up ticketless and fall prey to the counterfeiters. The end result is a crowd which can often swell to almost twice the recommended size. It is this, plus the restrictions of a site that at seven acres is just too small for a major rugby stadium, that has prompted thoughts of moving the home of Irish rugby away from Lansdowne Road. Certainly, further development of the ground is problematic: the rail route which runs under one of the two stands presents one insoluble problem, while the dogged resistance of the genteel residents of Ballsbridge to further building work provides another. With the IRFU's administrative offices housed in an old town house across the railway tracks, the thinking now is that the home of Irish rugby will be moved to an old horse racing venue on a greenbelt site on the outskirts of the city.

LOFTUS VERSFELD
PRETORIA, SOUTH AFRICA

Capacity: *60,000*
Opened: *1906*
Hosted: *1995 World Cup final third place play-off*

In these days of intense rivalry between provinces, it is interesting to note that the man who gave his name to the home of Northern Transvaal's Blue Bulls was in fact a dyed-in-the-wool Western Province man. One of four rugby-playing brothers, Loftus Versfeld was probably the least successful of the quartet. All four played against Bill Maclagan's British touring side in 1891, with Marthinus playing in all three Tests and the family's other cap, Hasie, scoring the only try conceded by the British in three gruelling months. The third brother, Charles, also represented Western Province (or Cape Town as it was then known) against the British.

But for all his relative underachievement on the field of play, Loftus Versfeld's impact as a rugby missionary will live for many years longer than any memories of his brothers' on-field heroics. As one of the men responsible for bringing rugby to Pretoria, and to the Transvaal in general, Versfeld ensured his posthumous fame by giving his name to Loftus Versfeld stadium in Pretoria and in starting up the Pretoria University Rugby Club, which remains the largest in the world with 60 teams playing every week. Situated just four miles from the city centre, the ground which was to become the Loftus Versfeld stadium was originally erected in 1906 to house the University rugby club. Two years later it also began to serve as the headquarters of the Pretoria subunion of the Transvaal Rugby Union, and by 1910 two wooden stands had been erected. However, the stadium stayed relatively undeveloped until Northern Transvaal finally pulled away from Transvaal in 1937, at which stage work began in earnest. In 1938 the ground was finished and the new stadium was officially named the Loftus Versfeld Stadium.

The first major match in the stadium was in 1938, when Sam Walker's British Lions beat the new Northern Transvaal union 20–12 in a match that was a lot closer than the scoreline suggests.

Walker's men found out early what the rest of the world's Test sides were soon to discover for themselves, that at 1,000 ft. above sea level and with a rock hard, grassless pitch Loftus Versfeld presents one of the most inhospitable environments in international rugby. The 1953 Wallabies were the first to be beaten at Loftus Versfeld, but Northern Transvaal soon claimed the scalps of the Lions, French, Welsh, English and All Blacks, the latter in a controversial match played in front of a crowd of almost 60,000 in 1976.

When Loftus Versfeld started to stage Test matches regularly after 1963, it became clear that the ramshackle stands fringing the ground had to be modernized. In the 1970s, a major renovation of the stadium was began. Each stand was

replaced and by 1976 a brand new all-seater stadium with acapacity of 60,000 supporters was unveiled, making Loftus Versfeld one of the four Test venues in South Africa alongside Ellis Park, Newlands and King's Park, Durban. Such is its importance that at the 1995 World Cup it was the venue for the third-place play-off between England and France, and the New Zealand versus Scotland quarter-final.

The rebuilding of Loftus Versfeld also coincided with a period of immense strength for the Northern Transvaal side. In the late 1970s, men such as Frik du Preez kept Northerns at the top of the pile, while the emergence of Naas Botha led to an unprecedented run of Currie Cup success in the 1980s and early 1990s (*see* page 105).

ON HIGH *At an altitude of 1,500 metres, Loftus Versfeld tests players to the limits of their endurance.*

MURRAYFIELD
EDINBURGH, SCOTLAND

Capacity: *67,500*
Opened: *1925*
Hosted: *1993 World Cup Sevens*

Situated three miles from the city centre in the western suburbs of Edinburgh, Murrayfield was originally the site of the Edinburgh Polo Club at Murray's Field until the ground was purchased by the Scottish Rugby Union in 1922 to provide a permanent home for Scottish rugby. The national side had first played at Edinburgh Academicals' Raeburn Place before making Inverleith the regular venue, but by end of the First World War it was clear that Inverleith was no longer suitable, and so the decision to move west was taken. The youngest of the Five Nations grounds, Murrayfield was first used to stage international rugby in March 1925, when Scotland reclaimed the Calcutta Cup after a seven-year losing streak beating England 14–11 in front of a crowd of some 30,000.

From that date, Murrayfield developed into a Caledonian fortress, helped no doubt by the fact that in the 1920s Scotland pos-

sessed an outstanding side in which the famous four Oxford three-quarters were peerless. The success of that era and the crowds it drew gave the SRU the funds to develop Murrayfield and in 1935 the West Stand was built, to be followed a year later by the North and East Stands. Since then, the ground has staged many memorable games in

front of some huge crowds. The biggest of them all was in 1975, when 104,000 crammed into Murrayfield to see Andy Irvine's Scotland defeat a Welsh side including such greats as Phil Bennett, Gareth Edwards and JPR Williams 12–10 in a match of breathtaking endeavour. So dangerous was that crush, however,

that the following season major matches were made all-ticket, a restriction that is still in force.

There have been many other great games to have been played at Murrayfield, not least the Grand Slam contest between England and Scotland in 1990, which Scotland famously won 13–7 against a powerful English side that was consid-

YOU'RE GORGEOUS *Murrayfield has developed into one of Europe's finest sports venues.*

ered overwhelming favourites. That English side was to have its revenge at Murrayfield 18 months later, however, when England beat Scotland 9–6 in the 1991 World Cup semi-final.

Since then the ground has undergone a complete rebuilding programme that cost almost £50 million. In 1993 the North, West and South Stands were completely rebuilt to add to the work completed on the East Stand in 1983, the final effect being to produce a stadium in the modern method – a bowl shape with all the stands completely covered. Despite being constructed in record time (certainly compared to Twickenham), with seats relatively distant from the field of play and a reduced all-seated capacity of 67,500, the "new" Murrayfield seems to have managed to retain far more of its old character than its soulless southern counterpart. Indeed, Murrayfield has the same intimidating atmosphere that made it such a difficult place to conquer (the French, for example, failed to win there between 1978 and 1994 despite producing some immensely powerful sides during that era). Just as importantly, perhaps, Murrayfield matches remain the same powerful social occasions that they have always been. The car park is still always full, the pubs are bulging at the seams and the city centre revelry goes on late into the night.

NEWLANDS
CAPE TOWN, SOUTH AFRICA

Capacity: *51,000*
Opened: *1888*
Hosted: *1995 World Cup semi-final*

Rugby in South Africa started in the Cape and to this day Western Province have remained arguably the single most dominant force in South Africa. Cape Town was the base for the British Isles side in 1891 after an invitation from the then governor of the province, Cecil Rhodes, led to South Africa's first incoming tour. Although the British toured the whole of southern Africa and played three Tests, they concentrated their efforts in Cape Town, where they played more than half their 20 games during their four-month tour, including the final Test at the Newlands ground, which was then three years old. In that Test, the British had to fight for a 4–0 win against a South African side which indulged in "fast and furious play" according to the Cape Times (this was hardly surprising as 11 of the side, including captain Alf Richards and H.H. Castens, were from Cape Town).

Although already an excellent playing surface, after winning the

BEAUTY SPOT *Cape Town's Newlands stadium: the world's most beautiful.*

Cape Town Test British vice-captain Johnny Hammond suggested that playing at Newlands was bound to cause problems for later sides, partly because of its "hard ground" but even more because of the "overwhelming hospitality" of the Cape Town rugby authorities. Needless to say, Hammond's words have proved prophetic.When the British next came back in 1896 with Hammond as captain, the 5–0 fourth Test defeat at Newlands was their only loss. In 1903, Cape Town was once again the only Test loss for the British tourists and in 1910 Irishman Tom Smyth's Lions lost their final Test by the unprecedented score of 21–5.

Yet for all the South Africans' early successes at Newlands, the ground is considered unlucky by followers of the national side because of the high number of Test defeats suffered at the venue. The reason for the run of losses is put down to the un-South African conditions that exist at the Cape Town stadium. Not only is the ground not at altitude (as are Loftus Versfeld and Ellis Park, Test venues where tourists have traditionally struggled) but Cape Town's temperate weather means that the ground is softer than almost anywhere else in South Africa, with lush grass and a

cool breeze. In short, conditions that are far closer to what New Zealanders and British players are used to than anywhere else in South Africa.

But whether or not Newlands is a place where the Springboks have the best chance of success, it is certainly the most beautiful ground in South Africa, and possibly the world. Nestling at the foot of Table Mountain, Newlands is a beautiful ground in a quiet residential area less than a kilometre from the equally famous Newlands Cricket Stadium, also the finest in South Africa. Both stadiums have been renovated extensively over the past decade, with Newlands now a gleaming testament to the financial power of Western Province rugby. Although capacity has been reduced by 5,000 to 51,000, the stadium is now fully enclosed and an all-seater venue to rival the best in the world. The stadium also continues to be the centre of South African rugby. The old South African Rugby Board was housed there from its formation in 1889, as is the present post-Apartheid South African Rugby Football Union. That pre-eminence stems from the dominance of Western Province, winners of the Currie Cup a record 29 times.

PARC DES PRINCES
PARIS, FRANCE

Capacity: *50,000*
Opened: *1906*
Hosted: *1991 World Cup quarter-final*

One of the most intimidating arenas in world sport, the Parc des

Princes in the west of Paris was built in 1897 and first used as the home of French rugby in 1906, when a young French side were thrashed 38–8 by Dave Gallaher's New Zealand "Originals". Although all matches against the Home Unions continued to be played there until 1920, it was then the French Federation's policy to

stage half of the major internationals against touring sides in the south of the country, where rugby is infinitely more popular than in the more soccer-friendly north of France. This policy continues today, and in recent seasons internationals have been held in Lyons, Toulouse and Nantes.

In 1920, however, the primitive

facilities of the Parc des Princes were being overshadowed by Racing Club de France's Stade Colombes to the north west of the city, and the French Federation eventually switched grounds when a programme of redevelopment had begun at the already impressive Stade Colombes ahead of the 1924 Olympics (at which the French were beaten 17–3 by the USA in the final. The writing had been on the wall for the Parc as early as 1914, when England had played their Five Nations match at Colombes, winning 39–13 in what was to be the last major international before the outbreak of the First World War.

As ever in France, it was the decision by the Parisian municipal authorities to pump in funds which led to Colombes being abandoned in favour of Parc des Princes once again. The decision to return to the Parc was taken in 1971, more than half a century after the last international game was played there, and owed much to the £10 million

RIP *Parc des Princes in Paris*

reconstruction which was taking place for the purpose of staging international soccer matches. Indeed, rugby and soccer have been bed-mates ever since in France, with the Parc des Princes also playing host to top soccer outfit Paris Saint Germain, plus at least two other top Parisian sides at various stages.

Soccer has had yet another role to play in the history of the Parc des Princes, and this time it is a terminal one. Demolition started on the Parc in the spring of 1997 and as of 1998, the home of French rugby will be across the city at the purpose built stadium which is to house the 1998 World Cup soccer tournament.

The decision to demolish the ground was taken largely because it was felt that the Parc des Princes, with its capacity of 50,000, was simply too small to cater for the huge following that Five Nations rugby now commands. Yet in many ways it was the size of the Parc which gave it a special intensity unrivalled

in Test rugby venues.

The steep, towering sides of the concrete edifice, and the cauldron-like feel that comes from the tight bowl shape (the Parc is fully enclosed), make this a naturally gladiatorial amphitheatre. Extra spice is also added by the presence of the Dax Brass Band, a four-piece which strikes up from the terraces every time France score. The end product is a ground at which France have proved phenomenally difficult to beat, and of the regular visitors, Ireland, Scotland and Wales all have dismal records at the Parc, with Scotland only winning once (in 1995) in the 25 years of rugby at the ground.

TWICKENHAM
SURREY, ENGLAND

Capacity: *75,000*
Opened: *1909*
Hosted: *1991 World Cup final*

There is a temptation to think of Twickenham as a part of rugby's furniture, a stadium that has been standing since the game began. Yet it is not so. England had already been playing international rugby for 36 years when the late, great referee Billy Williams began looking for a site on which to build a monument to English rugby. Up to that point, internationals had been played all over the country, initially using the London cricket venue of The Oval, but spreading the honour around so that Blackheath, Richmond, Manchester, Leeds,

Dewsbury, Birkenhead, Bristol, Leicester and Crystal Palace had all hosted England internationals.

Even with a mandate from the Rugby Football Union committee, of which Williams was a prominent member, it took more than a year to find a suitable spot. But when Williams alighted upon a ten and a half acre site in Twickenham the search was over and in 1907 the RFU handed over the considerable sum of £5,572 12s 6d and work started immediately. The purchase of what was then a cabbage patch was fairly controversial, for the ground is almost 15 miles from the centre of London. Yet so desperate were the RFU for a permanent home that the dissent soon died down, and by 1909 the ground was finished.

Although Harlequins were the

first side to play on the pitch when they met Richmond on 10 October 1909, the first Test match played on the sumptuous turf of "HQ" was in January 1910 against Wales. Crowds grew steadily from the 17,000 that watched that international and by 1932, when the North Stand and West Stands had been built, and a second tier added to the East Stand, the ground could hold 72,500, of which almost half were seated (although 75,000 did crush in for the England vs. Wales match of 1950).

Until the new South Stand was built in 1981, Twickenham remained virtually lost in time, unchanged except for small touches such as the erection of the "Rowland Hill Memorial Gates", topped by a pair of famous golden lions, or the lavish refurbishment of

the Royal Retiring Room, the cost of which was borne by Shanghai RFC. Yet when change started, it moved on apace. By 1995 the distinctively green West, East and North Stands had been rebuilt to form a distinctive horseshoe at a cost of £30 million. Within the next year, work will begin on rebuilding the South Stand so that the whole stadium forms a bowl. This, plus the sliding roof which will cover the whole stadium, will cost a further £16 million, but will give Twickenham an all-seated capacity of 85,000 (from its present 75,000) making it one of the outstanding venues for sport in the world.

Although many players and supporters feel that the enlarged stadium has been de-personalized by the changes, the clamour to play at Twickenham and to watch games there has never been greater. In the 1970s spectators could arrive on the day and buy a ticket, yet today despite rapidly escalating ticket prices virtually every match is sold out many times over, with black market tickets changing hands for ten times face value. The only way for many fans to see matches is to use the burgeoning corporate hospitality sector. While this ensures the pennies keep rolling in to the RFU's account, it has left many fans unhappy at the increasingly difficult procedure for obtaining tickets for International matches.

THE OLD CABBAGE PATCH *Twickenham has come a long way since it was used to grow vegetables.*

THE BUSINESS OF RUGBY

For more than a century, rugby union paraded the principle of amateurism almost in defiance of the money it has always attracted. Even though many of the game's institutions had commercial origins, its establishment resolutely upheld the Corinthian ideal. The arrival of the World Cup a decade ago signalled the end of a philosophy which had long been an anachronism, and in 1995 rugby union went 'open'. But the transition has hardly been smooth due to its suddenness and the failure of many traditionalists to adapt.

When rugby decided to bite the bullet and stage a World Cup competition in 1987, the game changed fundamentally and forever. Within four years, the competition had become the fourth most watched event in the history of sports television with more than two billion viewers. The 1995 World Cup, held in post-Apartheid South Africa, grossed the undreamt of figure of £250 million and within a month of that tournament's showpiece final in Johannesburg rugby union had become a fully professionalized sport.

Another month later the southern hemisphere completely restructured its domestic game and sold the end result to Rupert Murdoch's News Corporation for £340 million for a ten-year deal, and six months after that the Northern Hemisphere club scene exploded, with millionaire backers buying the game's top clubs on an almost monthly basis. After a century in self-imposed penury, Rugby Union had become very big business indeed.

The fact that rugby had been small beer in business terms until the catalyst of World Cup competition swept away the floodgates of the amateur ethos was no accident though. From its earliest days, the founding fathers of rugby union eschewed the concept of players being paid to play rugby, a sticking point that led to the formation of the Rugby League in 1895. Any device that might lead to professionalism was always kept at arms length by the British unions, whether it be domestic leagues, the Hong Kong Sevens or broken time payments, and it is no coincidence that it was England and Ireland who were the last nations to be arm-twisted into participating in the inaugural World Cup.

Worldwide rugby administration has always been governed by the British elite, and that group has always held the Corinthian principle of playing for the sheer glory as one of its central tenets. Much as athletics and cricket held out against professionalism for many years before eventually succumbing, so too did Rugby Union. Yet that is not to say that money was not an important consideration in the game's early development. Many of the earliest and most significant developments in the game were as a result of the lure of lucre.

When Melrose butcher Ned Haig came up with the idea of playing an abbreviated code of rugby at his local club's sporting tournament in 1883, it was not altruism or Corinthian ideals which drove him, but the need to scrape together funds for Melrose rugby club.

As he later recalled in an article entitled 'An old Melrose player's recollections', "Want of money made us rack our brains as to what was to be done to keep the club from going to the wall, and the idea struck me that a football tournament might prove attractive. But it was hopeless to think of having several games in one afternoon with 15 players on each side, so the teams were reduced to seven men. It was an instant success and saved the club from bankruptcy."

THE BRITISH LIONS

The British Lions also owes its existence to the determination of two Nineteenth Century entrepreneurs to turn a quick buck. In 1888, when the first British touring side to travel to Australia and New Zealand left on board a steamer from Southampton, it was at the initiative of Alfred Shaw and Arthur Shrewsbury, two England cricketers who had been a part of the early England cricket teams to have toured Down Under. Staggered by the enthusiasm of the colonials for sporting contact with the wider world, and convinced that the format could be transferred to rugby, the two men brought over a side from Britain, drawn almost exclusively from the northern clubs and the Scottish Borders cotton town of Hawick.

Although a suspicious RFU ensured the players signed affidavits to say that they were not paid at any stage, with hindsight it is clear that the whole concept was driven by the prospect of making a turn and that it was basically a professional tour. Certainly, the tour was organized with all the efficiency of a business operation. Some of the players were paid, with Dewsbury forward AJ Stuart admitting receiving an advance of £15 to "kit himself out" before the party left, while the revelation that the Halifax forward JP Clowes had also received expenses further angered the RFU and led to the first shot in the war between the pro- and anti-broken time lobbies that was eventually to lead to the formation of the Rugby League in 1895. If any further evidence were needed of the underlying reason for the tour, it came in Melbourne, where the tourists played 19 games of Victorian (now Australian) Rules Football on the basis that it was the code which could draw the biggest crowds!

It was perhaps a taste of things to come that this pioneering tour party was dominated by men from the northern strongholds that were later to break away to form the Rugby League. The party, which was described as being made up mainly of "working men" was one which could never have been put together unless many of the players were paid

for their time. Indeed, by 1888, the practice of paying players had already set in despite the strict official line on amateurism, and for most of the players from northern clubs it would

WE HAVE LIFT-OFF *The World Cup has transformed rugby into a genuinely professional global sport.*

a well-paid job at a pub that was usually owned by a supporter of his new club. By the time that the broken-time dispute came to a head in 1895, the business footing of the northern

have been perfectly normal to be paid, or paid in kind, for their efforts.

At the time, Association Football and rugby were vying for crowds, and in many cases it was the oval ball game which was attracting the biggest gates. The first floodlit game was played between Broughton and Swinton in 1878 and the intense rivalries of the close-knit northern towns and the ferocity with which clubs contested the county cups led to huge crowds and an unofficial transfer market that was an open secret. The general quid pro quo was that talented players moved to clubs in return for

clubs and their flouting of amateur regulations in this way was a standing joke. Speaking against the broken-time proposal, Cheshire representative the mischevious Rev Frank Frank Marshall raised howls of laughter when he said that he "knew one club in Yorkshire where there were *seven* publicans in one team ... it is an open secret in Yorkshire that there are many players in receipt of funds from clubs or their supporters."

But if by the late 1880s the game was beginning to take on many of the aspects of a professional sport in its northern heartland of Lancashire

and Yorkshire, so was the same process being repeated in South Wales, where huge crowds meant huge revenues for clubs and a brisk trade in players. As Phil Bennett said many years later: "Weekends were the same for everybody in Wales. Saturday was for playing rugby, and the Sabbath was for chapel. And if you weren't playing rugby, you were almost certain to be watching it." The upshot was that top grounds like Stradey Park, the Arms Park, Rodney Parade and St Helen's regularly hosted crowds well in excess of 20,000 for top matches, with that number rising to close on 50,000 in the years after the First World War.

Accurate figures for gate receipts are hard to come by in Wales, although gate receipts of £50 per game at Leicester, which had average crowds of around 10,000 throughout the 1890s, would suggest that the top Welsh clubs were bringing in well in excess of £100 per game over a century ago. With such comparatively huge sums floating around, it was no surprise that there has always been a large amount of player movement and player payment in Wales.

THE CASE OF 'MONKEY' GOULD

That Wales was a different world was made crystal clear by the case of Arthur "Monkey" Gould which divided British rugby in 1896, the year after the Great Schism between Union and League. Gould, the outstanding Newport and Wales captain and the finest of three brothers who all played international rugby, was a living legend west of Offa's Dyke, so when he retired in 1896 the Welsh Rugby Union marked the occasion by presenting Gould with a house. Although the WRU argued that its gift was a spontaneous token of esteem rather than payment for playing, the furore was immediate, with Ireland and Scotland refusing to play Wales again until 1899, although England, still scarred from the ructions of the Great Schism, had no stomach for a further fight and dismissed the affair as an internal Welsh matter.

The episode was instructive for both sides. Those who wanted to pay their players realised that there were ways in which they could do so and

DRAGON ARMY *This group of Welshmen gather in London ahead of the 1935 Five Nations clash with England at Twickenham.*

ways in which they could not, while the guardians of the amateur spirit asked questions only when they were unavoidable. So it was, for instance, that as well as a cap Wales gave each of its internationals a medal to commemorate many of their early Five Nations matches – it's just that the medals were made out of gold with a value of around £500 at today's prices when melted down (indeed, there are so few left intact that they are one of the chief prizes for any rugby memorabilia hunters!). From the turn of the century the incursions of Rugby League scouts heightened the pressure to "do something" for top players in Wales. As well as rival clubs poaching their stars, the Welsh now had to put up with northern chequebooks, and the lure of the League dollar was certainly an attractive one

for the Welsh, who have to date seen one in every six of their internationals "head north".

Although there were undoubtedly abuses of the amateur code, particularly in Wales, they were relatively minor and despite the ceaseless innuendo proved the exception rather than the rule. The cash that flowed through the clubs' turnstiles was used to provide better facilities. Many of the top clubs still have the large city centre sites they purchased a century ago (clubs as diverse as Hamiltons, Ponsonby, Easts, Cardiff, Leicester, Bective Rangers, Edinburgh Academicals and Racing Club de France all spring to mind) while the cost of erecting stands and terracing was a heavy burden in the early years. A closer examination of the finances of top clubs shows that the running

costs were sufficiently high that few could have afforded to pay players, a conclusion which was reached only on the (usually erroneous) assumption that all clubs are and were run efficiently!

CHECKING THE ACCOUNTS

An examination of the finances of the Leicester club is a useful example of the concerns that exercised clubmen in the game's early years. Before the turn of the century the usual offer to visiting teams was £10 or half of the gate, whichever was greater, while entrance was sixpence. As well as the cost of building up Welford Road, there were full-time officials to consider (cost £25 per year), medical insurance for the players (£50 per year) as well as travelling costs. Despite crowds of up to 10,000, 1893

saw a deficit of £473, and for many years only the energetic patronage of a wealthy local merchant Tom Crumbie ensured the club's financial well-being.

It seems strange to relate now, but back then most players paid their own way, even at clubs like Leicester. The New Zealand Maoris side which toured Britain and France in 1888–9, for instance, made every tour member pay £62 for the privilege, a huge sum in those days. For the most part, the concept of players paying their own way was vigorously upheld. When it was discovered by the Scots that every member of Dave Gallaher's 1905 All Blacks "Originals" was being given an subsistence expenses allowance of £3 a week, the SRU denounced the tourists as professionals, and refused to play the "All

Black "Invincibles" on their return in 1924. There are some unkind souls who ascribe that decision as much to Scotland's 12–7 defeat at Inverleith in 1905 as to a principled stand on the question of expenses, but there was also another aspect to Scotland's pique at the New Zealanders.

GATE RECEIPTS

When the 1905 New Zealanders' management broached the subject of expenses with the Scottish Rugby Union, they were told that their request for a guaranteed £200 was way out of line with the expected gate and that, instead, they could have the total gate receipts. Given that it was a take it or leave it offer, the New Zealanders turned up on spec only to find the Inverleith venue packed and a take of £1,200 awaiting them after their victory (equivalent to around £150,000 today). The SRU were not amused, but learnt the lesson that has since held true – that the international game is rugby union's cash cow.

It was a lesson they would not have needed to have been taught had they looked at the balance sheet for other international matches at the time. When England played France at the Parc des Princes earlier that year, for instance, 5,500 spectators paid almost £300 to watch the game, while the average receipts for internationals in the five years directly before the First World War were up to over £500. In the years after 1918, rugby's popularity at international level began to soar and crowds did likewise. When the Scots took on the French at a sell-out Stades Colombes in 1922, the day's receipts of 253,000FF were the highest for any sporting event ever held in France. As major grounds capable of holding well in excess of 50,000 spectators were constructed in the first half of the century, so crowds grew and the stadiums were in turn ever enlarged and improved.

Enlargement and improvement were constant themes in the first 100 years of rugby after the first international was played in 1871. With the British administrators holding the whip hand and the subject of pay for play not on the agenda, admission prices were kept low and the rev-

enue raised from the game went into developing the infra-structure of the game. With the game as introspective as ever, little or no conscious effort was taken to develop the sport beyond its traditional boundaries of the Big Eight countries (the four Home Unions, France, South Africa, New Zealand and Australia) and so the basic structure of the game stayed pretty much unchanged for nigh on 100 years.

After all, rugby union had made its bed in the mid 1890s when it refused to come to an accommodation with those elements which wanted to temper the amateur ethos through so-called "broken time" payments, and paid the price when they split away to set up the a fully professional Rugby League in 1895. For mighty England it was a devastating blow, with 20 of its top clubs disappearing overnight and a 15-year slump in international form following swiftly on. But it was not just England who were to suffer from the struggle that developed with the new semi-professional code (only in the last decade have there been any more than five full-time league players outside Australia).

While South Africa, Ireland, Scotland and New Zealand remained largely unaffected, rugby union in both Wales and Australia has faced

continual harassment from the league scouts. Despite league never taking root on Welsh soil, more than 100 Welsh internationals have defected to league, including players such as Lewis Jones, who went to Leeds for a world record £6,000 in 1952, Sixties Lions fly-half Dai Watkins and more recently, halfbacks Terry Holmes and Jonathan Davies. The impact upon Australia, where the game took root after the 1907 Kiwi tourists passed through, was even more far reaching as League established itself as by far the dominant code there. So devastating was the impact that union ceased for over 20 years in Queensland, while it was decimated in New South Wales. The result in Australia, as in virtually all of the rugby-playing world, was that those who wanted to play professional rugby played League, and those that remained were generally fervent in their desire for Union to stay an amateur sport.

The determination to remain amateur was an overriding feature of rugby union. Even when spiritual brothers athletics and cricket took the plunge, rugby held back. Players were not allowed to take anything but the most meagre expenses, while they were also banned from writing newspaper or magazine columns, or from appear-

ing in any forms of advertising. Any contravention was swiftly punished as the Welsh student Alban Davies found out in 1938 after trying to claim £3 for loss of earnings while playing for Major Stanley's XV. In a celebrated case, Davies was found guilty and banned from the game worldwide *sine die*.

FRENCH BOYCOTT

Such treatment was not reserved for individuals, but was also meted out to countries as well. In 1931, the top 12 French clubs – "Le Douze" – challenged the union over player payments. This, combined with the blatant transfer market and the appalling annual violence of the French Championship, led the Home Unions to cut off playing relations with France until after the Second World War. A period outside the International Board's jurisdiction, however, was probably not the best solution to the problem of professionalism and after 1945 the shamateurism in French rugby was in virtually open defiance of the IB regulations.

Italy presented a similar problem in that it was clearly buying in top players from the early Fifties onwards. A legal loophole meant that sportsmans' salaries could be funded as a tax break, and it was for many years

BOOMERANG BOY *Welsh fly-half Jonathan Davies was the first player who "went North" ever to be allowed back.*

a haven for top Southern Hemisphere players looking to make a quick buck in their off-season. Carwyn James and Pierre Villepreux coached there, but the list of players who have played there is almost endless and includes legends such as Naas Botha, David Campese and John Kirwan. Japan, which has one of the biggest concentration of rugby players in the world, also has a long history of paying its players, if only in kind, through its system of "work clubs" sponsored by companies such as Kobe Steel and Sanyo.

THE SPRINGBOK INFLUENCE

Of all the countries to help push rugby towards professionalism, however, the strongest impetus came from South Africa in the years of international isolation. Acting in a vacuum in which the International Board held no sway and in an environment in which the Currie Cup and provincial rivalries became paramount, the game in South Africa soon became semi-professional as the top six provinces competed for the services of the leading players. Danie Craven, the elder statesman of South African rugby, was the first to admit that the SARB had little or no control over the all-powerful provinces and unless that was changed by allowing the Springboks back into mainstream international competition, the game in South Africa would be the first to go fully professional.

The situation came to a head when South Africa, desperate to lure Test sides to the country in defiance of the Gleneagles Agreement which banned sporting links with South Africa while Apartheid was still in place, invited the Cavaliers – an All Blacks side in all but name – to tour in 1986, thus following in the footsteps of the South American Jaguars, who had toured South Africa in 1982. It was clear that the Cavaliers had all been paid, and equally clear that the tour could not be stopped. "If we insist that the provinces call off the tour," said Craven "they will break away and we will have professional rugby union. That is not a possibility, it's a fact." As later events were to prove, Craven need not have bothered using the future tense – South

Africa already *had* professional rugby by this stage.

The Cavaliers tour to South Africa and the hired hands of the World XV who celebrated the Centenary of the SARB in 1989, had proved to the world's top players that rugby at the top level could become a lucrative profession, and they began to make increasingly outspoken statements on the subject of professionalism. Player power was taking off, but it was also being fed by changes at all levels in the game.

THE 1987 WORLD CUP

At the grass roots, the introduction of structured league competitions in the Home Unions and the reorganisation of the National Provincial Championship in New Zealand put an enormous strain upon playing resources. Training methods got better and more rigorous, taking up an increasing amount of players' time. Matches became more frequent as competitions proliferated, and by the time the first World Cup dawned in 1987, the world's top players were being asked to train and compete as unpaid professionals and hold down jobs at the same time. For many, the pressures were immense and the contradictions all too clear.

The 1987 World Cup changed rugby forever by demonstrating its potential to establish itself as the third biggest sport in the world after soccer and basketball. Only the Olympics, the Soccer World Cup and the Asian Football Tournament had attracted more television viewers than the first Rugby World Cup, and all of a sudden the world of big business woke up to rugby.

Not only did advertisers and sponsors like the sport, they loved the fact that the people who follow rugby tend to be from the middle classes and therefore have a higher disposable income to spend on their respective products.

The upsurge in interest coincided with the resurgence in 1988 of England, the single most economically powerful of the major rugby-playing nations. Not only were the rugby side the only English sports team to be doing well, but in Will Carling they had a young squeaky-clean standard

bearer who helped portray the sport in a new light to millions of the non-converted. By the time England contested and lost the 1991 World Cup final to Australia at Twickenham, commercial interest in the sport had reached fever pitch. Not that a lack of commercial interest was ever the only problem as former RFU secretary Bob Weighill noted when he told an instructive anecdote regarding the RFU's first ever sponsorship deal.

"In the mid-Seventies we needed some new clocks for the East and North stands. A minor problem you might say. In fact, the total cost was about £2,000 which was a fair sum of money. Somehow or other a company got to hear of our needs and offered to donate two clocks to us. I was impressed by their generosity and put the offer to the committee. On my assurance that there were no strings attached the committee, albeit reluctantly, agreed to accept the gift. This was an era when there was no perimeter advertising, no such thing at all as sponsorship and when TV was only let into Twickenham on sufferance. The company put their name on the clock face, but it was so small that you could only make it out if you were a few feet away."

The RFU Weighill talks of is a far cry from the money-motivated organisations which governed rugby by the time of the 1991 World Cup. England, which by 1994 had a turnover of £75 million per annum, had already done the unthinkable by adding to their all-white strip in the name of commercial progress and were busy selling the rights to anything that could be sold. Down South, the All Blacks and Wallabies were pushing the boundaries of the amateur regulations with innovations such as the All Black Club, which marketed the All Blacks and then put the money into trust funds for the time that they finished playing.

With its constituent bodies ignoring its own regulations, the International Board stood by, turning a blind eye in most cases while professionalism became a reality.

With the international scene enjoying an unprecedented prestige and profile, the whole game in Britain and Australasia was given a lift. Crowds

at National Provincial Championship games in New Zealand were at their highest ever, as they were for Inter-State matches in Australia. In Britain the Varsity Match and the National Cup final, matches which would once struggle to half fill Twickenham, were many times oversubscribed. A far cry from the Seventies when it was possible to turn up at Twickenham on match days to pick up a ticket.

RUPERT MURDOCH

In Britain, the quality national newspapers ran as many pages on rugby as on football, rugby magazines were launched and for the first time rugby players became household names. Rugby had arrived and the game was soon having money thrown at it. At the heart of the expansion of the game of rugby has been a very eighties phenomenon, satellite television, and in particular the Sky network of Australian media magnate Rupert Murdoch. Launched over a decade ago, Sky has established a base of subscribers by buying up all available sport. It has paid vast sums to secure the rights to American Football's NFL, English football's Premier League and virtually all of the cricket played at international level. Willing to pay vast sums for showpiece sporting action, the prospect of tapping into the World Cup and other prestige tournaments such as the Five Nations and the Bledisloe Cup was just too inviting to resist.

Ironically, it was Sky's setting up of the Super League Rugby League series that precipitated rugby union's long overdue move to a professional status. The Super League called for more teams, which meant more players – and there had been no attempt to hide the fact that Union would be the first port of call as the League clubs looked for top quality recruits. Even worse, one of the Super League franchises was to be in Auckland, a prospect that scared the NZRFU witless, particularly when former great John Kirwan signed for them. Without stopping to worry about the technicalities, the three giants of the Southern Hemisphere joined together and approached Sky with a deal to sell a package that included a tri-nations six-Test series between the

LIONHEART *Traditional tours, such as the Lions, can be huge money-spinners in the new professional era.*

three and a provincial tournament to be called the Super 12. The scheme hit a huge problem almost as soon as it was conceived when Sky's bitterest media rival Kerry Packer launched a bid to start up a professional rugby circus in opposition to the established unions. It was an audacious scheme, and one which came within a whisker of succeeding, yet as its details became public the official unions were able to harness sufficient public opinion to apply enough pressure upon the players who had signed up with Packer's rival World Rugby Corporation to ensure that they remained within the fold.

It turned into a monumental struggle between the two camps, and one which almost destroyed the game, but it had also significantly upped the ante. By the time the Australian, New Zealand and South African unions had signed up to a ten-year deal with Sky, the price had risen to £340 million for rugby union's first fully professional tournament.

The results, though, have been stunning, with the average crowds for Super 12 games steady at almost 30,000 and the six-Test Tri-Nations series sold out many times over.

BATTLE OF BRITAIN

The teething pains in the Northern Hemisphere as the game went professional have been almost as painful as those in the Southern Hemisphere, and they have certainly been more protracted.

Even as this encyclopedia goes to print there seems no end in sight to the political disputes that have seen England thrown out of the Five Nations and then reinstated after doing a deal with Sky which was not to the liking of the other Home Unions. Riven by infighting, the RFU has also been unable to function properly as first it fought its senior clubs over the £87.5 million Sky paid for the rights to games at Twickenham, and then its junior clubs over allegations that the Sky deal was against the interests of the game.

Whatever the administrative ructions, though, the finances of the club game are in rude health. Virtually every major club in Britain has picked up a shirt sponsor over the past decade, and with the game going professional in 1995, nearly all of the top English clubs picked up an owner as in soccer. In fact soccer has been the role model for the entry of British rugby into the professional age, not least because the expansion of rugby has been driven by television money in the same way as soccer's recent expansion. Sir John Hall, the man who made the first move by buying Newcastle Gosforth and employing Rob Andrew on a £750,000 five-year contract, made £100 million out of his share in Newcastle United FC and now appears to be trying to work his magic in rugby, as are a host of other hopeful sugar daddies who have paid up to £3 million for the right to own a rugby club. Yet a cautioning tale comes from London club Harlequins who announced a loss of almost half a million pounds at the end of their first season in professionalism in 1996–97.

The result of this commercial explosion in English rugby has been profound. Supporters have seen ticket prices double at some clubs, ground-sharing with football clubs has become increasingly popular and the exorbitant salaries paid to top players have seen many of the best players in the world turn up on England's doorstep.

The money involved is staggering – top players such as Ben Clarke can earn up to £250,000 per season, while the sponsorship package of a club such as Harlequins approaches £1 million per season.

Even Rugby League has felt the power of the Union chequebook as many of its top stars have been signed to play for top English and Welsh clubs, the most high profile and the most expensive remaining the £1 million signing of former All Black Va'aiga Tuigamala from Wigan by Newcastle in February 1997.

BIG SPENDER *Since being appointed Newcastle's Director of Rugby, Rob Andrew has spent £5 million on players.*

THE LAWS AND TACTICS OF RUGBY UNION

Few sports are governed by a code of laws (never rules) as complex as those of rugby union. From their simple origins a century and a half ago, the laws have mushroomed into a dense thicket of subordinate clauses. The upshot is that refereeing decisions and infringements are sometimes difficult for the casual observer to understand amid the often chaotic appearance of events on the field of play.

If there is one single impediment to rugby union becoming a truly global sport, it is the fact that its laws are virtually incomprehensible to the uninitiated. In fact rugby has almost prided itself on the fact that it is so difficult to understand – it was supposed to mean that the game was one to play rather than watch. What started 150 years ago as a simple game with ten simple laws quickly became a bafflingly complicated game and even now, in the professional era, its laws are still in need of revision.

Ironically, the Rugby School code became the pre-eminent carrying code precisely because its laws (never rules)

were so easy to understand and because it was the only set of laws to have been codified at an early stage. Although the game is now very different to that played by Webb Ellis's immediate successors, many of the terms – such as knock-on, off-side, mark and try – are the same ones that were in common usage when Webb Ellis picked up the ball and ran with it during a Bigside Game at Rugby School in 1823. It was another 18 years before Webb Ellis's innovation of running with the ball was recognised, and even then the practice of "handing on" (passing) was illegal, with players having to wait to pick the ball up on the bounce.

For many years, the various codes of football co-existed and it was not until 1863 that Association Football and Rugby Football became two separate games. Strangely, that split only came about when Blackheath, Richmond and a number of other London clubs refused to accept a ban on "hacking", the brutal practice of kicking an opponent's shins or tripping him from behind. This practice was to be banned in 1866 after the particularly gruesome death of a player in a London derby, but by the then rugby had broken irrevocably from Association Football.

The Laws of Rugby Football were eventually set down in stone shortly

after the formation of the Rugby Football Union in 1871, a task entrusted to three Old Rugbeians, Richmond's EC Holmes and AE Rutter, and Wimbledon Hornets' LJ Maton. Since then, there has been endless tinkering with the laws, although after 1890 that was done under the auspices of the International Board which ensured that all laws were common throughout the world. Although administrators such as Derek Robinson have recently taken steps to try to make the game's 28 laws more accessible through books such as "The Laws in Plain English" or "A Player's Guide to the Laws", the definitive lawbook remains a small, densely-

ALPHABET SOUP *Bristol, whose players wear letters instead of numbers, take on neighbours Bath, who have no number 13 shirt.*

written book entitled "The Laws of Rugby Football", a virtually incomprehensible figment of some deranged lawyer's twisted imagination badly in need of complete rephrasing.

Although the following guide to the laws and tactics of Rugby Union is by no means a definitive one (and is not meant to be), it will provide a snapshot look at the evolution of laws over the years and a easy-to-follow precis of the salient features of rugby football.

NUMBER OF PLAYERS AND NUMBERING OF PLAYERS

In William Webb Ellis's day, the number of players was restricted only by the number of boys who wanted to play and were eligible to do so. Once the game moved outside the confines of Rugby School, however, standard sizes for teams had to be agreed upon and after 1863 the size of a team dropped from 25 to 20 players. That was further reduced to 15 in 1876 after Oxford managed to persuade Cambridge to play the Varsity Match with reduced numbers in 1875. The switch was a huge success, with the reduction in the number of players

turning the game from a forward battle of attrition into a genuine running code. The next year all club matches were played with teams of 15 and in 1877 the first 15-a-side game was played between England and Ireland at The Oval, and the size of sides has remained constant ever since. Rugby League also had 15 players per side until the number was reduced to 13 in 1906.

The numbering of players' shirts is a practice which goes back to the first tour match, in 1897, when New Zealand played Queensland in Brisbane. The practice did not catch on in Britain until 1922, when England and Wales met in Cardiff, and even then it was many years before the Scots accepted the innovation.

In the early years, the system of numbering players started with the fullback wearing the number one shirt, the front row forwards wearing numbers 8–10 and the back row 13–15. Today, the system is reversed, with the front row wearing 1–3, the back row 6–8 and the fullback 15.

Although the system of numbering players applies virtually everywhere in the rugby world, English

clubs Leicester and Bristol both retain their tradition of ascribing letters to their players instead of numbers.

Other quirks are based around tradition and superstition: Bath, for instance, refuse to have a No.13 shirt, while West Hartlepool have recently hung up the No.5 shirt for ever in memory of their lock john How who tragically died of a heart condition during a 1994 League match.

SCRUM

A scrum is essentially a method of restarting a game and is awarded when play breaks down for some reason, usually because the ball will not come back from a ruck or maul, or because of a minor infringement such as a forward pass or knock-on. In the game's early stages, players lined up at scrums in the order in which they arrived. In the 1920s, however, England's Wavell Wakefield introduced the idea of players specialising in a given position and the modern scrum was formed. After 1932, when the 3–2–3 formation favoured in Britain went out of favour and the Home Unions banned the 2–3–2 diamond formation (plus roving wing forward)

which the New Zealanders had used so effectively, the standard formation of the scrum followed the South African model of 3–4–1 and has remained so ever since.

The scrum has never appeared to outsiders to be an overt offensive weapon, but the sapping trial of strength it entails is one of the key reasons why one set of forwards will eventually be able to grind another into submission. Particularly skilled scrummaging exponents over many years have been the Argentines, whose eight–man shove (the "bajada") made them feared opponents. One of the most destructive scrummaging displays ever seen was that of the British Lions in the Fourth Test in 1977, when the All Blacks were pushed off their own ball so frequently that they resorted to three-man scrummages in order to ensure that the ball came back quickly enough.

This would now be impossible, as recent law changes demand that all eight forwards have to stay bound until the ball leaves the scrum. This, in tandem with regulations which state that front rows have to have their shoulders at the same height as their hips and which prohibit "wheeling" the scrum past 90 degrees, have restored the attacking potential of the scrum which had been reduced by the widespread practice of crooked feeds into the front row by scrum-halves. The willingness of referees to award penalty tries against sides which collapse the scrummage from five-metre scrums has also helped the scrum retain its importance.

Safety implications also mean that only specialist front row players are allowed to play there in the event of injury (the absence of just such a replacement once meant that Canterbury and Auckland played non-pushing scrums during a Ranfurly Shield clash).

An interesting innovation in scrummaging was one that was pioneered by Neath during the Eighties, when up to five backs would rush forward to lend their weight to an attacking five-metre scrum. Although almost always successful, it is now banned.

LINEOUT

The lineout is the method of restarting the game once the ball has gone out of play and is now considered the key phase in the modern game. With the number of strikes against the head at the scrum declining to the point where the side with the put-in is virtually guaranteed possession, the lineout is now the main battleground for primary possession.

For many years the lineout was a mass of heaving bodies all clambering over each other to ensure that their opponents gained as little clean ball as possible on their own throw-in. However, the 1995 adoption of the South African dispensation, which allows supporting (lifting, in other words), has managed to clear a lot of the wood from the lineout jungle and it has become a source of much quality possession. This tendency has been reinforced by the rise of the lineout specialists. Where once locks – the main catchers of the ball at the lineout – were no more than 6ft 3in, it is now rare indeed to see a top level lock under 6ft 6in and, in Martin Bayfield, and Simon Shaw Eng-

land had the first pair of international second rows who both topped the 6ft 10in mark.

Where once the ball was thrown into the lineout by wingers, the hooker now takes over this duty (except in France during the Seventies and Eighties when they experimented with using the scrum-half to throw in).

The one major innovation in lineout play has been the introduction of shortened lineouts, first used by Australian coach Des Connor in 1968 in the Bledisloe Cup series against the All Blacks.

THE RUCK AND MAUL

The ruck and the maul are formed after a tackle, the former when the tackled player has gone to ground with the ball and the latter when the tackled player remains standing. The maul has always been the essence of the game, and in its infancy before the concept of heeling the ball back from the maul became widely accepted. Mauls often lasted for several minutes as players grappled for the ball. The ruck, where the ball-carrier goes to ground and his forwards walk over him, has a more recent history. It was effectively introduced

by the New Zealand province of Otago in the years leading up to the Second World War and then going on to become the national style for the All Blacks. It has the useful effect of producing far quicker ball than the maul, thus giving more attacking opportunities.

What happens after a player has been tackled is one of the game's most difficult areas (at one time a player had to touch the ball with his foot before he could play it again, hence the famous phrase "Feet, Scotland, feet!"). There have been constant attempts to ensure that all players, except the tackler and the tackled, stay on their feet in order to ensure quick and clean ball, but with the possibilities of delaying the ball coming out virtually endless, both the ruck and maul have proved difficult to police. In 1992 the "nudge" law, where the side going forward gets the scrum put-in should the ball not become available, gave way to the "use it or lose it" interpretation, where the ball-carrying side has to use the ball if it is not going forward at a maul, but gets the put-in at the scrum if a ruck forms. This has produced faster ball from the breakdown and a more fluent attacking game.

CLOSE QUARTERS *The England and Wallaby packs prepare to enagage at the scrummage.*

FORMATION AND POSITIONS

The current positions are vastly different from those the early sides once used. Mention has already been made of the way in which Wavell Wakefield revolutionised the forwards by assigning players specific roles and of the way in which he used the back-row as one unit, but the role of the backs is also vastly different today than it was at the game's outset. If nothing else, in the early days there was no passing and so the backs' main occupation was as tacklers of the forwards! All of that changed in 1877 when Scotland's H.H. Johnston adopted the role of a fullback for the first time. That innovation was shortly followed by the emergence of the fly-half position, developed by Alan Rotherham at Oxford and Richmond. And when, in 1884, Cardiff back J Conway Rees introduced the concept of the four-man threequarter line, the playing pattern which is still used today had emerged.

POINTS SYSTEM

England were the first country to attempt to introduce a points system to determine the outcome of games in 1886, when they designated a try as worth one point and a goal (ie: try and conversion) three points. At this stage, a match was declared a draw unless a goal had been scored. At first the other Unions refused to accept the system, and it only gained widespread acceptance in 1892, when the value of a try was changed to two points, penalties and conversions were worth three points, and dropped goals and field goals worth four points. The scoring system was amended yet further in 1905, when the value of a try was increased to three points and the value of a conversion reduced to two points.

The change was accompanied by the abolition in 1905 of the field goal, the scoring move whereby the ball was kicked soccer-style off the floor in open play and over the crossbar. The next major change in the scoring system came in 1973 when the value of a try was increased to four points, a change that was further amended in 1992 with the continued upgrading of the try to be worth five points.

FOUL PLAY

It is generally held that the game is as clean today as it has ever been. Television cameras, the presence of two touch judges, the legal implications of on-field violence and the desire to appeal to youngsters (and their mothers !) has meant that the game has been radically cleaned up. Violent episodes such as the Lions' famous 99 call, or England and Australia's 1975 Battle of Brisbane are less likely than ever before to be seen in major games, and the determination to stamp out foul play also accounts for the rapid rise in the number of players sent off at all levels of the game.

A player can only be sent from the field for foul play, and despite the excesses of matches such as the 1914 Wales v Ireland match, which is generally reckoned to be the most violent Test ever played, the only man to be sent off in the first half of this century of international play was New Zealand forward Cyril Brownlie against England in 1925. Referees have certainly made up for it since, though, and the highest profile of the 50 or so internationals to have taken the long walk include Colin Meads against Scotland (1967), Englishman Mike Burton in Australia (1975), Welsh flanker Paul Ringer against England (1980), Wallaby David Codey in the 1987 World Cup semi-final and the biggest shock of them all, Philipe Sella, the world's most capped player, against Canada in 1994.

In the New Zealand of the Nineties, the crackdown on foul play has extended to viewers and spectators who can "cite" those responsible for violent play. So it was in 1993 that prop Richard Loe was banned for a year for eye-gouging after complaints from spectators. Other methods of warning players have also been introduced around the world, most notably the soccer-style yellow and red card system and, most recently, the sin-bin concept has been experimented with during the 1997 Super-12 series. Any player who commits a foul not serious enough to warrant dismissal, but worthy of some form of punishment, is told to sit in the sin-bin for 10 minutes to cool-off.

One of the main deterrents to violent play, however, has been the threat of legal sanctions. Gloucester lock Simon Devereux spent nine months in prison after a punch smashed Rosslyn Park player Jamie Cowie's jaw, while England flanker Gary Rees was lucky to escape jail for a similar punch on London Irish player Stefan Marty, while both Welsh and Scottish players have been given custodial sentences for violent acts on the rugby field of play.

REFEREES

Originally, there was no such thing as a referee. The two sides agreed on what laws they would play under and only paused when they disagreed on interpretation. That was a recipe for conflict, however, and soon the practice of appointing two umpires (one from either side) became commonplace. Inevitably, though, there was the need for an independent arbiter and after 1885 a referee was routinely added to the mix to adjudicate on disputes between the umpires! Eventually, the referee was given a whistle to blow and in 1892 was declared the "sole arbiter of fact", effectively sidelining the umpires to roles as touch judges (this traditional role is kept up during the Varsity Match, when the previous year's captains run the line in club blazers). For the first time the referee could blow his whistle regardless of whether one of the captains had appealed to him, and was able to allow play to continue if the offence was likely to help the infringed-against side – the foundation of the advantage law.

Matters have not changed materially between 1892 and today, although there are no longer any referees who officiate in "mufti" as Scottish referee Dallas Seymour did in 1905 when the All Blacks were controversially denied a try in their 3–0 loss to Wales. The All Blacks were as amazed that Dallas was wearing knickerbockers as they were that he was 30 yards behind the play! The one change has been the appointment of neutral referees for major games after persistent accusations of bias, particularly in South Africa. Touch judges can also flag for a wider variety of offences (there have even been

experiments to "wire up" the referees and touch judges to give hard-pressed referees two extra pairs of eyes) and since professionalism, the top referees are now paid.

OFF-SIDE

The most contentious area in law-making concerns offside. More than any other offence it can disrupt games by slowing down the release of ball from rucks and mauls and by giving backs no room in which to run or pass. Unfortunately, offside is also one of the most difficult areas on which to legislate effectively, although the latest guidelines of entering a maul or ruck behind the back foot seems to be the best compromise. More important has been the willingness of referees to penalise persistent offside to the point when Oxford were denied victory in the 81st minute of the 1996 Varsity Match by a penalty try awarded by referee Tony Spreadbury.

REPLACEMENTS AND INJURIES

When Mike Gibson stepped in for the injured Barry John in the Lions First Test against South Africa in 1968, he became the first official replacement in a Test match. Up until that point there were no replacements allowed for players who were too badly injured to continue, although such a system did operate informally in New Zealand, South Africa and Australia. There have been occasions when victories were won against the odds, such as in 1955 when the Lions rallied to take the First Test against South Africa after Lion Reg Higgins was carried off shortly into the second half, but the usual outcome was defeat for a side which lost a player. The concept of replacements was extended yet further in 1996 when each side was allowed to make up to three substitutions during a match, thereby legalizing a practice that had been tacitly employed by sides the world over for years. In the past, however, players were merely told by their coaches to develop a mysterious injury that would necessiate their removal from the pitch.

OFF! *Wasps' Kevin Dunn prepares for the long walk vs. Gloucester.*

EQUIPMENT

One hundred years ago, rugby players took to the field wearing nothing but the clothes they scrummed in. How times have changed. Rugby Union in the fag end of the twentieth century has never seen such a proliferation of equipment. Although the basics – such as goalposts, ball and pitch dimensions – have more or less stayed the same, it is the players' equipment that has undergone the most radical change. Mouthguards have been *de rigeur* for the last quarter of a century, but

in the last few years, especially since the sport went professional in 1995, there has also been the introduction of several other pieces of protective equipment. Head protectors and shoulder pads have both featured prominently during the 1997 British Lions tour to South Africa. These innovations have often been ridiculed, in particular by former players, who say that if they didn't need them in their day, then they don't need them now. But this is a blithe assumption that

misses the point. Rugby players have never been so big and powerful as they are today. Whereas 50 years ago it was rare to come across a forward who was taller than 6ft 4in, it is now unusual to find an international forward who is under that height. The professional age has meant players have longer to work on their fitness, and as a result the hits and tackles are that much harder.

Then there is the playing kit itself. Rugby jerseys now are made from

lightweight cotton or acrylic materials and in the last few years, international teams such as England, Scotland and South Africa have their sponsors' name emblazoned on their shirts. While, thankfully, the playing shirts of the international teams have remained faithful to tradition and kept their original colours, it must be hoped that rugby never follows football and changes its colours more times than a Chameleon just to please the governing body's bank manager.

Despite the protestations of a minority of old-fashioned diehards, rugby union is at last beginning to move with the times. Now the sport is professional and televsion audiences are soaring playing shirts have the sponsors' logo featured prominently, while kit designs have also undergone subtle transformations to make them more attractive

1997 *(right)*
Huge French second-row Olivier Merle shows off the latest rugby accessory during the 1997 Five Nations match against Scotland – the nasal strip. First designed as an aid to people who kept the neighbours awake with their snoring, the strip soon proved a hit with sportsmen as an aid to breathing. It was originally introduced in the high altitude of the 1995 World Cup in South Africa, The strip purports to increase oxygen flow through the nose by opening up the nostrils. Sceptics, however, claim that the strip is nothing more than a gimmick and does little to improve oxygen intake for the wearer.

1895 *(left)*
The rough and tumble of early rugby football is illustrated in this picture from 1895, the year of the Great Split. The clothes are rudimentary with trousers being the order of the day – it must have been tricky getting the grass stains out – and hats were an option usually only taken up by the sartorially–minded.

It is also worth noting the goalpost in the background, nothing more than an elongated version of a soccer goalpost.

Rugby players have never had it so good when it comes to choosing a boot. The range is huge nowadays, with each brand claiming to make the wearer run faster, tackle harder and score more tries.

1910

A gaggle of balls from Rugby School at the beginning of this century. The names on each ball refer to houses at Rugby. Made of pure leather and with no grip on them, it required great skill to catch and kick with one of these balls, particularly in wet conditions when it was more like handling a bar of soap.

1967

These boots were made for walking...and most of the time they walked over the opposition. They belong to arguably the greatest player in the sport's history, Colin Meads of New Zealand. They were worn by 'Pinetree' Meads on the All Black's 1967 tour to the UK when, unfortunately, Meads was sent off against Scotland. Note the way the studs are nailed to the sole, meaning the lifespan of the boots was equal only to that of the studs.

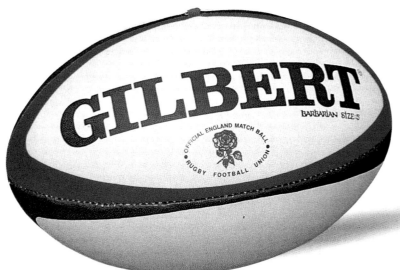

1997

Gilbert, the world's oldest manufacturer of rugby balls, are the official supplier to the English RFU, and here is their 1997 offering. Matching the colours of the England team's shirts, the ball has thousands of minute 'goosebumps' which provide a much better grip than the Gilbert balls of 1910 (see previous picture). Despite the improved grip, balls such as these are dropped with alarming regularity during international matches, perhaps giving credence to the theory that handling skills have deteriorated in the modern game.

1997

Waisale Serevi, the Fijian Sevens wizard, played in these boots during Fiji's successful 1997 World Cup Sevens campaign. The difference to the previous picture of Colin Mead's boots are obvious with removable studs and softer, more pliable leather being the two main differences. Low-cut, with the makers' name emblazoned prominently, the boots are designed for the modern era.

SCANDALS
AND CONTROVERSIES

Rugby Union scandals have not proliferated in the last few years, it just seems that way. As the popularity of the game has increased so have the column inches in the world's newspapers. Scandal requires public outrage to give it the air to live. Now that the media is largely financing if not controlling the game, there is an endless supply of oxygen. Where once rugby tours were accompanied by a handful of rugby journalists, they now carry with them a plane-load of hard news reporters. The remit from their editors is scandal.

WILL CARLING AND THE "OLD FARTS"

There is no better example of this than the sacking and subsequent reinstatement of Will Carling as England captain. The issue was not just reported by the media, it was created by the media. In an interview for an English television documentary "*Fair Game*" in 1995, Will Carling described the executive of the Rugby Football Union as "fifty-seven old farts". In days past Carling's comments would not only have been edited, but such a loaded question would never have been asked in the first place. But it was and the RFU decided that Carling had to go.

The RFU statement read: "It has been decided with regret that Will Carling's captaincy of the England team will be terminated forthwith and an announcement concerning his replacement will be made shortly. In the light of the view recently expressed regarding administrators, it is considered inappropriate for him to continue to represent, as England captain, the RFU, England and, indeed, English sport."

In actual fact, despite the public outrage provoked, the RFU had some justification for the decision. Some may have been moved that Carling had already been subjected to a couple of investigations regarding professionalism, but that should have been disregarded as Carling was never found to have transgressed. Far more significant was that, following the Five Nations game against Wales in 1991, the entire England team had boycotted the post-match press conference. This was unheard of and was contrary to the requirements of a captain and his team.

Carling himself claimed that it was nothing to do with money and was a reaction to the constant press harassment that the players had been subjected to. Others suggested that the action had rather more to do with the squad's dispute with the BBC over a fee that their agent was seeking for post-match interviews. There were members of the RFU who wanted to sack Carling there and then, but instead it was decided to put him on what was effectively a final warning. But yet again it was a media issue. It is strange that Carling should have been twice so inept in this field given that he was a man who ran a promotions company.

KISS AND MAKE UP *Denis Easby and Will Carling reconciliate in public.*

214

But the RFU were to prove themselves equally inept. For a start they announced Carling's sacking a couple of hours before the Pilkington Cup final. If they hoped that the match would subdue reporting of it they were hopelessly wrong. They compounded that error by at no stage bringing up the subject of 1991. If they had done so there might have been greater public understanding of their reaction, but as it was they were reviled.

Instead the RFU official line was relatively bland. The president, Denis Easby, said: "The decision has been made, I stand by it, and there is no chance whatsoever that it will be reversed". It was not only bland, it was hopelessly wrong. Dudley Wood, the secretary, added: "Will has lost the confidence of the RFU committee who appointed him in the first place. In view of his attitude to the committee, his position as England captain is untenable." Wheels were put in motion.

The England squad, soon to leave for South Africa and the World Cup, made it clear that almost to a man none of them was prepared to accept the role of England captain. If the RFU had handled the media that much better and made the history behind the sacking available one wonders if the public would have been so appalled and if the England players would have taken the same stance. As it was, the RFU had only one choice: to back down. Just two days after the original sacking an RFU statement was released which read: "Will Carling wishes to apologize to every member of the Committee for his inappropriate and gratuitously offensive comments at the end of a recent television programme. All 25 members of the England squad have indicated their support for Will Carling as captain and have respectfully requested the RFU officers to reconsider their decision to terminate his appointment. Will Carling would like to thank the squad for their support and also Denis Easby for his courage in reconsidering his original decision, thus enabling the England squad to have a settled and successful build-up to the World Cup. In the light of these circumstances, the RFU are agreeable to reinstating Will Carling

as England's captain for the period of the World Cup."

What circumstances? The attitude of the squad had to be ignored. If the RFU gave in then they gave in forever. And what of the apology? Did anyone really believe that Carling did not believe what he had said? He might have regretted saying it, after all the position of England captain is extremely lucrative, but did anyone truly believe that he did not mean it when he said it? If any proof were needed "old farts" has now become synonymous with sporting administrators. If only Carling could have chosen a wittier or more elegant phrase given that it is now repeated *ad nauseam*.

Easby's subsequent statement was a monument of fatuousness: "Will and I had a very good meeting at Twickenham. He gave me all the assurances I needed and I am delighted to be able to ask him to take on the captaincy of the World Cup. I regret what happened, but Will's original apology was not quite sufficient". It was a craven moment.

Further comments from the RFU executive members suggested that Carling had initially been quoted out of context, that he was led up the garden path with no right of redress, that he was cornered and coerced into saying something that he did not really mean and even that they were not offended by the remarks. This was insulting. It insulted Carling to suggest that as an England captain of seven years and a successful businessman he could so easily be manipulated, and it insulted the public's intelligence to expect them to believe such wimpishness.

Ten months later, Easby was heard again: "Will Carling is the most successful captain England will ever have. He has been an absolute credit to English rugby in eight marvellous years". As scandals go it lacked the sex and wit of the Profumo affair even if it rivalled it for political incompetence. At least Carling added a little of the missing mystique through his subsequently reported liaison with Princess Diana. But it was the scandal true to the times. Created by television, controlled by the press, finished by public opinion.

SORRY TALE *Andrew Markgraaf.*

ANDRE MARKGRAAFF'S GAFFE

It was television again that provided a podium from which Andre Markgraaff, the coach of South Africa, unceremoniously fell from grace. Markgraaff was secretly taped by former Griqualand West captain, Andre Bester, referring to black players as "f*****g kaffirs". The South African Broadcasting Corporation broadcast excerpts from the tape in its main news bulletin.

Markgraaff had originally threatened legal action against the company if they proceeded with the broadcast. The appearance of the tape in February 1997, four months after it was made, coincided with an edict from Steve Tshwete, the minister of sport, ordering an investigation into the administration of South African rugby.

He did not have long to wait or far to look. An extract from the tape states: "Naturally it's the whole f*****g country behind him in terms of the press. Now I hear that Mluleki George (senior SARFU vice-president and an ANC member of parliament) also wants to resign. It's kaffirs man, it's the f*****g NSC, the f*****g kaffirs." As a testimony to illiteracy, racism and bigotry, this was almost unrivalled. Sadly, only almost. The "him" in question was Francois Pienaar, the captain of South Africa's winning 1995 World Cup team, who was dropped by Markgraaff. Pienaar, who subsequently joined English club side Saracens,

would be near the top of anyone's list of men who demand respect rather than ridicule. But Markgraaff had proved to be not just anyone.

Mluleki George himself responded by saying: "How could we have a man selecting and coaching our national team who would talk about black people as kaffirs?" After remaining incommunicado at his home Markgraaff eventually had no option but to resign. It was one of the more popular decisions of his brief time as South Africa's coach. He was not exactly fitted after becoming the first coach to lose a home series against New Zealand, and he was widely disliked after removing Pienaar both from the squad and the captaincy. But there was a belief that Markgraaff himself was the victim of spite.

Andre Bester, who made the tape available, and his brother Piet played for Griqualand West for three seasons before departing for Orange Free State. It is claimed that Andre Bester left when Markgraaff refused to re-negotiate his contract and was deeply hurt by such a rejection. If all had gone smoothly the tape would probably never have been heard. When Pienaar was told of the scandal he said: "It is a serious blow to South African rugby. We spent a lot of time building up trust among the communities and now this happens. I can't make any sense out of it, but people must remember it is the irresponsible view of one person and not the views of the whole country, nor the views of the players. Even so, the feeling here now is going to be, have there actually been so many changes in sport in South Africa? It's a serious blow."

The problem was, contrary to what Pienaar said, the authorities in South Africa were far from convinced that the Markgraaff tape represented the views of just one person. At the same time that SARFU accepted the resignation of Markgraaff, the ANC demanded the additional resignation of Dr Louis Luyt, the president of the union. Lulu Xingwana, the chairwoman of an ANC study group set up to investigate the union, said that Luyt had known of Markgraaff's comments at least two months before they were published and had tried

VIOLENCE ON THE PITCH

to cover them up. She said that the matter was: "part of an on-going saga involving allegations of the racism, mismanagement, power abuse, lack of diplomacy and autocratic behaviour that has characterized Mr Luyt's involvement in South African rugby". She called the conduct scandalous and added, "We believe Luyt's resignation will be a positive step in the process of cleansing rugby, and sport in general for that matter, in this country." The chief executive officer of SARFU, Rian Oberholzer, said: "If Mr Markgraaff had not chosen to step down we would have forced him to do so. As I have said there is no place for racism in SARFU and we will take all steps necessary to eradicate it from our sport." If that took some swallowing, Markgraaff's comments were utterly indigestible when he said that he was not a racist and he believed there was no racism in South African rugby. But again the whole sorry affair was an example of how technology has increased the likelihood of revelation in all walks of life.

There is a certain misapprehension that the modern game is somehow more violent than the gentleman's game of yore. Apart from simple facts that hacking used to be legal, we are now living in an age of video evidence when foul play is constantly analysed and re-shown.

Now that players are so much more easily identified there seems to be an unending list of unsavoury incidents. Indeed, so often are individuals cited for foul play that one wonders if the latest incident is scandalous any more, or just a tedious reprise.

In recent seasons, Irishman, Peter Clohessy, and South Africans, Johan Le Roux and Kobus Wiese, have all being punished for violent conduct as a result of video evidence after match officials failed to notice their crimes during the game. Contrast this with the 1960s and 1970s when, for example, British Lion Sandy Carmichael was so brutally battered throughout a match against Canterbury in 1971, that he was later found

to have five fractures of his cheek-bone. Yet no opposition player was ever brought to book over Carmichael's injuries because television cameras were not present to record the assault.

One country which has always acted with alacrity in disciplining its players is France. French club rugby is probably the most vicious in the world. Yet Richard Dourthe, Olivier Merle and others have all been cited and suspended in recent seasons. Even the coaches can get involved in France. After their quarter-final defeat against England in the 1991 World Cup, coach Daniel Dubroca was so incensed that he tried to assault David Bishop, the New Zealand referee, in the tunnel after the game, finishing his international coaching career in that moment of madness. What incenses the French, is that while England react with pious outrage when one of their own is harmed, they are slow to penalize their own transgressors.

Jamie Joseph, the New Zealand flanker, can stamp on Kyran Bracken's

ankle and the whole of England is out-raged. Phil de Glanville's face is raked open and again the is talk of dirty foreigners. But when it is an Englishman ... What happened when a round arm punch from Wade Dooley perforated Doddie Weir's eardrum in a match against Scotland? What was Tim Rodber's punishment when he was sent off against Eastern Province in South Africa in '94? What happened when Brian Moore was convicted of a serious offence off the pitch shortly before the 1991 World Cup? Not a lot is the short answer.

Increasingly players have felt the need to take court action themselves. The problem for the courts is that they are not necessarily qualified to make a reasonable judgement. In the early 1990s, Gary Rees, the former England flanker, was sued by London Irish back-rower Stefan Marty whose jaw was broken. Rees had been obstructed at a line-out and swung round to hit Marty.

Not particularly vicious, not premeditated, it happens every week if

GOING TOO FAR *It's all too easy to make the rugby ruck into its less savoury version. Increased TV coverage will hopefully pinpoint the real culprits.*

NOT SO GENTLE GIANT *Olivier Merle is France's "enforcer".*

not with such destructive consequences. But without a great deal of expert testimony to support his actions and his character Rees might have gone to prison.

Simon Devereux of Gloucester did "Go straight to jail". In February 1995, Jamie Cowie of Rosslyn Park was walking back to take a tap penalty following a line-out infringement when he was punched in the jaw from behind. The jaw came out of its socket and was broken in three places. Even now, Cowie suffers excruciating headaches and has trouble eating. Needless to say, his rugby career is over. Devereux was charged with GBH with intent and received a nine-month sentence. The court is not the place to resolve the huge majority of violent exchanges, but at times there is no alternative.

When Richard Loe, the notorious New Zealand prop, crunched into wing Paul Carozza of Australia just after he had touched down for a try, breaking his nose, what sort of punishment is sufficient within the game? The crucial phrase within the law is "with intent". If that is clearly the case then the player should not go before a disciplinary panel, he should be sent before the courts.

DRUG TAKING
Drugs are more widely used because they are better understood and they are in some instances detectable. The drug problem had been most widespread in South Africa, where Transvaal and Springbok prop Balie Swart

and Orange Free State flanker Elandre Van Den Bergh were two of the highest profile players to be caught. There are more, as the tally of five top provincial players caught in 1997 would suggest. Paul Jones, the Llanelli lock, tested positive for an anabolic steroid in 1996. The irony was that Jones was found out, but had already told the club doctor himself. He said he took the drug to help a persistent shoulder problem, but realized his error and confessed. He received a two-year ban. He feels he was made a scapegoat, penalized for honesty. What he might say, and have far more of a case, is that while he was punished, and was not the first in Wales to be so, there are other unions around who turn a blind eye to the problem.

HIGH JINKS
On another scale altogether are the frivolous scandals. Foremost among these is the story of the Calcutta Cup. The magnificent trophy, which dates back to 1879, is made of silver rupees melted down from the last coins of the Calcutta Rugby Football Club. In 1988, after England had ground out a dull 9–6 victory over Scotland, two of the players, Englishman Dean Richards and John Jeffrey of Scotland, took the cup on a tour of Edinburgh's many pubs. Before long it was decided that the cup bore a striking resemblance to a football and an impromptu game was played out around the streets of Edinburgh's capital. Several goals later the cup was eventually recovered by the Unions who had to repair it at a cost of £1,000. The outcome was that Richards received a one match ban, a punishment that infuriated the SRU, who had suspended Jeffrey for six months. Once again, the English were accused of double standards in the matter of discipline.

A few years before in Paris another dinner ended with potentially far more serious consequences. The England players had been presented with a bottle of aftershave each as a complimentary gift by their French hosts. Several of the players decided to play a practical joke on one of their team-mates. They emptied the contents, replacing the cologne with

water. Unaware of what had transpired, Colin Smart, the England prop, was then challenged to down his in one as others did the same. He soon discovered that the alcohol in aftershave is accompanied by some far less agreeable substances and had to be rushed off to hospital to have his stomach pumped.

Another incidence of poisoning happened on the eve of the 1995 World Cup when nearly the entire New Zealand team went down with food poisoning following a meal in their hotel. There have been many subsequent theories as to the perpetrators of the deed that almost certainly cost them the match. Betting rings, backers who stood to benefit heavily financially if South Africa became world champions, patriotic saboteurs, plain malice or just a simple accident.

The coach of that New Zealand team, Laurie Mains, does not believe in the latter theory. Indeed he has become so fixated with the whole affair that he is still investigating the incident. But it seems unlikely that he will be able to come up with definitive proof as to those involved.

SHAMATEURS AND PROFESSIONALS
If money was the reason for the 1995 World Cup "poisoning" it would be no surprise in a game that throughout its predominantly amateur history has continuously been maligned by the mischief of Mammon. It began in 1893 when the northern unions argued that the only way to resist professionalism was to compensate players for their loss of working hours. At the time Yorkshire, and to a slightly less extent Lancashire, were the powers of the game. They dominated the early County Championships. But when they put their views to the AGM of the RFU at the Westminster Palace Hotel they were told that the principle of compensation was contrary to the spirit and ethos of the game. The argument continued for two years until in August 1895 12 of Yorkshire's senior clubs broke away. A Northern league was founded, membership of which meant isolation from the rest of the game. The great schism had occurred. Rugby Union and Rugby League and

never the twain shall meet.

France was the next to be accused of financially rewarding their players. In 1931 they were found guilty of not complying with amateur rules. The control and conduct of their game was not in keeping with the strictly amateur rules of the International Board. As a result France was expelled from the Five Nations Championship by the four home unions. The home unions began to modify their position in 1938, some would say because the impending war rather altered the world's sense of perspective. They had received certain assurances regarding the amateur structure of French clubs. "Of course, we don't pay our players," they would argue. "And it is pure coincidence that our star fly-half is paid to be the non-working manager of a lucrative bar owned by the club president." In the 1946–47 season France was officially reinstated, although allegations about professionalism were hardly quelled.

Even the British parliament has become involved in recent years. Tony Banks, a Labour MP, submitted a motion objecting to the sacking of Will Carling. An all-party bill, motivated by Dave Hinchcliffe, Labour's health spokesman and a former amateur rugby league player, was produced, objecting to the exclusion of Rugby League players from Uunion.

Michael Lord, the Conservative MP for Central Suffolk, used his position to speak out against professionalism. They all sounded rather like Prince Charles on the subject of architecture: both men held their own strong opinions, they were not over qualified to express them, and whether they were using or abusing their position to enter the argument was a point of some conjecture.

However, scandal offers publicity and there is scarcely an institution in the world that prefers publicity in the Houses of Parliament. With an ever increasing number of television stations hitting the air, and with more money entering rugby, it will seem like the number of scandals just continues to grow.

It is an illusion. It is just that more of them are discovered these days and there is more time and space in the media to promote them.

CHRONOLOGY

1175 First record of the "famous game of ball" being played in London

1314–1527 Nine European monarchs make it a specific offence to play "foote balle", ordering their subjects to pursue archery instead. Punishments range from fines to imprisonment.

1618 James I issues Declaration of Sports, which encourages sport on Sabbath leading to increased participation

1823 William Webb Ellis catches the ball and runs with it at Rugby School. The practice did not catch on immediately

1839 Old Rugbeian Arthur Pell sets up first rugby club at Cambridge

1843 Rugby club formed at Guy's Hospital in London

1845 Laws of the game codified in simple terms. It was the act of committing these to paper which almost certainly accounted for the Rugby School code's ascendancy over the unwritten codes from other schools

1850 Rev Rowland Williams introduces rugby into Wales via St David's College, Lampeter

1854 Old Rugbeian RH Scott starts Ireland's first rugby club at Trinity College, Dublin

1858 The world's first independent rugby club founded at Blackheath

1858 Merchiston School first play Edinburgh Academicals in world's oldest surviving fixture

1863 Rugby Football and Association Football split when Blackheath and Richmond refuse to agree to ban on running with the ball

1863 Blackheath play Richmond in oldest surviving top-class fixture

1864 First game played in Australia at the Sydney University club

1870 First ever representative fixture takes place when Yorkshire meet Lancashire, thus also initiating the County Championship

1870 Charles John Munro introduces rugby to New Zealand, and schools such as Christ's College, Christchurch, which were already playing football, accept the rugby code

1871 The Rugby Football Union is formed after 20 clubs meet at the Pall Mall Restaurant on January 26th at the behest of Richmond's Edwin Hash

1871 England accept Edinburgh Academical FJ Moncrieff's challenge to meet Scotland at Raeburn Place in Edinburgh and are beaten by a goal and a try to one try. After 1879 the fixture was played for the Calcutta Cup.

1872 The first Varsity Match takes place at Oxford, with the home side winning by a goal and a try to nil

1872 Rugby introduced to France by British wine merchants in Le Havre

1874 American University Harvard take on Canada's McGill University in first match in North America

1875 Size of teams begins to be dropped from 20 to 15 at behest of Varsity Match pioneers Oxford. This becomes standard practice a year later, and is adopted at international level in 1877 when England take on Ireland

1875 Hospitals Cup commences in England

1875 Hamilton RFC, South Africa's first open and independent club, is formed

1875 Ireland play their first international, losing to England by a goal, a try and a drop goal to nil at The Oval

1877 Scotland's HH Johnstone is the first to play as a single full-back

1878 Broughton v Swinton is the first floodlit match

1878 Swansea win the first South Wales Cup, beating Newport by a goal to nil

1879 First Unions formed in new Zealand in Canterbury and Wellington

1881 Eleven Welsh clubs form Welsh Rugby Union at Castle Hotel Neath on March 12

1882 New South Wales tour New Zealand for the first overseas tour, winning four games but losing to Otago and Auckland (twice)

1883 Melrose butcher Ned Haig invents sevens and stages first tournament

1883 England win the Triple Crown. They have won it 19 times since

1884 Cardiff take up the four three-quarters system first tried by Coventry in 1893. It is soon taken up by all Welsh clubs and the top West Country clubs

1886 Despite opposition from Home Unions, the RFU adopts points system in which try is worth one, and a conversion two. Matches still cannot be won unless a goal (i.e: a converted try) is scored

1886 International Board formed in Manchester, but RFU refuse to join so Home Unions suspend matches against England

1888 Embryonic Lions side tours Australia and New Zealand under captaincy of R.L. Seddon, who is drowned in Australia. 15 of party are from Northern clubs which later leave for League, but Hawick send three players, while Wales and the Isle of Man also have one representative

1889 A close season is established in Northern Hemisphere, running from May 1 until September 1

1889 New Zealand Natives tour New Zealand, Australia and Britain, playing 107 games in 14 months, of which they drew six and won 78. Victims include Ireland

1889 Touch judges introduced at international level to complement neutral referees first used in 1881

1889 South African Rugby Board is formed, including areas that are now Kenya, Zimbabwe and Namibia

1890 The Barbarians founded in January and play their first fixture in December, beating Hartlepool Rovers 9–4.

1890 England join the International Board, but take six of the 12 seats

1891 Scot Bill Maclagan leads English-dominated side to South Africa at invitation of Cecil Rhodes, and wins all 19 matches, scoring 223 points and conceding only one. The tourists award the Currie Cup, donated by the Castle Shipping Line, to their hardest opponents Griqualand West, and the Cup is then played for every year. When British return in 1896, side is half Irish and half English

1892 New Zealand Rugby Football Union is formed

1893 Northern clubs' motion in favour of broken time payments is defeated

1894 Try becomes worth three points and conversion two points

1895 22 clubs from Yorkshire and Lancashire break away to form the Northern Union in Huddersfield.

1897 Jerseys become numbered

1897 Scotland and Ireland refuse to play Wales because of allegations of professionalism

1899 The first British Isles side to contain representatives from all four Home Unions tours Australia, winning all but three games.

1903 The Ranfurly Shield is given to NZRFU and awarded to unbeaten Auckland. The first challenge is in 1904, when Wellington win 6–3

1903 New Zealand play Australia for the first time, winning 22–3 in front of 30,000 crowd in Sydney.

1903 Mark Morrison's British team lose last Test against South Africa to be beaten in a series for the first time

1904 Scot Darkie Bedell-Sivright leads Welsh-dominated British side to Australia, winning all 14 matches but losing the Test in New Zealand

1905 Dave Gallaher's "Originals" tour Britain, starting off with a 55–4 win over Devon and winning all but one of their matches, a controversial 3–0 loss to Wales after Bob Deans is dragged back after grounding the ball. Gallaher himself plays as a wing forward or "rover", an unknown role in Britain and one that excites much controversy

1906 France play their first official international (they had earlier put a side into the 1900 Olympics), but lose 35–8 to England at the Parc des Princes

1907 Paul Roos' powerful Springboks tour Britain and France, winning 27 games out of 30. They beat Ireland, Wales and a French XV, but lose to Scotland and Cardiff and draw with England

1908 Wales are the first side to win a Grand Slam

1908 Berkeley, from California, beat France to win the Olympic gold, sparking a riot

1908 Anglo-Welsh side fails to win a Test in New Zealand

1909 Australians beat England on their first tour of Britain. They win 25 of 31 games

1910 England play first game at Twickenham, beating Wales for the first time since 1898

1912 Springboks beat all four Home Countries

1914–18 Official internationals cease, although unofficial military internationals continue in which League players are also allowed to participate. 111 internationals lose their lives, including All Blacks captain Dave Gallaher and Ronnie Poulton Palmer

1921 Springboks tour Australia and New Zealand for first time, winning all four matches in Australia and drawing the three-match series in New Zealand. In all, the Springboks lost only two matches on the tour

1924–5 Cliff Porter's All Black "Invincibles" sweep through the British Isles and France undefeated, but fail to notch a Grand Slam as Scotland refuse to play a team they consider professionalised. The New Zealanders win all 30 matches, scoring 721 points and conceding 109

1926 Australia, South Africa and New Zealand join International Board

1929 The Wallabies whitewash New Zealand in the Bledisloe Cup for the first time

1930 The Lions lose series in new Zealand by 5–1

1931 France thrown out of the Five Nations for violence and professionalism. They were not allowed to rejoin until after the Second World War, and formed FIRA in 1934 to ensure international fixtures

1932 Danie Craven and the Springboks complete Grand Slam tour of Britain, a feat they repeated twenty years later, memorably thrashing Scotland 44–0 at Murrayfield

1937 The All Blacks are beaten 2–1 on home soil by South Africa, the New Zealanders' first series loss on home soil

1938 Sam Walker's British Lions lose series 2–1 in South Africa

1939–45 Series of wartime matches, in the first of which The Army beat an Empire XV 27–9 at Richmond. League players represent their countries (except Scotland) in the Red Cross Internationals and Rugby League XV beat a Rugby Union XV 15–10 in Bradford

1949 Bill Allen's All Blacks are whitewashed 4–0 in South Africa. Controversy over refereeing standards ensures that rivalry between the two countries is even greater than ever

1949 Australian Rugby Union founded

1950 Karl Mullen's Lions fail to win a Test in New Zealand, but win in Australia

1951 France beat England at Twickenham for the first time

1953 All Blacks are beaten twice at Cardiff Arms Park – by Cardiff and Wales – within a month

1955 Springboks and Lions share series marked by brilliant open play

1956 New Zealand get revenge for the whitewash of Bill Allen's "49ers" when they beat South Africa 3–1

1958 France win series in South Africa at first attempt

1960 Scotland become the first Home Union to tour overseas when they leave for South Africa

1963 Wales tour for the first time, losing Test in South Africa

1965 Dawie de Villiers' Springboks tour Britain and fail to win a match, losing five and drawing one. They then lose the series in Australia 2–0 before rounding off the year with a 20–3 defeat at Eden Park and a 3–1 series loss to New Zealand

1966 Lions whitewashed 4–0 for the first time in a series in New Zealand

1968 Replacements allowed for injured players

1971 Inspired by Barry John, Lions win a series in New Zealand for first time

1972 "The Troubles" in Ulster are so intense that Scotland and Wales refuse to travel to Ireland. England travel and are beaten 16–12 in the year in which a try becomes worth four points

1972 Despite being beaten in all of their games against top class provincial opposition, England stun the Springboks by winning 18–9 at Ellis Park

1973 Once again miserable in the run-up to the Test, England once again beggar belief by beating New Zealand 16–10 at Eden Park

1973 New Zealand end British tour with a rematch against 1971 Lions masquerading as Barbarians. In one of the most memorable games of running rugby ever played, Barbarians win 23–11

1973 Wallabies lose 16–11 to Tonga in Brisbane in Australian rugby's lowest ebb

1974 Cantabrians from New Zealand win the first Hong Kong Sevens tournament

1974 Lions are only denied whitewash of South Africa when Fergus Slattery's last minute try in the Fourth Test is controversially disallowed and the game ends a draw

1977 A Lions party containing 18 Welshmen suffers an unhappy tour of New Zealand and loses the series 3–1

1978 All Blacks complete Grand Slam tour of Britain

1980 Lions salvage last Test win to avoid whitewash in South Africa

1981 All Blacks win third Test against South Africa in remarkable fashion to win series 2–1, but the tour is disrupted by anti-Apartheid demonstrations and divides New Zealand opinion. Nicknamed the "Barbed Wire Tour".

1983 Lions whitewashed in New Zealand

1984 The Ella brothers star for the Wallabies on their Grand Slam tour of Britain

1986 Denied the chance to tour South Africa as the All Blacks, New Zealand's top players join under the banner of the Cavaliers and tour the Republic, but are comprehensively beaten by the Springboks in three of the four Tests. Argentina, disguised as the South American Jaguars, also tour South Africa three times between 1980–84, while a World XV attends the SARB Centenary Celebrations in 1989 in defiance of sporting sanctions

1987 The inaugural World Cup is held, and New Zealand are convincing winners. France and Australia stage one of the best ever games in the semi-final

1989 The Lions come back from a devastating First Test defeat to physically overwhelm the Wallabies and take the series 2–1

1990 Unbeaten underdogs Scotland surprise the rugby world by beating in-form England at Murrayfield in a Grand Slam showdown. Over the next two seasons England go on to win back-to-back Grand Slams for the first time since 1923–4

1991 Fresh from inflicting a record defeat on the Welsh, beating England 40–15 and sharing the Bledisloe Cup with New Zealand, Australia are the class act of a World Cup held in the Five Nations, beating hosts England 12–6 in the final

1991 The USA win the inaugural Women's World Cup, beating England 19–6 at Cardiff ARms Park

1992 Post-Apartheid South Africa re-commence international competition, but are comfortably beaten by New Zealand, Australia and England. Series defeats follow in 1993 against New Zealand, Australia and France, the last on home soil

1993 Lions are crushed by the All Blacks, who come back from a 10–0 half-time deficit, to win the decisive last Test 30–13

1993 England upset the form book by winning the inaugural World Cup Sevens at Murrayfield, beating Australia 21–17 in the final

1994 Queensland win inaugural Super 10 Championship, beating Natal 21–10

1994 England lose 2–1 in South Africa, but France are the first national side since the 1937 Springboks to win a series in New Zealand.

1995 England captain Will Carling is sacked for calling the RFU committee "57 old farts", only to be reinstated

1995 South Africa beat favourites New Zealand 15–12 in extra-time to win the World Cup on their own soil. Jonah Lomu emerges as the most high profile superstar ever in the game

1995 The onset of professionalism cannot be halted, and with Rugby League's Super League threatening to engulf Australasian Union, the three Southern Hemisphere giants sell a 10-year package to Rupert Murdoch's News Corporation for £340 million. The formation of the Super 12 provincial competition and the Tri-Nations tournament is professional rugby union.

1995 The International Board rubber stamps the de facto professionalism of the game and declares it "open"

1995 Jonathan Davies becomes the first man to be transferred back across the "free gangway" between League and Union when he signs for Cardiff from Warrington for £90,000. He is later followed by players such as Scott Gibbs and Allan Bateman

1995 Famous English club Newcastle Gosforth is sold to local entrepreneur Sir John Hall for £2 million, sparking a series of takeovers of top English clubs that make English rugby the richest in the world. The process culminates in Newcastle paying £1 million to buy former All Black wing Tuigamala out of his League contract

1996 RFU sign exclusive deal which gives TV rights to their Five Nations games to sattelivet TV and are thrown out of the competition by the other Home Unions. The RFU recant and then face a challenge to their authority from the top clubs.

1996 Rugby is in the law courts. Gloucester forward Simon Devereux is jailed for nine months for a punch that shatters a London Irish opponent's jaw and a referee is held liable for a Colt's injury after a collapsed scrum.

1996 New Zealand win the inaugural Tri-Nations series remaining unbeaten in their four matches against South Africa and Australia. The All Blacks then travel to South Africa and become the first New Zealand side to beat the Springboks in a Test series on their home turf.

1997 South African coach Andre Markgraaf is forced to resign after tape recordings of his racist tirade are leaked

1997 Fiji win the second World Cup Sevens, held in Hong Kong

1997 The first professional British Lions tour party proves the cynics wrong by contesting a hard-fought series in South Africa.

INDEX

The publishers would like to thank the following sources for their kind permission to reproduce the pictures in this book:

Action Photographics, Australia /Cox; **Allsport** /Shaun Botterill /Simon Bruty /David Cannon /Russell Cheyne /Chris Cole /Mike Cooper /John Gichigi /Mike Hewitt /Hulton-Getty /Clive Mason /Adrian Murrell /Mike Powell /Andrew Redington /Dave Rogers /Billy Stickland /Anton Want; **Peter Bush, NewZealand**; **Camarthen Athletic Club** /Mark Lewis;

Coloursport/Tom David /Jerome Provost /Schipper /Sipa Press; **Edinburgh Academical Football Club**; **Empics** /Kenny Rodger; **ET Archive**; **Mary Evans Picture Library**; **The James Gilbert Rugby Football Museum**; **Chris Greyvenstein** /New Holland Publishers; **Image Select/**Ann Ronan Collection; **Inpho Photography** /Tom Honan /Billy Stickland; **Mark Leech** /Photosport, NZ /Joanna Caird; **Museum of Rugby, Twikenham, England**; **Natal Newspapers Ltd., South Africa**; **Otago Daily Times, Dunedin, New Zealand**; **Popperfoto** /Brunskill /Rogers; **Chris**

Thau; **Touchline Photo** /Anne Laing /Tertius Pickard; **Wales News Service, Cardiff**; **Western Mail and Echo, Cardiff, Wales**.

Every effort has been made to acknowledge correctly and contact the source and/copyright holder of each picture, and Carlton Books Limited apologises for any unintentional errors or omissions which will be corrected in future editions of this book.

040-852

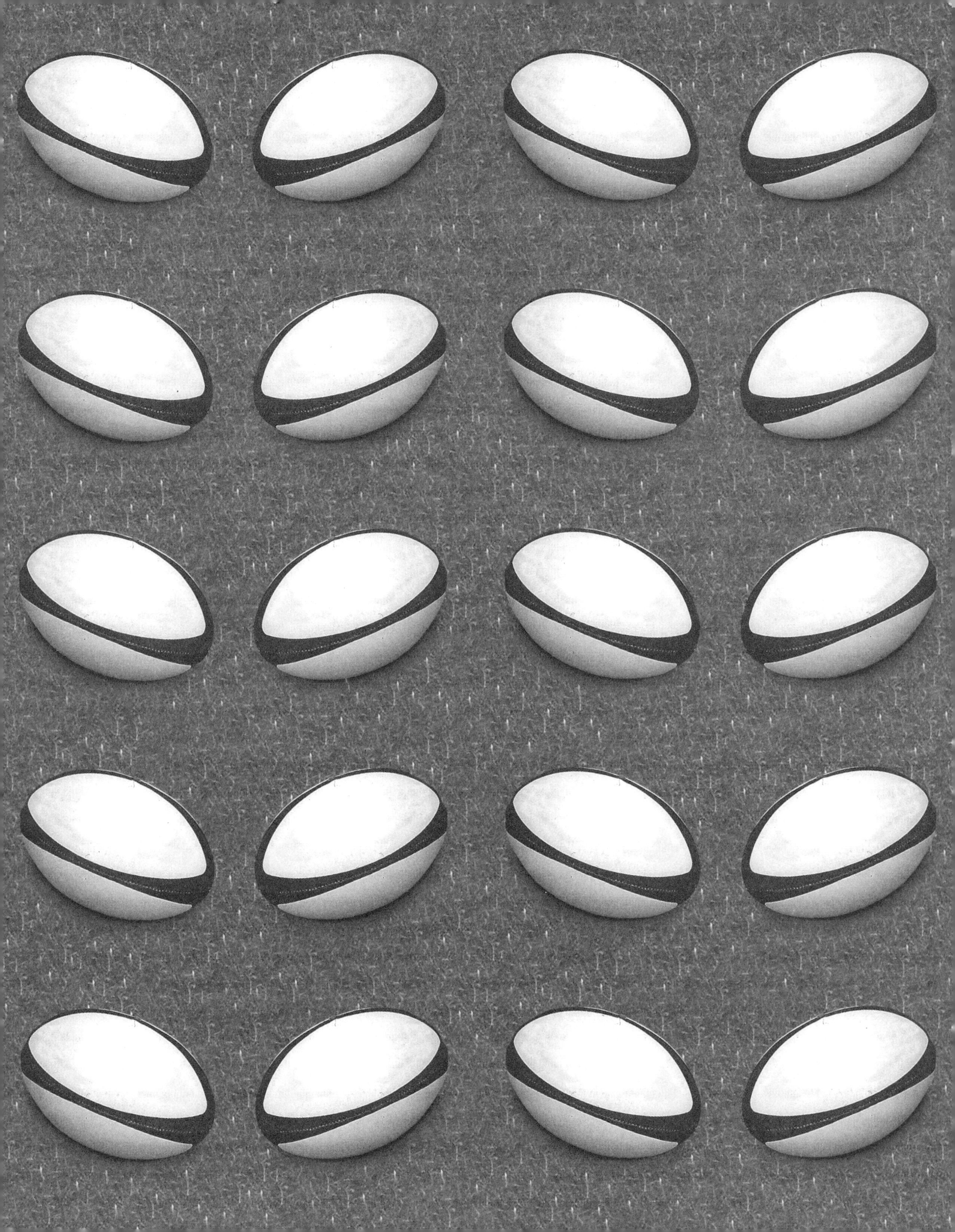